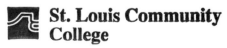

# Emily Faithfull

# Emily Faithfull

Victorian Champion of
Women's Rights

James S. Stone

P.D. Meany Publishers
Toronto

Canadian Cataloguing in Publication Data

Stone, James S. (James Stuart), 1919-
    Emily Faithfull, Victorian champion of women's rights

Includes bibliographical references and index.
ISBN 0-88835-040-6

1. Faithfull, Emily, 1835-1895. 2. Women's rights - Great
Britain - History - 19th century. 3. Women social reformers -
Great Britain - Biography. 4. Feminists - Great Britain - Bio-
graphy. I. Title.

HQ1595.F35S78 1994              305.42'092      C94-930618-5

ISBN 0-88835-040-6

*Jacket design is based on a sketch of the Victoria Press offices in the
December 15, 1861 issue of* The Queen. *The frontispiece photo of
Emily Faithfull was taken at the W. & D. Downey studio in London
c. 1886; thanks are due to Professor Laurence A. Cummings for
unearthing this photo.*

Jacket designed and typeset by Glen Patchet.

Printed on acid-free paper in Canada
*for*
P.D. Meany Publishers
Box 118, Streetsville
Ontario, Canada
L5M 2B7.

For my beloved wife Joan, Emily Faithfull's
great-great-niece.

# Contents

# Acknowledgements

First I wish to acknowledge the help and encouragement William E. Fredeman, professor of English at the University of British Columbia, gave me. Though I had done some research prior to reading his excellent article "Emily Faithfull and the Victoria Press" in 1974, it inspired me to delve deeper and write a book-length work rather than a series of articles. I am particularly grateful for his detailed criticism of the first draft of my manuscript and for the project assessments that he and Professor Margaret Fulton, Principal of Mount Saint Vincent University, submitted in support of my application for a research grant in 1984.

Thanks also to Sister Martha Westwater of Mount Saint Vincent University for sending me a copy of a paper on Emily Faithfull that she presented at the University of California (Santa Barbara) in 1981 and for making me aware of the chapter on Emily in her book, *The Wilson Sisters*.

I am also in debt to these librarians: Victor A. Berch, formerly Special Collections Librarian in Brandeis University Library, Waltham, Massachusetts, for providing me with thirty-two titles of Victoria Press publications (see Appendix); David Doughan, Assistant Librarian in the Fawcett Library, London, for setting me on the trail of some of Emily's letters; and Kate Perry, Archivist at Girton College, Cambridge, for letting me see Bessie Parkes's private papers, especially those concerning the Codrington divorce case.

These were the libraries in which I carried out most of my research: the British Library, especially their newspaper library in Colindale, North London; the Bodleian (Oxford); the University of Sussex Library; and the Manchester Central Library. My thanks to all of them, as well as to the library at my home university, the University of Waterloo.

I also wish to thank the University of Waterloo for providing me with working space, supplies, research money, and sabbatical leaves during the nineteen years I spent on this project.

Finally, I owe a debt of gratitude to the late Elizabeth (Betty) Whitbourn (née Faithfull) of Storrington, Sussex, keeper and interpreter of the Faithfull family tree, who uncovered valuable snippets of family history for me. Only her death in 1990 interrupted the welcome flow.

# Preface

My interest in Emily Faithfull was sparked by a passage in one of William Hardman's gossipy biographies that I was reading while researching my book on George Meredith. Referring to the "most sensational" British divorce of the 1860's, namely, the Codrington case, Hardman identified Emily Faithfull, manager of the Victoria Press, as alleged co-respondent and predicted her reputation would be damaged beyond repair. By coincidence, just before I read Hardman's comments, I was poring over the Faithfull family tree with Betty Whitbourn (née Faithfull) and wondering why she said so little about her great-aunt. Apparently the family had continued to regard Emily as a black sheep even in 1900 when Mrs. Whitbourn was born; she admitted that her involvement in the divorce case was still cause for family shame in the 1970's and 1980's. Yet Mrs. Whitbourn was proud of Emily's pioneer work in the British women's movement; so her reaction to my proposal that I bring her into the limelight again was ambivalent. However, I think I convinced her that, because Emily's achievements greatly outshone her shortcomings, her story should be told.

While conducting my research, I was frustrated by the lack of primary materials in archives and elsewhere. Particularly annoying was the absence of personal letters; Emily's "public" letters were available in the *Times*, the *Queen*, etc., and I found several others in the Fawcett Library and the Manchester Public Library--but nothing personal. Moreover, documents that she willed to her friend Charlotte Robinson for transfer (upon Charlotte's death) to Ferdinand Faithfull Begg seem to have disappeared. To make matters worse, non-standard biographical sources provided informal, sketchy, often inaccurate information about Emily, and standard works like the *Dictionary of National Biography* overlooked her. Faced with this situation, I realized that there were not enough facts about the private person Emily Faithfull to justify a conventional biography. But there was plenty of material concerning her public life. So I decided to write a survey of the diverse activities of this Victorian reformer whose important role in the women's movement has been unjustly minimized by her contemporaries and most twentieth-century feminist critics.

Now for an apology, or at least a justification. Very few articles have been written about Emily Faithfull, and no book-length work has appeared prior to this one. So I feel constrained to be definitive, that is, to cite most of my sources. Hence the spate of annoying citations within the text and in endnotes. I suggest that general readers ignore the textual citations. Many of the notes at the back of the book do, however, offer additional information that both general readers and scholars may find interesting. Scholars who want more evidence about sources may write me; my first draft contained ten times as many textual references as the final one.

I have used many abbreviations. "EF" appears in the Notes as substitute for "Emily Faithfull," and dates are abbreviated to Month/Day/Year, for example, "12/3/90" in place of "December 3, 1890." The names of journals and newspapers are also given in truncated form, but usually only after the full title has been used at least once, for instance, *EWJ* (*English Woman's Journal*), *ER* (*Englishwoman's Review*), *W & W* (*Women and Work*), *VM* (*Victoria Magazine*), *WLE* (*West London Express*), *LE* (*London Express*), *LP* (*Lady's Pictorial*), and *ILN* (*Illustrated London News*). Names of clubs, societies, and associations are likewise shortened: SPEW (Society for Promoting the Employment of Women), NAPSS (National Association for the Promotion of Social Science) a.k.a. SSA (Social Science Association), VDS (Victoria Discussion Society), WLA (Women's Liberal Association), NHS (National Health Society), LSA (Ladies' Sanitary Association), WPPL (Women's Protective and Provident League), and FMCES (Female Middle Class Emigration Society).

A final note: as my Emily Faithfull manuscript, twenty years in the making, was going to press, I learned that Eric Ratcliffe had just published a book entitled *The Caxton of Her Age: The Career and Family Background of Emily Faithfull (1835-1895)*. I immediately got hold of a copy and read it carefully. To my delight and relief, it consisted of only eighty-eight pages of text and dealt with Emily's career very briefly, confining itself to her Victoria Press, *Victoria Magazine*, and her three visits to America. Thus it serves as a valuable preamble to my more detailed scholarly work.

# Emily Faithfull

*Chapter 1*

# Introduction

Most people assume that the women's movement in Britain originated with the suffragettes, those militant suffragists who made life uncomfortable for Winston Churchill and his ilk from sometime just after the end of the Boer War. In fact, the movement began much earlier with the struggles of individual women that eventually combined with circumstances from 1855 on to produce a rich harvest in the efforts of a remarkable group of women. The suffragettes, important as they were in obtaining the franchise for women, were only the final straw that, momentarily at least, appeared to have broken the camel's back of male domination.

Or perhaps one should speak not of breaking backs but of changing an image, a concept of femininity that had held sway in the minds of British men and the hearts of most British women since the eighteenth century and had thus constituted "the major ideological agent in enforcing the subordination of women."[1] The chief components of this femininity were nobility, purity, "majestic childishness,"[2] and mental and physical fragility (hence inferiority). Because it was so difficult to maintain these delicate, spiritual qualities,[3] woman's sphere was designed to be private and domestic, essentially confined to the home, where evil could "be thrust out of sight" and this paragon of feminine virtues could remain "incapable of error."[4] Indeed, she would be the "Angel in the House" that Coventry Patmore had eulogized in his popular poem.

Of course, this angel had to be married to qualify as fit guardian of a home and of the moral upbringing of children. Yet she could not be held responsible for those children; for, according to the best medical knowledge of the day, her menstrual cycle inevitably weakened her body and mind. Therefore, her strong, rational husband had legal custody of their offspring;[5] her purpose in life was to produce children, serve her lord and master, and, if she were of the middle or upper class, be his "pretty, defenceless toy."[6] Single women were not part of this image of femininity, except for their aspiring to the married state; old maids were objects of pity and scorn. The fact that this "Angel in the House" was "nowhere to be found among living women"[7] did not alter the image one jot.

During the first half of the nineteenth century the education of young ladies was, for the most part, consonant with this concept of femininity.[8] It could be rigorous, especially if it were conducted in papa's study or at boarding school, where most middle- and upper-class girls spent one or two years in their early teens. But the Young Ladies' Academies and most boarding schools educated girls for the domestic setting (sans cooking and housekeeping[9]), with no thought of gainful employment, though a few of the graduates could conceivably become *amateur* scholars, musicians, or artists. To further emphasize the private sphere of women, their lessons included no "public" knowledge, for example, Geography, History, and Political Economy; even in 1859 the curriculum of the City of London College for Ladies consisted of these traditional subjects: English, Arithmetic, French, German, Drawing, Music, and Good Conduct.[10] And only a year earlier the *Saturday Review*, though it agreed that girls' schools needed to be improved, nevertheless insisted that the sole aim of these schools was to produce "better wives and mothers."[11]

What the architects of female education ignored in their devotion to the ideal of femininity were the economic crises produced by both the Industrial Revolution and the manpower requirements of Britain's budding empire. The former forced millions of working-class and middle-class women to work for pay; the latter resulted in a serious imbalance[12] in the ratio of males to females and hence an increasing number of spinsters and widows, most of whom were also dumped on the labour market.

Middle-class women were hardest hit by these crises, for they were not trained for any occupations outside the home and they could not accept the loss of caste involved in taking jobs that working-class women were already undertaking, e.g., factory work, mining jobs, and domestic service. Besides, middle- and upper-class women had been taught that work was degrading. As late as 1860 *Fraser's Magazine* averred that female labour was a hard necessity and that leisure and refinement were better for women than work of any sort; remunerative work, of course, was out of the question.

Early Victorian ladies had been allowed to play at philanthropy — Dorothea Brooke in George Eliot's novel *Middlemarch* is a case in point — but were not permitted to go "beyond parlour charity."[13] Governessing was acceptable as a job for ladies, but governesses by and large were poorly paid, partly because most ladies were not trained to be governesses and partly because the supply of governesses greatly exceeded the demand. Ladies could do needlework at home, thus avoiding the censure of society, but this enforced secrecy encouraged the sweatshops to pay these lady seamstresses starvation wages.

Other alternatives apparently existed in the 1850's (in theory, at least). Dinah Craik, author of *John Halifax, Gentleman,* suggested in 1858 that young women could be trained in teaching, painting or art, literature, and public entertainment (as actress, singer, or musician) and could take jobs in those professions — The Female School of Art and Design had been established in 1842 — but she entered a caveat that, though public entertainment could be "respectable," it was "dangerous to temperament, character and mode of thought."[14] Most people would have found Dinah Craik's proposal too radical, though; so only a few enterprising women took advantage of these alternatives. Not until 1862 did the *English Journal of Education* approve of the "honourable livehood" ladies could obtain from the pursuit of art, and it recommended that occupation chiefly because of its "requiring so little merely physical exertion, but so much cultivation and delicacy of mind and hand" as to be "particularly adapted to ladies."[15] The writer of this article still entertained the "menstrual myth."[16]

Thus the position of British women by the mid-1850's had changed little from that in the late eighteenth century. Wives were still legally part of their husbands' goods and chattels; ladies lost caste if they accepted any jobs other than governess, teacher, or

amateur artist — indeed, society preferred that they not work at all;
and women's education was geared to their future roles as wives and
mothers, despite the increasing surplus of women over men that made
marriage impossible for many women. Finally, as women's
weaknesses of mind and body supposedly incapacitated them for
public activities, there was no question of extending the franchise to
them. Even Queen Victoria, who had successfully united the
discharge of public duties with the cares of domestic life, abhorred
the idea of women voting.[17]

Significant protest[18] against this state of affairs had begun with
Mary Wollstonecraft's *A Vindication of the Rights of Women* (1792)
and her *On the Education of Daughters* (1787), particularly the
former. In the *Vindication* she advocated an extensive education for
women that would enable them to define themselves, the right to
work to achieve economic independence, and civic rights, including
the franchise and the right to stand for civic office. She was also in
favour of gymnastics for women and co-education to age twenty-one.
Her ideas, which were a hundred years ahead of their time, were
regarded in her day as "heretical and blasphemous"[19] and this
perception was maintained throughout most of the nineteenth century,
chiefly by character assassination. That is, she was vilified for her
ideas and actions concerning free love. As a result, pioneers in
women's work from the 1850's on avoided mentioning her name
while borrowing her ideas.[20]

An American woman, Margaret Fuller Ossoli (1810-1850),
deserves special mention[21] here because of her personal achievements and her influence on the British women's movement. Literary
critic for the *New York Tribune*, teacher, founding editor of *Dial*,
nurse in the Italian revolutions of 1848-49, foreign correspondent for
the *New York Tribune,* she also wrote *Woman in the Nineteenth
Century* and started a series of "Conversations" for women to
broaden their education. *Woman in the Nineteenth Century* exposed
the tyranny of men and the myths concerning women, and attempted
to construct a feminist framework for women to "encode their own
reality," to define their own sphere.[22]

Caroline Norton also merits attention for bringing the unjust laws
governing marriage, divorce, and child custody to the attention of
feminists. After her husband tried to sue her for divorce in the late

1830's for consorting with a cabinet minister, she discovered that she could neither get free of him nor get custody of her children. Her pleas concerning infant custody in 1838 resulted in the first Infants' Custody Act of 1839, which stated that a non-adulterous mother *might* be granted custody of children under seven and have access to older children. And her complaints about unequal treatment of women in divorce courts led to the Divorce and Matrimonial Causes Act (a.k.a. the Marriage and Divorce Act) of 1857, which permitted a wife to divorce her husband if she could prove adultery in conjunction with cruelty, desertion, sodomy, bestiality, rape, or incest. Of more importance for feminists,[23] though, was the inspiration Barbara Leigh Smith derived from Caroline Norton's plight that caused her in 1854 to write *A Brief Summary in Plain Language of the Most Important Laws Concerning Women* and in 1855 to work with a committee of women to obtain 3,000 signatures to a Married Women's Property petition that got as far as a second reading in Parliament before it was shelved in favour of the Marriage and Divorce Act. Thus Caroline Norton was in small measure responsible for the establishment of the group that I have been referring to as the pioneers of the Women's Movement in Britain.

Another important precursor of that movement was Harriet Taylor Mill (1807-1858), author in 1851 of "The Enfranchisement of Women," a *Westminster Review* essay that expressed the same ideas her husband John Stuart Mill adumbrated more forcefully in his book *The Subjection of Women* (written in 1861, but not published until 1869), namely, the need for employment, education, and votes for women as well as for legislation to raise married women from a state of virtual slavery. "The Enfranchisement of Women" put Mary Wollstonecraft's ideas into a Victorian context.

More widely read than Harriet Mill's essay was *Eliza Cook's Journal* (1849-1856). In this weekly publication Eliza Cook covered a gamut of subjects, most of which related to women. For example, in her October 5, 1850 article "Wrongs of Englishwomen" and a sequel to it in the February 5, 1853 issue she condemned those English laws — citing Blackstone to support her case — that granted wives no legal rights, permitted the ill treatment of women of all classes, and deprived single women of representation in government, even though they paid taxes. Eliza also spoke out about women's education: working women, she contended, should receive intellectual as well as domestic education; governesses should be better trained; "after education" of men and women of the working class should occur in mutual improvement societies, people's colleges, and mechanics' institutes;[24] defective education is "the real cause of [women's] helplessness as producers and workers;" wives' and mothers' "usefulness would be extended by their improved moral and intellectual culture;"[25] above all, the "menstrual myth" should be laid to rest by cultivating a woman's strengths instead of her weaknesses — a "woman's intellect should be systematically strengthened by culture, exercise, and discipline"[26] through exposing her to as broad an education as possible.

Cook agreed that the proper sphere of woman was the home, but she recognized that "for a large number of women, this is but a beautiful theory, and yet very far from being realized in practice."[27] Moreover, she noted that the greatest deficiency of employment occurred among middle-class women, whose occupations were confined to teaching (governessing), dressmaking, and millinery. She recommended that these "poor genteel women" should put aside their false pride concerning work and, with some practical training to make amends for their "neglected or perverted education," enter the job market as "shopwomen, designers, wood engravers, watchmakers, and compositors in printing offices."[28] Failing that, they should emigrate. All in all, Eliza Cook appears to have been the originator of many of the general and specific proposals that the "pioneers" translated into action from 1858 on.[29]

But the immediate[30] precursors of the nineteenth-century British women's movement were Florence Nightingale and Anna Jameson.[31] The former's heroism convinced even Queen Victoria that there might be some place for women in public life. Furthermore, though she was broken in health after her experiences in the Crimea, the "lady with the lamp" did yeoman duty in organizing departments of public service in England and abroad — hospitals, nursing, army barracks' sanitation, etc. Above all, her example in nursing and her insistence on rigorous training for women nurses made the occupation of nursing suitable for all women, including gentlewomen.

Florence Nightingale, Barbara Leigh Smith's cousin, preferred to work on her own. Therefore, Anna Jameson, a gregarious person who was closely associated with the young women who formed the nucleus of the women's movement, influenced them more directly than Nightingale did. Anna was a member of Barbara Leigh Smith's committee formed in December 1855 to obtain signatures for the unsuccessful Married Women's Property petition of 1857, and she encouraged the young women on this committee and in the subsequent Langham Place Circle "to make her stopping place their headquarters . . . She was their patroness and she called them her nieces."[32] They, in turn, considered her to be "one of the best and brightest women of the earlier Victorian era."[33]

Already an established writer and art critic, Anna Jameson got involved in the early 1840's with the education and employment of women. In an 1843 article summing up the 1842 *Report of the Royal Commission on the Employment of Women and Young People in Mines* she "demanded [that] public support come to the aid of working women and provide increased educational facilities for all women."[34] And in 1855 and 1856 she gave two remarkable lectures entitled "Sisters of Charity" and "The Communion of Labour" in which she proposed that the growing philanthropic work of women be extended to include the social employment of women in public institutions. In a prefatory letter to Lord John Russell, President of NAPSS (the National Association for the Promotion of Social Science established in 1857), she summed up these "requirements" of the women of England as follows: (1) "Some part of the government of public institutions (charitable, educational, sanitary) in which women and children are congregated . . . should be in the hands of able and intelligent women . . . e.g., prisons, workhouses, asylums, factories, hospitals, industrial schools," including departments of medical science, e.g., nursing, civil and military; management of rural hospitals; district visiting by Sisters of Charity. (2) Training to work in the above departments to be provided. (3) Higher kinds of industrial, professional and artistic training to be made freely accessible to women. (4) Boys to be taught "some principle of conscientious duty toward women." (5)"The woman's sphere of knowledge and activity . . . be limited only by her capacities."[35]

Anna also suggested that her "nieces" publish a journal setting forth the needs and claims of women and that they accept an invitation to join NAPSS in 1858. As her lecture "The Communion of Labour" emphasized, she believed that men and women could work together for the good of humanity if only women were allowed to shoulder their share of the burden. Her hope in this instance was that the men of NAPSS would permit the women to get directly involved in their activities.

Inspired by Jameson, the young women who comprised the Ladies' Circle (later called the Langham Place Circle because of the location of their first permanent headquarters) initiated the sweeping reforms concerning jobs, education and votes for women, married women's property, and the custody of children that were enacted between 1858 and 1895. Not all of them had been members of Barbara Leigh Smith's Married Women's Property petition committee — only Bessie Rayner Parkes, Barbara Leigh Smith, and Matilda Mary Hays could claim that honour — but Maria Rye and (very likely) Adelaide Procter had assisted with the preparation of that petition.[36] Isa Craig came on the scene in 1857, Emily Faithfull in 1858, Jessie Boucherett in 1859, and Emily Davies and Elizabeth Garrett in 1862. Of course, there were lesser lights in the group (e.g., Sarah Lewin, Jane Crowe, and Anna Mary Howitt); but these were the ones whose achievements were most manifest: Bessie Parkes and Barbara Smith as leaders and as founders of the first women's magazine in Britain, the *English Woman's Journal*; Matilda Hays as co-editor of this journal (with Bessie Parkes); Maria Rye, who dedicated her life to the emigration of "surplus" women and pauper children; Isa Craig, first secretary of the Social Science Association (NAPSS); Jessie Boucherett, founder of the Society for Promoting the Employment of Women — with the unfortunate acronym SPEW; Elizabeth Garrett (later Dr. Elizabeth Garrett Anderson),who fought for the right of women to become medical doctors; Emily Davies, one of the founders of Girton College, Cambridge; and Emily Faithfull, who, though primarily concerned with getting suitable jobs for women in occupations and professions from which they had formerly been excluded, was associated with every venture that the Langham Place ladies embarked upon, as well as some of her own making.

Barbara Leigh Smith, a financially independent rebel and free spirit who often had to brave the censures of society because of her illegitimacy and her outspoken advocacy of women's rights, was the acknowledged leader of the group, even after her marriage in 1857 resulted in her spending eight months of every year in Algeria. For she originated the ideas that the others acted upon. The Married Women's Property petition of 1855 is a good example of her originality; inspired by John Stuart Mill's *Political Economy* (1849) but disappointed with his too brief allusions to "marriage and the laws affecting women,"[37] she investigated those laws and subsequently produced a well-documented petition that was approved by the Society for Amendments to the Law and sponsored by two members of that Society (Lord Brougham in the House of Lords and Sir Erskine Perry in the House of Commons). Unfortunately, the petition was superseded by the Marriage and Divorce Act, but its very presence caused an amendment to that Act concerning deserted wives — one small success for womankind.

In 1857 Barbara Leigh Smith also came up with a grandiose plan for the remunerative employment of middle-class women entitled *Women and Work*. She proposed that 10,000 women be apprenticed to watchmakers; 10,000 be trained as teachers of the young; 10,000 as accountants; 10,000 as nurses under deaconesses trained by Florence Nightingale; several thousands in telegraph offices; 10,000 as lecturers in Mechanics' Institutes; 1,000 as readers of the best books to working people; 10,000 as managers of washing machines, sewing machines, etc. "Then the distressed needle-women would vanish; the decayed gentlewomen and broken-down governesses would not exist."[38] Barbara also extolled the virtues of work — "WORK . . . the great beautifier . . . makes women fit to be the mothers of children"[39] — and she contended that women should be able to work even after marriage, as many professions (e.g., medicine, decorative art, woodcutting, watchmaking, engraving) could be carried on at home. *Women and Work* caught the attention of Lord Brougham, president of the recently founded Social Science Association (NAPSS) who already knew Barbara through her father, Benjamin Smith. He therefore invited her and the other Langham Place ladies to become members of the SSA, and they did so in 1858. Consequently, the SSA soon came to consider the employment of educated women "a subject hardly to be surpassed in importance."[40]

Bessie Rayner Parkes's early work[41] in the women's movement also deserves comment. Because she was a close friend of Barbara

Leigh Smith, she became a charter member of the Ladies' Circle. A "handsome, sensitive, literary,"[42] intelligent person, with a "sweetness of nature"[43] that appealed strongly to George Eliot, Bessie differed markedly from Barbara Leigh Smith in being politically cautious. This caution made her less outspoken than Barbara; however, she did not shy away from exposing the unsatisfactory conditions under which women laboured.

Bessie Parkes, Barbara Smith, and Anna Jameson all realized that there should be a journal to publicize the women's movement. Early in 1857 Bessie agreed to edit the *Waverley Journal* in Edinburgh with a view to purchasing it (with Barbara's money). Negotiations took place from April to December, but finally, with the advice of a lawyer, George Woodyatt Hastings, they dropped the whole idea. Instead, Bessie and Matilda Hays undertook to edit a new magazine, the *English Woman's Journal*, with the primary aim of promoting the employment of women. Thus Bessie Parkes became *de facto* head of the women's movement, for she was in charge of the office on Princes Street where the journal was published, and where a women's club and employment register were established. Barbara was available to provide money and give advice in person or by letter; but Bessie had to make on-the-spot decisions. For example, though George Eliot told Bessie she was not impressed with the work Matilda Hays had done on the first issue of the journal (March 1858) and Barbara thought little of Matilda's efforts, Bessie kept her on staff until 1863. She also opened up the pages of the journal to the Ladies' Sanitary Association and she assumed full responsibility for 1858 journal articles on the plight of governesses, the implications for women of the 1851 census, female pauperism in workhouses, the need for female emigration and more avenues of work for women, the flaws in the new Marriage and Divorce Act, the proposed Workhouse Visiting Society, the need to connect female nursing with a large public institution, and the proceedings of the 1858 SSA meeting, especially the papers presented by Louisa Twining on Workhouses, by Mary Carpenter on Ragged Schools and Reformatories, by Florence Nightingale on Health and the Construction of Hospitals, and by Isa Craig on Emigration. All in all, Bessie did a fine job of conducting the *English Woman's Journal* and directing the little band of workers gathered round her during that first year of publication of the journal.

Cautious as Bessie Parkes was in exposing the wrongs of women in 1858, both she and Barbara were strongly criticized for their "women's rights' cry" by the *Saturday Review of Politics, Literature, and Art*, a journal which was to remain critical of the women's movement for the next thirty years and more. The *Saturday Review* likewise treated Barbara's *Women and Work* and Bessie's *Remarks on the Education of Girls* with contempt, branding the two writers and their circle as "strong-minded women,"[44] a term of reproach which implied that they had gone so far in their education, their radical ideas, and their actions that they had "unsexed" themselves. John Morley, reviewing Bessie Parkes's *Essays on Woman's Work* in 1865, voiced much the same prejudice when he referred to the "unwritten laws of social etiquette or sentiment" that do not permit women to work. Morley was particularly concerned about women "outraging . . . the plain dictates of nature" by "rushing into professions."[45]

The majority of Victorian women also condemned these advocates of women's rights. Even in 1879 the phrase "women's rights" was anathema to women who otherwise believed in the general advancement of their sex. And certainly in 1858 most women would have agreed with Margaret Oliphant's 1866 answer to John Stuart Mill in *Blackwood's Edinburgh Magazine* wherein she favoured emigration of women over their working for pay, education of women with marriage only in mind, a laissez-faire approach to the laws affecting married women, and, as a comfortable, middle-aged householder, utter rejection of the franchise that Mr. Mill was trying to obtain for her. Martha Westwater notes "the inexorable force of antifeminist thought among Victorian upperclass women"[46] when they contemplated having to exchange their class worth for individual worth; and that ultra-conservative attitude infected middle-class women as well.

Yet the Langham Place ladies would not have considered themselves radical, despite their wanting to change society. They might have accepted a compromise label "radical conservative," though some would have found even that designation too strong. No doubt all except Matilda Hays would have approved of the verbal slap on the wrist the editor of the *Spectator* gave Matilda for her "injudicious" statement that it was degrading for women to be wives, mothers, and sisters: "If Miss Craig, Miss Rye, and Miss Faithfull are to succeed in their efforts to find a place for the surplus, unattached female labourers, the fewer of these letters [to the editor] . . . the better."[47] Far better, they would have concurred, to uphold the concept of "the English Gentlewoman" set forth in the June 1864 edition of the *English Woman's Journal*: "Apart from politics, we have a conservatism in England, a right royal, true blue opinion, which holds its ground in spite of every shade of Whiggism, and Liberalism, and sectarianism. It is that feeling which preserves our gentlewomen as a recognized body among us, and gives it a place of such social importance that it may well claim to be an 'Estate of the realm.'"[48] The Langham Place ladies were tenacious in their criticism of injustices to women and in their non-militant attempts to remedy those injustices, but they were equally adamant about upholding their reputations as English gentlewomen. For them there was nothing more important to the cause of women than preserving their "good name[s] . . . at home and abroad."[49] Thus conservatism with a small "c" was as much the order of the day as was the necessity of getting the men in the Social Science Association to support them in their endeavours to readjust the social machinery.

*Chapter 2*

# A Brief Biographical Survey

The paucity of material concerning Emily Faithfull's personal life, the absence of formal biographies, and her exclusion from standard biographical sources such as the *Dictionary of National Biography* all militate against a conventional biography. Indeed, after an introduction concerning the British women's movement, the following structure seems appropriate: a chapter dealing chronologically with the few known facts and credible opinions about Emily's private life; succeeded by a systematic survey of her public activities over several chapters; then a concluding chapter assessing her overall contribution to the cause of women.

Youngest daughter of Reverend Ferdinand Faithfull, Emily was born in Headley, Surrey, on May 27, 1835. Her family tree[1] reveals an upper middle-class respectability dating back at least to the middle of the eighteenth century when her great-grandfather William Faithfull, an innkeeper who later became a corn merchant, was listed as "gent." Family gentility was given a further boost in Emily's grandfather, John Faithfull (1752-1827), a scholar of Merton College, Oxford, and later rector[2] of Warfield (near Eton and Windsor), where he conducted a "prep" school for Eton.

Three of John Faithfull's sons entered the Church: Francis Joseph Faithfull (1786-1854) became rector of a rich living at Hatfield (near St. Alban's), where he too ran a "prep" school for boys; another uncle, Robert, assumed the rectorship of Warfield when his father retired; and Emily's father, Ferdinand (1789-1871), was rector of Headley (near Epsom) from 1830 until his death. Several of Emily's male cousins also became rectors and a few of her female cousins married rectors. And Emily's brother George, a graduate of Oxford and rector of Storrington, founded a "crammer" school to prepare boys for army officer training. So the family as a whole got deeply involved with church and education, and this dual interest manifested itself again and again in succeeding generations.[3] For example, Emily's second cousin, Lilian, was principal of Cheltenham Ladies' College[4] from 1907 to 1922; and George's son and grandson kept the "crammer" at Storrington going until the Second World War.

In interviews granted after she had achieved fame as lecturer and reformer, Emily said little about her childhood except that she was sent at age thirteen to a boarding school in Kensington and presented at court when she was twenty-one.[5] She seems to have been a happy child. In her journalistic columns she recalled with pleasure the gallops with her father over the Surrey Downs, holidays with her family on the continent, and an enjoyable visit to the Great Exhibition of 1851. Yet she chafed at the restrictions imposed by her father, brothers, and other figures of authority. For instance, her "dear old governess" read her a lecture and sent her to bed when she "caught her secretly playing cricket with the boys" (*LP*, 9/8/88, 258). And her elder brother was furious with her for riding alone in a hansom cab after seeing a friend off on the train: "In fact I had to vacate the hansom, which he duly paid, and to take a modest four-wheel cab, very much to my chagrin" (*LP*, 6/18/92, 964). She was also indignant at not being allowed to walk unescorted with a young female friend in London's Belgrave district. And she remembered her "misery when a devout elder brother of mine" — George, who was seven years older than Emily, is probably the one referred to in both instances — "burnt the copy of Longfellow's 'Golden Legend'[6] I had spent all my pocket-money in purchasing" (*LP*, 6/19/86, 557). Still, in later years Emily recognized these restrictions as part and parcel of the conventions of the early Victorian Age, and she only alluded to them to demonstrate the welcome changes that had occurred, especially in sporting pastimes, reading, and the chaperoning of girls and young ladies.

Referring to her elementary education, she castigated the teachers who made her suffer because they "never troubled themselves about the individuality of their pupil" (*LP*, 5/6/93, 692). She said no more about the boarding school in Kensington. Yet, coming from a family so involved with education, she doubtless learned something at her father's or brother's knee or at her uncle's school in Hatfield.

There is only one mention of sickness in her nonage. From early childhood she suffered from asthma and the killer bronchitis that often succeeded it. In fact, Emily's early lessons in swimming and whatever swims she enjoyed in later years had to take place in southern France and Spain because she did not dare swim in the cool waters and cool weather of England.

As for juvenile bugbears, she admitted in later years that she had had the "utmost fear since childhood" (*W&W*, 12/11/75, 4) of black mourning garb — especially "the hideous monstrosity called widow's weeds" (*LP*, 4/10/86, 315). And "the idea of the 'cold grave' and its train of ghastly horrors [had] always filled [her] with a repugnance the process of cleansing fires quite [failed] to inspire" (*LP*, 11/29/90, 910). So even as a child she appears to have preferred cremation to burial.

In 1853 Emily made her début into London society at the house of Lady Morgan (Sidney Owenson), novelist and feminist,[7] and commenced upon a round of parties, balls, Queen's drawing rooms, and so on. She soon struck up a strong friendship with Helen Jane Codrington,[8] wife of Henry John Codrington, a naval Captain who later rose to the rank of Admiral and became a Knight Commander of the Bath. As Emily stated at the Codrington divorce trial in 1864, she stayed "with Mrs. Codrington more or less from 1854 to 1857" (*Times*, 11/21/64, 10). The Codringtons moved to Malta in 1858, but Emily's friendship with Helen Jane apparently continued unabated until May 1864.

Emily was presented at court in 1856, a confirmation of her position as untitled gentlewoman which no doubt resulted in more parties and balls. But this social life, especially after Helen Jane left England, began to pall. She told an interviewer in 1890 that, having for a time enjoyed the "usual aimless existence which most girls lead," she "determined to do some literary work."[9] That resolution guided her to the offices of the *English Woman's Journal* and its editor, Bessie Parkes, in November 1858. Bessie welcomed Emily as a "hearty young worker" for the *Journal*; in fact, she informed Barbara Bodichon in January 1859 that "Emily Faithfull is the nearest approach to my ideal of a canvasser I have yet got hold of. A clergyman's daughter, aged 23, & rather strong-minded; carried her own huge carpet bag, etc."[10] This impression of her as a woman to be reckoned with accords well with a reporter's 1860 description of the apparent contradiction between Emily's appearance and personality:

She . . . is very simple looking — has somewhat the appearance of a
farmer's daughter who did not spend her whole life over a piano or in
wasting coloured worsted — has expressive dark eyes and a very sweet
smile. When she began to read one could see that she had a character
fitted to command and energy enough underlying her appearance of
simplicity.[11]

Emily soon made friends with most of her new colleagues, but
Bessie Parkes remained aloof. Though Emily took her to her Headley
home in August [1859][12] and Bessie still regarded Emily as "a
splendid worker," the conservative editor of the *Journal* apparently
found her a bit too bold, perhaps even, as she wrote Barbara in
December 1861, "unsettled morally."[13] In another letter to Barbara
in September 1862 she stated that, although Emily was "*very* clever
and *very* kind in many ways," she had detected "a particular screw
loose which might . . . some day bring her to Millbank [an insane
asylum] . . . . At the same time, the character is so strong that it
might be most noble, but I fear it never will unless by some
unforeseen grace of God."[14] So Bessie decided to exercise caution
in her private dealings with Emily, though she was quite willing to
work closely with her in public endeavours like the Victoria Press,
the Society for Promoting the Employment of Women, and the
committee attempting to get women admitted to the universities as
students.

    Adelaide Procter had no such qualms. She got Emily into the
Portfolio Club, in which members read their (or other members')
poems or exhibited their paintings.[15] Adelaide and Emily also served
on SPEW and SSA committees, wrote for the *English Woman's
Journal*, and worked together at the Victoria Press. All of Adelaide's
co-workers agreed that she was a lively, cheerful person with a good
sense of humour; Emily, though not such an extrovert as Adelaide,
had the same characteristics. So from 1859 to 1862 they were good
friends. Then sometime in 1862, probably in the summer before
Adelaide caught the tuberculosis that killed her in 1864, something
happened to end their friendship. I believe that Adelaide unearthed
some details about Emily's relationship with the Codringtons, Emily
tried to cover up with a lie, and Adelaide caught her out in that
lie.[16] Whatever the explanation, Adelaide made it clear in letters to
Bessie Parkes[17] that her friendship with Emily was over: "The break
with Emily Faithfull is made and is a great one. . . . [It] occurred

when I thought ill enough of E.F. to drop her and to break my friendship with her."[18] This intimate friendship apparently fell victim to the scandalous divorce case even before it went to court.

The year 1863, during most of which Emily basked in public praise for her work with the Victoria Press and her launching of the *Victoria Magazine,* began calmly enough in the offices of the *English Woman's Journal.* Emily Davies, almost through her brief term as editor of the *Journal,* waxed sanguine about Emily Faithfull, despite Adelaide's unexplained breakup with her. To Barbara Bodichon she wrote, "I don't think there is any fear now, of her turning out badly. Miss Lewin spoke to me very strongly to-day about the great improvement she had seen in her. . . . She says Miss Parkes does not do Miss Faithfull justice yet, but she thinks she will by and by."[19]

But storm clouds were gathering in Bessie Parkes's mind,[20] as this comment in her letter of 18 May 63 to Barbara Bodichon indicates: "The Portfolio [Club] is asked to meet tomorrow night at Emily Faithfull's, a sore vexation, for I don't like to go; & yet just now it is doubly ungracious to stay away" (*Parkes Papers,* BRP V 117/1). She was not caught completely off guard, then, when the story of Emily's involvement with the Codringtons darkened the public horizon six months later. Here is Bessie's undated letter to Barbara Bodichon that refers to the coming scandal without naming names:

> Isa [Craig] burst out one day by accident with part of it to my astonished ears! and little by little the other two [Matilda (Max) Hays and Emily Davies?] let out what they knew!
> Sometimes I think she is mad; a mere case of "Folie Lucide"; but whether she is mad or bad, & whether what she says is true or false is more than I can tell.
> Now this is all I can or dare tell you; and more perhaps than I ought to say. I do not think you will do harm by visiting her; but I am publicly involved; & must keep clear of the blow-up which I think must by all the laws of chances, come some day . . . Max knows the whole" (*Parkes Papers,* BRP V, 159 [November 1863]).

Bessie's first public act of separation from Emily Faithfull occurred a month later (December 1863) when she cancelled the Victoria Press contract to print the *English Woman's Journal.*[21]

Other members of the Langham Place Circle remained loyal to Emily until the summer or fall of 1864. Emily Davies, who knew her well enough to call her "Fido" and served as editor of Fido's *Victoria Magazine* until March 1864, observed that "Some months [after my resignation], Miss Faithfull was obliged, owing to some references to her in reports of a divorce case, to withdraw for a time, from society, & I, & others, ceased to be associated with her."[22] Isa Craig and Matilda Hays held out longest — Isa because of a genuine feeling of friendship for Emily,[23] and Matilda because her own reputation was teetering on the knife edge of respectability[24] — but by the time of the Codrington divorce trial they too accepted the inevitable.

One person who did not desert Emily was Emilie Wilson. Their intense friendship[25] had begun in 1862 when Emilie, one of six sisters in an upper middle-class family, abandoned her rather vague philanthropic attempts to improve the quality of country life and embraced Emily's chief cause, getting jobs for women. She and Emily were inseparable during the mid-1860's. They stayed at each other's homes, vacationed together, visited friends together, listened to concerts and lectures together, and so on.[26] More than anyone else, Emilie and her family sustained Emily during the agonizing days of the Codrington divorce trial.

This trial commenced on July 29, 1864. Admiral Codrington's initial petition, filed November 14, 1863, had accused his wife of adultery with two co-respondents, chief of whom was Colonel David Anderson. Mrs. Codrington's response of June 4, 1864 "denied the adultery, accused her husband of extreme cruelty, and offered in extenuation of any adultery that may have transpired, that Admiral Codrington had 'by his wilful neglect and misconduct' conduced to it" (Fredeman, p. 143). In his suit the Admiral further alleged that the adulteries took place in Malta during his posting there and in London on their return; he also suggested that in 1863 Emily Faithfull may have provided a trysting place for his wife and Colonel Anderson. Mrs. Codrington countercharged that he had neglected her in Malta for a Mrs. Watson and that one night [in London] in October 1856, while she was occupying "the same room and sleeping in the same Bed" with Miss Emily Faithfull, her husband had come into that room,

got into the Bed in which [she] and the said Miss Faithfull were then sleeping and then attempted to have connexion with the said Miss

Faithfull while asleep. And [he] was only prevented effecting his purpose by the resistance of the said Miss Faithfull.

Ever after the said occasion and in consequence thereof [she] refused to allow [him] to occupy the same Bed with her and all conjugal intercourse between her and the [Admiral] from that time forward ceased (Public Records Office, J77.11, ff.5-6, paragraphs 2-3).

An adjournment was granted on August 1 for two reasons: first, the respondent (Mrs. Codrington) needed time to collect evidence from witnesses in Malta; second, Miss Faithfull was "not forthcoming" on July 29, having fled the country. The case broke in the newspapers right after the adjournment. Scandal sheets had a heyday, and even the normally sedate *Times* reported the trial "with extraordinary fullness of salacious detail."[27] In Fredeman's words, the "acres of type devoted to the trial by *The times* [reflected] a widespread public interest, no doubt intensified by the social position of the two principals and the countersuit by Mrs. Codrington, a novelty made possible by the Marriage and Divorce Bill of 1857" (Fredeman, p. 143).

More to our purpose, Bessie Parkes's lawyer father began a string of letters to his daughter concerning the "dirty Codrington case" (*Parkes Papers*, BRP II 80/3, August 2, 1864) that pre-judged Emily for her part in it. On August 3 he opined that "[whatever happens] E.F. is ruined and in exile from all Society respecting herself," and he gave his daughter some fatherly advice about the dangers that encompass virtuous women who take up with bad company: "Everybody compromises herself, of your sex, who keeps company with any who have publicly violated the great cardinal rules of morality" (*Parkes Papers*, BRP II 80/5). Nevertheless, his letter of August 11 disagreed with a scandal magazine's contention that the case was "injurious to Ladies' work," for he believed the "decline and fall of Emily Faithful (sic) won't stay the gradual rise of your Sex in their proper scale" (*Parkes Papers*, BRP II/82).

When the trial was reconvened on November 17, Emily appeared as a hostile witness. She conceded that in 1858 she had given evidence to Mr. Few, Mrs. Codrington's lawyer, about the Admiral's having taken liberties with her in 1856. But she argued that in so doing she was merely repeating what Mrs. Codrington had told her about the incident, that she had no recollection of any attempted rape, and that she woke up just as the Admiral was leaving the bedroom.

The idea of his behaving improperly had come to her from Mrs. Codrington and Mr. Few, and she had believed their story until she read the copy of the affidavit she had signed — without reading it — on May 12, 1864. She had then consulted a lawyer and, on his advice, left the country to avoid being subpocnaed by Mr. Few. On her return — again, doubtless, advised by her lawyer — she decided to contradict the evidence given in the affidavit.

Why did Emily change sides? Fredeman believes that the Admiral had intimidated her. Admittedly, there are grounds for this hypothesis. Early testimony for the Petitioner referred to Miss Faithfull's leaving his house of her own accord or his sending her away in early 1857, and his then placing a sealed package "in the hands of his brother, the General, containing an explanation of the cause of her dismissal, which remains in his custody with the seals unbroken" (*Times*, 11/18/64, 8). This statement implied a lesbian relationship[28] between Emily and Mrs. Codrington and threatened to reveal it if Emily's evidence favoured Mrs. Codrington.

Emily denied any knowledge of the package and insisted she had remained on friendly terms with the Admiral. She even introduced as evidence a letter from him to her sister "stating that in consequence of the differences between his wife and himself he objected to any third person domiciled in his house, and assuring her that in wishing Miss Faithfull to leave he was not actuated by any personal feeling towards her" (*Times*, 11/21/64, 11). Emily likewise denied that she had allowed Mrs. Codrington to use her home for assignations with Colonel Anderson.[29] In fact, she stated, on November 1, 1863 she had admonished her friend for being "excessively indiscreet and imprudent" and told her plainly that she (Emily) "did not like to be mixed up in the affair." Consequently, she and Mrs. Codrington had exchanged "unpleasant words." Yet they had remained friends until May 1864 when, according to Emily, she had signed the aforementioned affidavit after Mrs. Codrington promised not to involve her in the upcoming divorce case.

But Mrs. Codrington did involve her, and that, I believe, was the reason for Emily's defection. By dragging her into court to give evidence, Mrs. Codrington had abrogated their agreement. Friendship could not survive the fact that she (Emily) was being used as a pawn[30] by Mrs. Codrington and her lawyer.[31] So she decided to save herself if possible, though her chances of doing so were very slim in a society that condemned a woman for merely being cited in a divorce case.

The court allowed the Admiral's petition,[32] and the judge directed that there was no evidence to support the "charges" against Emily Faithfull. But despite the judge's further assertion that Emily was innocent though foolish, and at least one newspaper reporter's suggestion that she was led astray by a woman older and more experienced in the ways of the world, her reputation was thoroughly sullied. As S.M. Ellis says of the outcome of this "most sensational Divorce Case of the 'Sixties,"[33] Emily's "name was bruited abroad to the far ends of the world with much coarse jest and innuendo in the year 1864 and long after."[34]

Quidnuncs like Robert Browning assumed the worst of her: "As for Miss Emily . . . one of the counsel in the case told an acquaintance of mine that the 'sealed letter' contained a charge I shall be excused from even hinting to you — fear of the explosion of which, caused the shift of Miss Emily from one side to the other."[35] Sir William Hardman, somewhat less gossipy, still wrote off the "Lady Manager of the Victoria Press [as] simply a fool."[36] And Joseph Parkes, who had judged her so harshly in his August letters to Bessie, maintained this course in letters written during the trial —

"Most here [in the lawyers' office] and in the Court thought that she swore much falsehood and concealed the real facts. . ." (*Parkes Papers*, BRP II 83/2, 11/19/64)
and "E.F. will have her partisans, tho' I think most men and nearly all your sex will give her up as a dangerous woman and of impure mind." (*Parkes Papers*, BRP II 83/3, 11/20/64).

But he was a trifle kinder to her when sentence was passed on January 29, 1865: "I don't believe now E.F. ever did confess such supposed act [adultery with Admiral Codrington] or even approve the draft Affs [affidavits] shown her by [Mr.] Few . . . I believe the truth to be that she kept back much fact and truth of both husband and wife in her evidence, and that forced into the box she made up her tale to cut the best figure for *herself* in her painful, ambiguous and contradictory relations to both. E.F.'s worst plight is being so long the friend if not companion of so loose a woman as Mrs. C. and palpably continuing so late to herd with her; and I don't doubt she did lend her premises to assignations. On the whole the dirty case

will take all the enamel off of Emily's reputation and ruin her
business. If wise she will at once retire from business and her
Printership to the Queen. Still one pities her as a wild girl thrown
into such society at the early mad age of nineteen. . . . E.F. is bold,
and may try to brazen it out, but the Social Science Association +c
can't continue printing with her" (*Parkes Papers*, BRP II 79/3).

Bessie Parkes agreed with her father that, despite her feeling of
pity for Emily, she and the other Langham Place ladies[37] had to
continue to shun her. Bessie was not sure whether the Queen would
take away the Printership or refuse to admit her at court, but, as she
wrote to her friend Mary Merryweather on November 30, 1864, she
feared that Emily would "brazen it out" by showing up at "the very
next [Queen's] drawing room" (*Parkes Papers*, BRP VI 86). In the
event, she did not try to regain admittance to court gatherings, the
Queen did not cancel the Royal Printership, and the SSA[38] had their
*Transactions* printed by the Victoria Press for several years longer,
though the reference to Emily as publisher was disguised from 1866
on. Furthermore, though Victorian decorum demanded that the
Langham Place ladies terminate personal relationships, some resumed
public dealings with her in the 1870's. For example, Elizabeth Garrett
Anderson took part in several Victoria Discussion Society meetings,
and Emily Davies received a "Scotch (sic) lady" that Emily had sent
to her concerning employment.

Yet they were careful to disclaim their connection with her and
to depreciate her achievements. In the November 1864 *Alexandra
Magazine* (an offshoot of *EWJ*) Bessie Parkes, the editor, made it
abundantly clear that Miss Faithfull had not been a member of SPEW
for over four years, the Victoria Press had always been a private
enterprise under Miss Faithfull's direction,[39] and letters to Miss
Faithfull concerning employment must not be addressed to SPEW
(*Alexandra Magazine*, 11/64, 445-446). Bessie did not mention the
important role she had played in purchasing a small printing press
and working with Emily during the feasibility study that led to the
establishment of the Victoria Press. Nor did she confess that she had
long entertained a dream of establishing a Press organized and
operated by women under the management of a woman.[40]

Emily's family appear to have broken ranks concerning her
disgrace. Her sisters, Esther Faithfull Fleet and Maria Faithfull Begg,
stood by her during the trial and later, though, according to Bessie
Parkes's letter to Mary Merryweather, Esther "went home to bed very

ill after [Emily's final court appearance], & no wonder" (*Parkes Papers*, BRP VI 86). And Emily's mother doubtless gave her all the support she could. As Emily told an interviewer in 1890, her "two most cherished possessions" were an engraved portrait of the Queen and a pen-and-ink likeness of her mother (*Women's Penny Paper*, 8/2/90, 482), and another interviewer who visited her home in Manchester noted these two items plus a portrait of her grandfather and grandmother (*Manchester Faces & Places*, 1892, 133-4) — but none of her father.[41] Therefore, we may assume that he disowned or at least ignored her during the last seven years of his life.[42] Indeed, nowhere in Emily's writings does she say anything about her adult relationship with her father; so he may have disapproved of her lifestyle from the time she left home.

Here one encounters difficulties, though. For, after the trauma of the divorce trial, Emily seems to have destroyed all of her private papers; in particular, there are no letters from or to members of her family. She saved several volumes of autograph letters as well as thirty-five years of newspaper clippings about the progress of women,[43] but nothing of a personal nature. So one can only speculate about relationships with her family during and following the Codrington fiasco, except for shared public experiences with nieces, nephews, and cousins from the 1870's on and meetings with her brother George in the 1880's, all of which she recorded in her journalistic columns.

The scandalous divorce case may also have been partly responsible for Emily's financial difficulties with the Victoria Press and the *Victoria Magazine* in 1863 and 1864. But she continued to live in respectable, even fashionable, London neighbourhoods[44] with a small but adequate complement of servants; so some family money very likely filtered through to her. Still, as she insisted in interviews, she had to earn her own living from 1858 onward.

Lack of support from some members of her family and exile from the Langham Place Circle seem to have had little effect on her work for the cause of women. The long-term consequences of the Codrington divorce trial proved very damaging to her reputation, however. For after her death in 1895 her fellow pioneers and others following their lead chose to damn her accomplishments with faint praise or ignore them completely. To illustrate the former, Mrs. Fenwick Miller, a contemporary of Emily's and a fellow journalist, referred in her "eulogy" of Emily to the "*partial* success" of the Victoria Press and the *"relative inactivity"* (Italics mine) of Miss Faithfull in recent years; and she concluded with an unkind reference to Emily's personal appearance: "she did cause some mischief by appearing always as *manly* (Italics Mrs. Miller's) as possible; her torso portrait looks like that of a stout, serious gentleman — such a mistake!" (*Illustrated London News*, 6/15/95, 750).

Bessie Parkes (Belloc), in her book *A Passing World*, written in the year of Emily's death, alluded to close personal friends about whom she could have said more if she had wanted to reveal iniquities; instead she had chosen "to observe rigorously the old fashioned rule, *De mortuis nil nisi bonum*."[45] I believe she was referring to Emily here, and that she chose to say nothing[46] rather than risk saying something good about her. Similarly restrained, Caroline Biggs and Helen Blackburn[47] (both of whom served as editors of the *Englishwoman's Review*[48]) did not mention her in their "Great Britain" chapters in the *History of Woman Suffrage*; in fact, Blackburn noted the demise of Lydia Becker, Caroline Biggs and Isabella Tod in 1889, 1890 and 1896 but did not record Emily's death in 1895. And, though she listed a number of English women who made lecture tours of America in the 1880's and 1890's, she omitted any reference to Emily's triumphal tours there in the 1870's and 1880's. Blackburn also ignored her in compiling her pamphlet collection, even under headings clearly pertinent to Emily, for example, "Women and Their Work," "Periodicals," "Employment of Women," and "Education of Women."[49]

Other women closely connected with the Langham Place Circle who chose to say nothing about Emily after her death were Frances Power Cobbe in her autobiography; Louisa Twining in "Fifty Years of Women's Work,"[50] and Millicent Garrett Fawcett in *Women's Suffrage*.[51] The upshot of this conspiracy of silence was that her achievements have been slighted or ignored in major biographies and in most twentieth-century accounts of the British women's movement. The *Dictionary of National Biography*, which contains entries for all important members of the Langham Place Circle except Emily and, ironically, Bessie Parkes Belloc, merely notes Emily's ability as an entertainer and then only in an entry on Rutland Barrington, Emily's nephew who got his first acting engagement through her good offices. Among our contemporaries, Christopher Kent also stresses her dramatic ability but reveals its negative value by reminding us that the Victorian feminist movement paid little attention to the "stage as a career for women, which probably reflects the movement's concern with respectability and the stage's want of it."[52] Lee Holcombe wrongly credits SPEW with training the Victoria Press compositors[53] and mistakenly asserts that Queen Victoria gave the title "Printer and Publisher in Ordinary to her Majesty" to the Victoria Press (rather than to Emily Faithfull, whom Holcombe does not mention at all except in endnotes).[54] And Duncan Crow emphasizes the scandal of the divorce case while disparaging Emily's establishment of the Victoria Press[55]: "Miss Faithfull herself, who might be considered the very epitome of respectable spinsterhood — apart, that is, from her strong-minded establishment of a printing press run by women — a few years later became the bizarre performer in a scurrilous divorce case in which she was cited as a co-respondent by Lady Codrington."[56] Note the prudishness of "bizarre" and "scurrilous" and the male chauvinism of "strong-minded"!

Only in the last eighteen years have a few of Emily's accomplishments been given the credit they deserve: articles by William Fredeman[57] and the present writer[58] emphasize her success with the Victoria Press; and Pauline Nestor[59] and Martha Westwater[60] deal in some detail with the *Victoria Magazine*. But the full range of her contributions has not yet been understood.[61] The object of this book is to open the way to that *terra incognita*, for Emily Faithfull deserves to be recognized as a major figure in the British women's movement.

In the late 1860's Emily of course had no inkling of the long-term detrimental effects of the Codrington divorce case. Enough for her that the Victoria Press and the *Victoria Magazine* were relatively successful, though business had slackened off and she was forced to sell part of the operation. By 1868 she also had a novel to her credit and was embarking on a public-speaking career, the effectiveness of which would soon induce offers of an American lecture tour.

In 1869 Emily founded the Ladies' Work Society and the Victoria Discussion Society, and she struck up friendships with Alice Bell Le Geyt and Kate Pattison.[62] She resigned as head of the Ladies' Work Society after only two years, for she had considered it impracticable from the beginning. On the other hand, the Victoria Discussion Society (1869-75) was a great success, and Emily was deservedly praised as its prime mover and shaker. This society was also the means of introducing her to leaders of the American women's movement visiting Britain in the early 'seventies, in particular, Laura Curtis Bullard, Kate Hillard,[63] and Julia Ward Howe.

By keeping American women in general aware of Emily's activities and personality in her "Letter from England" column in the *Woman's Journal*, a Boston periodical, Alice Le Geyt seconded the good impressions these visitors took back home. Her column of July 1, 1871 praised this "wonderful person" who got through "such an amount of good work" and ended with a not-so-subtle suggestion that Americans should invite Emily to visit their country so that they might judge "her appearance and good elocution" for themselves. And that of July 15 referred to wonderful lectures and poetry readings she was giving in England.

In 1869 Emily also got involved in more public controversy than the Victoria Discussion Society could offer: first, a debate about the merits of John Stuart Mill's *The Subjection of Women* with half a dozen men at a "conversazione" (*VM*, 7/69, 263) and second, "a very interesting discussion" of women's education with five men at a Social Science Association meeting (*VM*, 11/69, 40). She was definitely "out of the closet."

Emily must have been occupied in 1871-2 with preparations for her first visit to America, but her accounts reveal little of this. She records that she reassumed ownership of the half of the Victoria Press that she had previously sold, worked out a detailed plan for a Training Institute in Domestic Economy, gave elocution lessons, and carried on her work with the Victoria Discussion Society and the *Victoria Magazine*. Also, in the first half of 1872 she and a new friend, Amelia Lewis,[64] teamed up in several endeavours, but none of these had anything to do with the upcoming American tour.

By September 1872 Emily and Kate Pattison were ready for their voyage to America. Their friends and associates — 150 strong — held a farewell soirée at which an American woman, Miss Beedy, told Emily that her hospitality to American women in London guaranteed her a warm welcome in the United States, and Moncure D. Conway assured her that she was already well known in America for opening employments to women. Two weeks later, they departed from Liverpool aboard the *Oceanic*.

Emily's objectives for visiting America in 1872 were to investigate employment of women in factories and elsewhere, "co-education of the sexes" (*VM*, 2/73, 351), and the political position of women. On her return home she reported that American women were in much the same position as their English counterparts with respect to unfit employment, low wages, intermittent work, lack of training, and the need for female factory inspectors. She noted too that the hours of work were higher in America and that there were fewer safety regulations.[65] She also described her visits to the Elgin Watch Factory near Chicago and the Riverside Press in Cambridge, Massachusetts, both of which employed as many women as men.

Emily observed at first hand that not all schools and universities in America had embraced co-education. Harvard, for example, isolated its women in an "Annex," and even the University of Michigan,[66] though otherwise co-educational, had reverted to separate lectures for female medical students because of the bad behaviour of male medical students in mixed classes. Nevertheless, she praised mid-western and western American universities for opening all but medical classes to women, singled out the model schools of Chicago and the free schools of other States for their successful adoption of co-education, and noted the excellent facilities and academic programmes of women's colleges like Vassar and Evanston.

As 1872 was an election year, she had the opportunity of talking to both presidential candidates, Horace Greeley and Ulysses S. Grant. After the election she concluded that the American Women's Suffrage Society had been unfair to Greeley; for, though he opposed female suffrage, he advocated both industrial employment and fair remuneration of women. He also had opened journalism to women in America by hiring Margaret Fuller as a reporter for his *Tribune* newspaper. Besides, Emily's interview with President Grant in March 1873 revealed that he too was against female suffrage. More to her political liking was a two-hour session with Senator Charles Sumner, "A man who stands head and shoulders above his fellows in intellectual culture and personal graces . . . it is owing largely to his labours . . . that the United States are really free, and the war has ended, and peace and union been restored" (*VM*, 5/73, 37).

She also visited Congress and the Massachusetts House of Representatives. Of the former she observed that, whereas the Senate was "decorous," the Hall of Representatives was "very noisy;" still, ladies in the visitors' gallery were not "wired off from mortal view" as they were in the "suspended cage" of the British House of Commons (*VM*, 5/73, 30). In Boston she had the seat of honour beside the Speaker during a debate on female suffrage[67] that resulted in a losing vote for supporters of the franchise for women (84 yeas, 142 nays).

Emily's lectures appear to have been her chief means of financing this visit to America — at $250 per lecture.[68] Most were presented in big cities (New York, Chicago, Boston, Philadelphia, Washington, Cincinnati), but some took place in smaller towns like Peterborough and Geneva, New York. And, though audiences usually consisted of society people, intellectuals, and professional women, Emily sometimes addressed groups of working women or students, usually without fee.

Asthma was her chief bane. A combination of sea-sickness and asthma during the thirteen-day voyage to America had so debilitated her that she had to be lifted ashore. In November Chicago's cold winds made her so ill that she had to cancel five of every six lectures. A third attack in December brought on by cold weather, coal dust, and smoke, inescapable concomitants of winter travel by rail,[69] forced her to cancel a southern junket to St. Louis, Memphis, and New Orleans and return to New York, where asthma struck again. Then it laid her low once more in Boston and Washington in February. The wonder is that she was able to continue with her truncated tour, especially as she was scheduled to lecture almost every night.

What made it bearable was the generous hospitality of the American women who helped Kate Pattison take care of her, particularly Laura Curtis Bullard, whose New York home was Emily's American headquarters, and Louise Chandler Moulton, who played host to her and Kate during the last month of their stay in America,[70] that is, the period between the loss of the *Atlantic*, on which they were due to sail in early April, and their eventual departure on the *Oceanic* on May 10.

Other marks of American hospitality were the receptions and farewell tributes arranged by leading American feminists, for example, the Sorosis Club's gathering at Delmonico's on November 4, 1872. American newspapers reported that on this occasion two hundred ladies welcomed Emily as "one of [Sorosis's] eldest and most distinguished honorary members," and Mrs. Wilbour, club President, gave special commendation to Emily's *Victoria Magazine* and Victoria Discussion Society. These newspapers also reported a reception at Steinway Hall, New York on January 25, where female representatives of various professions in literature, art, science, and industry gathered to applaud a "brilliant address" by Emily that stressed the "dignity of labour for women" (*VM*, 3/73, 463-71). And Emily herself recorded further tributes at the New England Women's Club, Boston, at Steinway Hall again for her planned farewell lecture, and aboard the *Oceanic* on the day before Kate's and her departure for England. During this final farewell Louise Chandler Moulton read her poem, "For Miss Faithfull's Dinner," various people praised Emily, and Mr. W.F. Wilder presented her with a gold watch from the women at the American Watch Manufactory at Elgin, Illinois, in deep 'appreciation of that noblest of good works, which you are doing for your sex, "*helping others to help themselves.*"'[71]

Though Emily was pleased about meeting eminent men on this first visit to America, she delighted in the many new female friends she made. Of particular note were Jane C. ("Jennie June") Croly,[72] Mary Booth, Grace Greenwood,[73] and Kate Field,[74] American journalists with whom she spent a good deal of her time; Susan B. Anthony and Elizabeth Cady Stanton, the most radical of American female reformers, whom Emily met at Mrs. Bullard's soon after she arrived in America;[75] Drs. Sarah Hackett Stevenson[76] and Mary Putnam; Miss E.P. Peabody, an expert on Froebel kindergartens; Anna Dickinson, Charlotte Cushman, and Ella Dietz Clymer, actresses; Lucretia Mott and Lucy Stone; and Maria Mitchell, Professor of Astronomy and Director of the observatory at Vassar, who played host to Emily and Kate when they visited that women's college.

These women undoubtedly helped Emily form a favourable impression of Americans in general. She disapproved of the corrupt politics of the American election in 1872, and was glad she lived in monarchical England. Yet, though she withheld "judgment of the American system for the present," she still proclaimed it "a wonderful country, full of possibilities and glorious promises . . . [that has] not yet reached an advanced stage of its growth" (*VM*, 1/73, 209).

Apart from some fulsome (hence untrustworthy) accolades concerning Emily, most Americans in 1873 seem to have formed a good opinion of this "frank and genial interpreter [of their country]" (American newspaper, rpt. *VM*, 5/73, 116). Working women were grateful for her abiding interest in their struggle to get and keep remunerative jobs: assistant librarians at Harvard University Library asked for her autograph, watchmakers fashioned a commemorative timepiece for her, telegraph operators gave her flowers, and "a large representation of . . . working women . . . eager to honour this practical, warm-hearted Englishwoman" (*VM*, 3/73, 465) attended one of her lectures. Feminists appreciated her "intellectual and moral force" (*VM*, 5/73, 120) and observed that, though she was "conservative in manner, [she was] radical in principle" (*VM*, 1/73, 209). Anti-feminists grudgingly admitted that she had "never been disagreeably loud in her affirmations" (*VM*, 12/72, 167). And leaders in the American women's movement were pleased that, when challenged, Emily was willing to affirm her support of women's suffrage.

Back in England at the end of May 1873, she stayed at the home of her friend Richard Peacock in Gorton (near Manchester) for several weeks before returning to London with an enhanced view of the condition of women in Britain and America. She had left behind a legacy of sorts, namely, a slightly revised version of her novel *Change Upon Change*, entitled for American readers *A Reed Shaken With the Wind*, which was published in New York in 1873.

Emily resumed her lectures and dramatic readings upon her return from America. But a more important contribution to the women's movement was the Industrial and Educational Bureau for Women, which was designed to train women for particular jobs, find work for them and, if no jobs were available, arrange for their emigration to the colonies. To advertise this Bureau she began publishing *Women and Work*, a weekly newspaper, in June 1874, and she hired Caroline Howard (later Mrs. Edward L. Blanchard) to take care of emigration problems.

The period from 1875 to 1879 was a busy one for Emily. Always interested in culture, she got actively involved in drama and dramatic reform. In 1875 she formed a small drama company that successfully toured the provinces after several performances in London. And, after espousing a reform movement in favour of "classic" (legitimate, literary) plays, she became an active member of both the Manchester Dramatic Reform Association and the Church and Stage Guild.

She terminated the Victoria Discussion Society in 1875 and *Women and Work* in 1876: the former had served its purpose; the latter, though worthwhile, had proven too expensive. The Victoria Press and *Victoria Magazine* were still going strong, as were Emily's lectures. In fact, in June 1878 she gave a lecture on modern extravagance that caught the public's fancy to such an extent that it crowded out her other lecture topics for the rest of the year. To fill the vacuum left by the demise of *Women and Work* she founded the *West London*

*Express*, a weekly newspaper which aspired to national news coverage and circulation. Unfortunately, it attracted too few subscribers; so it lasted only eighteen months.

After being so busy in the 1870's, Emily must have found the early 'eighties rather dull, for they witnessed a winding down of two of her major activities, the *Victoria Magazine* and the Victoria Press. She was still giving lectures, but from mid-1881 she had ample time to prepare for her next visit to America, which had been mooted as early as 1880 but did not materialize until October 1882. Now forty-seven years old, she very likely counted on this second trip to provide a fresh perspective and renewed energy to carry on with her women's work.

She undertook this voyage alone, though Kate Pattison, now an actress with Mr. Abbey's theatrical company, was aboard the same ship, the *City of Brussels*. As usual, bad weather brought on Emily's asthma and sea-sickness, but she took them in stride, as she later did bronchitis in Philadelphia and influenza during a brief visit to Canada. This time her journalistic reports were published in the *Lady's Pictorial*. Her salary for these columns and the fees for her lectures no doubt paid for the trip, with money to spare.

Receptions for Emily were, as in 1872-3, "delightful" (*LP*, 1/27/83, 59). Mrs. Croly arranged the New York welcome, Julia Ward Howe the Boston ceremony,[77] the New Century Women's Club the one in Philadelphia. In Chicago several ladies, including Dr. Sarah Hackett Stevenson, at whose house Emily "shook hands with over 300 people in two hours" (*LP*, 2/10/83, 103), hosted separate receptions.

One gets the impression that Emily gave many lectures during this 1882-3 visit, even though she recorded only four notable ones. The first took place at the Tremont Temple in Boston, where she was received by a gathering of learned men and women, Oliver Wendell Holmes among them. The second occurred at the Grand Opera House in Cincinnati while the Ohio River was in full flood — some of her audience arrived by skiff. The third was at Vassar College, and the fourth in "the famous Plymouth Church at Brooklyn, . . . the Rev. H. Ward Beecher [presiding]. . . . The church holds more than 2,000 people, and will probably be well filled" (*LP*, 5/5/83, 304).

In Boston, "the acknowledged centre of intellectual culture and literary work," Emily noted a "great stir" about "co-education of the sexes." Columbia College would not admit women to its classes, and

Harvard still relegated them to an "Annex." But petitions to improve the situation had been presented (*LP*, 1/6/83, 7). And there were many women students in Boston University's School of Medicine.

Emily again reported several new jobs for women in America, e.g., "thirty ladies . . . in the Index Department of the [Boston] Public Library . . . receiving very good salaries, and giving thorough satisfaction" (*LP*, 1/13/83, 26-7), and eighty in the Boston Title Company, making abstracts of public deeds. In New York she visited Kate Field's Co-operative Dress Association, a "hive of feminine industry" (*LP*, 11/25/82, 234), and in Philadelphia, a flourishing School of Young Lady Potters. She also spent a morning at the Mint in Philadelphia, observing that many women worked there, but were poorly paid. She approved too of the number of women involved in "artistic" occupations like decorative art, manufacturing perfume from flowers, and making limoges jugs. And, while reflecting on the American public's general approval of women working, she attacked "clerical Christians"[78] like Reverend Morgan Dix, an "American theological Rip Van Winkle," who still maintained, despite statistical evidence to the contrary, that marriage was the only career for women. According to these clerics, women should not work outside the home, nor should they seek education beyond a few lessons in domestic economy. "Offensively absurd and illogical" was the way Emily categorized Reverend Dix's patronizing attitude (*LP*, 4/21/83, 257).

On this second visit she made a special point of exploring the American cultural scene — theatre, opera, and concerts, in particular. For example, she enjoyed the dramatic performances of Mr. Abbey's company in New York, Boston, Philadelphia and Cincinnati, waxed enthusiastic about the American actor Laurence Barrett after seeing him in two leading roles, attended several other plays, a classical concert in Boston, and a performance of *La Traviata* in New York.

Besides meeting the American men and women already referred to, Emily reacquainted herself with "Mrs. Lucy Stone, the valiant female-suffragist, who, though happily married to the husband of her choice, Mr. Blackwell, stoutly 'maintains her individuality' by keeping her maiden name," and she made a new friend in "Mrs. Diaz, the heart and soul of the 'Woman's Educational and Industrial Union'" (*LP*, 1/13/83, 27). She also enjoyed Joaquin Miller, "that most eccentric erratic poet," who, like Emily, belonged to "a small band sworn to see that those belonging to the self-chosen brotherhood are decently and discreetly burnt instead of buried after death, in the simplest, most inexpensive manner" (*LP*, 4/14/83, 252).

In January 1883 Emily must have wondered if she was pure jinx or one of God's elect. For the *City of Brussels*, in which she had sailed to America a few months earlier, was lost at sea. Emily had arranged her homeward passage aboard that ship, "and the loss . . . is rendered doubly strange by the fact that when I was in America before, I had secured a stateroom in the White Star steamer Atlantic, which went down on her passage out, and with a far greater loss of life." Furthermore, Emily continued, "Just as I was about to close this letter, news came that the Planter's House, the St. Louis hotel in which we[79] had engaged rooms, had been burnt down twenty-four hours before we were due there" (*LP*, 2/10/83, 103).

Whether Emily believed in jinxes or not, she wrote nothing about her arrangements to return to England in the Spring of 1883. To judge by "Across the Atlantic" references to her being in Canada on April 10, then in Vassar, and finally in New York, she seems to have left for home aboard an unnamed ship about the third week in April. But she had arranged another lecture tour of America to commence in October 1883.

This third visit to America began auspiciously enough aboard the *City of Rome*, which, after some delay in Queenstown, Ireland, took only seven days to get to Sandy Hook. Emily again suffered from asthma at sea, but recovered quickly once she and her companion, Charlotte Robinson,[80] were comfortably settled in the New York Hotel (*LP*, 11/10/83, 305). The new Metropolitan Opera House and the arrival of Henry Irving, Ellen Terry and Matthew Arnold engrossed Emily during October. Then, after giving only a few lectures in early November, she succumbed to bronchitis, which left her voiceless for almost two months.

Respite from nightly lectures gave Emily a chance while in Philadelphia to listen to young university women and others[81] discuss important matters with Walt Whitman, who, to Emily's surprise, was a "cherished guest" of a Quaker family that believed in total abstinence from alcohol and tobacco (*LP*, 12/22/83, 391). In Chicago she further indulged in receptions and dances (this last for Charlotte's pleasure), a side trip to Minnesota, and a pleasant evening with General Palmer, owner of Chicago's Palmer House where the two women were staying. Noting Emily's continuing illness, Palmer suggested she undergo a "cure" over the Christmas season at his mansion near Colorado Springs. She accepted his offer, with heartfelt thanks.

Emily was delighted with Colorado's pure air, beautiful scenery, and weather so sunny and warm that she and her friends were able to picnic outdoors in the snow on January 12, without "overcoats and sealskins" (*LP*, 2/16/84, 151). Yet, though she felt much better, she did not consider resuming her lecture tour. For she was bent on investigating the Mormons in Salt Lake City and writing a series of articles about them for the *Lady's Pictorial*.

After Charlotte and she had spent several weeks as guests of the Mormons, Emily concluded that Mormon women were enslaved — physically and spiritually — by their polygamous husbands. And polygamy, that "crime against nature," (*Three Visits*, 197), was still on her mind when their train crossed the Sierras and rolled into San Francisco. Noting that the Chinese in that city were celebrating their New Year in February, she observed that "The Chinaman, like the Mormon, indulges in polygamy, and the 'small-feet' wives are never seen in the streets" (*LP*, 3/15/84, 254).

During her stay in San Francisco she helped that city's kindergarten movement by giving a benefit lecture and took keen interest in the silk culture in California, "which promises to prove so grand an opening for the employment of women." She also visited Mills' Seminary, "the Vassar College of the Pacific," and an Oakland ladies' club, the Ebell Society, honoured her at an afternoon reception (*LP*, 3/22/84, 279).

Writing from Los Angeles, Emily reported that she and Charlotte had each been offered twenty acres of vineyard in the San Joaquin Valley in Fresno County, along with a house "after our own plans to be built for us — if we would promise to spend four months in every year in this delightful locality" (*LP*, 4/5/84, 319). Given the fine weather and the clean air in this valley between two ranges of high mountains, they must have been strongly tempted.

On their way back to New York they passed through Las Vegas, Kansas, Chicago, Milwaukee, Buffalo, Niagara Falls, Auburn, Utica, and Albany. In Lawrence, Kansas, she lectured at Kansas State University, "the first university to thrown (sic) open its doors to women[82] as well as men" (*LP*, 4/19/84, 367). And she devoted her last "Across the Atlantic" column to Niagara Falls, especially the "new bridge across the turbulent river . . . 500 feet from shore to shore, at an altitude of 240 feet" (*LP*, 5/3/84, 415).

Her journalistic reports during this last visit to America were frankly critical of American society and its customs. For instance, she and Charlotte had been forced to include a spirit lamp and hot pot in their baggage to counter the despotism of American hotels concerning meal hours: "The unhappy traveller who arrives after the supper-room is closed must go to bed fasting; and still worse is the plight of those who leave before the breakfast hour" (*LP*, 3/15/84, 254). Emily also found society in Philadelphia and San Francisco too "fast." Indeed, in the former city, she noted, "moderation seems an unknown virtue. . . . People are either extreme abstainers or hard drinkers" (*LP*, 12/22/83, 391). Lastly, in a more philosophical vein, she observed that the American aristocracy of wealth had not yet "accepted the obligations of its position. . . . There is a terrible undercurrent seething already in the hearts of the poorer classes. The envious selfishness of poverty is rising in natural reaction against the ostentatious selfishness of wealth" (*LP*, 12/8/83, 366).

Yet she tempered her criticism by crediting Americans with generosity and benevolence. In the context in which she berated San Francisco for being too "fast" she also praised that city for "works of true benevolence" like the kindergarten and school systems that rescued poor waifs and strays and trained them "to become industrious and valuable members of the community" (*LP*, 3/22/84, 279). And she recorded many instances of ordinary Americans helping her and Charlotte — on trains, in hotels, at receptions, in homes, everywhere. So, all in all, her comments were constructive, and Americans seem to have accepted them in that light.

On April 16, 1884 Emily and Charlotte departed for England aboard the *Scythia*, arriving on May 3. This time they were treated to a "recherche" dinner arranged by Carina Blanchard and attended by "ladies, representative of art, music, literature, or some other department in which the fair sex has won its 'right to eminent domain'" (*LP*, 5/10/84, 435). Emily spent that summer writing her travel book *Three Visits to America* and a series of articles entitled "Life Among the Mormons."[83] She apparently started *Three Visits* at Richard Peacock's[84] home in Gorton, but wrote most of it in London.[85]

In December 1884 Emily and Charlotte Robinson established a decorative art business and school and a mutual home in Manchester. The business was successful right from the start. Not only did Charlotte gain recognition for her teaching; she also convinced members of the nobility, politicians, businessmen, civil servants, and others that they should get her and her graduates to beautify their houses, banks, hotels, and town halls both inside and out with painted friezes, carved oak furniture, and pretty knick knacks. In so doing, she opened up a new source of employment for women.

Emily ensured that the exhibitions of Charlotte's Manchester Society of Artists in Liverpool, Manchester, Glasgow, Edinburgh, Chester, Skipton, and London were well advertised. For instance, writing about the Musical and Fine Arts Exhibition in Manchester in October 1885 she quoted the *Manchester Courier* concerning Charlotte's nicely arranged assortment of pottery, painted mirrors, tables, brackets, draught and fire screens, and other furniture, "which arrest the attention of everybody who enters, and which it would be difficult to match in London or the provinces" (*LP*, 10/3/85, 291). Again, describing Manchester's Jubilee Exhibition in 1887 she singled out her friend's entry: "a constant group of admirers surround the dainty exhibit of Miss Charlotte Robinson. That lady has good cause to be proud of her artists" (*LP*, 5/21/87, 530). This Jubilee exhibition greatly impressed Queen Victoria — so much so that early in December 1887 she asked Charlotte to submit more decorative art work to her. The subsequent submission prompted an expression of "the Queen's warm interest in Miss Robinson's spirited efforts to increase in this appropriate direction the remunerative sphere of trained lady artists" (*The Queen*, 12/17/87, 821) and culminated in Charlotte's appointment[86] as Home Decorator to Her Majesty.

Emily was proud of her beloved friend Charlotte's artistic accomplishments. But, as she stated in her will, in which she named Charlotte as both an executor and sole beneficiary, she was above all profoundly grateful for the "countless services for which I am indebted to [Charlotte Robinson] as well as for the affectionate tenderness and care which made the last few years of my life the happiest I ever spent" (*Last Will & Testament of Emily Faithfull* dated October 18, 1892, Somerset House, London). With Charlotte taking such good care of her, Emily was able to resume her journalistic career with two weekly columns in the *Lady's Pictorial*: "Northern Gossip" from June 1885 and "Woman" from September 1888. Both dealt with women's issues as well as Manchester news, and both were very successful in spite of Emily's increasingly frequent asthma attacks.

Manchester, city of cold, foggy weather and pollution of various kinds (especially coal dust and smoke) was responsible for most of these afflictions. Emily recorded that she was ill off and on through the winter of 1886-87, kept a "bronchitis kettle in full blast by night and day" (*LP*, 1/21/88, 58) in January of 1888, and suffered five attacks of asthma in 1890 which left her so weak in early 1891 that a subsequent bout with Russian influenza almost killed her. A combination of Manchester fog and Emily's growing weakness brought on asthma and bronchitis again in December 1891 and severe bronchitis in May 1892. In January 1893 Emily reported in her *Lady's Pictorial* column (which she continued to submit throughout her illnesses) that fog "tries the strongest and is death to the weak-lunged and asthmatic. . . . I gasp for breath" (*LP*, 1/14/93, 70) and eight months later she noted that asthma compelled her to stay home and shut all the windows. Thus she was sorely tried during the last years of her life.

Like most victims of asthma, Emily was eager to try remedies. In 1885 she used her *Lady's Pictorial* column to recommend an "inhalant of Dr. Churchill's" (*LP*, 8/15/85, 144) and to report that burning "Himrod's Powder" helped her breathe more easily (*LP*, 8/21/86, 151). Also, and this gives credence to her great niece's memory of her,[87] she often referred to the "blessed relief" obtained by smoking the "fragrant weed" (tobacco), "the priceless gift from tropical climes brought to his English home by the elegant Raleigh" which she used only "under medical advice. . . . I have no desire to conceal the fact, although I hope I exercise discretion in its indulgence" (*LP*, 10/29/92, 660). Of course, the remedy most likely to be efficacious, as Emily realized from her Colorado "cure," was to move to a climate less conducive to asthma attacks than Manchester or London (or England for that matter). But her work was in England; so she had to take her chances there.

One must not conclude that Emily effectively retired when asthma laid her low in Manchester. Between and even during these onslaughts she maintained work habits that put to shame most of her contemporaries. In 1888 she told an interviewer that she worked "an average of eight hours a day at her writing table" (*The World*, 10/31/88, 6); in June 1889 she commented on the great advantage of having electric light on the Manchester-London train so that people like herself who "are accompanied by a bag full of letters and papers" can arrange and answer them "during the four hours' journey" (*LP*, 6/8/89, 834); and in 1890 she informed her readers that she travelled with a library and a blank book to record observations, experiences and anecdotes.

In what was no doubt a further attempt to deal with her asthma, Emily overcame what she called her "sybaritic tendencies" and tried to bring discipline into her diet. Having expressed her distrust of tea in 1874 and a preference for mochara (Cafe de Santé) over coffee in 1879, she began moving toward vegetarianism in 1886, although she could not accept the dogmatic approach of complete vegetarians — "some reformers ride their hobby-horses to death," she averred. She admitted to a "practical, not theoretical, dislike of meat" (*LP*, 2/26/87, 212), but was not yet "ready to give up eggs, fish, fowl, or game" (*LP*, 10/23/86, 351). By 1892, however, she was "almost a total abstainer of meat," though not of fish (*LP*, 4/9/92, 546) and she supported the Vegetarian Society's plea for funds, even if she could not agree that "it is inhuman, unhealthy, and irreligious to eat animal food" (*LP*, 6/11/92, 951). She also recommended that "the ordinary English housewife [cease to neglect] the vegetable and fruit diet which is of such value to the family" (*LP*, 7/14/94, 48). Yet Emily had her well-spaced moments when sybaritic tendencies came to the fore. In 1892, for example, she recorded her pleasure in consuming such gourmet Christmas delicacies as New York oysters, venison, and choice liqueurs.

She renewed another career in 1886 when she joined forces with Mrs. Blanchard and Lady Emily Strangford,[88] who had established the Colonial Emigration Society in 1881. Emily Faithfull agreed to organize and administer the Manchester branch of this society. At the same time she accepted an executive position in a State-directed association.

During the period 1885-95 Emily admitted to several pet "loves" and "hates." She confessed that she was an evening person who wished "the general ghastly breakfast could be abandoned, and the repast either served singly or in very judicious detachments" (*LP*, 1/1/87, 19). She also hated the song "Home Sweet Home," probably because of its extreme sentimentality. Conversely, she loved long coach rides: on one occasion, she took a coach to Epsom for the Oaks, and her "complexion suffered!" (*LP*, 6/9/88, 638). Another time she spent twelve hours on a coach trip, but would not recommend it to her readers. Still, she insisted, "I know of nothing more delightful than the journey by coach from London to Dorking or Brighton" (*LP*, 4/26/90, 632).

Four interviews of Emily in the last years of her life uncovered more of her likes and dislikes. Her chief displeasure was that Queen Victoria had not sufficiently recognized her achievements. Though Emily was grateful that her Majesty had awarded her £100 from the Royal Bounty in 1886 and had sent her an engraved portrait of herself with the inscription, "To Miss Faithfull, from Victoria R.I., 1888, a gift which commemorates the thirtieth year of her voluntary labours in promoting the industrial and educational interests of women" (*Woman's Signal*, 3/1/94, 138), she had hoped for something more substantial. After all, an 1884 memorial to the Queen signed by "statesmen and writers, Bishops and judges, peers and philanthropists" had strongly recommended that Emily Faithfull be granted a "literary pension in consideration of her services . . . both as a writer and a worker . . ." (*The World*, 10/31/88, 6-7). Emily's interviewers concluded that she thought the Civil List pension of £50 per annum awarded her in 1889 was too little, somewhat grudging, and several years too late.

Charlotte Robinson's friendship and the comfortable home that Charlotte had redecorated to suit Emily's needs were her greatest pleasures in these last years. One interviewer took particular note of the combined library and drawing room: "An unusually thick carpet ensures a maximum of quiet; Miss Charlotte Robinson has carefully planned everything from the tiled fireplace and cream-coloured overmantel, laden with old china, down to the bookcases, deftly broken by cupboards, the 'dog' lounge,[89] the cozy armchair shaded by palms, and the delicate paper which covers the ceiling. She has, of course, taken special pains with the serviceable writing-table and the dainty racks for newspapers and Blue-books . . ." (*Manchester Faces and Places*, 1892, 133). Thus, observed the *World* reporter, the bright and beautiful interior of 10 Plymouth Grove belied the "depressing ugliness" of the street and the property's poor gardening soil. In this haven she spent enjoyable days working on her *Lady's Pictorial* columns (with Charlotte no doubt doing some of the leg work), administering the Colonial Emigration Society, and dealing with correspondence. "I write from 10 to seven [letters] every day; and you would be surprised at the way strangers consult me upon all kinds of out-of-the-way subjects," she informed one reporter (*Women's Penny Paper*, op. cit., 481).

Whenever health permitted, she attended plays and concerts and delivered her weekly *Lady's Pictorial* columns to the head office in London. While in that metropolis, she often visited her nephew Ferdinand Faithfull Begg and his family, who had moved there in 1887. Sometimes she stayed with the Beggs, but she apparently preferred the "Hotel Victoria. . . . They make me thoroughly comfortable and always keep the same room for me" (Ibid.). She loved Begg's children, but they were young, numerous and boisterous. She also kept busy with such matters as liaison with Owen's College concerning women's education at Victoria University, being guest of honour at the official opening of the Prescot Watch Factory in 1889, and conducting a fund-raising campaign for the Romley Wright School of Domestic Economy in 1890.

During the last year of her life Emily indulged in thoughts about death. In March 1894, for example, she announced the sudden death of Mme Patey, a singer, in words that applied equally well to herself: "The lives of those who appear before the public, and to a certain extent live on the applause they obtain, the long journeys, constant changes of temperature, the draughts on the platform, &c., cannot be conducive to length of days" (*LP*, 3/10/94, 336). But her Cassandra voice is even more audible in references to dead fellow pioneers in the women's movement, especially Barbara Bodichon, Frances Buss, Adelaide Procter, Lady Stanley of Alderley, and Mary Thornycroft. Worried that the contributions of these and other women, including herself, would be forgotten, she also reminisced about her associations with women's workers still living: Elizabeth Cady Stanton, Susan B. Anthony, and Jessie Boucherett.

Thus anticipating death,[90] Emily made definite arrangements for her funeral. In her will she requested cremation at the Chorlton-cum-Hardy crematorium. Also, by supporting the Mourning Reform Association's proposal that "costly and senseless [mourning] customs" be abolished (*LP*, 6/9/94, 897), she made it clear that her funeral rites should be inexpensive and unsentimental. For, she had written three years earlier, "Real grief needs no outward symbols," and "To live in the hearts we leave behind us is a worthier ambition than to be buried in all the pomp and ceremony the undertaker can devise" (*LP*, 2/7/91, 216).

She died of bronchitis on May 31, 1895 and was cremated without delay and apparently without undue ceremony. According to the *Manchester Evening News* of that date, The Very Reverend Dr.

Maclure, Dean of Manchester, conducted the service. Chief mourners were Charlotte Robinson, Charlotte's sister Mrs. McLelland, and five of Emily's nephews and nieces — Ferdinand Faithfull Begg, Rev. Arthur Ferdinand Faithfull, Mrs. Isabel Cramer Roberts, Miss [Evelyn] Faithfull, and Miss Constance Faithfull.[91] Letters of apology came from the Mayor of Manchester, Judge and Mrs. Parry, and others.

Eulogies by her fellow pioneers and contemporaries were either half-hearted or non-existent. So "Miranda," editor of the *Lady's Pictorial*, took it upon herself to recognize Emily as "one of the universally acknowledged pioneers in the cause of woman's progress. . . . women workers of all ranks and conditions have lost one of their earliest, staunchest, and most indefatigable friends." (*LP*, 6/8/95, 855).

*Chapter 3*

# Early Involvement with Women's Work: SPEW and SSA

By the spring of 1859 the *English Woman's Journal*, increasingly involved in all stages of the women's movement, could no longer deal specifically with its main objective, promoting jobs for women. So, when Jessie Boucherett[1] proposed that a Society for Promoting the Employment of Women (SPEW) be established in London, Bessie Parkes and her co-workers in the *Journal* office welcomed this more concentrated approach to the problem.

SPEW held its first formal meeting on July 7, 1859.[2] The SPEW committee — at this stage an all-female group — consisted of Anna Jameson, Jessie Boucherett, Bessie Parkes, Adelaide Procter, Emily Faithfull, and Isa Craig, assistant secretary to the Social Science Association (SSA), with Boucherett and Procter serving as honorary secretaries and Sarah Lewin as assistant secretary. Noting that only three remunerative employments[3] were open to middle-class women, namely, teaching, domestic service and needlework, they decided to promote a range of suitable occupations for these women: printing (i.e., composing), law copying (i.e., copying law papers), domestic art, and perhaps hairdressing and watch-making. Boucherett also announced that she intended to establish a school[4] to train women in accounts and book-keeping, thus qualifying them for jobs as clerks, cashiers, ticket sellers, and saleswomen. The SPEW Register (for employers and for women seeking employment) was to remain for the present in the offices of the *English Woman's Journal*. They also agreed on three overriding issues: first, SPEW was established to promote, not provide, employment for women; second, the provision of jobs — especially those in occupations normally not open to women — had to depend almost entirely on the way SPEW's promotion (and that of other interested individuals or groups) affected public opinion. Third, because there were not enough jobs available in Britain, some middle-class, educated women would have to emigrate to the colonies or to America.

This group of women also knew full well that, for SPEW to succeed, it had to involve the Social Science Association in its operations. For, as Maria Rye reported soon after SPEW was established, "remonstrances were made by no inconsiderable portion of the press against the movement. . . ." And, she continued, when it was proved that there were thousands of educated women thrown upon their own resources with no chance of employment, the advice was invariably, "Teach your protégés to emigrate."[5] Evidently a male-dominated society would only listen, if at all, to men. Therefore, in November 1859 at the third annual SSA Conference at Bradford the women of SPEW "forcibly called" the attention of the SSA "to the necessity of providing new channels for the remunerative employment of women. . . . The miserable condition of the women employed in several branches of industry and the artificial obstacles raised to any extension of their employment by social prejudice or trade jealousies, certainly called for inquiry, and, if that were found practicable, for redress."[6]

The SSA acted in typical corporate fashion — but just as the women had planned[7] — by setting up a committee and empowering it to take over SPEW. The president of that committee was Lord Shaftesbury[8] and the secretary was Emily Faithfull, who had previously served as secretary of SPEW from August to November 1859.[9] The five other women on the original committee were appointed as members of the SSA committee, as were five other men — a total of twelve[10] in all, according to Emily Faithfull.[11] This committee took several months to appraise the operations of SPEW before subsuming it. In the process it put its male stamp on that Society. For example, though the SSA permitted women to read their own conference papers from as early as 1859, the men of SPEW read the women's papers. As Hester Burton reports of the June 29, 1860 meeting, "The gentlemen . . . read the reports of Miss Faithfull, Miss Rye, and Miss Boucherett[12] while the ladies concerned remained modestly in the background."[13]

Nevertheless, the women appear to have controlled the agenda, for they undertook the spade work that led to SPEW's decisions and conference papers. One decision was that branches of the Society should be formed in other large cities, e.g., Glasgow, Edinburgh, Dublin, Manchester, Newcastle, Leicester, Nottingham, and Aberdeen. Bessie Parkes and Emily Faithfull were chiefly responsible for founding the Edinburgh branch[14] in 1860, "on their visit to Edinburgh after attending meetings of the SPEW in Glasgow" (*EWJ*, 2/1/64, 427). The Dublin local[15] came into being during the SSA Conference in Dublin in 1861, with Frances Power Cobbe, Emily Faithfull, Bessie Parkes, and Louisa Twining as prime movers and honorary members.

The London SPEW soon had a number of offspring: the Law Copying Office directed by Maria Rye for the first two years of its operation; Emily Faithfull's Victoria Press; and the Telegraph Station, staffed by Isa Craig to ensure that qualified women got jobs as Telegraph Clerks. Employment Registers were set up at all three of these locations, as well as at the offices of the *English Woman's Journal*, which doubled as SPEW headquarters in the early years. All Registers were jammed with applicants from the day their doors opened — to such an extent that the Society had to face the necessity of middle-class female emigration by late 1861. Thus we find Emily writing letters[16] to the *Times* in December to publicize and solicit funds for a plan to send women to the colonies.

SPEW did not have to rely entirely on institutional support from the SSA. John Stuart Mill gave the Society his blessing and a donation in 1864. Henry Fawcett, a friend of Mill's and a well-known Member of Parliament, extended help to SPEW and the women's movement during the 1860's and 1870's, especially in such matters as women's education, employment, and legal status.[17] And by 1869 Queen Victoria[18] and other Royals had become patrons. Yet the executive must have been greatly relieved when the City of London incorporated the Society in 1879; for they desperately needed the consequent subsidy to establish classes in mechanical and industrial training. By this time private donations had almost dried up and the SSA was on its last legs.

Part of the problem was that the achievements of the Society were not obvious enough to inspire liberality among private donors. The London SPEW was directly responsible for finding permanent jobs for fifty to seventy-five women per year, and temporary jobs for fifty to a hundred women per year — hardly an impressive total. As for the promotion of jobs for women, the Society could not claim to have done more than encourage employers to hire women when the time was ripe, e.g., as law-copiers, telegraph clerks, compositors, shop assistants, nurses, photographers, and hairdressers in the 1860's; post-office clerks, shorthand writers, accountants, and wood engravers in the 1870's; and typists, telephonists, waitresses, decorative artists, librarians, and fruit pickers in the 1880's. To make matters worse, the emigration of middle-class women had not worked out very well; the colonies wanted women who could apply themselves to all types of work, not governesses with lily-white hands. All in all, SPEW had a tough row to hoe financially, especially since many potential supporters disapproved of middle-class women working for a living. Nevertheless, SPEW and mavericks like Emily Faithfull did teach Victorian society a valuable lesson through constant repetition: that every girl whose parents could not provide for her should be trained for a job.

Emily played an important part in the activities of SPEW from 1859 to 1864 — as charter member; secretary of the original committee for a few months; secretary of the SSA committee and hence a useful bridge between women on the original committee and the men who eventually took over; founder of the Victoria Press which, according to both Boucherett and Parkes in 1861, was the "most successful experiment [of SPEW]"[19] and "part of the whole undertaking";[20] director from 1860 to 1864 of one of the employ-ment Registers; active promoter of local branches; and chief publicist of the Society's activities in the *Times*, etc. Moreover, Emily remained a proponent of SPEW for the rest of her life — reporting annual meetings, recommending it to correspondents seeking employment, and giving it credit for being "parent . . . of most of the enterprises springing up in various directions for finding remunerative occupations for women [e.g., the Society of Type Writers[21]] — a fact some of the younger workers too often forget" (*LP*, 5/31/90, 865).

By 1890 some of these youngsters no doubt had also forgotten the part played by the Social Science Association (SSA)[22] in forwarding the cause of women. The SSA, an offshoot of the British Association for the Advancement of Science, became the political arm of its parent association in 1857 when it merged with the National Reformatory Union. Its objective was to study "as a science the solemn problems of human misery and its possible relief"[23] and to take action, if possible, to solve those problems. But the Association's philosophy was conservative;[24] it wanted a "re-adjustment of social machinery," not a "social revolution."[25] Besides, it was male-dominated; women were not elected to its executive, nor could they always expect a friendly ear. For example, the *Times* reporter attending Emily Faithfull's 1863 SSA Congress paper, "The Unfit Employments in which Women are now Engaged," noted during the discussion following the paper that the men in the audience did not pay enough attention[26] to the crux of the problem, i.e., the fit employments that should be opened up to women to replace the unfit ones. Still, the SSA accepted women[27] as members from its inception and encouraged them to speak out on "subjects of social importance."[28]

The Association was planned in five departments, in all of which the problems of women were involved: Jurisprudence and Amendment of the Law,[29] Education, Punishment and Reformation, Public Health, and Social Economy. And subsidiaries of some of these departments were set up to serve the more immediate needs of women: the Ladies' National Association for the Diffusion of Sanitary Knowledge (1857), SPEW (1859), the Workhouse Visiting Society (c. 1859), and the Female Middle-Class Emigration Society (1861).

Any action taken by the SSA had to be initiated or approved by that body's annual Congress,[30] at which papers were presented in each of the departments of the Association. A perusal of the papers concerned with the condition of women indicates that the following general topics were dealt with over the twenty-eight congresses (1857-1884)[31] of the Association: education and training (higher, secondary, technical, and domestic economy); employment (in factories, civil service, teaching, printing, medicine, etc.); female suffrage; female prisoners (treatment of); hospitals for women and children; legal status, especially of married women (concerning property rights and custody of children); Protective and Provident Leagues (i.e., women's trade unions); the state of public opinion concerning women; recreation (in public parks, swimming pools, and playgrounds); representation of women on School Boards, Boards of Guardians, County Councils, etc.; sanitation; Workhouse Visiting Societies and Workhouse education.

Despite its favouring the status quo, the SSA raised public consciousness and influenced legislation concerning the position of women with respect to education, prison administration, public health and the law. And it eventually paid attention to the necessity for women in financial need to be employed in suitable occupations. But, according to Emily Faithfull, the SSA, "after doing a great deal of useful work, was sacrificed to 'faddists' of steadily increasing dulness, and finally killed by ponderous papers and hopelessly desultory debates" (*LP*, 9/17/87, 283).

The part Emily played in the SSA, other than as secretary of the ad hoc committee involved with women's employment, was apparently confined to attendance at SSA congresses[32] and presentation of papers. But mere attendance was never enough for her. She appears to have been relatively quiet at both the 1859 Congress at Bradford[33] when Parkes and Boucherett read their papers on the employment of women (or, rather, the lack of employment of women) and the 1875 Congress in Brighton that she found dull and boring.[34] But at the 1869 Congress in Bristol she got involved in the aforementioned hot discussion concerning women's education, and in 1871 she spoke out in a Congress session about the need to train women, especially those in "higher classes of society, . . . in some avocation (sic) by which they could earn a livelihood" (*VM*, 11/71). And she presented provocative papers at all the other congresses she attended.

Her 1860 and 1861[35] SSA papers,[36] "The Victoria Press" and "Women Compositors," reported on the success of the Victoria Press during the first year and a half of its existence, difficulties encountered, and other jobs related to printing that women could undertake.[37] Her 1862 paper, "On Some of the Drawbacks Connected with the Present Employment of Women," stressed the importance of early training for women: "this want of training is the first and greatest drawback to the employment of women."[38] The other drawbacks were the popular prejudices concerning women, especially middle-class women: that it is "undignified for a woman to receive payment for her labour," that "public life is injurious to women," and that "indolence is a permissible foible in women."[39] Get rid of these prejudices, Emily contended, give women the training they need, and they will be able to compete with men for jobs. "Unfit Employments in Which Women are Now Engaged," her 1863 paper, noted that women were working at boring, badly paid, or physically unsuitable jobs. Emily believed that women should not undertake hard manual labour; therefore mining jobs (e.g., the pit-brow work[40] undertaken by women), chain-making, and factory work demanding long hours were all unsuitable. Dull, repetitive jobs such as the manufacture of pincushions or counting sheets of paper were also unfit employment. Governessing and home work (needlework, dressmaking, etc.) were not suitable because they were subject to the indignities and overwork that accompany low wages. Emily's 1870 paper entitled "The Influence of Working Men's Clubs on Their Homes" emphasized the "dangers of a divided interest" to the family and the home if wives were excluded from their husbands' social clubs. In reading this paper, Emily referred to a workman's remark that wives of members of working men's clubs preferred that their husbands spend ten minutes at the public house rather than an evening of improvement in the club reading room. Her rejoinder was that "this proved that wives were as yet insensible to the great value of institutions of this nature; and [she] thought that this insensibility would be best cured by giving women a share in the advantages men are learning to prize."[41] That is, let the wives join these clubs too.

*Chapter 4*

# Printer and Publisher: the Victoria Press "Non Nobis Solum"

When the women of SPEW decided to promote the employment of women in the printing trade, they were concerned that Emily Faithfull, who volunteered to supervise this experiment, would have to combat attitudes ranging from uncertain support and suspicion to savage opposition. As an *Illustrated London News* article stated in 1861, Emily's Victoria Press (for the Employment of Women) was "at first viewed with considerable distrust" (*ILN*, 11/30/61, 538), for the public held doggedly to the conviction that woman's sphere was the home and that printing, like every other blue-collar job, was decidedly unfeminine. Even firm supporters of the movement to get women into the trade seemed to begrudge the success of the Victoria Press, or at least some of them wanted to erect a barrier to women's employment at that point. A *Dublin Review* reporter said he rejoiced that the Victoria Press was "a complete success" and advocated more female printing presses; then he observed that "here too, woman's work must be limited" (*Dublin Review*, 11/62, 30), and though he approved of training and education for women, he was not in favour of "women's abstract rights" (Ibid., 36). So it is not surprising that Emily felt constrained in 1862 to appeal to the highest authorities through a letter to a Miss Bethell, requesting that she bring a petition before Lord Westbury, the Lord Chancellor, in which his Lordship was asked to promote the interests of women printers.[1] There is no record of any action by Westbury; however, the mere act of forwarding the petition probably relieved some of Emily's frustrations.

Male chauvinists averse to the venture tended to hide behind masks of protectiveness (of "delicate women") or its opposite. Anthony Trollope epitomizes the former approach, Arthur Munby the latter. As Fredeman states, "Early in his chapter on 'The rights of women' in his travel recollections of America, Anthony Trollope records a confrontation with an American lady who charges him, 'You are doing nothing in England towards the employment of females'.

'Pardon me', I answered. 'I think we are doing much, perhaps too much. At any rate we are doing something'. I then explained to her how Miss Faithfull had instituted a printing establishment in London; how all the work in that concern was done by females, except such heavy tasks as those for which women could not be fitted, and I handed to her one of Miss Faithfull's cards. 'Ah', said my American friend, 'poor creatures. I have no doubt their very flesh will be worked off their bones'. I thought this a little unjust on her part; but nevertheless it occurred to me as an answer not unfit to be made by some other lady, — by some woman who had not already advocated the increased employment of women. Let Miss Faithfull look to that. Not that she will work the flesh off her young women's bones, or allow such terrible consequences to take place in Coram Street; not that she or those connected with her in that enterprise will do ought but good to those employed therein. It will not even be said of her individually, or of her partners, that they have worked the flesh off women's bones; but may it not come to this, that when the tasks now done by men have been shifted to the shoulders of women, women themselves will so complain. May it not go further, and even come to this, that women will have cause for such complaint? I do not think that such a result will come, because I do not think that the object desired by those who are active in the matter will be attained. Men, as a general rule among civilized nations, have elected to earn their own bread and the bread of the women also, and from this resolve on their part I do not think that they will be beaten off."[2]

Munby, "nursing his own private penchant for working-class girls" (Fredeman, p. 148), goes to the other extreme in expressing contempt for Emily's decision to hire men for tasks that Munby's improbable amazons could easily undertake. Here is his diary entry after visiting the Victoria Press in May 1863:

In the afternoon I went to Farringdon Street, to make enquiries at the Victoria Press. It is much enlarged in influence since Miss Faithfull showed me over the Coram Street house some years ago but it is no more a *female* press than it was then. Fifteen or sixteen female compositors are all the women they have on the premises: and the actual printing, which is done here, is all done by men. The clerk in charge, whom I saw, was a man: the office boys *were* boys. This, I apprehend, is little better than trifling with the female labour question. We dont want — at least *I* dont — to disturb the 'wages fund' by making women printers or clerks or what not: that which I want is, liberty for any woman who has the strength and the mind for it, to turn her hand to any manual employment whatever.[3]

"All or nothing" for Munby; "nothing at all" for Trollope — neither solution could answer the needs of millions of British women in search of remunerative employment such as printing could offer.

Male printers constituted the group most vehemently opposed to Emily's enterprise. Miss Thackeray (cousin of the famous novelist), who inspected the Press in 1860, suggested that there was a 50-50 split among printers approving and disapproving of the Victoria Press.[4] But the recalcitrance of the printers' union and the sabotage visited upon Emily's establishment (of which more later) indicate that the majority of printers were trying to put her out of business. In any case, it is abundantly clear that "of all the experiments that were commenced explicitly to implement the social theories of the leaders of the women's movement, none was more hotly contested than the formation of the Victoria Press" (Fredeman, p. 140).

Most of the details concerning the origin and early success of the Press may be found in Emily Faithfull's SSA papers, "Victoria Press" (1860) and "Women Compositors" (1861). The former revealed that, though the women of SPEW were well aware of earlier failures to train women to be printers, Bessie Parkes undertook to purchase a small press and some type and hired a printer to instruct Emily and herself in the craft of printing. Both were quickly convinced that women (preferably young girls) could be trained as compositors. So Emily and George W. Hastings[5] undertook jointly to finance a press for the employment of women and to begin operations as soon as possible, with Emily in full control. A house in a respectable, "light and airy" neighbourhood (Russell Square) was refurbished as a printing office, and they ventured to call it the Victoria Press in the assurance that Queen Victoria would approve.[6] The business opened on March 25, 1860 with five apprentices from SPEW at premiums of £10 each[7] and others apprenticed by friends and relatives, the total rising to sixteen by September 1860, of whom one, daughter of an Irish printer, was experienced and three were semi-experienced. Male printers were employed to "make up and impose the matter, and carry forms to the press-room" (*EWJ*, 10/60, 123); the women were confined to the composing of type, though Emily suggested in her "Victoria Press" paper that experienced women compositors could undertake jobs like reading and correcting for the press. She also stated in this initial report that she had taken special care with sanitary arrangements and had provided stools for the compositors, as well as a dining room where women working overtime could have tea at 5:30 p.m. But she did not know what to do about the dust expelled by the antimony-lead type when it was heated.[8] "Women Compositors," Emily's 1861 SSA paper, updated the earlier paper by reporting that the Victoria Press was now self-supporting and busy, the wages for women at the Press were the same as those for the men,[9] Miss Matilda Hays was now a partner[10] in the Victoria Press, and the Press's first prestige book, *The Victoria Regia*, was forthcoming (*EWJ*, 9/61, 37-41).

Other sources provide further information about the genesis of the Press. An exchange of letters concerned with Emily's libel action against James Grant in August 1869 identified the printer who helped Bessie Parkes and Emily Faithfull carry out their feasibility test as Austin Holyoake,[11] Radical brother of George Jacob Holyoake, one of the most active Radical Freethinkers of the nineteenth century. And Bessie Parkes may have contributed something else of value to the Victoria Press, namely, the system of Major Beniowski, through the use of which, according to her, one could learn the job of compositor in a week.[12] Certainly Bessie had hoped in December 1859 that her morning's examination of Beniowski's patents could "help to bring the matter of the employment of women in printing to some practical issue" (*EWJ*, 12/59, 276). Thus Emily, following Bessie's lead, probably used some of the Major's ideas in the instruction of female apprentices, though she contended the apprenticeship period should be much longer than a week.[13]

There are no figures for the wages paid compositors at the Press during the years 1860 to 1868. William Wilfred Head did provide some in *The Victoria Press Almanack*, a broadside published in 1868: 10 shillings a week after a six-months apprenticeship, rising to 25 shillings a week for a competent workwoman. And he went into more detail in an 1869 publication, *The Victoria Press: Its History and Vindication*,[14] in which he said the range of women's wages was 18 to 25 shillings per week, "when fully employed."[15] But, as Fredeman notes, "In practice they earned less: a sampling of the wages of twelve compositors, with experience varying between eighteen months and nine years, which appeared in the *Printer's Register* in 1869, revealed a low of six and a high of twenty shillings[16] as the average weekly wage, based on hourly earnings of between 2 1/2 and 5 pence [for an eight-hour day and five-day week]. Under Head's management, premiums were dispensed with for apprentices, and each new girl underwent a month's training with an experienced hand, who received any earnings that might accrue to the novice during that period. Overtime was paid extra during Emily Faithfull's management, but this practice had to be abandoned after the Factory Act amendment of 1867" (Fredeman, pp. 149-50).

Concerned with public opinion, especially when the printers' union was trying to laugh the Victoria Press out of existence, Emily encouraged visitors to witness its operation. Miss Thackeray was impressed by the physical layout and the apparent efficiency of the workers in 1860:

On the first floor are work-rooms. The front one is filled up with wooden desks, like pews, running from the windows, and each holding three or four young women. At right angles with the pews run long tables, loaded with iron frames and black sheets of type, which are being manipulated by two or three men . . . a table of rules is hanging up on the wall, and I see NO TALKING ALLOWED printed up in fiery letters.[17]

Both the *Illustrated London News* and the *Queen*[18] reported visits to the Press in 1861, and both provided sketches[19] of the printing-office that bore out Miss Thackeray's description. Prompted by Emily no doubt, both journals also observed that the Victoria Press was wisely acquiring a special character to ensure its continued existence,[20] namely, a close connection with the SSA through publication not only of that Association's *Transactions* but also of "plain and popular tracts on the great social questions of the day" (*The Queen*, 12/7/61, 261) with which the SSA concerned itself, e.g., "Post Office Savings-banks," "Friendless Girls, and How to Help Them," "Prison

Discipline," "Poor Laws and Workhouses," "Emigration of Educated Women," and "Life Insurance by Small Payments'" (*ILN*, 11/30/61, 538). And, lest readers think this concentration on tracts rather demeaning for a reputable publisher, both reporters commented on the production pending of "a work of more ambitious character . . . *The Victoria Regia*, a handsome Christmas book of prose and verse, to which all the leading writers of the day have furnished contributions" (*The Queen*, 12/7/61, 261). Emily was keenly aware of the necessity for good public relations.

There also is evidence that she was concerned about good relations with her workers, beyond sanitary conditions, stools to sit on, facilities for cooking, short hours, decent wages, and so on. In February 1862 the *English Woman's Journal* noted that Emily Faithfull had entertained her compositors at her private residence and had given prizes to three apprentices (*EWJ*, 2/62, 429). And in August 1878 the *West London Express* referred to the annual dinner of the Victoria Press employees at the Alexandra Palace, presided over by Miss Emily Faithfull. So we may assume that there were a number of these entertainments over the twenty-two years the Victoria Press existed.

Because Emily had concluded by June 1860 that the compositors' trade was "eminently suited to women,"[21] she entertained high hopes that large numbers of women would soon be employed in printing establishments. On the basis of these reasonable expectations she advertised for another six to eight apprentices (*Times*, 7/23/60, 9). And G.W. Hastings echoed her optimism in a SPEW meeting, giving Emily full credit for achieving her objective: "it was owing to her energy, perseverance and discretion that the [establishment of the Press] had proved so successful, and . . . it was to her efforts we now owed the fact that the first woman's printing office was so well organized and regulated, and had been conducted with such skill for the business, and such kind thought for the workers, that most, if not all, the objections urged against such a scheme had been proved futile at once and forever" (*EWJ*, 8/60, 392).

But male printers were not so willing to accept defeat as Emily and Hastings believed. From the outset their trade union (or, more specifically, the Society of Compositors) had justified W.E. Gladstone's adverse opinion of it: "The printer's monopoly is a powerful combination, which has for its first principle that no woman shall be employed — for reasons obvious enough — viz., that women are admirably suited for that trade, having a niceness of touch which would enable them to handle type better than men."[22]

The "determined hostility" of the male printers[23] to the employment of women in the Victoria Press soon manifested itself in sabotage: in Emily's words,

> The opposition was not only directed at the capitalist, but the girl apprentices were subjected to all kinds of annoyance. Tricks of a most unwomanly nature were resorted to, their frames and stools were covered with ink, to destroy their dresses unawares, the letters were mixed up in their boxes, and the cases were emptied of "sorts" (*Three Visits*, 26).
>
> . . .
>
> Again and again the machinery was wilfully injured and destroyed, and the waste of capital was simply ruinous (*The Women's Penny Paper*, 8/2/90, 481).

Also, the "men who were induced to come into the office to work the presses and teach the girls, had to assume false names to avoid detection, as the printers' union forbade their aiding the obnoxious scheme" (*Three Visits*, 26). Furthermore, "printers resorted to personal intimidation and scurrilous attacks in the trade journals."[24] As Fredeman observes: "It may have been the news of the formation in America of a Women's Typographical Union in June 1869, or the establishment in the same year, by Austin Holyoake, of the competitive Female [Women's] Printing Office, that sparked the most extensive controversy on the subject. The Victoria Press, as the only working example of an office expressly operating 'For the Employment of Women', was at the storm centre. It bore the brunt of the attack from such journals as the *Publishers' circular*, the *Scottish typographical circular*, and the French journal *L'imprimerie*; but it was also the principal object of defence by the influential *Printer's register* in a long and impartial examination entitled 'The female compositors' question' in October 1969" (Fredeman, p. 151).

The writer of the subsequent report for the *Printer's Register* conceded "that the Victoria Press 'does not testify much to the advancement of a movement, which after nine years can only point to a couple of dozen people benefited by it,' but his over-all reaction, based in part on interviews with the girls themselves, [was] favourable and forward-looking."[25]

We found the girls apparently comfortable and contented; well in health, respectable in appearance; turning out good work, and drawing good wages. If these are only to be enjoyed by men, we are able to understand their objections; but if girls and women are to be allowed to share in the comforts of existence; to be enabled to live decently and honourably, by the exercise of a trade, which is, as we maintain, suited to their physical, intellectual, and social requirements, we see no reason whatever to join in the narrow-minded, selfish and cruel outcry against Female Compositors.[26]

Nevertheless, the union remained antagonistic. Male compositors in Newcastle-on-Tyne went on strike in 1875 because a printer employed women as compositors. "Even in 1879, in response to my appeal for an extra hand to fulfil some urgent orders," Emily Faithfull recalled in 1892, "the secretary of the Society [of Compositors] stated that, unless an assurance was given that the said compositor would not be called upon to assist the females in any way, no Society man would be allowed to come" (*LP*, 9/17/92, 411). And if a sympathetic printer wished to hire a woman compositor, he had to advertise in a deliberately unspecific way or suffer the consequences, e.g., this advertisement in *Women and Work* in 1875 — "Wanted - Women compositors for a City printing office. Apply 85, Praed St., Paddington [the address of the Victoria Press[27]]" (*W & W*, 7/10/75).

Male ranks closed even tighter when female membership in the union was proposed. In 1886 this motion was passed at a Conference of the Typographical Societies, which included among its membership the London Society of Compositors:

That while strongly of the opinion that women are not physically capable of performing the duties of compositor,[28] this confederation recommends their admission to membership of the various typographical unions, upon the same conditions as journeymen, provided always the females are paid strictly in accordance with scale.

The effect of this motion, as Ramsay Macdonald pointed out, was "to make it practically impossible for any women to join the society"[29] because very few male printers were willing to pay female employees more than 50% of "scale." Yet one woman was admitted to the London Society of Compositors in 1892, in accordance with the conditions imposed by the motion. Emily Faithfull immediately expressed her delight, and noted the "contrast to the attitude of the

Union in the days when I opened the Victoria Press" (*LP*, 9/17/92, 411). But the union had not changed as much as she assumed;[30] even in 1941 the Society of Compositors excluded women from its membership.[31]

This hostility (both covert and overt) on the part of the printers' union resulted in a "serious loss of money" for the Victoria Press. Emily had to get help from "rich and generous friends"[32] or the Press would have failed. These financial difficulties were most pressing in the winter of 1861-62, partly because of sabotage but also because of having to work with half-trained apprentices while trying to cope with more and more work and increasingly difficult printing jobs, for example, *The Victoria Regia*. Letters from Adelaide Procter to Bessie Parkes and from Bessie Parkes to Barbara Bodichon underscore these problems. Here is Adelaide on the bad effects of working long hours at the press in 1861: "The women are enough to make any one swear. I wd not have believed how careless they are — such disgraceful carelessness. Emily is quite triumphant that I am forced to admit what a trial they are" (*Parkes Papers*, BRP VIII 11). And this is Bessie in a letter dated 1 Apr 62: "the source of my chief worry this winter has been the Press, which never by any chance keeps an engagement as to time, while Emily Faithfull is herself worried by 20 half-trained female printers & I often wonder she gets through at all" (*Parkes Papers*, BRP V 114/1). Small wonder that Emily was trying to take shelter under the ample financial roof of the SSA[33] and was concentrating on contract printing of pamphlets and bread-and-butter publications like the *Transactions* and the *English Woman's Journal*. Yet 1861 was a momentous year for both Emily and the Press, for it witnessed a major change of emphasis from printing to publishing. In addition to the *Victoria Regia*, five titles issued in that year bore the imprint, "Printed and Published by Emily Faithfull & Co., Victoria Press, (for the Employment of Women), Great Coram Street, W.C."

The highlights of 1862 for the Victoria Press were first, the appointment by Royal Warrant of Miss Faithfull as "Printer and Publisher in Ordinary to Her Majesty"[34] and second, a medal for good printing from the Jurors of the International Exhibition. The *Victoria Regia* was the immediate reason for both awards; the Royal Warrant clearly stemmed from its publication and the good Jurors singled out that work for the prize, even though Emily had submitted a book on growing and cooking gourds to illustrate the printing skills of her women compositors. This third year of the Press's existence was also the busiest in terms of works printed and/or published. But, though this activity resulted in a heightened reputation, it was artistic, not commercial, success. So Emily decided to expand the operation to see if increased business would improve the financial situation. The first step was to open a steam-printing office at 83a Farringdon Street in November 1862 and hire ten more apprentices to help staff it; the second was to inaugurate the *Victoria Magazine*, a monthly journal to be printed at the Press along with all the other publications. With the advent of the *Victoria*, Emily moved her editorial offices from 9 Great Coram Street to 14 Princes St., Hanover Square.

Because of the added expense of this magazine in 1863, the impending cancellation of the printing contract with the *English Woman's Journal*, and what Emily Davies referred to as "cheating"[35] by Victoria Press printers (male and female), Emily was forced to sell part of the Press in January 1864. William Wilfred Head, a journeyman printer, became a partner for £1,000 (one-third of the evaluation) and was given an equal share in the profits (*VM*, 1/70, 262). But business did not pick up as much as Emily and Head had anticipated. By 1867 it was clear that there was not enough custom for two; therefore, at Head's urging Emily "withdrew from the business for the nominal sum of £1500" (*VM*, 1/70, 263) in August 1867.[36] Or, rather, she said she had withdrawn. In point of fact, she had only sold him half of the firm, specifically the steam printing press at 83a Farringdon Street, the office at 1a Princes Mews, and the use of the name Victoria Press, though not of the title "Emily Faithfull, Printer and Publisher in Ordinary to Her Majesty," which had been conferred on her personally, as she reminded Head in 1868. She retained the editorial offices in Princes Street, the imprint of the Victoria Press, and the right to continue to publish under that name. This interesting and apparently legal partition of the Press is borne out by the citation in Emily's novel, *Change Upon Change*, published in 1868, to the effect that Emily Faithfull was the publisher of record and W.W. Head the printer.

Though Head appears to have done most of the printing for the Press in the years 1867-71, he published only two items, the *Victoria Press Almanack* (1868), a large, one-page broadside (or handbill), and *The Victoria Press: Its History and Vindication*. Furthermore, aside from *Change Upon Change* and the *Victoria Magazine*, which was printed at Head's steam press from 1867 to 1871, he appears to have printed relatively few items during those years: a few SSA papers, Motley's *Dutch Republic*, Emily Davies's *Report of an Examination of Girls*, Thomas Beggs's *International Arbitration and Reduction of Armaments*, and sundry other tracts — a recorded total of sixteen[37] in four years.

Emily reassumed ownership of the Victoria Press, sans 83a Farringdon Street,[38] sometime in 1871; yet the three located titles for the years 1871-73 (Emily Faithfull's "Woman's Work," *38 Texts*, and Fitch's "Working Women's College") provide little evidence of publishing activity. The *Victoria Magazine*, now expanded to do justice to the activities of the Victoria Discussion Society, seems to have been the focus of these years.[39] Nevertheless, Emily enlarged the Press in 1874 when she began publishing her penny weekly, *Women and Work* (1874-76), and she extended it again with her weekly newspaper *West London Express* (1877-78). She opened up a new Victoria Steam Printing Press at 85 Praed Street in 1874[40] to accommodate the former, and, after moving this Press to 117 Praed St. in late 1877, enlarged the premises to handle the latter.[41] The *Victoria Magazine*, of course, continued publication during the years that these two newspapers served their turns.

In no year from 1874 to 1881 were more than three titles[42] published; in some years only the *Victoria Magazine* and one of Emily's other journalistic enterprises bore the Victoria Press imprint. By 1880, even the magazine had ceased publication, and Emily was planning another tour of America. Sensing that it was time to wind up a venture that had enabled her to achieve her principal objectives, she sold the Victoria Press to the Queen Printing and Publishing Company in April 1881. Her decision brought to an end three decades of involvement as a publisher in the cause of women's rights.

Emily had not succeeded in getting women accepted as card-carrying members of the printers' union. But she had proved that her apprentices could do quality work and that she could utilize their printing skills in the production of beautiful and thought-provoking publications, thus living up to her title as "printer and publisher . . . to her Majesty." Indeed, the artifacts of the Victoria Press were what made her efforts worthy of respect and emulation.

Let us consider her prestige productions first. Fully cognizant that the eyes of Britain were upon her and her protégés, Emily wasted no time in bringing out the first of these less than a year after getting her business under way. *The Victoria Regia*, was, as William Fredeman points out, "probably the high point of all the printing done at the Victoria Press."[43] This Victorian table-book, an anthology of "original contributions in prose and verse" by the best (or, at least, best known) authors[44] of the day, was, as Emily Faithfull noted in her Preface to the book (p. vii), "a choice specimen of the skill attained by my compositors." Adelaide Procter's 1861 letters to Bessie Parkes indicate that she,[45] as editor of *The Victoria Regia*, worked very hard to convince these "best authors" that they should contribute to this anthology. Moreover, she got Bessie Parkes and the other Langham Place ladies to canvass for contributions; for instance, she asked Bessie (*Parkes Papers*, BRP VIII 17/2) to approach William Allingham, George Eliot, Elizabeth Gaskell, Margaret Oliphant, Tom (T. Adolphus) Trollope and Theodora Trollope.[46] And she called at least one meeting of the canvassers to discuss their success or lack of it (*Parkes Papers*, BRP VIII 19). But Emily, ambitious to demonstrate her publishing skills, proved to be the linchpin of the project. Even the title-page and binding illustrate her concern that artistic form should complement practical function. To make the title-page interesting she introduced a "vignette combining [her initials with those of] the Victoria Press. . . . The design consists of an ivy-entwined shield . . . with 'E' and 'F' in interlocking and cross-blocked letters separated by an ampersand and followed by the abbreviation 'Co.' Across the top of the shield, on the inside, is the motto '*non nobis solum*'. A single ivy leaf is in the upper left corner; a second balances it in the right, part of a vine which runs diagonally behind the shield, extending at the top right with three leaves, and bottom left with ten. Standing on top of the shield, and continuing the ivy motif, are the letters 'VP'" (Fredeman, p. 153). In keeping with its dedication to Queen Victoria, the presentation binding is in full red morocco, with the royal crown prominently displayed in the centre of a carefully designed cover. Of that dedication Emily commented in her Preface, "I trust that the *Victoria Regia* will be found a not unworthy record of the literature adorning the rule of a Sovereign who has known how to unite the dignified discharge of public duties with a constant regard for the cares of domestic life; and who has thus borne a noble and enduring testimony to the value of women's intellect and heart." This restrained praise[47] of both the Queen and the cause of women was in sharp contrast to Bessie Parkes's fulsome dedication poem.[48]

Two of the books published in 1863 are also worthy of note: *A Welcome: Original Contributions in Poetry and Prose* and *Poems: An Offering to Lancashire*. The first celebrated the marriage of the Prince of Wales and Princess Alexandra of Denmark. The second was "Printed and Published for the Art Exhibition for the Relief of Distress in the Cotton Districts" (Title-page inscription), and the editor, Isa Craig, stated in a preface that "Miss Faithfull undertook to print and publish a thousand copies free of expense, the compositors of the Victoria Press volunteering their services, and Messrs. Richard Herring & Co. furnishing the paper gratuitously, so that the proceeds of the sale will be devoted to the object to which the volume is dedicated."[49] Both books were anthologies,[50] like *Victoria Regia*. And both had a host of contributors. *A Welcome* had contributions from Christina Rossetti, Dante Gabriel Rossetti, and Charles Kingsley, as well as from many of the contributors to *The Victoria Regia*, e.g., Harriet Martineau, Frederick Maurice, Caroline Norton, Edwin Arnold, Anthony Trollope, Isa Craig, and George Macdonald. *Poems: An offering to Lancashire* was smaller and plainer than *The Victoria Regia* and *A Welcome*. Yet it too was a fine example of the capabilities of women compositors at the Press and those of its publisher, Emily Faithfull.

William Fredeman gives special commendation to *Te Deum Laudamus* (1868) and *38 Texts* (1872), both of which were illuminated by Esther Faithfull Fleet[51]:

Probably the two most splendid works published by Emily Faithfull at the Victoria Press . . . As physical objects, they are superior to any book issued with the imprint of the press, and they compare favourably with similar books by Owen Jones and Noel Humphreys, but they are so uncharacteristic that it is difficult to be certain how much of their production was actually done on the premises. As publications of Emily Faithfull — and *38 Texts* is a very personal volume commemorating her father's death in August 1871 and his habit of sending Biblical texts as New Year's greetings — these two books must be regarded as the apogee of her publishing endeavours; as illustrations of either the compositorial talents of her women printers or of the normal production work of the Victoria Press they can only be classed as beautiful but eccentric exceptions (Fredeman, pp. 159-160).

The salient point here is that these beautiful books marked one limit to Emily's publishing skills; with these and the three anthologies to her credit, she could afford to devote most of her time and energy to "plain and pedestrian" (Fredeman, p. 157) publications designed to provoke thought rather than aesthetic pleasure.

Scaling down from prestige publications, one notes some productions that were not as ordinary as Fredeman's phrase implies. Of the books published in 1862, Amelia B. Edwards's *Sights and Stories: Being Some Account of a Holiday Tour through the North of Belgium* contained black-and-white illustrations; and *Birds and Flowers, or the Children's Guide to Gardening and Bird-keeping* was "the first and only book with a coloured illustration" (Fredeman, p. 154). Likewise, Frances Smith Marriott's *The Votive Offering*, with a lithographic frontispiece of Ulcombe Church and Rectory in Kent and six other lithographs, must have appealed to a reader's pictorial sense. And two titles were designed to arouse curiosity, if nothing else:

(1) Neptune, pseud. *Oyster tattle and truthful digest of the Herne Bay, Hampton & Reculver oyster fishery, read a third time and passed in the House of Lords, with a few words upon existing oyster companies, and their vexatious opposition.*

(2) [Mary Louisa Boyle], *The Court and Camp of QUEEN MARIAN.* By A Contemporaneous Historian. Dedicated *By (anticipated) permission* To the CROWN-PRINCE OF MARIAN LAND. *Done into English from the original Marianese* By A BUNGLER A.D. One Thousand Eight Hundred and Dash.

But these productions were few in number. There is no denying that the Press's output consisted chiefly of tracts, pamphlets, contract printing, and issues of Emily's journals and newspapers (the *Victoria Magazine, Women and Work,* and the *West London Express*).

Yet these ordinary publications were the chief means of making Emily Faithfull's name a household word in her time. As the Appendix[52] to this book illustrates, many of the tract pamphlets published by the Victoria Press dealt with women's issues, e.g., R.H. Hutton's "The Relative Value of Studies and Accomplishments in the Education of Women," Frances Power Cobbe's "Female Education and How it Would be Affected by University Examinations," Emily Faithfull's "On Some of the Drawbacks Connected with the Present Employment of Women," Emily Davies's "Medicine as a Profession for Women," Anne Jellicoe's "Woman Supervision of Women's Industry," Jessie Boucherett's "Shall My Daughter Learn a Business?," W.T. Blair's "Female Suffrage," and Maria Rye's "Emigration of Educated Women." Still, these pamphlets were read by relatively few people. Emily's journals and newspapers, fully devoted to the cause of women, were what caught the public eye and mind; through them she was able to use the Victoria Press as a forum for women's work. Indeed, only by establishing the Press as a foundation for her other enterprises could she become known as a publisher and hence as an effective spokesperson for women's rights.

Also, by proving that a woman could successfully manage a publishing business in the face of constant harassment,[53] she inspired other women to do likewise or at least to feel confident that, with proper training, they could undertake almost any non-supervisory job. This was a truly revolutionary idea in the 1860's, and supporters of the women's movement paid tribute to it in assessing the social impact of Emily's establishment of the Victoria Press. According to one commentator, she helped "to free her sex from the set groove in which they hitherto worked" (letter to editor of *Daily News*, rpt. in *W & W*, 9/19/74), or, as another writer put it, she laid "the foundation of the fuller opportunities and greater liberty enjoyed by women" (*Woman's Signal*, 11/1/94, 279). It is difficult for us in the 1990's to appreciate the inspiration of the Victoria Press to women in the 1860's, but perhaps this 1861 observation expresses it best: "Certainly among the wonders of the present day the Victoria Press claims a position" (*EWJ*, 5/61, 209). Even Lord Shaftesbury regarded the twenty or thirty capable young women at the press as representative of "the twenty thousand or the two hundred thousand in this country, who require employment in suitable branches of industrial occupation" (*EWJ*, 7/63, 422).

At a more mundane level, Emily did open the printing business to women in Britain,[54] and compositors trained by her got jobs in other printing offices, despite the opposition of the printers' union. H.W. Porter, a male printer, rightly noted the "deep obligations the public owe to [her] for her successful efforts in opening up to females so suitable and remunerative an employment" (*EWJ*, 9/60, 69). She also inspired American women's advocates like Mr. Houghton of Riverside Press to hire women as printers. Speaking of female compositors in 1892, Emily stated, "Mr. Houghton told me in 1873 that [women] had been introduced owing to what he had seen in my London office, and that in the interests of business he did not let them work in separate rooms; he not only acknowledged the value of their nimble fingers, but the moral effect of their presence and influence" (*LP*, 9/17/92, 411). Indeed, from 1870 on women were hired more readily as printers in the U.S.A. than they were in Britain.

*Chapter 5*

# Journalist and Lecturer

As important in its total effect as Emily Faithfull's establishment of the Victoria Press was her work as a journalist. Indeed, journalism occupied her throughout her working life — from 1858 when she began as occasional reporter for the *English Woman's Journal* to her last "Northern Gossip" column in the *Lady's Pictorial*. During this long career she undertook most of the tasks associated with newspaper writing: news reporter, correspondent,[1] interviewer,[2] writer of editorials and articles, columnist, and editor and publisher of the *Victoria Magazine*, *Women and Work*, and the *West London Express*. And she brought to all these jobs her broad, culturally-based perception of journalism: "a competition which involves reading as well as writing, and a familiarity with the current literature of the day" (*LP*, 2/24/94, 260), "wide experience of men and letters" (*LP*, 12/12/91, 1099), an ability to condense, and a need for absolute accuracy.

That she succeeded in putting these journalistic principles into practice is evident from the praise she and her journals, especially the *Victoria Magazine*, received. In 1875 "Jennie June" Croly included her among a select group of women journalists "known far and wide as successful editors and correspondents" (*W & W*, 11/13/75, 6). Antoinette Blackwell, presenting a paper at the Women's Congress in Paris in 1876, made special mention of the *Victoria Magazine* as an "excellent paper, emanating from the indefatigable Miss Faithfull, [that] has done and is doing good work" in enlarging the "field of women's work" (rpt. of Congress paper in *VM*, 1/77, 217). F.A. Smith referred to Emily and four other female journalists in 1889 as "incontrovertible evidence that in their profession women have proved their ability to take equal rank with their male compeers."[3]

She was also featured in an 1893 article on female journalists of international importance, as well as in Fanny Green's paper of that same year which made special note of her "careful, accurate, and intelligent verbatim reporting."[4]

In keeping with Emily's emphasis on accuracy and condensation, her writing may best be described as spare and unsentimental but "sprightly"[5] and effective. Here are three examples.[6] The first, a description of the mountains of Colorado, is vivid and enthusiastic; the second, an appraisal of John L. Sullivan's questionable merits, is critical but lively; the third, recording the death of Lord Shaftesbury, is highly appreciative of his contributions to the cause of women, but not sentimental or adulatory.

> I have spent my Christmas and New Year's Day under the shadow of the majestic range of the Rocky Mountains, in the midst of scenery more wild and magnificent than anything I ever imagined. We are more than 6,000 miles (sic) above the level of the sea, yet, thanks to the lightness and purity of the atmosphere, I can breathe with a freedom seldom vouchsafed to an asthmatic, and though the thermometer has been at zero, such is the power of the sun during morning hours, that it is far pleasanter to walk abroad without a sealskin than with one. No wonder that invalids have sought this as a land in which "life is worth living," and become enthusiasts about a climate which is cool in summer and balmy in winter — a place noted for its exquisite blue skies and transparent atmosphere as well as its grand scenery (*LP*, 1/26/84, 75).

· · ·

> Mr. J.L. Sullivan and I have met — in a limited sense — before! After travelling for two days and a night in a railway carriage while crossing the American continent, and having another twenty hours' journey before me, I was anxious to breakfast during a short delay at Denver, but on attempting to leave the Pullman drawing-room car I found myself in an immense crowd of Colorado roughs, who were preparing to greet the great prize-fighter, who at once stepped out of the next carriage with the air of one who evidently regarded himself as king of "the noble art" — of boxing. He monopolised the whole platform and station buffet, much to my discomfiture; but as I did not feel prepared to dispute this appropriation with a professional bruiser, I induced the negro conductor of our car to make a raid on my behalf while I retired to an obscure corner of our carriage, from which I watched the adulation lavished on the hero of mining "sports." Sullivan seems to be

received with much the same enthusiasm in kindred circles here [Manchester]; his Free Trade Hall reception was attended, I hear, by more than four thousand persons (*LP*, 12/3/87, 578).

. . .

There are few northern homes in which the loss has not been felt acutely of that noble-hearted worker whose mortal remains were peacefully laid to rest in his Dorsetshire grave last Friday. Lord Shaftesbury, during a long and beneficent career, identified himself with so many efforts for the good of humanity throughout the country, that men and women of every rank and creed feel that they are mourning a personal friend. . . . The pile of his letters lying on my table, representing a correspondence extending over twenty years, will never be needed to revive the gratitude I shall always feel for his cordial cooperation in all that concerns the interests of women. In days when both ridicule and disapprobation followed those who ventured to urge the higher education, and the need of finding fresh channels for the remunerative employment of women, Lord Shaftesbury by his personal presence and brave advocacy aided a movement at that time far from popular; and it would be difficult to say how much of the respect it now commands is due to his influence and countenance. His philanthropic efforts for factory labourers and ragged schools need no comment here, but in a newspaper devoted to ladies, this reminiscence is not out of place, from one who was for years intimately associated with him in removing those unfair restrictions which debar their industrial and professional progress (*LP*, 10/17/85, 336).

This is not to say that her style is without blemish. As the "6,000 miles" slip concerning the altitude of Colorado Springs demonstrates, her writing was subject to the odd journalistic boner, despite her often pedantic attitude concerning English usage.[7] And, as Martha Westwater points out with particular reference to the *Victoria Magazine*, Emily "wrote hurriedly, did not disdain clichés, and frequently repeated herself."[8] Yet, as Westwater admits, she was "an able synthesizer and a forceful writer."[9] So, all in all, she expresses herself well.

Less creditable was her tendency to pad her journals and columns with praise of self,[10] Royalty, family and friends. Advertising such personal achievements as the Victoria Press, *Victoria Magazine*, *Women and Work*, *West London Express*, the Industrial and Educational Bureau for the Employment of Women, and the Victoria Discussion Society[11] can of course be justified because of the need to promote these endeavours. But Emily often went beyond the bounds of mere publicity. For example, she appears to have reprinted every word of praise from newspapers and journals on both sides of the Atlantic concerning herself and her achievements. A case in point is Volume XX of the *Victoria Magazine*, written in accord with her policy of using its pages to celebrate the attainments of individual women, especially those of Emily Faithfull.[12] In this instance almost the entire volume[13] was devoted to her tour of America in 1872-3, from the opening poem "To Emily Faithfull" through her "Letters from America" and reprints from American newspapers severally entitled Miss Faithfull in America, Miss Faithfull the Guest of Sorosis, Miss Faithfull's interview by the *Chicago Evening Post*, Miss Faithfull as one of the English lecturers in America, to the tribute of the women of New York to Miss Emily Faithfull.

The *Athenaeum*'s review of this volume of the *Victoria* appeared under the heading "A Triumphal Progress," but the reviewer wondered how triumphal it really was, for he found the praise of Emily too fulsome and therefore, to him, questionable. "Letters from America," he said, were "full of [such] gratulatory items" as her being pleased to see a copy of the *Victoria Magazine* in Chicago; the New York World had lauded Emily as a "lion who is every inch a woman;" the women of New York had hailed her as "one who has done so much for the humblest of her sisters in England" and "one of the foremost representatives and advocates of the higher industrial and educational interests of women;" and the Sorosis Club had lavished high praise on her. The reviewer therefore felt constrained to register incredulity concerning these encomiums: "In the case of the editor of the *Victoria Magazine*, her vanity must be inordinate, unless the Transatlantic view of her position in the world does not exceed that she herself entertains" (*Athenaeum*, 7/26/73, 103.)

Martha Westwater also speaks of Emily Faithfull's "unpleasant shrewdness which made capital use of flattery,"[14] especially flattery of the Royal Family. Yet in this matter one must keep in mind that Queen Victoria was for Emily both a role model for British women and the embodiment of her argument that women should attain equal rights: "I do not think," she stated, "that women sufficiently appreciate the sympathy and interest of our Queen in their opportunities for self support and intellectual development. She is indeed a strong supporter of every good word and work, and especially of those that relate to the opening out of honourable and bread-winning careers."[15] Here she was giving Queen Victoria more credit than she deserved for advocacy of remunerative work for women; however, I do not regard this passage as "unpleasantly shrewd," and, if it is flattery, it is more subtle than "capital." Besides, where women's education was concerned, Queen Victoria did her best to approximate Emily's idealized conception of her as a monarch "exceptional among sovereigns as a responsible human being" (*LP*, 12/22/94, 959), a Queen modelled after the Princess in Tennyson's "Songs of the Princess."

Her treatment of the other "Royals" was at times straightforward, at other times somewhat obsequious (from a twentieth-century perspective, at least). A reference to the German Empress Frederick's visit to Girton and Newnham, the women's colleges at Cambridge, as proof of her never failing "during her visits to the land of her birth[16] to personally inspect some of the new enterprises by which useful and remunerative channels for the industry of women will be created" (*LP*, 3/10/94, 321) was in keeping with Emily's perception that female "Royals" should concern themselves with the cause of women. But her memory of Princess Alix (a grand-daughter of Queen Victoria who had married the Czar of Russia) as someone to whom she humbly presented some miners' hats in 1889 did her little credit. Nor did her account of the 1888 visit of the Prince and Princess of Wales to Blackburn — in this instance she revealed a somewhat unseemly family pride that Bishop and Mrs. Cramer Roberts (her nephew-in-law and niece) were lunching with their Highnesses in the Town Hall, while "Miss Faithfull of Storrington" (Mrs. Cramer Roberts's sister[17]) was entertaining lords and ladies at the Vicarage (*LP*, 5/19/88, 545). On another occasion she recorded the visit of the Duke and Duchess of Devonshire[18] to Manchester, with the observation that she had once met him "at a luncheon at the house of a mutual friend" (*LP*, 8/27/87, 171), thus rather snobbishly placing herself at the level of "untitled gentlewoman,"[19] just a notch or two below royalty.

In dealing with the lesser nobility, Emily again indulged in name-dropping. For example, she recalled meeting a titled artist, Count Gleichen (Prince Victor of Hohenlohe), at Lady Seymour's in Portsmouth "many years ago" (*LP*, 10/23/86, 351) and she remembered playing croquet "in the dim and distant past" with Lord and Lady Amberley at Lord Carlisle's viceregal residence in Dublin, where they were fellow guests (*LP*, 8/25/88, 209).

One can hardly apply the term "name-dropping" to journalistic references to her family. Yet they do qualify as "gratuitous family pride." The majority of these citations were to her siblings and their offspring, but even distant relatives got their due if they reflected minimal credit on the Faithfull name. Many items were devoted to the achievements of her sister Maria's family, in particular those of Maria's husband, the Right Reverend James Begg, D.D., and their sons Ferdinand Faithfull Begg and Walter Bentley.[20] In her paper on emigration to New Zealand Emily referred to Dr. Begg, the well-known Edinburgh divine,[21] as an expert on the subject;[22] and she later identified him as a member of a fund-raising committee for establishing an institution to train domestic servants in Edinburgh. Of Dr. Begg's son and her favourite nephew, Ferdinand Faithfull Begg,[23] Emily had much to say. From 1886 on she faithfully reported his activities as Primrose League Councillor and founder of the first Primrose Habitation in Scotland, chairman of the Edinburgh Stock Exchange and broker on the London Stock Exchange, moving spirit in the Imperial Federation League, and expert on emigration to British colonies because of the time he had spent in New Zealand, Australia, and Canada.[24] She displayed almost as much pride in Ferdinand's actor brother, Walter Bentley. But in his case she contented herself with reprinting comments from other newspapers,[25] for example, *The Queen* recording the start of his career, the *Scotsman* noting his success in *The Lady of Lyons* and in *Money*, and the *Dumfries Herald* reporting a dramatic recital that included items dear to his Aunt Emily's heart and voice like "Somebody's Darling and selections from Shakespeare" (*W & W* rpt 2/12/76, 2).

Her sister Esther Faithfull Fleet's family also got more than their due in her columns. Esther herself was praised for her illumination of books published by the Victoria Press and Marcus Ward[26] as well as for other illuminations, for example, a birthday gift of photographs and flowers and a presentation at the International Workmen's Exhibition. One of Esther's sons, J. Faithfull Fleet, was accorded two accolades by Emily, the first when he was appointed second assistant collector of Dhalwar, India, in 1875, the second when, after studying Canarese and Sanskrit literature at the University of Göttingen, he received a doctorate and was appointed Commissioner of the Central Division in India. But another son got more praise than his brother did, more even than Ferdinand Faithfull Begg. This was George Rutland Fleet, better known as Rutland Barrington, actor, vocalist, playwright, theatre manager, producer, and close friend of Sir Arthur Sullivan.[27] According to the *DNB*, Emily Faithfull helped him get his first engagement with the actor Henry Neville. Then she celebrated his successive triumphs in her columns — in Tom Taylor's *Clancarty*, with Mrs. Howard Paul's acting company from 1875 to 1877 (after a brief stint as leading man in Emily's short-lived acting company), and with D'Oyly Carte from 1877 to 1888. When her nephew took over the management of the St. James's Theatre in 1888, she merely reported that his adaptation of *Mr. Barnes of New York* was doing well at Newcastle. Thus she covered up the fact that the St. James's operation was going bankrupt[28] and that Rutland would have to resume his Gilbert and Sullivan and Savoy careers for another five years. For his doting aunt, Rutland Barrington's career in the theatre was always brilliant and successful.

The activities of her brother George's family were also publicized in her journals and newspaper columns. George received both credit and blame[29] for the operation of his "crammer." Still, she was pleased to inform her readers that she had had dinner with George and Bishop Cramer Roberts in January 1887, for she apparently had not seen much of him since the Codrington divorce scandal. She was, of course, very interested in Cramer Roberts, suffragan Bishop of Manchester in the late 1880's and early 1890's, for she had already worked closely with Bishop Moorhouse, the Bishop of Manchester, in matters having to do with women and poor people. Besides, Francis Cramer Roberts was married to her niece Isabel, one of George Faithfull's six daughters. So when he was inducted as suffragan Bishop in 1887, preached his first sermon in the cathedral, entertained and was entertained by Bishop Moorhouse, she recorded these events in her *Lady's Pictorial* column.

She also credited her niece Isabel with smoothing the way for her husband by holding "fortnightly receptions, with a view of enabling the hard-working Bishop to see something of his northern neighbours" (*LP*, 12/10/87, 619). Finally, in a news item designed to connect her brother George, his son Arthur, Isabel and her husband, she reported Arthur's clerical appointment to a Lancashire post: "Another clerical move brings a Yorkshire vicar into Lancashire, the Reverend A. Ferdinand Faithfull having accepted from the High Sheriff the living of Hornby near Lancashire (sic). Mr. Faithfull's sister is married to Bishop Cramer Roberts, of Blackburn, and his father is the well-known rector of Storrington, Sussex" (*LP*, 12/12/91, 1095).

The marriage of Emily's cousin Julia Faithfull to Sir Monier Monier Williams, K.C.I.E., D.C.L., L.L.D., professor of Sanskrit at Oxford, resulted in many journalistic references to the learned professor — his publication in the 1870's of books, articles and lectures on India and Afghanistan;[30] more lectures and a book on Buddhism in the 1890's, and Emily's pleasure both in lunching with him in 1895 and in her scholarly sister Elizabeth's having mastered Sanskrit with his help.[31] Mrs. Francis G. Faithfull, a cousin by marriage, likewise received encouragement for the "breezy freshness of style" of her novel, *Love Me or Love Me Not*.[32] And her daughter Lilian, who later became famous in educational circles as Principal of Cheltenham Ladies' College, got special commendation from Emily for her appointment as Vice-Principal of the Ladies' Department of King's College in Kensington Square. She even celebrated the achievements of two sons of a daughter of Reverend Fanshawe who happened to be a grand-niece of Reverend Ferdinand Faithfull, Emily's father. One of these sons was "Captain Henry Lucius Fanshawe Royle, (recent D.S.O.)." The other was the "great cricketer," Reverend Vernon Royle (*LP*, 1/28/93, 145). Reflected glory indeed!

Concluding this discussion of Emily's journalistic plethora of praise, I wish to note in her defence that most British and American women journalists of the day indulged in this practice, especially when it conceivably aided the cause of women. Louisa M. Hubbard, for example, dished out gobs of flattery to Queen Victoria in her journal, *Work and Leisure*. On its title page Hubbard coupled the Queen with Florence Nightingale, Mary Somerville, Rosa Bonheur and Jenny Lind, but gave Victoria preference over these other women because of her "perfectly balanced life" as "Wife, Mother, and Queen" (*Work and Leisure*, London: Hatchards, 1880). Hubbard, incidentally, had used this same title-page in her newspaper, the *Women's Gazette* (1875-79). And even an American woman, Frances Willard, gave high praise to Queen Victoria: "By the very fact of her existence and her character, aside from any work that she has wrought, she has been probably the most potent force in accustoming the great world-thought to the association of the word 'woman' with that most bewildering of all words — power" (*Woman's Signal*, 3/1/94, 138).

In an assessment of Emily's journalistic achievements in the *Victoria Magazine* (May 1863-June 1880),[33] the word that best describes her many roles is "conductor;" for, except for the first ten months when Emily Davies was editor,[34] she conducted this monthly journal in all of its phases (as publisher, editor, reporter, reviewer, and so on).[35] And, since the Victoria Press printed the *Victoria Magazine*, she supervised the printing as well. Mind you, because of financial difficulties, her control as publisher was hardly monolithic, though she alone decided on the contents of the magazine. For instance, she published the first volume herself, but the next four volumes were published by Ward and Lock, the following seventeen volumes by her, and volumes 23 to 35 by Simpkin, Marshall and Company (Fredeman, p. 154). Furthermore, as Westwater points out, by the late 1870's Emily was "slowly abandoning the editor's chair for that of writer and lecturer."[36]

Finances were a constant worry. Referring to the *Victoria Magazine* and *Women and Work* in 1893, Emily averred that "the [financial] loss was great, and but for the generous help of friends[37] they would not have lived to accomplish the good work they undoubtedly did" (*LP*, 6/10/93, 937). As early as January 1864 Emily Davies, still editor of the magazine, reported that things were going badly. She agreed with R.H. Hutton, editor of the *Spectator*, that Thomas Adolphus Trollope's second-rate novel, *Lindisfarn Chase*, for which the *Victoria* was paying top rates, had had a bad effect on circulation. But Trollope's poor novel could not be held accountable for the fact that, although the magazine had done "pretty well in London," it had been "a dead failure" in the country as a whole (*ED Papers*, 349), even though the Empress Frederick of Germany's name "headed its list of subscribers" (*The World*, 10/31/88, 6). After Emily Faithfull failed to convince Ward and Lock, publishers, that they should take over the magazine, she was forced to economize[38] just to keep it going. So she accepted Emily Davies's resignation as editor,[39] assumed that post herself, and concentrated more on the cause of women than on literary "rivalry with Fraser, Macmillan, and Blackwood"[40] (*ED Papers*, 3/12/63). The measures worked, for the *Victoria* stayed continuously alive for sixteen more years.

Because the magazine was initially designed to appeal to a wide audience (both male and female), the early volumes consisted of a traditional mix of poetry, novel or short story, a Literature-of-the-Month column that presented very brief book reviews, a Social

Science section[41] which dealt with social health and welfare (including women's issues), and a number of independent articles and news items. Other general headings were introduced as needed. "Miscellanea" came into being in November 1865 and lasted to the end. Under "Victoria Discussion Society" the minutes, papers presented, and discussions of the Society were reported in full detail from 1869 to 1875. In 1872 "Passing Events" held brief sway, as did "Letters from America," Emily's columns during her first trip there. "Women and Work" and its attendant "Guide to Employment for Women" were introduced in April and November 1876 respectively, after the demise of Emily's *Women and Work* newspaper. In September 1876 "Our Library Table," which headed up full book reviews, superseded "Literature" (which had earlier supplanted "Literature-of-the-Month"). "Music and Drama," a column intended to add culture to the magazine, commenced in November 1876. Portraits (and articles) of newsworthy men and women (under the name of the person being honored) began in January 1878. "Correspondence" and "Letters to the Editor" appeared occasionally, usually when Emily considered it important that a woman (or a man supporting the cause of women) should air their views.

Most of the poetry was mediocre to poor,[42] for example, the poems by Ella Dietz, Alice B. Le Geyt, Louise Chandler Moulton, and Edward L. Blanchard. The odd one was good, though: Christina Rossetti's "The Eleventh Hour" and Thomas Hood's "The Light-house-Keeper's Child," both published under Emily Davies's editorship, come to mind. The difference in quality appears to be due to the relative poverty of the *Victoria* during publication of the later issues: Dietz, Le Geyt, Moulton, and Blanchard, all friends of Emily Faithfull's, very likely were not paid for their poems, whereas Rossetti and Hood were.[43]

The second-class status of women, both civil and political, was always a matter of concern for the *Victoria*. Employments unfit for women, overworked and undernourished needleworkers and shop assistants, destitute governesses, discriminatory Factory Acts — all these evils were frequently exposed. And the claims of clerics (and others) that sexual equality was counter to the word of God were opposed at every turn. Also, as Emily believed the best way of improving the status of women was education, a good number of the articles focused on that important issue. The need to upgrade girls' education; to establish technical training centres (e.g., Emily's

Industrial Bureau, SPEW, and Schools of Domestic Economy) as well as colleges for women (or preferably, colleges for both men and women); and to convince the universities that girls should be allowed to write local university entrance examinations and eventually be eligible for academic degrees in all faculties, including medicine — all these matters received their full due in the magazine.

Jobs for women were very high on the *Victoria's* agenda. Emily was constantly on the watch for remunerative occupations suited to trained women, for example, cigar maker, watchmaker, pharmacist, nursery superintendent, nurse, midwife, photographer, clerk (in telegraphy, savings banks, government, insurance companies, etc.), shorthand writer, horticulturist, hairdresser, plan tracer, printer's reader, librarian, Poor Law Guardian, School Board Trustee, and so on. And for those women who could not find jobs the magazine provided a good deal of information about middle-class female emigration to New Zealand and Australia under Maria Rye's guidance.

Combination among women and female suffrage were prominent topics in the magazine. The Women's Provident and Protective League, women's unions that did not advocate strikes, and clubs for women all received the editor's approval, and she herself queried both the inequality of Civil Service salaries (men's versus women's) and women's rights in the Post Office. She also celebrated the granting of the municipal vote to women that enabled them to serve as Poor Law Guardians and School Board Trustees, and though she regarded herself as an "independent [advocate] of women's suffrage" (*VM*, 1/72, 283), she reported every meeting and every petition to Parliament favouring the women's franchise.

The "Literature-of-the-Month" column, which began with reviews of books by the great authors of the day, tended more and more toward reviews of books by and about women, for instance, Jessie Boucherett's *Tracts for Parents and Daughters*, Bessie Parkes's *Essays on Woman's Work* and *Vignettes*, Emily Davies's *The Higher Education of Women*, *The Handbook of Telegraph* (dealing with the employment of women as Post Office telegraph clerks), W.R. Greg's *Why Are Women Redundant?*, J.S. Mill's *The Subjection of Women*, Milne's *The Industrial Employment of Women*, etc. And the "Music and Drama" section registered appreciation of musicians and musical groups and featured articles on theatres, actresses, relations between Church and Stage, and dramatic reform.

The value of the *Victoria* may most clearly be seen through a comparison of nineteenth and twentieth century assessments. Emily Davies and Emily Faithfull had launched the magazine with a watchword ("Liberty") and a motto ("Let every woman do that which is right in her own eyes"),[44] both of which suggest a freethinking liberalism never evident in its pages. Yet it was not as conservative as Pauline Nestor says;[45] in fact, as Elizabeth Cady Stanton, revolutionary editor of *The Revolution*, an American women's journal, maintained, "No Woman's Rights library begins to be complete without [the *Victoria Magazine*]" and "Of the *Victoria Magazine* published by Miss Emily Faithfull, too much in commendation cannot be said."[46] And Mrs. Wilbour, president of the Sorosis Club in 1872, agreed with Mrs. Stanton: "At present I know of no paper or magazine that so faithfully reports all facts of interest[47] connected with women."[48]

Emily herself was no less laudatory of her *Victoria Magazine* in 1893 when she coupled it with the *English Woman's Journal* and *Women and Work* as publications that "forwarded the industrial and educational claims for women, . . . gradually moulded public opinion and at last led to reforms therein advocated as necessary for the free and harmonious development of women's physical, mental, and moral nature under the changed conditions of life in the nineteenth century" (*LP*, 9/2/93, 318). But what she neglected to point out was that the *English Woman's Journal* and its successor, the *Alexandra Magazine*, were in existence for only seven and a half years, whereas the *Victoria* provided continuous coverage of women's activities for seventeen years and two months. As Westwater says, the "chief value of the *Victoria Magazine* lies in its chronicling of events in the history of the women's movement . . . it is significant as a literary document of social history, giving ample coverage to twenty years of intense agitation for women's emancipation in Great Britain."[49]

Westwater's evaluation is, however, the rational judgement of a twentieth-century historian. Women of the nineteenth century regarded the *Victoria* as a constant inspiration[50] to British and American women in an ongoing struggle for their rights rather than as "a literary document of social history." Therefore, a broad measure of its worth must take account of both the emotional nineteenth- and the rational twentieth-century viewpoints.

Mrs. Wilbour also praised the *Victoria* for providing full coverage of the meetings of the Victoria Discussion Society (VDS),[51] an offshoot of the magazine that met monthly nine times a year (usually November to July) from 1869 to 1875, except for the 1872-3 season when Emily, its founder and director, was in America. Kate Pattison, in announcing that meetings of VDS would resume in November 1873, reminded members that the object of the society was "as before . . . the discussion of educational and industrial reforms" (*VM*, 9/73). But Emily defined its "two-fold object" in much broader terms[52]:

(1) to obtain from ladies the sympathy I fancied certain reformers required;

(2) to induce a free interchange of opinion, and provide safeguards against mistakes which might be made unless such subjects were well ventilated. All shades of opinion were invited, narrow cliques carefully avoided, and it may certainly be claimed that at these debates women learnt for the first time to publicly express their opinions on the subjects under discussion, for in those days hardly any lady ventured to speak, however competent to do so (*LP*, 10/21/93, 604).

One should note that in this definition she enjoined ladies to exercise caution in making public statements outside the confines of the VDS meeting room.[53] In 1869 Emily was still recovering from the public humiliation of the Codrington divorce case. So she was in effect telling VDS ladies not to speak out on matters of importance to women until they had their facts straight and were not too far in advance of public opinion. If they did not wish to be full of care, they had to be careful!

She took pains in organizing the society to provide it with a firm financial basis and a goodly number of prestigious members. The membership fee was originally 12 shillings per year (later one guinea), but that included a subscription to the *Victoria Magazine*; so membership fees hardly paid the secretary's salary, much less the expense of hiring a hall or publishing the proceedings of the society in the *Victoria*. The real financial underpinning consisted of liberal donations from rich and influential people like Lady Jane Franklin, one of "the earliest supporters of the Victoria Discussion Society" (*W & W*, 7/24/75, 5). Emily persuaded these benefactors to part with their money by enlisting eminent individuals as vice-presidents and chairmen of meetings. For example, Sir Charles Dilke and Mr. Nassau Senior agreed to be vice-presidents; and a whole string of famous people (mostly men[54]) were chairmen: the Earl of Shaftesbury, Lord Houghton, Sir George Grey, Sir John Bowring, Sir Erskine Perry, Sir John Swinburne, Sir Charles Clifford, Honourable Arthur Kinnaird, A.J. Mundella, M.P., Sir Charles Trevelyan, K.C.B., Dr. Heinemann, F.R.G.S., and Dr. Gladstone, F.R.S.[55] With such an impressive list to present to potential donors, a name like that of Julia Ward Howe of Boston, Mass., could be added without raising an eyebrow. For, though Mrs. Howe was a well-known women's rights' advocate, she had, after all, written the Battle Hymn of the Republic and was at present (July 1872) engaged in a campaign for world peace.

The papers presented and discussed at the VDS meetings dealt not only with every aspect of women's work but also with sundry political, social and cultural matters of interest to both men and women. In the category of women's work were "The Position of Women," "Women & Work," "Domestic Service," "Domestic Economy," "Medicine as a profession for Women," "Women in Art," "Watchmaking as Employment for Women," "Canada as a Field of Employment for Women," "Female Education," "Physiological Instruction and Physical Education for Women," "Emigration," "Women's Franchise," "Opposition to the Women's Movement," "Married Women's Property Bill 1870," and "Women in India." And, to ensure that "all shades of opinion" were represented, J. McGrigor Allan was invited to follow up the "Women's Franchise" paper with his paper entitled "A Protest Against Woman's Demand for the Privileges of Both Sexes." The more general papers dealt with such topics as "Play, Rational and Healthful," "Mutual Relations of Rich and Poor," "Coal Supply in its Relations to Domestic Economy," "The Poor Law-System," "Shorthand and Spelling Reform," "The Froebel System of Education," "Higher Education in Germany," "The Physical Sciences as a Key to the Social Sciences," "Spirit, Matter and Cosmic Force," "Temperance," "The Art of Reading," "The Sonnets of Shakespeare," "Poetry and Humour," and "Landscape Art in Poetry." Emily managed to maintain a balance between male and female presenters of papers.[56] And a perusal of the accounts of the discussions that followed the papers indicates that the women had the edge as discussants. So, all in all, women did participate fully.

Emily presented two VDS papers entitled "Women and Work" and "A Year's Experience in Emigration Work in Connection with New Zealand," and she played a major role in the discussions following these presentations. Moreover, she often got involved in the discussions of other papers,[57] despite her evident attempts to encourage other women to speak. For example, she disagreed strongly with Mrs. St. John's cheerful view of the position of women in 1870,[58] for she was not optimistic about an early victory over people opposed to or simply apathetic concerning the women's movement. Again, after listening impatiently to two papers on the proposed women's franchise, one man[59] vehemently opposing it and the other[60] acting like a wolf in sheep's clothing, she attacked both of them and freely acknowledged the necessity of the franchise. She did, however, express her confidence that education and training of women would produce results without the franchise, especially if the new approach to women's education encouraged thought, not just the accumulation of facts, and stressed thoroughness, not the hit-and-miss "smattering" hitherto considered suitable (*VM*, 1/71, 311). And she voiced her belief that teaching domestic economy to both mistresses and servants would result in well run homes in which servants would carry out their duties properly and mistresses, recognizing the changes that were occurring in social life, would grant servants more freedom.

Emily also stated her opinions in VDS sessions dealing with physiological instruction for women and with medicine as a suitable profession for women. Of the former she said that, as sanitation was chiefly the responsibility of women, women must receive instruction in physiology in order to prevent disease. As for women becoming medical doctors, she insisted that they were merely "returning to the usages of our forefathers," that the profession was well suited to woman's intellect and strength, and that female doctors could treat women's ailments better than male doctors (*VM*, 4/70, 519-521). Finally, she made VDS members aware that she was in the vanguard concerning female emigration. Four and a half years before she presented her paper on emigration to New Zealand, she spoke out strongly about the need for a government scheme of emigration that would provide "proper funds and proper escort . . . for these [women] who are ready to take their share in the exigencies of colonial life" (*VM*, 5/70, 22).

The members of VDS, male and female, did not doubt that the Society was one of her major accomplishments. At the end of its first year of operation, they moved a vote of thanks to Miss Faithfull for "the distinguished ability, courtesy, firmness, and judgment with which she has exercised all the duties belonging to her office" as president (*VM*, 8/70, 356). In the first meeting of the second year, Miss Downing recognized the importance of the Society and Miss Faithfull's part in it by describing it as a "*movement* which she so well leads and represents" (*VM*, 1/70, 125). At the outset of VDS's third year Arthur Kinnaird, treasurer of the Society, presented Emily with a testimonial consisting of a silver tea and coffee service, kettle, salver, and epergne "for her valuable services in promoting the Industrial and Educational Interests of Women" (*VM*, 11/71, 158), along with a scroll signed by members of VDS and other subscribers. And at the end of that third year, in a farewell soirée for Miss Faithfull, who was about to embark on her first visit to America, Mrs. Horace St. John spoke for the members of VDS in praising the "zeal, ability, and energy with which [Emily] had conducted the Society (Cheers). . . . She hoped it would be re-opened on Miss Faithfull's return, for it had done much good . . . it was most important that ladies should discuss questions relating to themselves" (*VM*, 10/72, 520).

So VDS was a great success. Why then did Emily terminate it in June 1875? The answer is that the Society had achieved its objective. As Emily said in 1893, "the debates of the Victoria Discussion Society led the way to the meetings and congresses at which women now speak without fear or hesitation" (*LP*, 6/10/93, 937). Besides, by mid-1875 Emily was much involved in acting, lecturing, editing the *Victoria* and *Women and Work*, and running the Industrial and Educational Bureau for Women. Moreover, SPEW had set up a Ladies' Debating Club to give women practice in public speaking, and Emily preferred not to duplicate any of SPEW's ventures.

She had established the Industrial and Educational Bureau for Women[61] in September 1873 "on the model of one[62] she recently saw working well in New York" (*Times*, 9/2/73, 9). The aim of the Bureau, according to this notice in the *Times*, was "to provide work for women through technical instruction; through a registry for professional, industrial and domestic employments; through emigration too; and through a practical course of training provided for young women in various families; also lectures to working women on household economy, cooking, treatment of children, and laws of health[63] . . . and a reading room, school for plain sewing, and cutting-out department . . . Miss Faithfull thinks the institution, if supported by the public, will help women to help themselves, the truest form of charity." Emily's letter of September 25, 1873 to the First Woman's Congress of the Association for the Advancement of Women provided details of this new venture of hers and suggested that American workers "form an office in New York in more complete connection with mine — to receive ladies who wish to emigrate, or domestic servants." She also mentioned in this letter that "the Earl of Shaftesbury, Lord Ormsthwaite, Lady Pollock, Reverend Basil Wilberforce, and others are working with me in this matter, but I have sole responsibility."[64]

Training women for jobs was the chief objective of the Bureau. Besides arranging for women to attend training schools (SPEW's school for clerks and bookkeepers, the Female School of Art, Teacher Training institutes, and so on), Emily set up some classes at the Bureau (e.g., Mr. J.B. Rundell's shorthand class,[65] the use of Wheeler and Wilson's sewing machines,[66] and dressmaking[67]). And in a series of short articles on the Bureau she continued to emphasize the need for women to be trained and ready to undertake jobs away from home.[68]

By October 1874[69] she was able to claim that the Bureau was a "wonderful success"[70]: by providing "a reliable and easy means of communication" between "those who need work and those who can give it," employment "has been obtained for ladies as cashiers, translators, sub-wardens in prisons, matrons in hospitals and emigrant ships, house decorators, designers, glass stainers, illuminators, law writers, china painters, copyists, proof-readers, compositors, sales-women, book-keepers, shorthand writers, machinists, etc., while others have been placed in positions of trust in connection with various companies and business enterprisers (sic)" (*W & W*, 10/10/74, 6).

The Industrial and Educational Bureau continued to be successful in training women and getting jobs for them. Financially, however, it was another millstone around Emily's neck. The subscription fee (one guinea per year) had to be kept low because many subscribers were women seeking jobs.[71] Furthermore, as not enough wealthy people chose to subscribe, Emily had to report a considerable deficit at the end of the second year of operation. So she organized a highly successful dramatic performance at St. George's Hall, Langham Place, on June 26, 1875 to defray the costs of the Bureau and its chief means of communication with the public, *Women and Work*, a "*Weekly Industrial, Educational and Household Register for Women,* Edited by Emily Faithfull. Price/1 penny" (*W & W*, 6/6/74, 1).

The immediate objective of *Women and Work* was to serve as a connecting link between employer and potential employee, and thus promote the "industrial pursuits of women." In a more personal vein, Emily wrote of its aim "to smooth the way for enlarged spheres of occupation [for women] and to secure fair play and equal treatment in the practical affairs of life . . . to help, if possible, those who desire to help themselves, to direct those who wish to tread the path of industry, and to encourage the faint-hearted, who have to fight the battle of life against overwhelming odds" (*W & W*, 6/6/74, 4). But she hoped *Women and Work* would be more than an industrial register; she intended to make it a "high-class Family Newspaper reflecting the growth of public opinion in all that tends to elevate the physical and moral welfare of [women]" (*VM*, 5/74, 93). So, though she eschewed party politics, controversial doctrines, and romance, she decided to add "art, literature, and science" to the articles on and guides to employments, thus providing the cultural overview she believed all women needed.

The "Guide to Employments" section of the newspaper listed both jobs available and training (apprenticeship, course, school) needed for those jobs. Also, in some issues of *Women and Work* "special commissioners" contributed articles on types of employment opening up to women, e.g., "Women Shoemakers" and "The Sewing Machinist." Then there were articles on education, emigration, domestic economy, women in factories, milliners and dressmakers, sanitation, cookery, artistic employment of women, the false pride of middle-class ladies concerning remunerative work, and so on. A column entitled "American Notes" dealt mostly with employment in the U.S.A., though women's rights and esprit de corps received their due, as did female suffrage.

Advertising was more prevalent in *Women and Work* than in the *Victoria Magazine*. For example, Messrs. Hatchard listed books they had published, especially those related to the cause of women, and William Robson encouraged ladies to sell his "Packet Tea." But most advertisements appear to have been non-paying notices about the activities or interests of Emily, her relatives, or her friends. She publicized her lectures, her lessons in reading and elocution, the Victoria Dressmaking Company, the contents of the *Victoria*

*Magazine*, the Victoria Press, the Victoria Discussion Society, and her need for women compositors. And she published notices for Amy Stewart, "pianiste," who had assisted at the June 1875 dramatic performance in aid of the Industrial and Educational Bureau, and for Mrs. Howard Paul's entertainments (which involved Rutland Barrington, Emily's nephew). Even an apparent advertisement for Dietz's Climax, a portable cooking stove which used oil and incorporated a coffee-filter, looks more like an enthusiastic recommendation by Emily the traveller than a bona fide advertisement. Thus, as was the case with the *Victoria Magazine*, advertising revenue apparently contributed little toward the operating expenses of *Women and Work*.

Several journals (*The Spectator*, *Pictorial World*, *Punch*, *The Lancet*, *The Daily News*) expressed their good wishes for the success of *Women and Work* (rpt. in *W & W*, 8/1/74). *Punch* went even further than the others: "An old and faithful worker in the cause of women (EMILY of that ilk) has started a weekly paper which, if it keeps up to its purpose and its promises, deserves *Punch's* support and that of all friends of the feebler and fairer, softer and sweeter, willinger and weaker, worse-used and worse-paid, harder-worked and harder-thrashed sex. . . . Miss FAITHFULL calls her paper *Women and Work*, its object being to make known the work to the women who want it and the women to the work that wants them. *Punch* can only wish good speed to the woman and her work; for it is sorely needed" (*Punch*, 6/13/74, 76).

*Women and Work* was, indeed, sorely needed; and certainly from a functional point of view it and its parent, the Industrial and Educational Bureau, were wonderful successes. But, as Emily later stated, "It is a terrible matter to have been in advance of your time. I was the first woman to start a weekly penny paper in the interests of the sex in England; but I scarcely care to recall to-day how much the experiment cost me. *Women and Work* struggled valiantly for a year or so,[72] but the time was not ripe, and after much anxiety my newspaper expired peacefully" (*LP*, 5/25/89, 726). Yet, despite the financial cost, she was proud that it had paved the way for penny papers like the *Women's Gazette* and the *Women's Penny Paper*.

Emily Faithfull's next journalistic venture was the *West London Express*, a weekly penny newspaper published from September 15, 1877 to December 28, 1878. It was a valiant attempt to produce a full-fledged newspaper[73] and to expand the Victoria Press. In Emily's words, the *Express* was founded in the belief that "there was room for a paper, which, not ignoring the features of local [West London] journalism, should yet take a wider view of current events than can be expected in a purely local journal" (*WLE*, 1/5/78, 6). Like the *Victoria*, the *Express* indulged in self-aggrandizement with its frequent reference to Emily's lectures and entertainments, though most of these items were confined to advertisements. But it did provide good local coverage of the activities of West End vestries, County and Police Courts, School Boards, Boards of Guardians, Workhouses, and recreation facilities. It also contained many lively columns, e.g., "Art Gossip," "The Stage," "Music," "Fiction," "Flashes of Fun," "The Court," "Our Telephone," "From the Strangers' Gallery [of the House of Commons]," "Pen and Ink Sketches [of West End Clergymen]," "Correspondence," and "Work for Women."[74]

In this newspaper Emily dealt with national and international news in several ways: a "Foreign News" column, hard-hitting editorials, and news stories. Editorials covered wide-ranging topics like the mass meeting of disgruntled agricultural labourers, Russian and Bulgarian atrocities in Turkey, Russian occupation of Afghanistan, unreasonable demands of male Trade Unions, "miserably defective sanitary organisation of our parishes" (*WLE*, 11/3/77), and the fine "Proms" of 1878. Many news items about the cause of women appeared in the *Express*, for example, meetings to promote women's suffrage, the University of London's decision to admit women to degrees in all faculties, the need for women's unions because of starvation wages, and the treatment of wives as nonpersons. Yet Emily did not allow these stories about the condition of women to upset the nice balance of local, national, and international news that she maintained throughout the brief existence of the newspaper.

Even though there were still many non-paying "ads,"[75] advertisements played a greater role in this newspaper than in either the *Victoria* or *Women and Work*. In fact, in May 1878 Emily announced that she was going to enlarge the newspaper because of the increasing demand for advertising space. A number of these paying "ads" very likely would have been non-paying in the other two journals, for instance, jobs for women (prior to Emily's inaugurating her "Work for Women" column), a Grand Concert in aid of the Indian Famine

Fund, a Grand Matinée in aid of the Vicarage Fund, courses offered at the College for Working Women, the London Museums, the West End shows, and free emigration for women to Australia and New Zealand. And perhaps some of them were non-payers in the *Express* as well. But others were clearly money makers, e.g., Messrs. Ricketts, dressmakers; Bliss's Asthma Remedy; and the General Expenditure Assurance Company's coupon system.[76]

The *Express* was a good newspaper, and for a while it prospered. In November 1877 Emily was pleased to report an increasing demand for the paper "in all parts of the West End of London and throughout the country" (*WLE*, 11/10/77, 102). And in a January 1878 editorial she referred to her New Year's "hopes [being] brightened by the past success" of the paper (*WLE*, 1/5/78, 6). But, though it was enlarged in May 1878 to accommodate an apparent demand for more advertising space, publication ceased at the end of 1878 with no warning and no explanation. The only reason I can think of is that it failed financially, despite last-ditch attempts to save it like a special prepaid rate for advertisements, the sudden opening of a "city office" at 84 Fleet Street (in addition to the "chief office" in the Victoria Press building) in late October 1878, and a rather desperate reminder that the newspaper was available at these two offices, as well as at city and district wholesale agents, railway bookstalls, and all news agents (*LE*, 10/26/78).

Emily Faithfull's last, and perhaps best, journalistic engagement was as reporter for the *Lady's Pictorial*, first with "Across the Atlantic" reports from America during her second and third visits to that country (1882-4), then with her "Northern Gossip" column every week from June 1885 to her death in 1895 and a second weekly column entitled "Woman: Her Interests and Pursuits" from September 1888 to May 1895. The "Across the Atlantic" columns, which appeared, for the most part, weekly or fortnightly from November 1882 to May 1883 and November 1883 to May 1884, dealt not only with matters of concern to women, e.g., kindergartens, co-education, women in medicine, Vassar College, Women's Clubs, jobs for women, "fast" women, the Temperance Movement, American divorces, etc., but also with other topics of interest to British people in general: Emily's sea voyages; railroad travel and accidents; the Cincinnati flood of 1883; evenings with leaders in learning and culture; theatrical and cultural events; visits to Congress; her stay in

Salt Lake City to investigate Mormonism; the free libraries of Topeka; the silk farms and vineyards of California; and so on.

A year after returning from her third visit to America, Emily began her "Northern Gossip"[77] column in the *Lady's Pictorial*. She used a pseudonym, "by a Lancashire Witch," but it was common knowledge that she was the author of this column of news and comments from the Manchester area. Three years later (September 15, 1888) the column "Woman: Her Interests and Pursuits" (later shortened to "Woman (by Miss Emily Faithfull)") made its début[78] "at the Editor's request." Emily prefaced the first submission of "Woman" with this comment: "In this department of the *Lady's Pictorial* I shall not only notice the serious pursuits of modern Englishwomen, but their popular amusements. Comments will be made on passing events relating to their domestic, social, educational, legal, and political welfare. Information will be given respecting professional and industrial careers, and new occupations suggested. Hints from practical workers will always be welcomed, and the progress made in similar directions in other countries duly recorded. The questions of correspondents will be answered to the best of my ability" (*LP*, 9/15/88. 272). She apparently intended to keep any observations about women's issues out of her "Northern Gossip" column and, by the same token, to confine the "Woman" column to such issues. In fact, both columns dealt with the "serious pursuits" and "popular amusements" of women as well as with local news. After all, "Northern Gossip" had covered women's concerns for three years before "Woman" came into existence. But why two columns instead of one? The editor of the *Lady's Pictorial* no doubt wanted more of Emily in the journal.

Aside from news of her own doings and praise of her relatives' and friends' accomplishments Emily allotted most space in her two columns to the women's topics she had been dealing with for more than twenty years. News of events in Manchester and district was something new and different. The restoration of the Manchester Cathedral, the local celebrations attending Parliament's passage of a Bill authorizing construction of the Manchester Ship Canal and the subsequent opening of the canal, Emily's day trips by rail from Manchester to London and return, her involvement in local political campaigns, her annoyance at women being excluded from celebrations of the Queen's birthday in 1885 and from the Manchester Town Hall dinner for Prince Albert Victor in 1888, her disclosure of corruption among contractors preparing the Exhibition site for the celebration of the Queen's Golden Jubilee, and her condemnation of Manchester's slippery streets and foul atmosphere — these lively reports on local events and conditions helped not only to put Manchester on the map but also to instill a sense of community in her Manchester readers.

Reading "Northern Gossip" and "Woman" makes one realize that these *Lady's Pictorial* columns do not represent a pre-retirement cushion for an erstwhile active person. Emily Faithfull worked hard to produce up-to-the-minute reports, first making good use of many volumes and magazines containing "the literature of the woman question" (*LP*, 9/15/88, 272) in her Manchester home,[79] then putting her columns together on the train[80] to London with the aid of a smaller travelling library before personally delivering them to the *Lady's Pictorial* office.

Because of the popularity of her *Lady's Pictorial* columns, Emily became something of a celebrity in Manchester and the North counties. In 1888 George Murray, taking part in some private theatricals at Eccles, made an off-the-cuff reference to the "Northern Gossip" in the *Lady's Pictorial*, and his audience immediately appreciated the allusion, as did Emily when she heard about it. She also was pleased by the many "pleasant comments on my contributions to the *Lady's Pictorial*" (*LP*, 12/28/89, 952) that she received in the mail.[81]

At least two of her articles appeared in journals[82] other than the ones with which she was closely associated: "Domestic Service in England" in *North American Review*, July 1891, pp. 23-31; and "The Progress of Woman in Industrial Employment" in the *Universal Review*, December 1888, pp. 637-643. The fact that both were solicited articles indicates the high regard in Britain and America for Emily Faithfull's knowledge of woman's condition, especially in such important matters as jobs and education. By 1888 she had become one of the sages of women's work, and her success as a journalist was in large part responsible for her acquiring that reputation.

But her journalistic endeavours were not confined to the written word. Just as we today view radio and television news as highly successful offspring of newspapers, so Victorians regarded public lectures as felicitous extensions of printed messages of all sorts. Thus, when Emily began to worry about the sluggish rate of change of public opinion concerning women's rights, she must have thought it both natural and logical that she, a recognized elocutionist, should try to alter public attitudes through a series of lectures as well as through published articles and editorials.

Her first lecture on the condition of women took place in the Hanover Square Rooms, London, in December 1868 and was well received by a large audience. Indeed, it marked "the first step . . . towards the inauguration of lectures by women throughout the United Kingdom" (*VM*, 5/72, 119) and established her as itinerant spokesperson for the cause of women. During the next twelve months she followed up this initial success by lecturing on the same topic to a total of 50,000 people throughout England. Assured that she had made some of them think about women's rights, she suggested at a VDS meeting in January 1870 that "the great thing now to be done was to educate public opinion respecting the difficulties and needs of women, to break in upon public apathy and indifference" (*VM*, 1/70, 214). Adding Scotland to her itinerary in late 1870, Emily maintained her busy schedule over the next two years with lectures variously entitled "The Position and Claims of Women,"[83] "Woman's Work and Woman's Sphere,"[84] "Woman's Work with Special Reference to Industrial Employment,"[85] "Woman's Work and Woman's Mission."[86] And she donated the proceeds[87] from several of these lectures to worthy causes, e.g., French and Prussian sick and wounded (October 1870), and French Female Refugees (February 1871). Her Exeter lecture on the "Position and Claims of Women" appears to have been typical of the many she gave during this 1868-72 period. Even though it was an hour and ten minutes long, a "very large audience" listened to it with "great attention and interest." In fact, the Exeter reporter continued, it was "a most successful address, for Queen Street seemed to teem with warm conversation and controversy on various points of the Woman Question for twenty minutes after the breaking up of the meeting" (*The Exeter and Plymouth Gazette Daily Telegram*, 4/7/70, 3).

Emily's lecture tour of America from October 1872 to May 1873 encompassed the north-eastern States and two mid-western ones (Illinois, Indiana), and it seems to have been as successful as her earlier tours in the United Kingdom. Of course, she altered some topics to suit her American audiences, producing such titles as "The Women's Movement in England in the Last Fifteen Years,"[88] "Queen Victoria and the Royal Family," "The Scope for Women's Faculties in England and America," "Movements Relating to

Women," "Glimpses of Great Men and Women I have Known,"[89] and "Last Words on the Woman Question, with English and American Experiences."[90]

Back in England she initially limited her condition-of-women lectures of 1873-4 to "The Present Aspect of the Women's Movement in America" and "Eight Months in America,"[91] and was duly praised for her "acuteness of observation" and "lively appreciation of Yankee humour" (*Falkirk Herald*, rpt. in *VM*, 2/74, 382). She did, however, present more general papers entitled "Women and Work" and "A Year's Experience in Emigration Work in Connection with New Zealand" at VDS meetings in June and December 1874; and by October she was again offering "Woman's Work and Mission."

Her lectures from 1875 to 1882 were, for the most part,[92] literary in nature. During her second and third lecture tours of America (1882-3 and 1883-4) she must have continued to lecture on the position of women. But she made few references to lecture topics; only two appear in the accounts of her 1880's travels in America: "The Changed Position of Women" (New York, December 1882) which is mentioned by Odell,[93] not by Emily, and "Woman's Work" (Cincinnati, February 1883), cited in *Three Visits to America*.[94] Yet it is clear that she lectured well[95] and frequently enough[96] in 1882-3 to merit a "brilliant offer" of a further six-months' lecture tour in 1883-4 (*LP*, 6/16/83, 403). As mentioned earlier, this third and last visit to America proved one too many.

When she began writing her "Northern Gossip" column in the *Lady's Pictorial* in 1885, she told a correspondent that she had "a great many engagements far a head (sic), lectures +c."[97] Once again she did not indicate the topics of these lectures, though no doubt some of them had to do with women's work. In 1892 she told an interviewer that from 1885 on she "was [also] in constant requisition as a speaker at the annual meetings of benevolent societies, but severe and persistent attacks of asthma and bronchitis [had] lately obliged her to decline the numerous requests received" (*Manchester Faces and Places*, 1892, 133). There is no record of her presenting regular lectures after 1889.

Emily turned more and more toward literary topics after 1875. She had inaugurated these cultural lectures in 1870 when she first presented "The Best Society: Your Bookshelf," and this topic[98] remained a staple commodity in her repertoire until the winter of 1888-89.[99] In this lecture she entreated her audience[100] to "shun mean books, sentimental rhymes, and tales of mere adventure;" instead she wanted them to read novels and poetry that "opened to us the entire kingdom of thought" (*VM*, 2/71, 473, rpt. from the *York Herald*). In 1871 she put three more literary arrows in her quiver: "The English Poets," "The Prose-Writing Poets" and "American Poets."[101] The last of these became very popular after she had experienced American poets and their poetry during her first visit to America. Thus she could announce that she intended to devote her entire lecture tour of February and March 1875 to her revised version of "American Poets." And this lecture held its own throughout 1876-78, even becoming one of the lectures in a course[102] given by the Misses White to "Daughters of Gentlemen" who had to be "carefully, religiously, and practically educated" (*WLE*, 11/24/77). "English and American Orators," which replaced the lost "English Orators"[103] in 1873, was ready for delivery to English audiences in July 1873. But it apparently did not enjoy as long a run as "American Poets," though rhetoric ranked as high with Victorian audiences as poetry did.

Emily also had considerable success with lectures not manifestly feminist or literary. The best example is "The Extravagance of Modern Life: Its Cause and Cure." She had written an editorial on this topic in 1875 in which she despaired of reform and simply pointed out the social and political price of such prodigality. However, by 1878 she realized that not only were a great many people really worried about the bad effects of extravagance, but they were also ready to listen to her proposals for a cure. So she orchestrated an afternoon lecture on June 19, 1878 in the Egyptian Hall of Mansion House (bailiwick of the Lord Mayor of London), and persuaded the Earl of Shaftesbury to be chairman and the Lord Mayor to be present. She even convinced Thomas Hughes, M.P., that he should add his comments after she had finished speaking.

The meeting turned out to be "one of the largest and most enthusiastic held for some time at the Mansion House" (*WLE*, 6/29/78, 2). Emily began by recounting some of her experiences with destitute widows and daughters to prove that though the English people were industrious they were also improvident. This improvidence, coupled with material prosperity, the spirit of equality, and a general love of money, had resulted in the hypocrisy — common to all classes and both sexes — of living beyond one's means, particularly through the credit system. Consequently, the nation as a whole was heading toward bankruptcy. The cure for this national disease was to encourage provident habits through lessons in thrift in the schools, education in cultural rather than monetary values, and accumulation of savings in savings banks, building funds, and insurance societies. In particular, she recommended the General Expenditure Assurance Co., established in 1874, which worked in co-operation with "legitimate traders" to promote the spending of "ready money" and thus make the credit system obsolete. These co-operating traders handed out General Expenditure Assurance Co. coupons when they received cash payment for goods, and these coupons could then be used as savings or as cash for the next purchase from another (or the same) trader. The more the public resorted to ready-money purchase, the bigger the list of traders involved in the General Expenditure Assurance scheme would become (*WLE*, 6/29/78, 1-2 and *VM*, 7/78, 250-54). In this speech Emily called upon the Press to expose the shams of the day and encouraged society to adopt a "braver spirit" in dealing with extravagance. When she finished, the applause was "loud and continued." Thomas Hughes, after agreeing with everything she had said, provided more details about the General Expenditure Assurance Company. Then Shaftesbury praised Emily for her "very able address" and "excellent advice" (*WLE*, 6/29/78, 1-2).

Every press report was positive. Emily was variously described as "noble-spirited," "outspoken," "clever," "sensible," and "a strenuous and fearless supporter of every good cause" (*WLE*, 6/29/78, 2). And her lecture was acclaimed "a capital address — good without being goody" (*WLE*, 7/6/78, 13). In fact, this "Modern Extravagance" lecture was so much in demand that she gave repeat performances during 1878 in more than twenty cities and towns in England and Scotland, and her audiences were uniformly large and appreciative. In almost every instance she got some eminent person to chair the meeting, e.g., the Duke of Devonshire in Buxton, the Mayor in Newcastle-upon-Tyne, the Bishop of Manchester in Manchester, and the Lord Provost in Glasgow. And the proceeds were often donated to deserving causes — hospitals, orphanages, convalescent homes, etc. Though this lecture's popularity appears to have waned over the next few years, Emily continued giving it until 1882.[104] For instance, in March 1881 it drew a "crowded audience" to the Kensington Vestry Hall, and the proceeds went to the National Thrift Society[105] (*LP*, 4/2/81, 116).

Incidentally, Emily opened her 1883-4 tour of America with a lecture[106] entitled "Modern Shams" that was probably an offshoot of this "Modern Extravagance" lecture. According to the *Lady's Pictorial*, this "Modern Shams" presentation in New York's Chickering Hall was "attended by a brilliant audience. The Reverend Robert Collyer presided and on the platform were to be seen some of the most notable clergymen and people in New York" (*LP*, 12/1/83, 343).

After writing her travel book, *Three Visits to America*, in 1884, Emily began her 1884-5 tour of the United Kingdom with a lecture entitled "The Mormons: their Social Life, Amusements, and Celestial Marriages."[107]    Her subsequent lectures were mostly one-shot performances. A notable example is her Jubilee address in the Manchester Town Hall on May 3, 1887,[108] which dealt with the political and social changes due to Queen Victoria's life and influence, particularly her influence on British women. After presenting this address to the Prince and Princess of Wales, assembled dignitaries, and ordinary citizens, she had an interview with the Princess in which the latter manifested "her kindly interest in Miss Faithfull's labours by conversing with her for some time on the subject. The strong sympathy shown by the Princess in women's work throughout the kingdom, as expressed to Miss Faithfull, was one of the most striking incidents of a remarkable day" (*The Queen*, 5/7/87, 566).

Emily also spoke at the inauguration of the South Manchester Primrose Habitation in 1887, and she made several speeches concerning her latest projects, the Colonial Emigration Society and the Imperial Institute. In a letter to Mr. Pritchard dated March 28 she mentioned her recent "address" to the Emigration Society (Fawcett Library, Vol. II), and her *Lady's Pictorial* columns informed her readers that, before Genevieve Ward began her benefit performance in October, Emily had enlightened the audience concerning that Society. Apropos of the Imperial Institute, she gave a speech in the Manchester Town Hall on July 21, and she followed that up in December with an address to the Lord Mayor of Manchester's meeting.

In 1889 she made at least two more public speeches, one at a huge political demonstration for Arthur Balfour and the second at the official opening of the Lancashire Watch Factory in Prescot. The latter was supposed to be merely a vote of thanks to Lady Margaret Cecil, who had laid the cornerstone. Emily transformed it into a stirring speech in which she alluded to her 1872-73 visits to American watch factories, her (and others') attempts to start a similar venture in 1874, and the great satisfaction of this achievement for Prescot and women watchmakers.

The newspapers were remarkably concordant about the worth of her lectures. Here are some comments on those concerning the position and claims of women:

"purity of its eloquence . . . . clearness of its reasoning" (*Hull and Eastern Counties Herald*, rpt. in *VM*, 4/70, 567)

"Scrupulously moderate at all points . . . lucid and irrefragable in argument . . . good choice of facts and illustrations" (*Exeter & Plymouth Gazette Daily Telegram*, 4/7/70, 3)

"brilliant address" (*New York Times*, rpt. in *VM*, 3/73, 469)

"a born orator" (*New York Herald*, rpt. in *VM*, 3/73, 468)

"clothed sound common-sense views in a most attractive and humorous form" (*Manchester Guardian*, rpt. in *LE*, 11/30/78, 348).

And they were equally complimentary about her literary topics:

*The Best Society* was "an eloquent lecture — a real intellectual treat" (*York Herald*, rpt. in *VM*, 3/71, 473)

*English Poets* was "concise and well defined . . . [Her] enunciation [was] clear and artistic and all sensationalism was avoided" (*Woman*, 7/13/72, 435)

*American Poets* was an "admirable critical discourse [that displayed] singular power of pathetic and humorous expression" (*The Era*, rpt. in *VM*, 4/75, 554).

Thus the *Illustrated London News*'s statement in 1895 that Emily was "very popular as a lecturer both in this country and in the United States" may be accepted verbatim, for there is no negative press report to contradict it.

*Chapter 6*

# Political Reformer: Education

To appreciate Emily Faithfull's contribution as a political reformer, one must scan a broad continuum of her activities, ranging from attempts to upgrade women's education, getting jobs for women, and supporting female suffrage, to advocating that women actively participate in politics, especially when the rights of married women and the health and welfare of the nation were involved.

In 1874 Emily wrote an editorial about difficulties encountered by School Boards trying to enforce compulsory school attendance. The chief difficulty was that many working-class children had to work or take care of brothers and sisters not of school age. She suggested low-cost infant nurseries (crèches) as a partial answer, for they would permit baby-sitting girls to attend school. But she despaired of any remedy being applied, for public indifference concerning education, especially girls' education, was proving a tough nut to crack. The House of Commons was dragging its feet, or, as she phrased it in reference to the defeat of the University of Scotland Bill[1] in 1875, the House was "not very much in earnest" (*W & W*, 3/6/75) about any matter relating to the welfare of women. Yet Parliament was merely reflecting public acceptance of the traditional view that women of all classes should be educated to be wives and mothers only. At its worst this "angel-in-the-house" education still consisted (for young ladies, at least) of "a mere smattering of languages, a little instrumental music, the use of globes and dumb-bells, and a few superficial general notions" (*Three Visits*, 64). At its best, it took cognizance of the recommendation of the Royal Commission Report of 1858 that "new and complex tasks of household management" should be part of the curriculum in middle-class girls' schools. This proposed addition of domestic economy as

94

a school subject seemed forward-looking, but it too merely added fuel to the argument that women should be educated for domesticity. And things were no better overseas. At the time Emily was worrying about girls' education in England, Elizabeth Cady Stanton was venting her frustration about a similarly narrow system of girls' education in America[2]: "The only way to end the race of dyspeptic, neuralgic mothers is to educate a generation of complete women, not toys, nor slaves, but reliable, responsible human beings" (E. C. Stanton, "American Notes," *W & W*, 1/2/75, 2).

Individuals dissatisfied with the state of women's education had established two women's colleges, two secondary schools, and some experimental schools by 1858. Queen's College, founded in 1848 by Rev. Frederick D. Maurice and other reformist members of the Church of England, stressed arts subjects more than sciences, but its curriculum did include Mathematics, Latin, and Greek. Bedford College, established in 1849, emphasized science and ethics in a non-denominational setting. The instructors at both institutions were professors from the University of London,[3] and the level of education at the beginning ranged of necessity from primary to secondary, for most of the students[4] had not previously been subjected to a broad, rigorous education. By 1880 Cheltenham Ladies' College (estab. 1858 by Miss Beale) and North London Collegiate (estab. 1850 by Miss Buss) had extended the usual girls' college offerings to include History, English Literature, Geography, Mathematics, French, German, Latin, Science and Calisthenics. Cheltenham, which prided itself on teaching daughters of gentlemen, also taught Natural Philosophy, Chemistry, and Greek, whereas North London Collegiate, more involved with middle-class students than Cheltenham, offered Health, Plain Needlework, Writing, Book-keeping, and Political and Domestic Economy.[5] One of the most innovative schools was Barbara Leigh Smith's[6] Portman Hall School in London, a co-educational, secular, student-centred institution whose curriculum was a far cry from the traditional "catechism" system of rote learning. Such experiments, however, had to be financed privately; so they proved too expensive for the long run.[7]

Despite this rather gloomy picture of the education of girls and women, beneficial changes did occur after 1858, and Emily either got directly involved in bringing them about or she gave them much-needed publicity. In the latter category she concentrated on general, primary and secondary education. For example, she publicized the

Working Women's College proposed by John Stuart Mill, Harriet Martineau, Frances Power Cobbe, Mme. Bodichon and others, brought into being by Mr. and Mrs. Malleson in 1864, and made co-educational in 1874;[8] and an evening college for working women (estab. 1874) sponsored by the Women's Educational Union that offered business correspondence, précis-writing and shorthand. Emily wished this evening college every success, for she contended that its business courses "[fall] well within women's sphere, and thoroughly competent female clerks and shorthand writers are sure to find employment" (*WLE*, 3/23/78, 137). She also was pleased when a National Home Reading Union was formed and when individuals concerned about working-class readers opened their reading rooms and libraries to them.[9] And though she does not appear to have been greatly interested in the deliberations of the Schools Inquiry Commission concerning primary[10] and secondary education,[11] she did give credit to Dorothea Beale for her *Report Issued by the Schools Inquiry Commission on the Education of Girls* (*VM*, 12/69), for she realized that some fundamental changes in girls' education would result from that report.

Of the chief agency of these changes, namely, the National Union for Improving the Education of Women of All Classes (a.k.a. the Women's Educational Union), she wrote at length. The first act of this Union, founded in 1871 by Mrs. Maria Grey with the help of her sister Emily Shirreff and the Social Science Association, was to establish the Girls' Public Day Schools Co. Ltd., a limited liability company financed by shares sold to the public. Over the decade from 1872 to 1882 this company built and staffed some twenty-seven schools[12] for girls wherever they were most needed in England. Emily Faithfull was clearly impressed by their record, for she reprinted a long letter from Maria Grey that had been published in the *Times* in 1877; here are a few excerpts from that letter: "In these schools nearly 1,700 girls are receiving a first-class education at a *maximum* fee of fifteen guineas per annum . . . the company recognizes no social distinctions; its schools are public schools, open to all who choose to pay the fees, and in all the daughters of gentlemen . . . sit side by side with the daughters of the smallest tradesmen . . . . [These schools are] benefiting girls of all classes above those provided for by the public elementary schools" (*VM*, 4/77, 551). She also kept her readers informed of the expansion of this company (shares sold, number of schools constructed). And in

1875 she published a full report of Emily Shirreff's SSA paper, "Is a fair Proportion of the Endowments of the Country made applicable to Female Education?," in which Miss Shirreff demanded either better educational endowments[13] for girls' schools or a manifest change in public opinion that would result in better education for girls. Emily Faithfull was particularly pleased that "Miss Sheriff (sic) concluded her excellent paper with an eloquent protest against the 'enfeebling' system now prevalent of educating girls" (*W & W*, 10/16/75, 3).

Closely associated with the Girls' Public Day Schools Co. Ltd. (and hence with the National Union[14]) were Froebel Kindergartens; indeed, one of the kindergartens was attached to the Girls' Public Day School at Croydon in 1874, and other company schools followed suit.[15] Emily was, if anything, more interested in kindergartens than in elementary and secondary education. In 1874 she made special mention of Mrs. Schwabe's kindergarten school in Italy which that lady hoped to make into a model school by attaching it to a training school for teachers and an industrial school. Three years later she published an account of the annual meeting of the English branch of the Froebel Society in which she outlined Froebel's system[16] as set forth by Emily Shirreff, President of the Society, and informed *Victoria Magazine* readers of the need for subscriptions to train kindergarten teachers in that system. Then, during her second visit to America, she attended a lecture on kindergartens by Miss E.P. Peabody,[17] who had studied Froebel's ideas in Germany and introduced them to America. As a result she got directly involved with Chicago and San Francisco kindergartens,[18] particularly the latter under the aegis of Mrs. Sarah B. Cooper and the Golden Gate Kindergarten Association.[19]

Education of the poor was also a recurring topic in Emily's columns and editorials. For instance, in 1874 she expressed her firm agreement with Mrs. Nassau Senior's report on the training of pauper children. Like Mrs. Senior she believed that the existing Union schools were "fiascoes" and these children should be separated "entirely from the associations, the surroundings, the very walls of the workhouse" (*W & W*, 12/19/74, 4). She noted that a deputation of the National Committee for Promoting the Boarding-Out of Pauper Orphans was presently being received at Local Government Offices, and she trusted that these children, especially the girls, would soon be boarded-out.[20] Of the education of poor children in general she made the radical suggestion that those who were able should pay the full price of children's education, thus ensuring that the poor,[21] in particular the gutter-children who in 1878 did not attend school at all, would be better educated. Yet, though Emily believed in universal education,[22] she was not in favour of an education system that lumped all children together in national, secular schools. She was, after all, a product of an age that, as she herself expressed it, upheld "those distinctions of class which not only exist in fact, but are jealously insisted upon by the English people, and rightly. The members of the School Board [advocating a centralized public school system for all children] evidently know little or nothing of the 'gutter children' of whom they talk so glibly. . . . Those really acquainted with [the gutter child] know him to be — as a rule — sharp enough, but a liar, and generally a thief, dirty in his person, profane and obscene in his talk, a thorough little scamp, in short, with whom no respectable workman cares to have his children brought in contact" (*W & W*, 1/8/76, 4). Like Matthew Arnold, Emily feared the uncultured, often savage, "Populace;" therefore, though both she and Arnold wanted to give them the "Sweetness and Light" of education, they insisted on maintaining a careful distance from them until education made them civilized (or at least civil). Besides, as she stated on more than one occasion, John Stuart Mill himself was opposed to a monolithic education system because of the conformity and the lack of experimentation it engendered. So Emily, perhaps a little ashamed of her undemocratic sentiments concerning gutter children, cited danger of conformity as a second, and firmer, plank in her argument for retaining small private schools as an educational option.

Her idea of education for girls was essentially liberal. It stressed "precision of thought, work, and act" (*LP*, 11/21/91, 917) and thoroughness (hence not too many academic subjects), no cramming,[23] and no corporal punishment. She insisted that the curriculum for girls (and women) should be the same as for boys (and men); that is, it should aim at developing women as "human creatures," not as angels or toys[24] or as "mechanical wealth producers" (*LP*, 11/9/89, 622). In general she favoured a strongly classical curriculum[25] at the university level; however, if a particular university[26] concentrated on the sciences rather than the arts, Emily would permit a subject like Greek to be dropped. She also included a number of useful (hence "liberal") non-academic subjects like swimming and Physical Education (gymnastics, outdoor games), drawing and music, dancing and fencing, and elocution.[27] And she insisted that the female student's progress be checked by yearly examinations, thus giving definite direction to her studies. For she wanted women to compete (and be seen to compete) with men in educational matters.

Higher education of women was for Emily, as for all members of the Langham Place circle, the chief objective of the women's movement, both for the intellectual stimulus and culture it provided and for the vocational opportunities it afforded. Referring to women's education in 1889, she wrote, "Above all this confusion, one strong, intelligible cry has distinctly made itself heard — the demand for education, that women may be taught thoroughly, in order that they may be able to work[28] like reasonable beings at skilled labour and intellectual pursuits, and with some regard to their various positions in life" (*LP*, 3/23/89, 394). But she expected more of female university graduates than an ability to work efficiently: "it is to them that we must look in this age of fierce competition for the maintenance of cultivated and refined tastes, which will save the nation from degenerating into sensuous luxurious ease or a vast money-making machine for the gratification of this rapidly increasing passion for material display" (*LP*, 7/12/90, 66).

She also believed that higher education would bring other benefits in train. With statistics[29] to back her, she pointed out that university girls were healthier[30] and more efficient than other girls, both at university and after graduation, and that their children's health was above the national average. She also contended that because higher education was the "cure" for female apathy, it would help bring about a desired union of women. Moreover, she insisted, educated women would still get married,[31] beget and nurture children, and supervise their households; indeed, their higher education, which should include some knowledge of domestic economy, would make them better wives and mothers than they would have been without university education.

Her strong belief in the beneficial effects of education caused her to take a leading role in the struggle to get women admitted to universities. Early in 1862 Elizabeth Garrett and Emily Davies decided to apply[32] for permission to take the University of London matriculation examination which, if they passed, would constitute their admission[33] as medical students to that university. Uncertain of the reception of an unadorned application, they got Elizabeth's father, Newson Garrett, to write the accompanying petition, and

Emily Davies wrote a letter to enlist public support. Then they persuaded Emily Faithfull to host a series of parties at which influential people[34] were induced to form a committee to support their petition. She also wrote a letter to Mrs. Tail asking her to enlist the support of the Bishop of London, and her Victoria Press printed copies of the relevant motions, etc., to be considered by the University Council. As Emily Davies informs us, conferences were also going on "of Mrs. Bodichon, Miss Craig, E.F. [Faithfull], and Miss Parkes at Waterloo Place [headquarters of the Social Science Association]" (*ED Papers*, 262). But it was all in vain; the letter to Mrs. Tail was "answered in the negative for the Bishop" and the motion laid before the governing council of the University of London was lost by the tie-breaking vote of the Chancellor (*ED Papers*, 254).

An expanded committee, with Emily Davies as Honorary Secretary, met again in October. They decided to try to get girls admitted to the local (matriculation) examinations of the older universities, Cambridge and Oxford, in the hope that, if they were successful, the University of London and other universities would follow suit. Emily Faithfull was not a member of this committee, but she considered herself both a founder and an ex-officio member of the movement,[35] and her Victoria Press printed copies of the pamphlet entitled "Proposed Admission of Girls to University Local Examinations" that expounded the argument[36] presented to the Secretaries of the Universities of Oxford and Cambridge. The mills of these universities ground so slowly that a memorial from Cambridge dated October 23, 1863 which approved of the proposal to admit girls to Cambridge local examinations came as a total surprise to Emily Davies's committee. Of course, the Cambridge academics doubted that the girls would do very well in these examinations; so they only agreed to a one-year trial at first, then to a three-year trial,[37] and finally to a permanent arrangement.

Emily Faithfull published the eagerly awaited results of the December 1863 examinations: thirty-three of eighty-three girls had passed. "Good!" she wrote, considering the scant month and a half the girls had to get ready, and the fact that most of the failures were in arithmetic, a subject not normally taught to girls (*VM*, 3/64). By 1866 she could avouch that the results were truly excellent: the girls were better overall than the boys; they were now very good in arithmetic; and, despite prognostications by male doubters that such difficult examinations would prostrate these "fragile" girls, the young ladies had exhibited no signs of weariness or other ill effects (*VM*, 4/66, 571-2). Success followed success; after the University of London admitted girls to their local entrance exams in 1868,[38] Emily proudly announced that, of nine "ladies" who wrote the first London locals, six had passed with honours (*VM*, 7/69). This compared favourably with the twenty-five of thirty-six "women"[39] who had passed the 1869 Cambridge locals (*VM*, 9/69).

In addition to the part she played getting girls admitted to university local examinations, Emily actively promoted scholarships for women and noted all improvements in women's higher education at British and American universities. As late as 1874 scholarships for women were almost non-existent. Therefore, it was incumbent on her to praise the Clothworkers' Company for their decision to provide 200 guineas per annum in aid of higher education of women, the first contribution being targeted to help finance the North London Collegiate and Camden School for Girls, entrance examinations for Girton College, and two Exhibitions for the ladies of Merton Hall, Oxford. A year later she was pleased to list the winners of Girton College scholarships (benefactors not revealed). In January 1877 she reported that Eliza Orme had been awarded the "Hume Scholarship in Jurisprudence, of the value of £20 per annum, tenable for three years" (*VM*, 1/77, 262) and she printed Maria Grey's plea for more scholarships for women. From that time onward she faithfully recorded (usually with photographs of the recipients) an increasing number of scholarships and other awards for women.

In reporting improvements in higher education for women at British universities, she limited herself to Cambridge, Oxford, London, and Victoria University (Manchester). For women the chief points of interest at Cambridge were the two women's colleges, Girton and Newnham.[40] The need for a women's college at the university level had been recognized in 1867 when the Schools Inquiry Commission noted the poor quality of female teachers, especially in secondary schools. A working committee consisting of Emily Davies, Barbara Bodichon, and others was formed and a college costing £30,000 was projected at Girton, a few miles out of Cambridge. At first it appeared that the financial goal might be attained, but by mid-1868 little money had been donated after an initial surge brought in close to £2,000, of which £1,000 was contributed by Barbara Bodichon and £100 by Emily Davies. Emily Faithfull, after duly recording these contributions in the June 1868 issue of the *Victoria Magazine*, later implied that the disappointing level of contributions probably resulted from adverse public opinion as mirrored in an 1869 *Quarterly Review* article that voiced strong opposition to a women's college. She also reported that the sights of the committee had been lowered; therefore, the women's college was being established in Hitchin, some fifty miles from Cambridge, with Emily Davies as its principal. This institution opened in October 1869 in a refurbished house that accommodated only six students. For the next four years Cambridge dons had to commute to Hitchin twice a week to lecture to the young ladies. So conditions were far from ideal. Yet, as Emily Faithfull informed her readers, there were several Hitchin candidates for the Cambridge "Little-Go" examination in 1871.

A second campaign succeeded in raising the money needed to start building Girton in 1872, although Barbara Bodichon had to contribute £10,000 this time. Professor Henry Sidgwick, who was organizing University Extension lectures at Cambridge, tried to convince Emily Davies that she should locate her college in Cambridge rather than at Girton "to ease the problems of visiting lecturers" and "accommodate women attending Extension lectures."[41] But she refused (presumably with the backing of the Girton committee), chiefly because she wanted to "carry on a free, healthy, undisturbed student-life"[42] away from the distractions of the city.

Emily Faithfull celebrated the subsequent successes of Girton College[43] and its students. In 1876 she reported that students had to be turned away because of lack of space. And in 1878 she noted that, with forty students in residence and more clamouring to enter, the college would have to be enlarged at a cost of £7,000. She also gave graduates of Girton their due every year at convocation time, sometimes through reprints from other newspapers, for example, the *Daily News* in 1879, but usually in enthusiastic, first-hand reports of the triumphs of Cambridge women. Examples of the latter occur in successive issues of the *Lady's Pictorial* in 1894: on June 16 she applauded a woman "first" in the Historical Tripos and an "equal to a second first" in the Law Tripos; on June 23 she devoted a full page to comments on and photographs of successful women graduates, and spoke of her "liveliest satisfaction" in recording the distinguished successes of Cambridge women, especially the triumph of Miss A.M.J.E. Johnson of Newnham College, who had beaten *all* the men in the second part of the Mathematical Tripos.

One may note that, in giving these women credit from the late 1870's onward, Emily lumped Girton and Newnham students together, refusing to get involved in the ongoing controversy about the relative merits of these two colleges. She did refer to Emily Davies's letter to the *Times* in 1879 which pointed out that women at Girton were taking the male course of study and were writing degree examinations to prove they were capable of the same intellectual work as men, thus implying that women at Newnham, subject to a flexible curriculum and not required to write Cambridge Previous Examinations or final examinations, were not as fit academically as Girton students. But she gave equal space to a rebuttal by Henry Sidgwick,[44] who stated that Previous Examinations were not required of Newnham applicants because they included Greek, and he and other Cambridge professors disapproved of making Classics compulsory. "Therefore, [at Newnham] the 'Higher Local Examination' was taken to test the general fitness of students seeking academic training" (*VM*, 3/79, 499). Anne Clough, principal of Newnham, further confessed that not all students wrote the Higher Local Examinations; indeed, "they were not required to take any examination, and no subjects were compulsory,"[45] but Emily, though she generally favoured Emily Davies's philosophy of education, declined to take sides. She duly announced the opening of Newnham Hall in October 1875, reported that Newnham, like Girton, had been forced to turn away applicants for admission in 1876, and published an article on university education at Newnham in 1879. Also, when Anne Clough died in 1892, she eulogized her as having "[accomplished] much while appearing to do but little" (*LP*, 3/19/92, 428).

Her satisfaction concerning Cambridge women graduates was not unalloyed. After all, although they were competing successfully with male students, they were graduating with certificates, not degrees. Besides, there was little hope of Cambridge granting degrees to women, for several well-supported petitions to the governing University Council over the period 1887-1897[46] were either ignored or, if put to a motion, soundly defeated. In fact, Cambridge did not admit women to degrees[47] until 1948, a full twenty-eight years after Oxford. So it is not surprising that Emily compared the second-class status of Newnham students with that of the women students relegated to the Harvard "Annex" she inspected in 1882. And that comparison became invidious when Harvard University admitted women to full rights and privileges in 1894 (*LP*, 6/16/94, 925).

During the years 1863 to 1895 Oxford was even more reluctant than Cambridge to grant women equal privileges with men. It had instituted local examinations for women in 1870 but, though Lady Margaret Hall and Somerville College were established as women's colleges in 1879, the university did not see fit to grant certificates to women graduates until 1884. Moreover, as Emily noted, women students were not admitted to the medical faculty (and its examinations) until 1890, and even then their ultimate reward was a lowly certificate. Diplomas were introduced in 1894 but these were only glorified certificates.

Emily commented routinely on the progress of women at Oxford. For example, her *Lady's Pictorial* column in mid-1894 contained a photograph and a sketch of a Miss Gould who, receiving a "first" in natural sciences, was obviously a "brilliant success." But the accompanying description of this young woman as "bright, active, womanly, fond of sports, and well versed in the details of domestic management" (*LP*, 7/21/94, 90) hardly prognosticated a successful career in the natural sciences. As far as Emily was concerned, Oxford was moving too slowly in recognizing women's need for higher education.

She maintained an abiding interest in the University of London, however. For the 1862 petition to get women admitted to degrees had been defeated by only one vote, and that university had instituted both local examinations for girls in 1868 and extension lectures for ladies in 1869.[48] When the University Senate again rejected degree status for women in 1874, Emily deplored that body's "hasty decision" and commended Eliza Orme's "able" article in the *Examiner* that discussed the many requests from towns and cities all over England for university lectures and suggested that the steady demand for certificates would eventually persuade the Senate that women were in earnest about higher education (*W & W*, 7/11 and 7/18/74). The following year she noted "with no little pleasure" (*W & W*, 10/2/75, 3) the opening of another law class for women at University College (London), for male lawyers had mounted a strong lobby[49] to prevent women entering their profession in any capacity. And three years later she announced the inauguration of credit courses for women by King's College (London) professors in Kensington Square; these lectures differed from those previously provided in that they led to certificates which could presumably become degrees if a college were established in Kensington or if the women students satisfied University of London residence requirements at another college.[50]

But the most wonderful news to come out of the University of London was the January 1878 announcement of that University's decision — no false alarm[51] this time — to open up all its degrees to women. Noting the majority of 110 in the Convocation vote, Emily stated: "So large a majority plainly shows the extent to which public opinion has advanced as regards the claims of women to enter the lists with men in the professions. We hope after so marked a recognition of the rights long struggled for in vain, on the part of a body of learned and intelligent men, we shall hear less of the worn out platitudes against the higher education of women" (*WLE*, 1/19/78, 28). She also was pleased to report that "A memorial [had] been signed by more than 2,000 women, thanking the University of London for their honourable and generous conduct in admitting women to degrees" (*VM*, 3/78, 446).

This "conduct" resulted in other universities admitting women to degrees, for example, Victoria University (1880), the Royal University of Ireland (1882), Wales[52] (1889), Scotland[53] (1891) and Durham[54] (1895). But as Emily pointed out in 1891, only the University of London[55] gave women "in all respects . . . equal facilities with men" (*LP*, 10/3/91, 566). Victoria University, she added, had made the most generous provisions for women (as befitted a university founded in honour of the Queen), but it did not admit women to medical degrees; and the others imposed similar (or worse) restrictions. Oxford and Cambridge, of course, granted no degrees to women except the Cambridge degree in Music.[56]

During the last twelve years of her life, Emily manifested a keen interest in Victoria University, for her Manchester home was a few hundred yards from one of the Owen's College buildings,[57] and she knew many of the students and professors of that core college of the university[58] brought into being by royal charter in 1880. Owen's College had been strictly a male enclave before 1880. In 1877, as Emily reported in her *Victoria Magazine*, the Manchester Association for Promoting the Education of Women had sent a memorial to this college requesting access for women — merely to attend classes, not to receive degrees or even certificates. But the Court of Governors of the College rejected their plea. So it must have been a shock for the Governors and the professors of Owen's College to learn that the

Royal Charter demanded equal rights and privileges for men and women. No doubt economic realities accounted for their grudging acceptance of this requirement, though several of the professors[59] worked diligently to provide educational facilities for women in accord with the charter. More conservative faculty, however, ensured that women students were excluded from courses in science and medicine (science to 1888 at least, and medicine to 1899 and beyond).

Victoria University degrees for women at Owen's College had to await construction of a Women's Department in 1883; therefore, no degrees were granted until 1887. In the interim, women were allowed to compete with men for prizes: Emily reported that the first two prizes were awarded to women in 1885. When several students on "Alice Fay" scholarships were welcomed by the Vice-Chancellor the following year, she enthused about the opportunities for women at Owen's College (and the other two colleges making up the university). She was confident that if they made an "effective demand" for science courses, Owen's College would probably meet that demand (*LP*, 11/6/86, 397); and she expressed her firm belief that Owen's College women were getting "as thorough an education as their brothers" (*LP*, 9/18/86, 232).

Emily was present at the first Victoria University convocation where women received degrees; only four had been successful, but her sanguine expectations brightened up her *Lady's Pictorial* column. She even persuaded a number of American friends to join the "very large attendance of ladies" at the convocation and observed that "the [four] girls were cheered again and again" (*LP*, 11/12/87, 499). In 1892 she experienced similar delight when she received a special invitation from the President and Council of Owen's College to meet the new Chancellor of the University, Earl Spencer, for she no doubt viewed this invitation as recognition of her ongoing campaign to improve the higher education of women.

In 1893-4 she noted three interesting developments at Owen's College. First, women "associates,"[60] many of them with academic degrees, had been appointed members of the college. She regarded this as proof that higher education had enabled women "to use the power gained with tact and delicacy in a way different from and yet complementary to men's" (*LP*, 3/18/93, 390). The second development was more ordinary, yet equally important: Her Majesty the Queen's gift of £2,000 had been earmarked for the construction of a new building to house the women's department. The final reference to Owen's College was a further observation on the way the college was slowly changing for the better. For the first time ever women had been invited to an "open" meeting of the Owen's College Debating Society, at which the President of the Society expressed his hope that the day would come when they would be admitted to such meetings on equal footing with men. The subject of the debate was "The Living Wage" (*LP*, 2/3/94).

Sometimes Emily was interested in higher education for its own sake, but more often she had in mind its use as a means of access to the professions, particularly teaching (and governessing), pharmacy, and medicine. Female teaching and governessing had poor academic reputations until well into the 1870's. Queen's College had been established in 1848 because the majority of governesses were too ignorant to give their charges a meaningful education. And the situation had improved little by 1860 when Barbara Bodichon stressed the need to raise the educational level of mistresses of girls' schools by allowing them to take university "local" examinations.[61] Six years later Emily Davies founded the London Schoolmistresses' Society with a similar aim of raising the teaching standards that the Schools Inquiry Commission had labelled "abysmally low," particularly at girls' schools. To voice her concern about this matter, Emily Faithfull wrote an editorial in 1874 about the necessity for governesses and teachers to get a thorough training, and another one two years later about the majority of governesses being "miserably incompetent," hence deserving of[62] the low pay (£20 a year) they received (*W & W*, 1/15/76, 4). But apparently little was done to improve their training, so she complained again in 1893: "anything which can help to develop a more scientific and inspiriting process of elementary education [by governesses] is of vital consequence to every mother and child in England" (*LP*, 5/6/93, 692).

She also extolled the virtues of teacher training, for being able to "successfully impart requisite knowledge to children" was as important as possessing the knowledge itself (*W & W*, 1/15/76, 4). For instance, in 1874 she recommended a newly opened Devon and Cornwall Girls' School because it had hired three mistresses with first-class honours certificates from Cambridge, one of whom was trained in the Froebel kindergarten system; and the Drawing mistress at the school had a teacher's certificate from the South Kensington Department of Science and Art. Again, in 1877, the year that the

Teachers' Training and Registration Society was inaugurated, she announced the opening of "a new Training College for Mistresses, under the auspices of the National Society and the Society for Promoting Christian Knowledge" (*VM*, 11/77, 80). And she noted the 1893 establishment of a teacher training department at Bedford College, "pioneer in the promotion of higher education for women" (*LP*, 7/15/93, 104).

Pharmacy was another profession that accepted women after some initial opposition, though male pharmacists claimed there was none. It may even be that Emily helped break down the barriers. For when she contended in an 1871 lecture on women's work[63] that pharmacists did not want women to join their ranks, she managed to goad the editor of the *Chemist* into publicly refuting her statement and insisting that women would have no more trouble entering the profession of pharmacy than she had had in getting women compositors accepted by the printing trade. Naturally, she had a field day with this highly questionable comparison, and the editor took his lumps. Then, perhaps not by coincidence, the Pharmaceutical Society opened their examinations to women in 1874 and Emily was able to assure her readers that "women are not only admitted to the classes [of the South London School of Pharmacy], but every encouragement is afforded them to avail themselves of the advantages of the school;[64] every facility being provided for their comfort and convenience" (*W & W*, 10/31/74, 5). By 1891 she could report with satisfaction that "English ladies are now employed in London and elsewhere in this very suitable occupation with great success. Educated women are more to be trusted to dispense what contains, according to Professor Tyndall, the promise of life as well as death, than some of the careless boys trusted with such edged tools" (*LP*, 6/10/91, 1097).

Medical doctors were willing to allow women to become midwives, nurses, and members of the Ladies' Sanitary Association,[65] but not full-fledged practitioners. Even then they assumed that the British Medical Association would control midwives' activities.[66] In the face of these restrictions, Emily advocated better education for midwives[67] and took a strong stand concerning medicine as a suitable profession for women — by constantly comparing the American and British (and Russian) situations, by cataloguing the stages of Elizabeth Garrett Anderson's struggle to get a medical degree and be accepted by the BMA, and by keeping her readers aware of a more general struggle for women's education in medicine that culminated in the University of London's admitting women to medical degrees in 1878.

She painted a rosy picture of medical education in America, beginning with the "twelve women braving the ridicule" (*Three Visits*, 22) who registered in the first medical college for women in Boston in 1848.[68] From Brooklyn she wrote in November 1872 that "Philadelphia is great in women doctors. The principal one makes an income of £5,000 a year" (*VM*, 1/73, 211). Then from Ann Arbor she sent a letter to the *Times* about the fine "separate but equal" medical education provided for women at the University of Michigan, which had opened doors to both sexes in 1869 (*Times*, 12/31/72, 9). Admittedly she noted in 1875 that Dr. Mary Putnam Jacobi was "now labouring to collect a fund for promoting the higher medical education of women" (*W & W*, 8/14/75, 5); for, despite easier public acceptance of women medical doctors in America than in Britain, American female medical students were still experiencing problems. Nevertheless, in 1882 more than 400 women doctors plied their trade in America as compared with nineteen[69] in Britain; in Boston alone, Emily reported, there were "plenty of thoroughly qualified women practitioners for those who prefer them and the matter excites little or no comment" (*LP*, 1/20/83, 50).

The Britain-Russia comparison was not so convincingly weighted against the home country. For, though a Ladies' Medical Academy had existed in St. Petersburg prior to 1887, an edict of that year closed the college. It opened again in 1890, apparently because of the good work of women doctors. When it was closed once more in 1894, Emily hoped that the Czarina, one of Queen Victoria's granddaughters, would help restore the right of women to enter the medical profession (*LP*, 1/12/95, 64). All the same, the British women's cause had been subject to similar vicissitudes. For instance, Elizabeth Garrett Anderson had undergone many disappointments in her fight for medical recognition. After being refused admission to the University of London's School of Medicine, she suffered a second blow when the College of Physicians rejected her 1864 application to write their examinations. She partly surmounted this difficulty by taking private classes in medicine, writing the London Society of Apothecaries' examinations, and receiving their diploma in 1865. But this document restricted her to operating a dispensary for women and children and treating the diseases of women and children only. So she had to go to the University of Paris,[70] where she obtained her medical degree in 1870. Things went better from then on: the BMA made her a member in 1873, and she founded the London School of Medicine for women (with Sophia Jex-Blake) in 1874 and served as its Dean for twenty-three years. She also became senior physician at the New Hospital for Women, and President of the East Anglican Branch of the British Medical Association. In describing Elizabeth Garrett as an anomaly in 1865, merely "a special consulting practitioner," the *Lancet* had tried to belittle her role as a pioneer in the cause of women (*Lancet*, 10/7/65, 415-16); but the publicity surrounding her struggle pricked the collective consciences of the University of London Senate, members of the House of Commons, the British Medical Association, and the British public.[71] The consequence was the granting of medical degrees to women.

Emily not only made her readers cognizant of every aspect of Mrs. Garrett Anderson's conflict with medical (and other) authorities; she did a similar service for the young women[72] who registered at the University of Edinburgh in 1869, gained honours in 1870, but were cut off in 1871 because the university claimed that the male students would not take clinical instruction in company with female students. Despite criticism of their action even at the Parliamentary level and the obvious need for a women's medical college,[73] the University of Edinburgh refused to rescind its decision.[74] So the London School of Medicine for Women was established; though no medical college or hospital had offered to provide the mandatory clinical instruction, the school had enrolled twenty students by November 1875.

Meanwhile, as Emily reported in September 1875, the British Medical Council, no doubt prompted by the bad publicity resulting from their treatment of Mrs. Anderson, Edinburgh University's similar treatment of potential women doctors, and the growing need for women doctors in India,[75] determined that classes and examinations of female medical students should be conducted apart from those of male students and that, if universities would not admit them on this basis, other arrangements would be made. This decision of the Medical Council inspired Parliament to pass the Medical Act Amendment Bill of 1877 that made it possible for the University of London[76] to open its medical (and other) degrees to women in 1878.

The London School of Medicine for Women did not wait for these several authorities to sort this matter out. By the summer of

1877 it had concluded a five-year arrangement with the Royal Free Hospital for hospital (clinical) instruction of their students. As Emily pointed out in a long article on the School, all that remained was for the Medical Council and a university to approve of the school's curriculum (a foregone conclusion) and set the requisite examinations. Of course, it was essential that members of the British public who sympathized with the movement should contribute funds to pay for this education and hospital instruction — some £5,000 for the first five years. The money was raised, and the London School of Medicine for Women became an adjunct of the University of London in 1878.[77]

Yet, as Emily was well aware, jobs in the professions were available, if at all, to relatively few educated women. Most women had to be trained for trades. As she kept repeating in her columns, letters to the editor, SSA and VDS papers and pamphlets, "With training I yield to no one in a belief in woman's capacity. Without it I know from many a painful experience, she has no chance whatsoever" (*Times*, 4/4/74, 10). Again, pleading with parents (especially fathers[78]) to give their daughters and sons equal chances, she admitted there were difficulties in opening up jealously guarded trades to women, but she still insisted that every girl should be trained in some trade.[79] In 1888 she even wrote a special article entitled "Our Daughters" in which she considered Walter Besant's recommendation that fathers set up endowments or purchase insurance to ensure that their daughters would not be left destitute. She agreed in part with Besant, but declared that training for work[80] was a better solution because it fostered independence in women.

She regarded training as much more than the mere learning of mechanical skills, however, though these were very important.[81] She strongly approved of young women taking additional courses that challenged the intellect and fostered self-discipline, for example, courses in Science and Art at the Quebec Institute,[82] The Birkbeck Institute and the Working Women's College that were "designed to supplement the defective education of early years" (*W & W*, 11/28/74, 4). She also recommended the correspondence programme of the Cooper Institute in New York City as the "best means of self-education" (*LP*, 12/9/82, 273), and she gave high marks to a Birmingham firm for organizing a wide variety of lectures and classes for its employees: "If our artisan classes were better instructed there would be fewer strikes . . . and of the moral advantage to the people

at large there can be no question whatever" (*W & W*, 1/16/75, 4).
Thus it appears that she viewed education of the intellect and
technical training as inseparable parts of the educational continuum.

Still, technical training for particular jobs had priority. So she
concentrated on this practical matter[83] while recommending education for life as a later or parallel pursuit. For her, as "Industrial,
Educational and Domestic Bureau," the original name for her
employment bureau, denotes, the term "technical training"
encompassed the domestic arts (or "domestic economy," as it was
more commonly called); commercial applications of the arts like
wood engraving, illuminating, porcelain painting and gilding,
photograph painting, lace-making, and art needlework;[84] and more
obviously technical training like silk manufacture, nursing, and
telegraphy.

From 1860 she provided up-to-date information on the kinds of
training available to women. She kept her readers aware of SPEW's
activities and courses as well as those of her Industrial and
Educational Bureau; she publicized the Queen's Institute in Dublin,
which taught the Dublin SPEW's courses; she recommended courses
in nursing, especially one at the Nightingale Fund Training School
for Nurses, St. Thomas Hospital, London, during the 1870's, and,
after 1887, at Queen Victoria's Jubilee Institute for Nurses. In 1889
she suggested that upper-class women attend the Forsyth Technical
College, for it specialized in training gentlewomen in "domestic
arts . . . finance and functions of money . . . and upholstering;" more
importantly, some of its graduates had already been hired by
upholsterers and businessmen (*LP*, 1/26/89, 118). And in 1891 she
wrote several columns encouraging women to enroll at Swanley
Horticultural College, which taught its students farming, gardening,
and dairy work. Concurrently, two lady farmers near Horsham were
offering training in dairy and poultry work, gardening, and breaking-
in of ponies to ladies intending to lead a colonial life, and Emily
informed her readers of this opportunity.

She also provided information about wood engraving
apprenticeships and typewriter instruction. And, lest one should think
that she was providing little information about schools and courses,
she reminded readers that there were very few training centres,[85] let
alone courses, for women. Indeed, she felt she had to take the
initiative in proposing that training courses be set up for women
undertaking the following occupations, among others: sanitary

inspector,[86] silk manufacturing,[87] business and political work.[88] Furthermore, she editorialized in favour of women prisoners being trained in a trade that would enable them to earn a living after they were released from prison; for in 1874 they received no training at all.

The technical training course about which Emily was most enthusiastic was Domestic Economy,[89] for she, like nearly all Victorian women, took pride in the fact that being "mistress of a household" was "the one sphere in life which is [woman's] without dispute" (*LP*, 1/20/94, 80). Therefore, all girls without exception should be trained in domestic economy, that is in cookery, housework, hygiene, sanitation, and needlework.[90] For, besides being essential for domestic servants and working-class mothers, a "practical knowledge" of household duties would greatly improve relations between the lady of the house and her servants; in fact, it "would go far in bridging over the gulf which is widening between them . . . . Moreover, if middle-class girls knew more of domestic economy, many a difficulty would be spared the young wife who knows as much about the management of a house[91] as of a ship" (*VM*, 6/72, 245).

In 1871 she went so far as to lay plans for a Training Institute in Domestic Economy. Her letter to the *Times* in December 1870 had announced the founding of a National Association for the Formation of Industrial Homes throughout the Country "to aid in the establishment of training schools for instruction in every branch of domestic service in all our large towns, and rural parishes will be induced to unite for the maintenance of one [training school] for the benefit of four or six districts" (*Times*, 12/30/70, 3). At these schools popular lectures on cookery and household duties would be given to servants and to mistresses of households. But this announcement merely served as advance notice of an elaborate proposal that she presented to members of the Victoria Discussion Society at its meeting in February 1871.

This scheme postulated a "self-supporting Training School" in the West End of London where resident servants would be taught "the several duties of Cooks, Kitchen, House, Chamber and Parlour Maids," and "daily learners" would get instruction in "culinary and confectionary departments." Lectures would also be given "on food, cookery, housekeeping, the laws of health, and other subjects;" and ladies would receive practical lessons "in preparation and dressing of meat, poultry, fish, vegetables, & c, including the higher branches of the culinary art, such as made-dishes, confectionary, ices, setting of the table and dessert, & c." Functional requirements of the school — including accommodations for the ladies and the resident servants — would entail construction of a building with "bedrooms, elegantly and commodiously furnished, with bathroom . . . ; general morning and drawing rooms; a lecture hall; reading and parcels rooms, and handsomely fitted Restaurant" (*VM*, 2/71, 394-95). Capital costs would therefore be high, and the general public would have to contribute generously to defray these initial expenditures. Emily planned that operational costs would be fully recovered, though. Subscribers of £10 would become life members of the institution, and their servants could be trained for three shillings a week. Daily learners would pay two shillings a week. Lady subscribers of at least £1.1s could take the course of twenty-four lessons on the Art of Cooking and General Household Management for £2.2s, whereas non-subscribers would have to pay £5.5s. Resident ladies would pay £1.1s a week for accommodation, and they and the general public would buy the School's restaurant meals at a rate 25% below that of first-class London restaurants.

She had clearly worked hard on this detailed submission. And her efforts were recognized by *The Queen*, which published a brief abstract of the plan, and by the American publication *Woman's Journal* (in Alice Le Geyt's "Letter from England"[92]). As Emily was pleased to report, "Lord Shaftesbury, the Countess of Warwick, Lady Collier, Dr. Sieveking, and several friends promised to help" her bring the proposal to fruition (*VM*, 2/71, 394). Shaftesbury did in fact preside over a meeting at the Victoria Press offices on August 22 and a provisional committee,[93] presumably appointed to carry out a feasibility study, was instructed to meet with Emily and him later that month. At that juncture the project apparently folded, for it was not mentioned again. No doubt the committee had discovered that the general public was not ready for such an expensive solution to a problem it was not yet willing to acknowledge. Even Emily, enthusiastic as she was about the School, had not been particularly optimistic about the public's response, for she referred to the proposal as only "a suggestion, for whether it is ever carried into action depends on the amount of practical support it obtains from the general public" (*VM*, 2/71, 392). In the same context she said she was "ready to give some personal trouble to it, but the sinews of war must be forthcoming" (*VM*, 2/71, 395). Realizing after six months that the British public was not about to exercise its financial muscle, she transferred her "personal trouble" to other matters.

Yet she remained convinced that domestic economy was the most basic subject a woman could pursue; in fact, after 1871 she became a strong advocate of domestic economy courses, whether government-supported or not. In 1874, for example, she publicized a lecture on cookery for the working classes that was being promoted by the Ladies' Sanitary Association; in 1876 she was pleased to report that domestic economy was officially a school subject, though not all schools were teaching it and others were teaching it poorly; in 1878 she recommended the *Report of the Society of Arts Congress on Domestic Economy*, especially the papers on the need to improve school training of girls in health and plain needlework; and ten years later she proposed that classes be organized to instruct teachers in methods of teaching plain cooking, sewing, and dressmaking to workpeople.

She also helped several private schools of domestic economy that usually could not make ends meet. Miss Romley Wright's School of Domestic Economy in Manchester was one of these. In 1886 Emily congratulated Miss Wright on her excellent classes, and two years later she praised her for arranging special cookery classes for the poor that stretched her scant resources and forced her to apply for a grant from the Manchester Corporation. "Shame, Manchester!," Emily exclaimed in 1887 when she observed how short of funds Miss Wright's school was (*LP*, 10/8/87, 372). And she continued to cry "shame" as the Corporation deliberated. She reminded these Aldermen that Mr. Heywood, a local millionaire, was paying the School's rent of the larger premises needed to accommodate the increased number of Manchester students in 1889, and informed them that a fund-raising campaign in which she was directly involved[94] was under way. The Corporation no doubt heaved a collective sigh of relief when Emily informed the public they had finally approved a grant to this School which was performing a much-needed public service by "teaching the poor how to make the most of their food" (*LP*, 12/5/91, 1022). In the 1890's she meted out similar praise to two other schools of domestic economy: Mrs. Elder's school in Glasgow that was so efficiently run by Miss Gordon, and Miss Cock's school at Walthamstow which, by inculcating high ideals and self-discipline in its young female students, gave them "a good start in life" (*LP*, 7/21/94, 90).

Of the several courses taught at schools of domestic economy, Emily gave priority to cookery. In fact, though she approved of the establishment of a National School of Cookery in 1874 and of selected girls being sent there from all parts of Britain,[95] she was pleased when Education Department grants were given to girls taking "practical cookery" at provincial cookery schools[96] (*W & W*, 7/10/75, 5) and later at Board and other elementary schools. For she believed cookery was "so important that it might well be substituted for one of the more recondite topics[97] of public enlightenment" (*VM*, 4/77, 547). Besides, though Schools of Cookery might prove more effective in the long run for teaching high-class cookery,[98] it was more important that School Boards hire licensed teachers[99] to teach plain cookery to every girl in every local school. She knew, of course, that School Boards were not likely to introduce expensive domestic economy courses or other industrial arts classes for girls unless women serving on those Boards lobbied for them.[100] So she took every opportunity to report speeches by women members of School Boards, for example, Lydia Becker's[101] speech about improvements in school curricula since 1870, particularly through the introduction of cookery and dressmaking courses for girls, and Mrs. C.P. Scott's speech to Board School pupils and parents suggesting that industrial arts courses in drawing, "sloyd,"[102] and carpentry would be of value to girls (*LP*, 11/22/90, 874).

Mrs. Henry (Millicent Garrett) Fawcett stated in 1899 that "up to the present much more has been done to attain [women's] ideal in the educational field than on the field of professional and industrial employment."[103] Emily Faithfull, looking back in 1891, concurred. She was particularly impressed with the change in public opinion concerning higher education, for she could remember the days when "University degrees for women were still condemned as injurious to their health" (*LP*, 4/4/91, 518), when it was asserted that education would unfeminize them and "those who [won] independence or university distinction [would] scornfully reject the bare idea of marriage" (*LP*, 7/21/88, 79). Some people, she said, still held those mistaken beliefs, but most did not. She also took satisfaction in realizing that she had been partly responsible for that healthy improvement in public attitudes: as host of the breakfast meetings that resulted in Cambridge's admitting women to its local examinations (and all that followed) and as untiring publicist of every educational advancement by girls and women over a thirty-year period.

She likewise could be proud of the changes she had wrought in public opinion concerning the technical training of women for jobs and for healthier homes — through provision of technical training courses at her Industrial and Educational Bureau, promotion of training institutes in Domestic Economy in the schools and elsewhere, constant emphasis on the dignity of work for women and the need to train for every job, publishing information about the availability of that training, and initiating training in jobs where it had not been provided before.

*Chapter 7*

# Political Reformer: Jobs, Trade Unions, and Emigration

As her establishment of the Victoria Press demonstrates, Emily Faithfull's chief "political" concern from 1860 onward was the employment of women. But job availability was only a starting point. She also demanded adequate wages, security of tenure, and acceptable working conditions. And only slightly less important was the provision of jobs for British women in the colonies (Canada, Australia, and New Zealand) or the United States of America.

Emily realized that public attitudes would have to change, the first and most firmly held of these being that marriage was the only proper sphere for a woman. She was in favour of women being domestic, of "making a home;" but, as she asked a *Chicago Post* interviewer in 1873, "What shall we do with the four women in every five who cannot, if they would, become domestic?" (*VM*, 2/73, 354). So everyone had to recognize the economic (or physical)[1] necessity that forced a majority of women into the labour market. And, she went on, women in particular had to stop considering work as a temporary stopgap preceding marriage; instead, they should get the training needed to make a career of their work.

She also objected to the tendency to attribute particular faults to women, e.g., that their minds were "less adapted to industrial employments" than men's minds, that women were "inaccurate," and that their "exertions were of an intermittent nature." For Emily contended that these faults were "not inherent," though some people chose to believe they were (*VM*, 6/74, 193). More difficult to dispel was the prevalent fallacy that because women were by nature mentally and physically inferior to men they were fit to undertake

118

domestic work only. Emily recognized the physical inferiority of women in some instances, but not all; pit-brow women could undertake tasks as strenuous as those required of male miners, despite Parliament's attempt to restrict them.[2] But she strongly disputed the male claim that women could not do mental work as well as men. She also deplored the fact that, because of this fallacious belief, an educated governess was not as well paid as a housemaid or cook. In any event, she stated, "it will be time enough to determine the intellectual rank of woman, when she has had free admission to industrial employments and a fair opportunity of showing her inherent powers to rise higher [through education]" (*VM*, 7/70, 391).

Another foolish attitude she tried to change was an apparently ingrained belief among upper-class and middle-class women that they would lose caste if they undertook any job but that of governess (publicly avowed) or needleworker (secretly practised behind blinds at home). The consequences of such "false pride" were hosts of badly paid or unemployed governesses and thousands of overworked, starving needlewomen and other "home workers." Emily drew the line at ladies becoming domestic servants (in Britain, at least) but she believed they could undertake most industrial jobs without loss of respectability (*VM*, 2/73, 355).

As for women being paid to work, she could not comprehend the public prejudice that denoted a woman "spirited" if she did things for nothing (e.g., fox hunting and grouse hunting) but labelled her "bold and unfeminine" if she got paid for doing similar things (e.g., hunting for game in the Rocky Mountains) (*LP*, 8/29/85, 183). One result of this all-too-common opinion was that idleness was considered creditable (especially among upper- and middle-class women) and work was viewed as dishonourable or at least questionable. Another was that industrialists and other employers assumed that women in general constituted "a practically unlimited supply of cheap labour" (*LP*, 1/6/94, 25) — hence the hiring of women for unfit employment, as "scab" labour when men went out on strike, and as badly paid governesses,[3] "sweated" seamstresses, and miserably paid unskilled workers.

This bias against women working for pay was most evident when educated women tried to enter the professions. Emily had to confess she was "disheartened" in 1895 when she realized how few professions[4] were open to graduates of Girton and Newnham. Moreover, the women lucky enough to be admitted were not appointed to positions of authority.[5] As Mrs. Fawcett observed of the medical profession in 1899, "Women are ineligible to become Fellows of the College of Surgeons or the College of Physicians. With rare and unimportant exceptions they are kept out of paid posts or hospital staffs. Even hospital committees . . . seldom include any lady members."[6]

Thus public attitudes were changing slowly, so slowly that the women's rights' plea for a "fair field and no favour"[7] in hiring practices seemed but a cry in the night. Yet by 1890 paid work for women before marriage was considered respectable, even for ladies, especially if they had to work for a living.[8] Also, work, especially work for women, had assumed a dignity it had not had before.[9] Furthermore, training and education were making women more efficient, and that efficiency was being recognized, though it was not always rewarded.

One outcome of the tendency for ladies to undertake home work — mainly needlework, but also home-made articles of various sorts and even art work like wood carving and oil painting — was a proliferation of Ladies' Work Societies in the 1860's and 1870's. Emily viewed these societies "with considerable distrust" because their work was sold chiefly "at drawing-room sales,[10] where purchases are regarded as a charity," and because they pandered to "the false pride which still induces ladies to seek paid work as if they were ashamed of it . . . — fairly earned money must be regarded as far more dignified than the bounty of friends and relatives."[11] Yet so great was the distress, the utter destitution,[12] of the gentlewomen (chiefly "widows and daughters of clergymen, officers, and professional men"[13]) who applied to her for help[14] that she decided in 1869 to establish a Ladies' Work Society, "forlorn hope" (*VM*, 1/71, 370) though it might be.

The practical operation of this Work Society was simple enough. It involved the directors' buying materials at wholesale prices, having the anonymous[15] women perform the necessary needlework (or whatever home work was required), and selling the finished goods at a fair price.[16] Emily was not satisfied with this arrangement, however. So, with unemployed governesses particularly in mind, she hired a female superintendent (Miss Twynam) to organize "Ladies' Adult Training Classes . . . in connection with the Ladies' Work Society [that were] intended to train those desirous of earning an independence in other remunerative operation than that of tuition"

(*VM*, 11/69, 80). Some of these classes were single lectures on popular subjects; but most of them were training courses[17] in skills that could lead to paid employment. Miss Twynam was especially proud that the "Reading Class for training first-rate readers is undertaken by Miss Emily Faithfull, and as ladies are employed in reading to invalids and blind people, an improvement in so general an accomplishment is advocated on all sides" (*VM*, 11/69, 80).

The "home work" operation was moderately successful for a while. To advertise it, Emily took specimens of lace, woodcarving, and oil painting produced by the Society to an International Workmen's Exhibition. These received high praise, and Emily herself was "unanimously elected a Juror in Class 15, Textile Fabrics, of the . . . Exhibition" (*VM*, 9/70, 582). But the Society was bound to fail in the long run. Emily later described this venture as a "quixotic attempt to achieve the impossible" (*Three Visits*, 284), for the public did not buy enough of the goods to provide even meagre subsistence[18] to most of the ladies involved. So she abandoned the project in early 1871, though she resurrected the training courses associated with it when she founded her Industrial and Educational Bureau in 1873. She did continue to advertise ladies' work societies, especially those that encouraged members to take an honest pride in their work and not hide their identities, but by and large she disapproved of these groups.

For the same reason she objected to old style, hit-and-miss, unpaid philanthropy. Yet she lauded trained, dedicated philanthropists like Louise Michel in France, whom she described as "the representative of suffering, living for the poor, the disinherited, the famishing of the world" (*LP*, 7/16/92, 104). And she publicized the attempts of these gentlewomen to increase the scope of their work. For instance, she noted the work of volunteer female nurses in the 1870's — as parochial nurses among the sick poor, in Sisterhoods and as Deaconesses, in foreign hospitals, and in a mission for inebriate women. In the following decades she gave high marks to the new philanthropy that incorporated visits to workhouses and prisons, supervision of female prisoners, ladies' settlements among the poor,[19] and Houses of Help for the sick and distressed,[20] as well as supervision of recreation for working girls, jaunts to the country and the seaside for poor children, treats for crippled children,[21] and "boys' and girls' clubs and classes of all kinds" (*LP*, 1/18/90, 89). Still, she merely reported the activities of these philanthropists, for well-to-do women did not have to worry about where their next meal was coming from. Her chief concern was to obtain paid work for distressed ladies of the upper and middle classes whose very survival depended on their getting jobs.

To bolster the confidence of these unfortunate women she kept them informed of prestigious or unusual positions that trained women had acquired. In the first category were these occupations: astronomer (Caroline Herschel and Maria Mitchell were the best examples, but a "corps of trained women assistants" at Harvard (*LP*, 6/4/92, 908) also was worthy of note); archaeologist (Amelia Edwards[22]); entomologist (Eleanor Ormerod); antiquary (notably Lady Welby, who gave a learned address on folklore at a Congress of the Society of Antiquaries in 1891); conveyancing lawyer (Eliza Orme, a second-generation pioneer in women's work); Labour Correspondent for Women in the government's new Labour Department (Clara Collet); engineer (Millicent Fawcett, who had "adopted the profession of professional engineer" — *LP*, 5/13/93, 733); and professor (Miss Smith and Lilian Faithfull, both of whom occupied professorial chairs, if not professorial ranks[23]).

Under the heading of "unusual" occupations Emily listed these jobs American women had filled: State Librarian for Iowa; State Supreme Court Justice and State Postmistress; Enrolling Clerk in the Colorado House of Representatives and in the Legislature of Washington Territory; diamond cutter; switchman, steamboat captain, and taxidermist; President of a street railway in which the woman's husband was Treasurer; clergywoman;[24] and publishers[25] (of the *Chicago Evening Post* in 1878, Frances Willard being one of them).

Uncommon jobs for British ladies included Registrar of Births and Deaths; lighthousekeeper; hotel manager (especially in resort hotels in Blackpool, Buxton, and Llandudno); manager of an orphanage (Emily recommended a well-managed London orphanage run by two women, one of whom was the daughter of the late Dean of Manchester); and inventor — here she listed women inventors of an extension grate for ranges or cooking stoves and a travelling wardrobe, and noted with satisfaction that women had made 400 applications for patents in 1891.

Broadening the list to include occupations available to more than a few ladies, she dealt with potential jobs in Health and Welfare, especially those involving the care of poor people. Emily was one of the first to propose that women become Poor-Law Guardians: "There is no public function to which their influence would be so directly beneficial, as that of Guardians of the Poor" (*VM*, 1/70, 263). And when ladies were granted the right to be Guardians, she not only encouraged them to run for office but also provided details about jobs resulting from their new political power, e.g., work for trained, educated women in the wards of insane asylums; as matrons of workhouses and prisons; workhouse infirmary nurses; Assistant Inspectors of workhouses, Mrs. Nassau Senior having shown the way; and Inspectors of Industrial Schools.

In the field of medicine, Emily noted, opportunities for jobs were somewhat better than in workhouses and prisons. Appointments for women doctors in public hospitals were scarce. However, the New Hospital for Women, established in 1872 by Elizabeth Garrett Anderson and others, offered employment for a few doctors, as did the London School of Medicine for Women and several smaller hospitals for women and children. And two breakthroughs occurred in 1894 when Miss Cumming was made resident surgeon of the new Greenock Eye Infirmary and another female doctor was appointed Medical Examiner to the Imperial Life Insurance Company. Of course, the need for female doctors in India was urgent from 1877 on,[26] and many women took advantage of that employment opportunity.

Thanks chiefly to the efforts of Florence Nightingale, lady nurses got jobs other than at the seat of war. Emily could claim by 1874 that nursing represented "a wide field for female industry" (*W & W*, 7/18/74, 5). For the lady with the lamp had convinced authorities that trained female nurses were needed to nurse the sick poor in their homes,[27] thus avoiding large expenditures from the public purse for nursing them in hospitals and workhouse infirmaries.[28] Moreover, many private families had hired Deaconesses as nurses — "excellent nurses," according to Emily (*W & W*, 5/15/75, 5), and an idea broached by Emily and Louisa Hubbard — that private families hire lady nurses as nursery superintendents — had been tested and found workable. So here was another field of employment for gentlewomen. As Emily reported in 1890, "the idea is now carried out in various directions. . . . I am glad to say that I have had many applications from ladies who know what would be gained by having a cultured, responsible woman in a position which enables her to watch over the tender frames as well as the intellectual development of the children in her charge. . . Indian mothers, who have to send their children to the hills, are specially glad to have a lady at the head of the nursery" (*LP*, 5/3/90, 656). She could also affirm that trained lady nurses were needed in country districts to act as "skilled Midwives" and give lectures on "household matters and sanitary laws" (*LP*, 8/29/91, 367).

Emily likewise observed that there were a few prestige jobs to which nurses might aspire. For instance, in 1874 a Mrs. Black had established a Cottage Hospital at Northam (near Southampton) that specialized in treating ulcerated legs and eczema, ailments common among the poor. By 1889 the matron of this hospital and the head nurse had served under Mrs. Black for fifteen years and the junior nurses for seven. Also, Mrs. Hall, a trained nurse, was "head of the best medical home in Buxton" (*LP*, 6/4/92, 911), and, though one might doubt the desirability of these jobs, two nurses were serving as Superiors of Lepers' Hospitals, Miss Fowler in the South Seas and Miss Marsden in Siberia.

The election of educated ladies as School Board Trustees also pleased Emily, not only because these were "desirable and fairly remunerative" jobs in themselves (*W & W*, 7/11/74, 5), but because they opened up other positions for women in education, e.g., schoolmistresses in elementary schools, instructors in swimming and gymnastic exercises, and, once Lydia Becker's agitation as a member of the Manchester School Board had its desired effect, "the appointment of a few women [as] school attendance officers" (*LP*, 10/5/89, 442). Emily also looked forward to the day when women would serve as School Inspectors.

She was able to report limited success for another group closely connected with education, namely, women librarians. Here again women in America had been more successful than their British counterparts. Still, Emily could report that Mrs. Stamp was librarian of the Kensington Free Public Library in 1878 and that male opposition had apparently weakened on three fronts in 1894 with the precedent-setting appointment of a woman librarian at Manchester College, Oxford, the Obstetrical Society of London's hiring of a lady librarian, and the welcome statistic that "out of 140 officers employed by the Library Committee [of the Free Reference Library] 100 are women" (*LP*, 12/29/94, 999).

Because society considered culture to be a concomitant of femininity, feminists had promoted paid employment of women in jobs related to art, music, house decorating, etc. from the 1850's onward. Emily applauded this trend, and she dared to add employment of respectable actresses to the list. In the realm of art she advertised sales of works by female artists of the Royal Academy; the talents of a New York sculptress, Edmonia Lewis; and jobs in art pottery,[29] cameo-cutting, wood-engraving[30] and wood-carving, illuminating books, crayon photography, specimen mounting, etching,[31] decorative art,[32] glass painting[33] (also glass staining and enamelling), china painting (a well-paid job[34]), painting on other materials, and art photography.[35] She also noted that women were employed in ladies' or mixed orchestras (preferably as violinists), as singers, or as music therapists. Being particularly keen on music therapy for the sick because it had helped her during a bout of insomnia, she envisaged paid employment in that occupation for thousands of women musicians and hundreds of female directors. Indeed, she announced, the Guild of St. Cecilia had already sent musicians to hospitals and infirmaries thanks to gifts received from people (one of whom was Florence Nightingale) who were "interested in this scheme for comforting those who are in pain" (*LP*, 8/22/91, 334).

Returning to more ordinary concerns, she tried to increase the number of civil service jobs for women. Although the British government had hired female clerks in 1870 as copiers (i.e., hand-writers), their status was lowly. But after the postal telegraph companies, which had about 500 female clerks[36] on their staff, were taken over by the General Post Office in 1869, the situation improved greatly, for Lord John Manners, Postmaster-General at the time, took a personal interest in hiring women. In fact, Emily stated, the number of women employed by GPO Telegraph Stations doubled by 1871 to one thousand. Three years later 700 women served alongside 500 men in the Central London Station alone, and this number increased to 800 by 1877. Emily was disappointed in April 1877 when the Central Station stopped hiring women as telegraph clerks because it was inexpedient to put them on the night shift. However, she announced a few months later, Lord Manners had promised that "the introduction of female labour into the service would immediately be resumed when the proper proportions [of men and women] were obtained" (*VM*, 8/77, 366).

She does not appear to have been directly involved in the hiring of female telegraph clerks. But, as Janet Courtney[37] has confirmed, she persuaded both Manners and Henry Fawcett to employ women in the Post Office Savings Bank. The former, Emily reported, had hired "about thirty" ladies as postal sorters by August 1875[38] and assured her that that number would "shortly be increased" (*W & W*, 8/28/75, 2). A year later, she noted that women were also employed in the G.P.O.'s Returned Letter Office because of the "very satisfactory results" of the "experiment" with women in the Savings Bank Department (*VM*, 12/76, 175-6). By 1890 she felt confident that the efficiency of women in these government jobs would induce banks and offices to open up similar jobs to women. And in 1891 she registered her satisfaction that salaries paid to British female[39] civil servants were good, as were promotions, hours and working conditions.[40]

But the Civil Service employed relatively few women.[41] So Emily had to turn her attention to jobs for ladies in commerce, industry, and agriculture, where there were more opportunities. Among prestige commercial occupations were shopkeeper, translator, and stockbroker. It was permissible for a lady to open a shop, even if someone else financed its operations, but she could not serve as a shop assistant without losing caste. Likewise, a translator's job, which paid well, could rescue the odd educated governess from a life of destitution. Female stockbrokers, a group of whom formed their own brokers' association in San Francisco in 1876, were rare in Britain, but a few had crept past the male barriers. Emily merely glanced at these favoured few, though, focussing on clerical jobs that were opening up in large numbers by the late 1870's.

The Prudential Assurance Society appears to have been the first company to hire women as clerks after their initial success in the Civil Service; in 1876 Emily listed Prudential job requirements, salaries, and hours in her "Guide to Employments for Women" section of the *Victoria Magazine*: "Applicants must be gentlewomen; salaries commencing at £32, rising [to] £52; hours 10 to 5" (*VM*, 12/76, 182). Yet one should recall that women had taken the initiative much earlier: as law-copiers, cashiers, and book-keepers[42] from the early 1860's and as plan-tracers[43] of engineers' and architects' drawings from 1875 on. Clerks who could take shorthand also found employment from the mid-1870's onward. In 1875 Emily reported that jobs were available, and in 1876 she advertised a clerical position with a lawyer who wanted several female clerks trained in both shorthand and law-copying and was willing to pay a salary of £1 to £1 10s a week. By 1887 she could assert that shorthand offered "a remunerative professional career for women" (*LP*, 9/10/87, 266), and three years later, she affirmed that a trained woman could demand a very good salary as a "type-writer," an occupation which was now "an institution" (*LP*, 1/31/91, 178). This woman, Emily stated, could do even better if she offered shorthand too; if she was willing to carry her typewriting machine to ladies' homes to help with their correspondence, she could be guaranteed constant employment.

Telephone operators could not expect such a rosy future. Many women were employed in burgeoning telephone offices in 1888 but, according to Emily, "the wages given to female operators are in some instances disgraceful; it is quite impossible that they can live on the pittance paid."[44] On the other hand, saleswomen or, as Emily called them, "female sales agents," could make a good living, especially if they were vending packet tea,[45] or books,[46] or the new Singer sewing-machine, which even in 1874 was selling well in America and Europe.

Industrial jobs were also on the increase in the last quarter of the century and some of these were suitable for gentlewomen. Printing appears to have been a dubious candidate; Emily herself was apparently of two minds about whether a lady would lose caste if she engaged in printing, though she did view proof reading, layout, and editing as ladylike jobs.[47] Yet she did not reject printing out of hand as an occupation for gentlewomen. Therefore, courageous daughters of gentlewomen could presumably apply for apprenticeships in printing. There were only 4,500 women printers by 1889, but Emily still hoped that the trade would open up; besides, there were jobs for women in lithography and numerical printing,[48] skills closely allied with conventional printing.

Another occupation with which she got directly involved was watchmaking. Right after her first visit to America, where she had seen women watchmakers in action at the Elgin Watch Factory near Chicago, she spearheaded a campaign to get a similar factory established in Britain. In 1889 she personally witnessed the belated results of that campaign when she was a guest of honour at the laying of the foundation stone of the Lancashire Watch Factory in Prescot. On that occasion she spoke briefly to an assembled crowd of 3,000 people about what the factory would do for the town of Prescot and for the employment of women in general and was quoted by the local newspaper as saying, "This ceremony marks an epoch in the industrial condition of women,[49] quite as important as the laying of the foundation-stone of the new hospital for women in London last week by the Princess of Wales marked in the medical progress of women" (*LP*, 6/1/89, 773).

After 1873 Emily also displayed a strong interest in the manufacture and sale of silk; for, considering the employment figures in America (more than 6,000 women in silk factories in 1875, and more than 25,000 in 1884[50]), she foresaw a great number of jobs for gentlewomen. Now that the Victorian Ladies' Sericultural Company of Melbourne, Australia, had successfully established a silk farm and had proven their silk was equal to the best Italian silk, both "grain" (silkworm eggs) and "cocoon" (*W & W*, 9/12/74, 3), she looked forward to British women manufacturing the finished goods in Britain or Australia.

Other industrial jobs suited to gentlewomen were upholstery, though Emily could not answer for the respectability of some of the upholstery firms, working with gold, jewels, etc., and perfume manufacturing — "neat and eminently feminine work. . . . How far better is such work than the drudgery of the needle" (*W & W*, 7/18/74, 2).

Ladies could also undertake agricultural pursuits, particularly, as Emily pointed out, if they were self-employed, e.g., in bee-culture (or bee-keeping), "an industry peculiarly suitable to women" (*Three Visits*, 243); fruit growing — in 1889 she reported that 62,000 women were engaged in the cultivation of fruit in America[51] and that in Britain "clever women" were making money in this business; flower farming, especially in Australia, where flowers were transformed into perfumes and essences; dairying;[52] and poultry-keeping, "a very profitable pursuit" for a "really clever, energetic woman" (*LP*, 1/4/90, 20). In addition, gentlewomen were easing into horticultural jobs like market gardening, greenhouse work, and landscape gardening. Two years after recommending Swanley Horticultural College to women interested in market gardening, she noted that its first lady graduates had been "immediately engaged by a local nurseryman for greenhouse work" (*LP*, 3/25/93, 422). Landscape gardening, unfortunately, was still a male preserve; in 1891 Emily told Lancashire readers that the "only lady landscape gardener of which England can boast" (*LP*, 1/10/91, 56) was a Manchester woman.

She did not encourage ladies to accept any domestic jobs other than governess and nursery superintendent. But she did list some rather trivial "paid occupations for women" submitted by a Miss

Banks that desperate gentlewomen could perhaps undertake: tending china, etc., washing and mending fine laces, dusting bric-a-brac, etc., exercising and grooming pet dogs, and decorating dinner tables (*LP*, 9/29/94, 436).

Emily also publicized a few jobs for ladies that did not fit into any of the above categories, e.g., editor, reporter, public speaker, shopping chaperon, and guide. Although she was reluctant to recommend jobs in journalism — even in 1889 only a dozen British women had been invited to join the National Association of Journalists — she believed there should be some women reporters, for "in spite of the theory (masculine theory?) of their want of accuracy, observation has led us to believe that a trained woman is more accurate than most men, because, as a rule, more painstaking and conscientious. The woman who was a good reporter would find her services eagerly sought after" (*VM*, 6/78, 177). She was similarly proud of the lady editors of various newspapers and journals in America[53] and Britain, and, noting in 1890 that female public speakers and lecturers were much in demand, she expressed her pleasure concerning this marked change in public attitudes from "40 to 50 years ago" (*LP*, 12/13/90, 1010).

She also made London ladies aware that their country counterparts needed shopping chaperons to help them through the maze of London shops and that Miss Edith Davies had established a comprehensive lady guide service in London that would provide travellers with information (and guidance) concerning "everything from sight-seeing to insurances" (*LP*, 4/11/91, 566). Emily thought Miss Davies was trying to do too much; but she wished her well, for she was providing a service and opening up another occupation for gentlewomen.

Though she was mainly concerned about gentlewomen, Emily also tried to find suitable jobs for working-class and lower middle-class women. As early as 1859 she was cognizant of the poor working conditions, low pay, and lack of training for these women employed in mines or mine-related jobs, domestic service, and factories. As her 1863 SSA paper pointed out, working-class women were often forced by circumstances to accept unfit jobs that men were not willing to take, e.g., artificial flower making which, though it seemed to be a good job for women in 1874, proved dangerous to their health because of the use of arsenic in making the flowers. The same was true of match-making, where phosphorus was to blame, and chain-making, where white lead brought on lead-poisoning.

Emily considered some jobs suitable for both gentlewomen and lower middle-class women, e.g., printing, watchmaking, bookbinding, cashiering, telephone operating, and dressmaking.[54] But more clearly in the realm of working-class industrial jobs for women were cigar-making, about which she wrote a long article and later commended a Liverpool factory for providing good working conditions; black-smithing; operating an eyeing press in needle factories; working in dustyards (mostly "strong Irish women" — *W & W*, 8/22/74); and needleworking.[55]

All sorts of industrial jobs for women opened up in Britain between 1874 and 1880, and Emily listed most of them[56]: envelope making, paper-box making, paper staining and envelope folding; carpet sewing, tobacco-pipe making, clerking for a butcher, and cartridge-making; paper-making and bookbinding; machinist; embroiderer, electro-plater and polisher, and jewel case maker; book-folder, pickle-maker, jam-maker, and match-maker. In addition she reported that American employers had hired women in these industries: glass staining and enamelling, cutting ivory, pearl and tortoise shell work, carpet weaving, drapery manufacturing, umbrella manufacturing, hat making, and tobacco preparation.

She also advertised many commercial jobs for working-class and lower middle-class women. Hairdressing, an occupation beloved of SPEW in 1860, was one of her favourites, especially in 1876 when this career was finally opening up for women. And, though Emily disapproved of women serving in bars, she recognized that they were employed as barmaids in both England and America; so she accepted this innovation along with the introduction of women cab-drivers. More to her liking, however, was the 1880 proposal that women become waitresses (to wait on table and to carve) — surely a more dignified job than that of barmaid.

She likewise approved of working-class women taking these jobs: washerwoman,[57] window draper, counter woman, manicurist, tailor, and canal boat steerswoman.[58] Also, in an obvious attempt to open up more British railroad jobs for women, she reported that women were working on *Dutch* railways as "carriage-cleaners" and as "line watchers" (*LP*, 9/17/92, 411). And she advocated the continued hiring of women as domestic servants, for "domestic service" even in 1894 was "the best-paid branch of women's work" (*LP*, 7/28/94, 136), and there were many jobs available[59] — as housekeeper, cook, lady's maid, housemaid, chambermaid, general servant, and so on.

Realizing that paternal legislation would not guarantee a "fair field and no favour" to women seeking employment, Emily maintained an unremitting campaign to convince women to combine in meaningful fashion. She had much to say about the importance of combination in achieving women's "natural state" of equality with men (*LP*, 8/1/91, 208). For instance, in 1870 she opined that "women have yet to learn that union alone is strength" (*VM*, 11/70, 124), and she expressed the same opinion in 1894 when she admired Lady Aberdeen's "wise words respecting organisation without union, and the consequent waste of power" (*LP*, 10/27/88, 472). She also deplored the apathy of most women concerning combinations of any sort, especially trade unions. Emily certainly made her female readers aware of the urgent need for women's trade unions to counter bad working conditions and poor pay. In particular, she acquainted them with the suffering of "sweated" unskilled workers, with whom employers did what they pleased. For example, in 1878 she wrote an article, "Working Women," to expose the terrible conditions for seamstresses, button-hole makers, braid-makers, dressmakers, and white-lead workers; in some cases their wages were so low that they lost hope and committed suicide. Again, dealing with workers in London's East End, she strongly condemned landlords' and employers' treatment of these "toilers and their rack-rented, badly-ventilated and drained houses, and starvation wages . . . [living] lives of degradation, infamy, and misery too terrible to think of" and she insisted that the "total abolition of the sweater, combination and co-operation among the workwomen and the drastic remedy of no homework[60] seem the only remedies which are likely to strike at the root of the evil" (*LP*, 1/25/90, 107). She also worried about other "sweated" workers, e.g., shopkeepers' assistants, who worked in unsanitary conditions for too many hours[61] without sit-down[62] breaks and had to gulp down their meals on their employers' premises; overworked, exhausted fisher girls in the North; chain-makers, who worked in family shops for the usual pittance granted home workers; and such poorly paid groups as match-box girls (2 3/4 pence per gross of boxes), restaurant workers (5 shillings a week), and shirtmakers (6 shillings a week).

Women teachers could hardly be called "sweated" labour. Yet, though they had a union, their salaries were much lower than those of male colleagues. Emily pointed out that the average annual salary for a female teacher in Manchester in 1894 was less than £104, whereas a male teacher's was £257. And this difference was not abnormal; indeed, she asserted, "this may be taken as representing the difference in salaries paid to men and women throughout the country"[63] (*LP*, 10/13/94, 520). Fully qualified female teachers of infants received even less pay; and female technical instructors (teaching cookery, laundry-work, dressmaking, millinery, hygiene, and sick nursing) were paid in haphazard fashion — some received fairly good salaries, others were paid on an ad hoc basis. Apropos of the latter, Emily criticized the Lancashire County Council for paying instructors six shillings a lesson — "a niggardly system that lowers status and discourages thorough training" (*LP*, 2/10/94, 192).

The remedy for this injustice to women workers was equal pay for men and women doing the same jobs. With government workers in mind, Emily made this suggestion to a *Chicago Post* interviewer, and she voiced it again during a private interview with President Ulysses S. Grant, this time with reference to all women workers. She did not expect an equal pay proposal to be implemented immediately, but she did not regard it as "pie in the sky," for women teachers in California were about to get equal pay with men in 1875, and women in theatres and concert rooms in Britain had been accorded that status a few years earlier.

She disapproved of paternal legislation, particularly Factory Acts that restricted or extended the hours of work for women but not for men, for this government interference did nothing to improve women's working conditions and pay. In fact, it tended to make matters worse. For example, the Factory and Workshops Act of 1867 gave firms employing milliners and dressmakers the right to demand fourteen hours work per day from female employees, even though the Act of 1871 limited the hours of work to twelve; the Home Secretary dealt with this apparent anomaly by granting these firms special warrants to exceed the new limit. Some companies took full advantage of the resulting confusion, "to the great detriment of [the workers'] moral, mental, and physical condition," as Emily put it when she applied to the Home Secretary to withdraw his letters of permission. When he would not do so, she asked the *Times* to help her get the Factory and Workshops Act of 1871 changed so that dressmakers need not suffer hardship.

In 1878 she exposed the paternalistic nature of the consultations conducted by the new Home Secretary, Mr. Cross, before he presented another Factory and Workshops Bill to Parliament. Observing that he had listened to employers and deputations from male trade unions but refused audience to representatives of women's trade unions, she insisted that "women ought to have been allowed a hearing in a matter which concerns them so much" (*VM*, 5/78, 88). After noting the "inquisitorial" provisions of the sequent Bill, she expressed her fervent desire that "before many years, these Acts to 'protect' women, which means to heavily handicap them, will be repealed by the force of public opinion" (*VM*, 4/78, 545-6). Her wish was not granted. So she published a "manifesto" prepared by a group of laundrywomen in 1891 which demanded that "in future no legislative enactments shall be imposed upon women that are not equally imposed upon men"(*LP*, 3/21/91, 434). And in 1892 she condemned a Bill settling the conditions of labour for Shop Assistants because it treated them like children. The wheel had come full circle: the paternal legislation of 1892 was identical with that of 1867 and 1871.[64]

Yet, despite her conviction that women's trade unions were needed to combat this kind of legislation and improve working conditions, Emily did not want these unions to pattern themselves after the radical male unions that were alienating the British public in the 1870's. For at that time, she, like most Victorians, believed in a political economy that relegated the labourer to a subordinate position in the Capital-Labour relationship, an economy that ruled out strikes or even the threat of strikes.[65] Referring to a strike (and subsequent lockout) of coal miners in Wales in 1875, she observed that "coal famine [had] set in upon the locked-out miners of Merthyr Tydfil." Then she placed the blame squarely on the workers' shoulders: "It takes a good deal to teach miners common sense" (*W & W*, 4/10/75, 5). In like fashion she condemned the miners who were threatening a strike in 1878 if their wages were reduced 12½%. Let them and their families starve, said Emily; they have no claim to charity or pity. She had not been quite so severe with striking agricultural labourers in Kent a month earlier, for "the condition of these people is worthy of consideration, but the law of political economy says that when times are bad the poor must suffer." In fact, when she suggested that "wise and temperate arbitration might settle the present dispute between the farmers and the labourers" (*LE*,

11/16/78, 313) and then printed a letter from Alfred Simmons about unfair treatment of the agricultural labourers, who had been asked to take a double deduction in pay, she appeared to be relenting somewhat. But she returned to her firm stand when the striking agricultural labourers threatened to emigrate: "Good! Neither law nor charity can override the 'inexorable logic' of political economy" (*LE*, 12/28/78, 409).

Nevertheless, her compassion for the working man came to the fore in the late '80's and early '90's when she shifted the blame for strikes and riots to trade union leaders. Of an 1889 gas strike she stated, "there is a great difference between advocating trade unions because one is anxious to put a stop to 'sweating' and unlimited competition in labour, and supporting paid leaders, who stir up strife and force a quarrel when the cause is bad. Many of the men here, I am told, did not want to strike. There has been much suffering and distress by the foolish course into which our gas-makers have been betrayed" (*LP*, 12/21/89, 911). In similar vein, she expressed sympathy for striking colliers in 1890, citing their low wages and the danger associated with their work as valid reasons for the strike. This is a far cry from the "inexorable logic of political economy," as is her proposing arbitration to settle a coal strike in 1893 and praising Florence Balgarnie for organizing a fund drive for the coal miners' wives and children during that strike.

Emily also attacked male trade unions for not acting in the interest of either the public or women workers. All too often, she said, they tried to exclude women from their trades by striking, threatening to strike, or some other means. Over the years she kept careful record of the usually successful tactics of these unions: Kidderminster carpet weavers, porcelain makers, and watch makers (1874); compositors (1869, 1875, and 1879); silk dyers and confectioners (1880); pottery makers and china painters (1891); and telegraph clerks (1892). Yet she realized that a combination of men and women in trade unions would give women more clout in negotiations with employers. So in the last years of her life she advocated using the Trade Unions Congress (TUC) to improve the bargaining position of women, either through unions of men and women that abjured strikes, e.g., the London and Provincial Domestic Servants' Union formed in January 1894, or through women's unions joining the TUC.[66] For she recognized that this parent body, if not the individual male unions comprising it, was generally sympathetic to the cause of women; for instance, from 1879 on it supported the women workers' request for female factory inspectors.

Emily made it clear as early as 1874, the year of the first official women's trade union in Britain, that women's unions should avoid strikes. Therefore, she was confident that the great body of female mill workers on strike in Belfast would see the light and submit to a 10% reduction in wages, was pleased that the Women's Trade Union (Bookbinders) was "a society not intended in any way to promote strikes" (*W & W*, 10/17/74, 4) and believed that the Lancashire mill strike of 1878 would end quickly because "if the Lancashire operatives adopt the ballot . . . the women will surely out vote the men in favour of peace" (*WLE*, 5/25/78, 245). Still, she noted at least one exception to her dictum concerning strikes, namely, the chain-makers' predicament in Staffordshire in 1886. When she wrote her November 1886 column, these non-unionized "home workers" had been on strike for thirteen weeks and were starving. The masters, who, according to a Staffordshire industrialist, "go into the market and cut each other's throats, then come to the [home] factory and beat down the workpeople," refused to pay "the modest advance demanded" to augment the women's weekly pittance of four shillings for a sixty-hour working week. So, Emily concluded, "there is a point at which competition becomes criminal" and she termed this situation "a blot on the boasted civilisation of the nineteenth century" (*LP*, 11/20/86, 455).

Emily Faithfull was not only an outspoken proponent of women's trade unions; she also got directly involved with an embryo union that preceded the first official women's trade union by a full two years. This ad hoc society[67] had the grandiose title Amalgamated Milliners', Dressmakers', and Female Assistants' Benefit and Protection Society[68] and Emily served as its president for two months (May and June 1872), during which she hosted several meetings at her house, with Lord Shaftesbury as chairman of at least one session. At the first meeting the members requested that their newly elected leader deliver an address on "the grievances under which female workers suffer" (*Woman*, 6/1/72, 363). According to Amelia Lewis, this speech resulted in a firm decision to send a deputation consisting of Lord Shaftesbury, several M.P.'s, Emily Faithfull, and a number of other men and women to Mr. Bruce, the Home Secretary, to petition for a reduction from a 14-hour working day to twelve hours, with 1½ hours for meals (hence 10½ hours of actual work). Emily, who helped prepare this "memorial," was empowered to read it to Mr. Bruce. She did so, and Shaftesbury and the M.P.'s added their supporting arguments, to no avail (*VM*, 7/72, 357-362).

Though Mr. Bruce's refusal to restrict the working hours of these women effectively closed the books of the Society for the next three years, Emily felt that the British public should be made aware of this unjust treatment of milliners and dressmakers. So she published an article entitled "The Cry of the Needlewomen" that both criticized the faulty regulations governing their hours of work and revealed the bad working conditions in some of the factories — she cited medical evidence concerning polluted, dusty air, lack of sufficient light, bad food, etc. For good measure she quoted from a Report of the Inspectors of Factories that castigated employers for taking advantage of the 14-hour-day exemption granted by the Home Secretary.

Dame Anne Godwin described Emily Faithfull as an early trade unionist who "organised women in the printing trades" in the 1860's.[69] But Godwin's statement is misleading, for Emily did not organize a women's trade union at the Victoria Press; instead she hoped — in vain — that male compositors would welcome women printers (from the Victoria Press and elsewhere) into their trade union. Yet she did work with Emma Paterson, whom she met in 1872, in planning women's printing societies,[70] which were co-operatives rather than trade unions. And she was pleased when her protégé Paterson, who had learned her printing skills at the Victoria Press, opened her own co-operative press, the Women's Printing Society, in 1876.[71]

Emily also encouraged Emma to set up women's trade unions and was proud that Mrs. Paterson invited her as a charter member to attend the organizational meetings of the proposed national union that soon became the Women's Protective and Provident League, with Paterson as Honorary Secretary. She also made a point of visiting the central office of this League in Holborn, London, whenever she could. For the WPPL was a decorous group that accorded with Emily's (and John Ruskin's[72]) concept of trade unions: a league of "unobtrusive and peaceful organisations" (*W & W*, 1/23/75, 2) not intended in any way to promote strikes (*W & W*, 10/17/74, 4), but concerned with members' wages, hours of work, working conditions, sickness and unemployment insurance,[73] and mutual aid.[74]

After Mrs. Paterson died in 1886, Emily continued to keep her readers posted about the activities of the WPPL, now called the Women's Trade Union Provident League. She observed in 1889 that Clementina Black was trying to get the League on a good financial footing; in particular, she needed funds to set up a Labour Bureau. She also reported that Miss Black had founded a Manchester branch of the League to aid the Manchester Society for Women Shirt-Makers in negotiations with employers. In the same context Emily supported the Match Girls' Union that Annie Besant had founded in 1888.

Following that turbulent year (1889), Emily called for more women's trade unions — under the League or otherwise — all over the country and, to stress the urgency of the situation, she cited speeches by Lady Dilke, Clementina Black, and Florence Balgarnie, all of whom were members of the League's executive. For women were not joining trade unions in the numbers needed to convince employers they meant business. A Society of Typists and a union for women in the silk industry had recently been formed;[75] but, all in all, both the League and its individual trade unions were not dealing from strength.

The Co-operative Movement, which had been considered too radical a means of combination for both men and women in the 'forties, 'fifties, and 'sixties, had become relatively respectable by the 1880's when Socialism replaced it as political bogey. Even George Jacob Holyoake, once considered the most disreputable of English radicals during his Chartist and Rochdale Co-operative days, was given his due as "one of the oldest leaders of the [Co-operative] movement." For, as Emily noted, his Co-operative idea of an "equitable distribution of profits" in a "wholesale distributive society" was more in line with Capitalism than was the Fabian Socialists' proposal that there should be no profits in any commercial transaction (*LP*, 9/19/91, 494). Indeed, Emily and many other women regarded Co-operation as "a social and moral force" (*LP*, 10/4/90, 537). Therefore, they supported the establishment in 1883 of the Women's Co-operative Guild[76] as an adjunct to the Co-operative Movement;[77] for the purpose of this Guild was "to apply the principles of religion to commercial and industrial life" (*LP*, 8/6/92, 182) and its "main aim" was "to rouse aspirations and faculties of women up to a higher and broader stage" (*LP*, 8/6/92, 198). Who could quarrel with such high ideals? As Emily indicated in the same column, the Guild, which had a membership of 5,000 women by 1892, provided lectures on physical exercise, home reading, the education of children, sick nursing, cooking, women's suffrage, etc. And it arranged for the presentation of papers on business training, trade unionism, and co-operation — all with higher wages for women in mind.

Emily recognized three different kinds of Women's Co-operatives, some of which existed before the Women's Co-operative Guild. First, there were Co-operative homes, which took advantage of wholesale prices in providing board and lodging for their members; examples were the Dressmakers' Co-operative Homes and the Nurses' Co-operative Society that charged nurses only 7½% of their wages for board and lodging. Second were business Co-operatives like the Women's Printing Society; the Co-operative Washerwomen, whose chief customer was the Civil Service; the Co-operative Dress Association in New York established by Emily's friend Kate Field; the Co-operative Shirtmakers, founded by another friend, Mr. Montefiore, to get some of the shirtmakers out of the "sweatshops;" and the Union Confectionary Society,[78] a group of trained women who formed a Co-operative when they were "discarded by a well-known firm" for joining a trade union (*LP*, 7/16/92, 104). The third type of women's Co-operative functioned as both business and club, the Women's Co-operative Guild being the best example. The Co-operative Association of Lady Dressmakers, which *The Queen* proposed should be established in a "large provincial town, preferably Manchester, . . . to provide work for ladies who do not want to become teachers" also fitted into this category, for the plan involved a "house where these cultivated women can live together" (*The Queen*, 4/24/86, 431). In similar fashion the Ladies' Association for the Protection of Girls and Women developed a Co-operative scheme among philanthropic agencies to co-ordinate their charitable efforts, and the Central Association of Societies for Women and Girls established a Co-operative for mutual help among their member Societies.

Emily likewise considered women's and men's clubs to be social and moral forces in Britain, with the emphasis on social enjoyment. Women's clubs in America, she claimed as a result of her three trips to that country, had much broader aims[79] than those in Britain, but recreation was fairly high on their lists. She strongly favoured mixed social clubs. Indeed, she recommended that membership in some men's clubs be opened up to the whole family. Since "old puritanical tendencies" concerning amusement were gradually giving way, Emily stated at a meeting of the Manchester Presbytery, "men [should] . . . share their enjoyments [in clubs and elsewhere] with their wives" (*LP*, 12/20/90, 1056). Besides, some of the men's clubs offered sickness and unemployment insurance as well as retirement annuities, benefits not to be sniffed at if a woman did not belong to a strong trade union or if she were suddenly widowed.

Mixed clubs for the upper class were not plentiful; however, Emily recommended the Albemarle, which consisted of "an equal number of ladies and gentlemen" (*LP*, 12/15/88, 707). And she was glad to report that ladies had been admitted to several societies (ancient and modern) that functioned in the manner of clubs: the Royal Order of the Knights Hospitallers of St. John of Jerusalem, the Royal Geographical Society,[80] and the Ancient Order of Foresters.[81]

She identified a number of clubs for ladies only, most of them homes. For upper-class women with plenty of money there was the Alexandra, "a capital club [which] has an excellent *chef*." Lower on the scale came the Somerville, which "appeals to quite a different class of ladies, but . . . is the nucleus of some zealous workers" (*LP*, 12/15/88, 707). For gentlewomen visiting London, plans were being drawn up in 1889 for a "well-appointed home" that did not charge the "prohibitive rates" of the Albemarle and Alexandra Clubs (*LP*, 7/27/89, 120). Ladies who earned their living as civil servants, telegraphists, teachers, artists, nurses, and so on, would find the Brabazon House on Tottenham Court Road quite suitable and conveniently located. And governesses with jobs could get "cheap and respectable lodging and board" at the Victoria Home for Young Governesses (*W & W*, 2/12/76, 3); unemployed governesses would have to apply to the Governesses' Benevolent Institute for assistance.

Working-class and lower middle-class women's clubs were more social and educational than those for ladies. Some of them were homes, e.g., the Princess House, a women's lodging-house with restaurant and reading-room for women working in Knightsbridge and Brampton,[82] and a home for working girls in Clerkenwell. Those offering only club facilities to working girls appear to have been designed to inculcate order, discipline, and good manners, as well as provide amusement and instructive recreation.[83] For instance, the "admirable institute" opened in 1878 at Bromley-le-Bow[84] was "a pleasant and useful place of evening resort" (*WLE*, 3/2/78, 100). Emily also wished "God speed" to the Seymour Club for young women of the working-class, which was open from 6 p.m. to 10 p.m. on weekdays and all day on Sunday and charged "a subscription commensurate with [a working woman's] means," for it too supplied "a social want." Moreover, in accord with her ideas of self-reliance and independence, this club was run by the women themselves (*WLE*, 1/26/78, 40). On the other hand, the Countess of Aberdeen's "Household Club," which Emily advertised in 1895, probably was subject to intrusive patronage; its social evenings included instructional recreation in singing, woodcarving, home-reading, and sewing, along with classes and lectures in other matters.

She also promoted clubs that attempted to keep young girls — mostly those of the working class — out of trouble, e.g., the YWCA;[85] Girls' Friendly Society, which "kept a strong moral hold on young girls employed in business" (*WLE*, 8/17/78, 109); Travellers' Aid Society to protect respectable girls; and Metropolitan Association for Befriending Young Servants. All of these institutions provided night homes or refuges.

From 1860 onward Emily was similarly concerned about girls and women who, because they could not get jobs in Britain, had to emigrate to the "colonies" or America. For public opinion appeared to coincide with that of W.R. Greg, who, in an 1862 article entitled "Why are Women Redundant?",[86] proposed the wholesale emigration[87] of superfluous women to the colonies for husband-hunting purposes. Much involved with SPEW at that juncture and very sympathetic toward the hundreds of educated women applying to her for work at the Victoria Press or elsewhere, Emily was the chief publicist of SPEW's plan to establish a Female Middle Class Emigration Society headed by Maria Rye[88] and Jane Lewin to supply the colonies' need for public school teachers, schoolmistresses, and private governesses. In a letter to the *Times* (12/4/61, 7) she outlined SPEW's proposal to set up local committees in the colonies that would supply information to the London office about available positions and provide assistance and protection for the women when they arrived. The London committee, besides arranging special protection for single ladies, would try to procure "assisted passages" and "assist candidates from a special emigration fund." She also announced that "twenty ladies had already gone to the colonies and five others were awaiting funds" (*Times*, 12/6/61). All this would cost money; therefore donations from the public would be greatly appreciated.

This plan seemed to be working; indeed, in his "redundant women" article W.R. Greg singled out Emily and Maria Rye for special commendation: "two ladies . . . are pursuing a most useful career of judicious benevolence, for the service and to the credit of their sex, — Miss Emily Faithfull and Miss Maria Rye. They find plenty of women of all ranks willing and anxious to [emigrate]." But the local committees in the colonies — Australia and New Zealand in particular — were unable to convince the settlers that they needed educated ladies as teachers and governesses; what they wanted were working-class or middle-class women willing to pitch into any work that needed doing. Domestic servants, needlewomen, and hard-working companion-helps were the order of the day. So Maria Rye had to revise her policy to accommodate the colonists,[89] though Jane Lewin carried on with the original plan until 1881.[90] Emily, busy with other tasks, confined her 1860's emigration activities to providing information about the FMCES.[91]

The first volume of the *Victoria Magazine* informed readers that Miss Rye had experienced other difficulties, especially in New Zealand. According to her letter to the Langham Place ladies, the New Zealand colonists were so wanting in hospitality that they initially refused to accept her boatload of female immigrants (*VM*, 10/63, 570). Worse still, local committees in New Zealand and Australia had not made adequate arrangements for housing the young women. So Maria was very discouraged; but she gave notice that she intended to remain in the Antipodes for several years to discover what kinds of women would be welcome there, perhaps change the colonists' attitudes, get the co-operation of governments, and make proper arrangements for the reception of British women.

Emily also devoted a good deal of space to Maria's activities in her 1866 *Victoria Magazine*. First, she recorded her enthusiastic reception by the Langham Place ladies and representatives of the SSA when she returned from Australia; on this occasion Barbara Bodichon gave her £100 to help defray expenses. In August Emily dealt with Maria's plans to send 100 women to Australia in the near future,[92] and she praised the arrangements made with the Government of Australia to receive and house these women in a Government Emigrants' Home (an "excellent barracks") until they assumed their respective jobs (*VM*, 8/66). She also noted Maria's careful aboard-ship preparations and gave her credit for "prompt and business-like acuteness" (*VM*, 10/66, 562-4). At the end of the year she reported that the British government had put about £3,000 a month at Maria's disposal for the emigration of women, and she reprinted an article from the *Times* concerning her commendable mode of operation.

The New Zealand pipeline stayed plugged for Maria and the Australian one apparently dried up. In fact, there are only two further references to her taking women to the colonies: one in the *Victoria Magazine* in May 1868 about a voyage to Canada with 110 women who would help to satisfy a Canadian need for general servants, nursemaids, housemaids, washerwomen, dressmakers, and needle-women, and the other in the *Englishwoman's Review* of October 1868 concerning 100 servant girls she took to Canada in October. Thus SPEW's high hopes for middle-class female emigration appear to have come to nought by 1869; for, despite the money the British government had granted Maria Rye, everything conspired to defeat her efforts. As Emily said in presenting her 1874 VDS paper on emigration to New Zealand, neither governments nor citizens paid much attention to female emigration in the 1860's: "When Miss Rye first began her work, nothing could be more discreditable than the total want of order which prevailed at embarkation, nothing could exceed the confusion which prevailed on board the outbound ship before she weighed anchor. Nothing, in short, was wanting to bring emigration — especially female emigration — into unmitigated disrepute" (*VM*, 1/75, 201). Such a sad state of affairs could only be rectified, she had asserted five years earlier, by introducing a truly "judicious plan of emigration" in the 1870's: "we want fifty Miss Ryes, with Government aid and Government protection, before we can carry out any adequate plan of female emigration. But who will lead this forlorn hope?" (*Times*, 3/31/70, 6). Furthermore, something was needed in addition to establishing a special Government agency with sufficient funds to carry out its mandate, and that was to educate ladies in practical trades of the sort needed in the colonies. For "we have sufficient proof that the colonies are willing to receive active, useful women, though they naturally shrink from having those who are fit only for one kind of head work, and no kind of hand work, thrown upon their protection" (*VM*, 5/70, 22).

Despite her disappointment when Maria Rye abandoned adult female emigration, Emily did not give up hope that some adequate scheme would soon be pursued. For the success of her Industrial and Educational Bureau depended on emigration's being an option for unemployed women. Fortunately for her, the governments of Queensland and New Zealand realized that female emigrants, both single and married, were essential to their developing economies. By 1874 both countries were offering free passage to certain groups of women, e.g., domestic servants and dairywomen, and assisted passages to other women. And they were making every effort to ensure that the emigration process as a whole was "comfortable and honourable" (*VM*, 1/75, 201) — almost a complete reversal of government attitudes in the 1860's.

But of even more significance than a government's change of heart was Emily's relationship with Mrs. Caroline Howard (later Mrs. Edward L. Blanchard). This lady, who signed her missives concerning emigration with the pen name "Carina," had worked with Maria Rye from the early days of the FMCES; in fact, she had taken 75 of Rye's single women to New Zealand in 1862. She had spent the next ten years in the Antipodes, mostly in New Zealand as selecting agent for the New Zealand Government. Then, by coincidence, she came home to London at about the same time that Emily returned from her first visit to America and set up her Industrial and Educational Bureau.[93] So she was on hand when Emily wanted up-to-date information about emigration to New Zealand[94] and Australia.

They probably met in late 1873. But Emily apparently did not feel secure in her new-found knowledge of emigration until the summer of 1874, when she wrote an editorial about the connection between women's work and emigration, with particular reference to an American investigation of the treatment of female immigrants aboard ship that recommended the hiring of government matrons, better sanitary conditions, and separate boarded-off compartments for married couples, single men, and single women. In September of that year she published an article "from a correspondent" (probably Carina) entitled "On Board an Emigrant Ship." And she announced the departure on October 4 of the emigrant ship *Gauntlet*, the 142nd ship to depart for Queensland under the immediate direction of the Queensland Government Office, with its Captain, Surgeon Superintendent and Matron in charge of 305 emigrants — 109 members of families, 103 single men, and 93 single females.

In the same issue of *Women and Work* as the news item about the *Gauntlet*, Emily published her own article, "New Zealand Emigrants," which served as preview to the VDS paper she presented in December. This article described the excellent emigrant facilities provided in England by the New Zealand Government: the Brunswick Hotel at Blackwall (near Liverpool); the new clipper ship *Waimate* with its experienced Captain Rose; the government matron; separate compartments for married couples, single men, and single women; the doctor and government officer who carried out a strict health inspection as soon as the emigrants went aboard; and last (and perhaps most important) Mrs. Caroline Howard, "one of the most noble workers we ever met . . . dotting in and out among the various groups of emigrants aboard the *Waimate*, with an appropriate speech [and gift] for each . . . Emigration under such auspices, though everything human admits of improvement, is almost all that could be desired" (*W & W*, 10/31/74, 5). For those who might still be faint of heart, Emily cited statistics: 197 ships had departed for New Zealand since 1871, safely carrying 47,000 emigrants to their new country. She also reminded them that she and her Industrial and Educational Bureau, with the expert assistance of Mrs. Howard, were available to make all arrangements for emigration to New Zealand and Australia.

The VDS paper she delivered in the presence of Mrs. Caroline Howard and a large audience was entitled "A Year's Experience in Emigration Work in Connection with New Zealand." Along with the information presented in "New Zealand Emigrants," it conveyed this interesting idea: a well-educated girl with other skills, e.g., dressmaking, cooking, caring for children, and nursing, could prove her worth aboard ship and, with testimonials from the captain and matron, get herself a good job in New Zealand; therefore, emigration could be a great boon for educated middle-class girls (and even ladies) who were willing to turn their hands to any work (*VM*, 1/75, 189-207). The very notion of ladies working at "menial" jobs like domestic service elicited a sharp response from several newspapers; the *Hornet*, for example, scolded Emily, labelling her "more enthusiastic than discreet" (*W & W*, 12/12/74, 4, rpt. from the *Hornet*). However, the chairman of the VDS meeting, Sir Charles Clifford, who had lived in New Zealand, supported her, as did emigrants in letters to Emily. And Sir Thomas Tancred of Canterbury, New Zealand, agreed with her that if women came to New Zealand as domestic servants and were "young women of competency and respectability of character," they would be treated as "friends and members of the family" (*W & W*, 4/24/75, 2).

Emily concentrated on New Zealand emigration in 1874; the following year was Queensland's. In August 1875 she published a report from Carina concerning her July inspection of the *Great Queensland*, a "beautiful vessel," in fact the best she had ever seen in fourteen years of visiting hundreds of emigrant ships. She was fitted up to provide maximum comfort to the 700 souls inhabiting her for some 80 days. Carina was particularly impressed by the "excellent ventilation," "abundance of room for emigrants," and the special provisions made for the comfort of "free emigrants" (quite unlike the usual steerage arrangements). She also singled out the experienced Surgeon-Superintendent, a veteran of fourteen voyages, the "kindly, motherly" Matron, the "well-known and kind-hearted" Captain and the "excellent first officer," and she assured friends and relatives of the emigrants that they "need feel little anxiety" (*W & W*, 8/28/75, 2). All in all, a great (and apparently much-needed) confidence-builder from this lady whose chief responsibility to Emily's Industrial and Educational Bureau in 1875 was to visit all passenger ships sailing to Queensland and give last-minute aid and advice to the emigrants.[95]

The September 1875 copies of *Women and Work* featured both an advertisement offering free emigration to Queensland for domestic servants and an editorial by Emily. The advertisement provided details about Queensland wages in addition to free board, e.g., Cooks and Laundresses — £30 to £50 per annum, Housemaids — £20 to £25 per annum, General Servants — 12s to 15s per week, and Nursemaids — £18 to £25 per annum. Because these wages were higher than they could get in Britain if jobs were available, Emily's editorial strongly recommended that women emigrate to Queensland or New Zealand, where such jobs were guaranteed and there was no loss of caste for ladies undertaking domestic service.

During the last three months of the year she wrote about other departures. October issues of *Women and Work* reported a postponement of the voyage of the *Indus* from October 20 to October 29 and announced that anyone wanting to book one of the available berths should apply to Emily Faithfull's Emigration Office, 85 Praed Street.[96] A November issue disclosed that the *Indus* had left, the *Western Monarch* was due to depart soon and "emigrants who got their passages through the agency of Miss Faithfull's Bureau" could take heart from the comforting statistic that to date 100,000 people had been sent to Queensland by the Imperial (i.e., the British) Government without a single loss of life (*W & W*, 11/13/75, 2). Carina's Christmas message also spelled out the "very great improvements" made to the *Western Monarch*[97] before its departure for Queensland, especially the increase in domestic comfort by the provision of more space and privacy for married couples, and better arrangements for steadying hot water cans and tea urns when the weather was rough (*W & W*, 12/25/75, 5).

Emily's emigration activity, if not her interest in female emigration, tapered off after she stopped publishing *Women and Work* and transferred her Industrial and Educational Bureau to other members of the Faithfull family. She did continue to dispense information, though. In 1877 she told would-be emigrants to Colorado that they needed prior training in domestic economy, and she recommended Texas in 1878 because of its fine climate and its "people, [who were] if rough, [still] kind and hospitable. It certainly surpasses Canada [as a place to emigrate to]" (*WLE*, 9/14/78, 171). Also, while on her second and third visits to America, she gathered valuable information about conditions for emigrants in "Kansas, Colorado, New-Mexico, California, etc." (*The Queen*, 5/3/84, 497). Nor did she forget the labours of Carina: a letter from Edmund Yates, editor of *The World*, assured Emily, who presumably had asked for some publicity concerning Carina's expert handling of emigration matters, that "the charms of Mrs. Blanchard are advocated in today's issue" (Fawcett Library, Vol. IIB, 22/10/84).

Emily once again got directly involved with female emigration in May 1886 when Mrs. Blanchard and Viscountess Strangford[98] asked her to form (and head) the Manchester branch of the Colonial Emigration Society[99] they had established in London in 1881. Emily jumped at the chance, for she and Mrs. Blanchard realized that the "extraordinary increase of [Britain's] population," coupled with the urgent need of immigrants in Queensland and Canada, had by now made emigration a "glorious opportunity," not just a "remedy" (*LP*, 6/18/87, 652-3). As was true of their former partnership, Carina did the lion's share of the work, i.e., arranged passages and gave advice and moral support to the emigrants. And Emily gave her full credit for so doing: in 1887 she reported that Carina had interviewed more than 1000 persons in a single year, and in 1892 she referred to the "benevolent work carried on by that energetic lady. . . . Emigration needs careful supervision and personal knowledge, and under the auspices of this excellent lady it has proved a blessing to thousands[100] of English men and women" (*LP*, 6/11/92, 945).

Yet Emily herself did much to ensure the Society's success. As President of the Manchester branch, and later (July 1886) of the Northern and Midland Branch, Emily met regularly with Carina, presided over the operations of the Emigration Office[101] in Manchester, and undertook the difficult job of enlisting the support of influential aristocrats and high-ranking clerics, e.g., "the Earl and Countess of Lathom, Lord Derby, Lord and Lady Egerton of Tatton, Lord Frederic Hamilton, the Dean of Manchester, and the Bishop of Salford," not to mention "the local members of Parliament, and the leading citizens" of Manchester and other cities of the Midland and North of England (*The Queen*, 5/22/86, 575). This task alone necessitated a good deal of correspondence. For instance, she asked Lord Ripon to attend the inaugural meeting of the Manchester branch of the Society during his visit to Manchester in May 1886;[102] requested that Lord Egerton of Tatton undertake some task for the Society;[103] and invited Lord Carmarthen and Lord Rosebery to be patrons of a theatrical performance.[104] The aristocrats did not always offer to help; all the same, she maintained a barrage of letters to them.[105] She also had to worry about raising funds for this venture. Besides soliciting individuals for contributions, e.g., Lord Derby,[106] she supervised the sale of shares. At least, that is how I interpret her letter thanking Mr. Pritchard for his "kind reply and order" (Fawcett Library, Vol. II, 28/3/87). She also arranged a Benefit Performance in aid of the Society by her friend Genevieve Ward, the well-known actress, and sold tickets to that event. On the afternoon of this performance she preceded Miss Ward to the stage of the Prince's Theatre, Manchester, and, after stating the aims and objects of the Colonial Emigration Society, made a further plea for funds (*LP*, 11/5/87, 472).

During the time she was involved with the CES (1886-1895) Emily also kept her *Lady's Pictorial* audience aware of emigration opportunities and pitfalls. She cautioned would-be female emigrants concerning Manitoba in 1886, but cancelled that warning for dressmakers, tailors, and printers in 1889 and for domestic servants in 1892. She also apprised them of changing conditions in California — from assuring them there was room for thousands of women in 1884, to indicating that it had become a "survival of the fittest" situation in 1886 (*LP*, 4/10/86, 315), and expressing concern for the English ladies that a Mrs. Parker had sent to that State, when it wanted only strong farmers' daughters for domestic work. As for

New Zealand, she indicated opportunities for women in fruit, poultry, and honey farming. Finally, referring to the colonies in general in 1894 and 1895 she reported that women and girls were still needed as hard-working domestic servants, machinists, and seamstresses, and that ladies willing to do menial work could get jobs as companion-helps.

Yet, while Emily was deeply engaged in the operations of the Colonial Emigration Society, a privately-directed and funded group, she came to the conclusion that British emigration should be State-directed; for the colonies, especially Australia and New Zealand, had already taken this route. So when Lord Brabazon asked her in late 1886 to be Manchester Branch Secretary of the National Association for Promoting State-Directed Colonisation, she accepted the post with pleasure. The next year she arranged several meetings of the Manchester branch of this Association, at the first of which (with the Mayor of Manchester presiding) she agreed that for the present small personally-directed societies must carry on but "warmly advocated Lord Brabazon's scheme as one which is most likely adequately to relieve the labour market at home" (*LP*, 2/12/87, 174).

In May 1888 she reported that the proposal for State-directed colonisation was gathering steam. By this time, however, her perception of emigration had changed significantly. During the previous year the Prince of Wales had proposed an Imperial Institute that would use State-directed emigration to tighten the bonds of Empire and Emily immediately endorsed the idea. At a meeting in Manchester Town Hall in July 1887 she publicly lauded Prince Edward for his courageous suggestion, and the heir to the throne thanked her for promoting the Institute at the local (Manchester) level. A few months later she was asked to address a Manchester meeting of the newly formed Imperial Institute at which Arthur Balfour, M.P., the Dean of Manchester, and the Mayor of Manchester were present. On that occasion the guest speaker, Sir Frederick Abel, defined the Imperial Institute as emigration's "Intelligence Department" (*LP*, 12/24/87, 657).

By 1890 this Institute, renamed Imperial Federation League to accord the colonies a voice in its operations, had greatly expanded its mandate beyond State-directed emigration, though that remained its foundation. Emily, self-proclaimed "one of the earliest workers in connection with the Imperial Federation League" (*LP*, 5/14/92, 776), celebrated its success in attempting "to secure the permanent unity of the Empire" in various ways, one of which was to send some of its best speakers around the country to outline the League's objectives and sign up members. In October 1890 she recorded that one of the ablest speakers, her nephew Ferdinand Faithfull Begg, Canadian representative on the London Executive Committee of the League, had addressed a Manchester meeting chaired by herself. The gist of Begg's speech[107] was that an imperial body representing both Britain and the colonies was urgently needed to facilitate mutual defence, imperial tariffs, emigration, etc.; this powerful non-partisan[108] group presumably would be an offshoot of the Imperial Federation League. Again, in February 1891 Emily reported that she had been paid a visit by another noted lecturer, "Mr. Parkin of Imperial Federation fame," who was "delighted with the way in which the matter has been taken up in Yorkshire, and a northern branch is being rapidly formed to consolidate the success already won by his lectures" (*LP*, 2/28/91, 312).

Other ways of ensuring the success of the League (and hence the unity of the Empire) were spelled out in Emily's directions to members of the Britannia Roll, the women's branch of the League[109] formed in 1891: pay your membership fee (a minimum of 1s per year); subscribe to the journal and the other publications of the League; encourage debates at working men's clubs; see that your children are thoroughly grounded in the geography, history, and conditions of the British Empire; put matters affecting the Empire before your members of Parliament; hold drawing-room meetings to discuss these matters; and extend hospitality to colonial visitors.

This vast scheme of the League may seem peripheral to the more immediate problem of women's emigration, which had to be faced daily at Emily's Colonial Emigration Society office. Yet she considered it the ultimate solution to that problem. As she queried in 1888, "How much longer will it take to convince a foolish and perverse generation that colonisation is not merely proposed to relieve our congested population at home, but in order to develop the physical resources of the colonies themselves? The *laissez faire* policy is depriving us of men [and women] who, instead of building up our own nation, go to the United States. In less than twenty years 3,500,000 persons were thus lost to the British Empire" (*LP*, 12/22/88, 739).

It is appropriate to conclude this chapter with some unsolicited comments concerning Emily's ability to find employment for women, for everything she did with women's trade unions and emigration was subordinate to that commendable purpose. First, a commendatory letter from Mary Bird of South Carolina: "Madam, — Your name is so intimately connected with the movement for obtaining remunerative employment for women, that you cannot be surprised when strangers address you on the subject, even from the remotest corners of the earth" (*VM*, 12/71, 168). Next, the *Daily Telegraph*'s recognition of her "as a staunch friend of the interests of her sex, and a most useful assistant in all efforts made to multiply the channels of female employment" (*Daily Telegraph*, 2/23/78, rpt. in *VM*, 3/78, 451). Last, plaudits in an 1892 article: "To her, more than any woman we can name, belongs the credit of the opening up [of] independent careers in industrial and artistic directions, and hundreds of women are now enjoying the fruits of her persistent labours throughout the United Kingdom" (*Manchester Faces and Places*, 1892, 134).

*Chapter 8*

# Political Reformer: Suffrage, Other Political Interests, Health and Welfare

Most nineteenth- and twentieth-century commentators have wrongly assumed that Emily Faithfull was either opposed to female suffrage[1] or indifferent concerning the matter,[2] the latter viewpoint being more common. For example, a *New York Tribune* reporter who attended one of her lectures in 1872 averred that "her useful life is given to the industrial and educational advancement of women rather than to demands for suffrage — to duties rather than to so-called political rights" (*VM*, 12/72, 167). And this idea gained credence from statements of interviewers from *The World* (1888) and *Manchester Faces and Places* (1892), both of whom recorded her observation that the "true remedy for women's wrongs lay rather in enlarging their sphere of usefulness than in endowing them with the suffrage" (*Manchester Faces and Places*, 1892, 133).

The fact that these two interviews and the report of her lecture in America were published in journals with large readerships is significant. I believe that in these instances she was laying down a public smokescreen behind which she could both reveal her increasing advocacy of female suffrage to those committed to women's rights and continue to link that support with women's ongoing need for jobs and higher education. A more accurate statement of her attitude was printed in the *Manchester Evening News* on the day of her death: "With regard to women's suffrage Miss Emily Faithfull was strongly in favour of it, but did not give it the enormous prominence some do" (*Manchester Evening News*, 5/31/95).[3]

This is not to say that she advocated votes for women from the moment she joined the Langham Place Circle. From 1858 to 1864 she followed the lead of the *English Woman's Journal* in maintaining a discreet silence concerning this unpopular topic. And even after John Stuart Mill campaigned for election to Parliament in 1865 with the enthusiastic support of the Langham Place ladies, was duly elected and inspired the formation of the Kensington Society, a Women's Suffrage Committee composed chiefly of these same ladies[4] — even after this exciting turn of events Emily remained apparently neutral, though in the July 1865 *Victoria* she did publish excerpts from a letter to the editor proposing extension of the franchise to women. However, when Mill handed Parliament a petition drawn up by the Kensington Society and signed by 1,500 women which proposed the enfranchisement of single women ratepayers and widows with property, Emily admitted that, though still holding education to be more important than votes for women,[5] she was prepared to reconsider the matter. Subsequently she published Barbara Bodichon's SSA paper on the extension of suffrage to qualified women in the November 1866 *Victoria Magazine* and a detailed report on the loss of Mill's motion in Parliament in the May 1867 issue. The following year she made a somewhat tentative, but nonetheless clear, commitment to the cause[6]: in the July 1868 *Victoria* she countered the *Saturday Review* attacks on women's suffrage,[7] and in December, as she recalled in 1872, she undertook her first public lecture[8] before a large audience because she thought it was time to locate "this matter of female franchise" in its full context of "women's rights" (*VM*, 5/72, 119-120).

Emily remained an independent advocate of female suffrage for the rest of her life. Nevertheless, she strongly upheld the stand of the National Society for Female Suffrage that female householders and ratepayers — single women and widows — who paid taxes should be represented in Parliament by men or women and should have the right to vote for their representatives.[9] Indeed, she described the first public meeting of the National Society in London on July 17, 1869, which John Stuart Mill and some other M.P.'s attended, as "eminently calculated to advance a cause we have at heart" (*VM*, 7/69, 356); for, as she asserted two months later,[10] "the importance of gaining the suffrage for educated women can scarcely be over-rated" (*VM*, 9/69, 478). She even felt confident enough by July 1870 to state in friendly public forum, namely, a VDS meeting, that "the experience gained by more than twelve years of practical work" in the cause of women had compelled her "to acknowledge the necessity[11] of making the franchise the great and central point of all our efforts, for without it, women will never make way against trade monopolies, nor obtain their fair share in the educational endowments of their country" (*VM*, 7/70, 239).

Still she did not join the National Society for Female Suffrage; nor did she agitate for the franchise or sign petitions[12] favoring it. Furthermore, in other public forums she tended to hedge her bets. For example, confessing in a letter to the *Times* that she was in favour of women's suffrage and was convinced it was "of great importance both from an educational and industrial point of view," she hastened to add that she utterly "[repudiated] any sympathy with those who are discontented with 'home duties'" (*Times*, 6/11/70, 6).[13] One consequence of this balancing act was that she often had to reassure doubting strangers that she really was a strong supporter of women's suffrage. In July 1872, for instance, Julia Ward Howe, a recent convert to the suffrage cause, asked Emily in a VDS meeting for public assurance that she favoured the franchise. And another well-known American feminist, Lucretia Mott, requested that she include her views on votes for women in her farewell American lecture in 1873. "At the close Mrs. Mott arose and expressed her great pleasure . . . and confessed that all her doubts as to Miss Faithfull's soundness in the faith on the woman suffrage question had been removed, and said (turning to her), 'I don't see but what you go just as far as the rest of us'" (*The New York Tribune*, rpt. in *VM*, 5/73, 125).

Yet, despite these many queries about the strength of her advocacy, Emily never wavered in her support of female suffrage from 1870 on.[14] Even during her first trip to America she took advantage of several opportunities (other than her lectures) to spread the word. In a *Chicago Evening Post* interview she stressed the necessity of the franchise for self-dependent British women of property. And she at least broached the subject in her interview with President Ulysses S. Grant,[15] only to accede to his wish to discuss "the industrial interests of women."

She also kept readers informed of her reasons for supporting female suffrage. Referring to ignorant male voters in an 1875 editorial she opined, "When any drunken costermonger, who pays a paltry sum for a shelter, and cannot write his own name, can vote for a member of Parliament, it is a ludicrous paradox to deny the same privilege to women rate payers" (*W & W*, 4/10/75, 1). Ten years later she recorded objections of lady farmers to their illiterate male employees being newly enfranchised, whereas they themselves were still without the vote. In similar fashion she turned anti-suffrage arguments inside out:

> The Census has long since compelled everyone to acknowledge that from year to year more and more women are becoming self-depend-ent[16] members of the community: the fact that women are weak is an additional reason for protecting their interests; and the argument that they are essentially different from men only makes it the more necessary to permit them to express their own opinions and not to hand over their concerns to those who see from a different point of view matters relating to their education, employment, and property. . . . The enfranchisement of women stands on a totally different footing now to the day when it was received in the House of Commons as "an entirely artificial appetite" or "a female fancy for forbidden fruit." The matter must be regarded from the standpoints of right and expediency.
> (*LP*, 11/10/88, 534).

She also reminded faint-hearted women that female suffrage was not just a matter of individual preference: "it matters little enough to any individual woman personally whether she has a vote or not, but it is of vital consequence to the interests of women as a class that they should have representative government" (*LP*, 7/15/93, 104). And she answered Mrs. Eliza Lynn Linton's objections to women taking part in "actual politics" by observing that the unsatisfactory position of women which had inspired the Langham Place ladies to undertake their revolution in 1855 had not changed greatly over the years: "The laws now protecting women are inadequate, and surely it is time that the noblest women in the state had a direct voice in the laws which dispose of their property, their persons, and their children" (*LP*, 3/24/94, 409).

Whenever she deemed it appropriate, Emily cited other strong advocates of female suffrage,[17] e.g., Elizabeth Cady Stanton, who considered the enfranchisement of women to be the "most important of all reforms . . . . For there can be no valid women's work in any direction" without it (*W & W*, 2/20/75, 2); Isabella Tod, who contended that women must have the franchise to counter the increasing paternal legislation that interfered with the daily lives of women; Mrs. Mona Caird, who deplored the sort of civilization represented by a State that condemned half its citizens (its women) to "inequality of rights" evident in "hindered moments, fettered intelligence, [and] artificial determination of work through lack of choice" (*LP*, 7/18/91, 119); Jessie Boucherett, whose article, "County Council Elections and Women Householders," stressed the need for women to have the vote "to protect their right to work and earn their living" (*LP*, 3/12/92, 392); and even a mere male, a certain Mr. Hall, who, though in no hurry to enfranchise women, "could not for the life of him see why a woman who was the head of a household and paid rates should not have a vote for a member of Parliament as well as for other purposes" (*LP*, 10/13/91, 798).

Yet Emily always tempered her advocacy of female suffrage with common sense. In 1878 she noted that a martyr to the cause of women's suffrage had refused to pay her taxes and had allowed her property to be seized. Then she sensibly observed that this woman could "hardly expect her heroic example to be followed by women to whom the seizure of goods means the workhouse" (*LE*, 12/7/78, 357). And she entered this caveat in 1894: "that all evils complained of are to disappear with the possession of the franchise is a dream in which I have never indulged" (*LP*, 3/24/94, 409).

But, caution and common sense aside, the franchise was an important feature in all of her lectures on the condition of women. In fact, in an 1870 letter to Elizabeth Cady Stanton and Mrs. P.W. Davis, in which she regretfully declined to attend the Twentieth Annual Celebration of the Woman Suffrage Movement in the U.S.A. to which they had invited her, she stated that she was "at present the only regular lecturer here on this subject [Woman Suffrage]."[18] So Dr. Brewer was apparently not overstating the importance of her contribution to female enfranchisement when he said in his introduction to the discussion of a VDS paper entitled "Franchise for Women" that "the great speakers who have most influenced public opinion upon the subject are Miss Faithfull and Miss Helen Taylor" (*VM*, 2/72, 394).

During the 1870's Emily also agreed to chair two meetings of female suffrage groups, though only at a local, low-profile level. One of these was the West Middlesex Affiliated Association (Woman's Franchise), which under her guidance drew up a petition to Parliament and empowered her to sign it on behalf of the Women's Disabilities Bill (*Woman*, 4/20/72, 268). The other was a gathering of

Islington supporters of the 1875 Forsyth Bill for the Removal of the Electoral Disabilities of Women. At this meeting Emily stated that her work promoting the industrial and higher education interests of women "compelled her to sympathize with the movement which would be brought prominently forward by those who were connected with the Suffrage Society" (*W & W*, 2/13/75, 4), for she had experienced at first hand the adamant opposition of male-dominated trades and professions to the idea of women joining their ranks.

As a rational champion of female suffrage she also felt it was her duty to counter-attack those opposed to it. In an editorial criticizing Professor Goldwin Smith's premise that men would (and should) prevent women getting the vote because physical force was, is, and shall be the ruling force in the world, Emily's apt rejoinder was, "it is no homage to any one to say they cannot exercise the full rights of citizenship because, in a peaceful land, they are not the warlike power" (*W & W*, 7/4/74, 4). Her answer[19] to Captain Maxse's irrational argument "That those should keep who have the power,/And those should take who can" (*W & W*, 9/21/74, 4) was similarly worded. On another tack, she poured scorn on a Mr. Chaplin who had approved of ladies "purifying" the horse races but not the polling booth (*W & W*, 6/12/75).

In 1889 she took on a much tougher opponent than any of these men, namely, the ladies[20] who had signed the "Appeal Against Female Suffrage" published in *Nineteenth Century* in June. Emily first presented their arguments, viz. (1) "to men belongs the political struggle," (2) "women should stay out of the fight and exercise sympathy and impartiality," (3) "there are grave practical difficulties in enfranchising women (married versus unmarried women, moral versus immoral women, etc.)," and (4) "almost all the principal injustices against women have been amended." Then she pointed out that arguments (1) and (2) were outdated, since by 1889 women were very much involved in politics, even at the national level;[21] number (3) was covered, as it was for men, by the property qualification; and number (4) was downright wrong (*LP*, 6/8/89, 834). A month later she associated herself squarely with Lydia Becker's Counter-Appeal.

Dealing with Samuel Smith, an anti-feminist M.P. who had opposed Mr. Woodall's Women's Disabilities Removal Bill of 1890-1891 with a Manifesto decrying the way even minimal participation in politics had produced a lowering effect on women's naturally submissive but noble natures, Emily devoted two columns to

refutation of Smith's Rip Van Winkle arguments. Of female submiss-
iveness she suggested that higher education of women was slowly but
surely altering this *unnatural* attitude. Of the alleged threat to
women's nobility she cited Queen Victoria as living proof that
involvement in politics need not affect a woman's personality, for
who would "dare say that the discharge of her public duties has
weakened one chord in her womanly nature?" (*LP*, 5/9/91, 762).

Though not a member of the National Society for Women's
Suffrage, Emily gave it indirect support, chiefly by reporting its
meetings[22] but also by deploring the several splits in its ranks.
Examples of the latter abound. For instance, in late 1871 the
Manchester branch broke away from its London parent,[23] apparently
because of "little cliques and jealousies" (*VM*, "The Women's
Suffrage Campaign," 5/72, 119). Five years later the two groups
patched up their differences and the reunited Society gave solid
backing to Leonard Courtney's Women's Suffrage Bill. In 1885
another schism was in the offing, this time due to Lydia Becker's
"secret feud" with other members of the Society who tried to unseat
her. On this occasion Emily observed: "Miss Becker has done some
excellent work in her day, but it is to be deeply deplored that she is
not ready to give others the credit and forbearance . . . they deserve"
(*LP*, 12/19/85, 513). Over a year later, Lydia apparently saw the
light, for she arranged for a healing "At Home" gathering to which
she invited all members of the National Society for Women's
Suffrage. However, the feud broke out again in December 1888, and
Lydia again appears to have been the instigator. As Emily reported
in January 1889, she had received a circular accusing her of "misrep-
resentations" and had concluded that she was "too high-handed" (*LP*,
1/12/89, 54). This "serious disruption" led to another London-
Manchester split of the National Society that lasted until 1892 and
opened the door to the 1889 formation of the Women's Franchise
Society (the Pankhursts, Mrs. Jacob Bright, Mrs. Fenwick Miller,
etc.) which favored votes for all women. Emily believed that such a
radical approach was "likely to postpone Women's Suffrage
indefinitely" (*LP*, 12/12/91, 1099), though she briefly entertained a
proposal to grant the franchise to some married women. Fortunately,
"delightful reunion" of the two National Societies (Manchester &
London) in May 1892 made such an unpalatable compromise
unnecessary (*LP*, 5/7/92, 685), even if it left two women's suffrage
societies in the field. Still, there was hope for one strong society; in

1894 Emily was pleased to report a "very notable meeting" of the Manchester Society for Women's Suffrage with Dr. Pankhurst in the chair, flanked by such platform guests as Mrs. Fawcett, Mrs. Wolstenholme Elmy, and Mrs. Emmeline Pankhurst — in other words, a mixed bag from both Societies (*LP*, 5/19/94, 765).

Parliament, of course, was the focus of the suffrage society's activities; so Emily faithfully recorded that august body's treatment of every Women's Suffrage Bill: the fleeting success of the Bill of 1870, which passed second reading by a vote of 124-91, only to be defeated later 220-94; the 1871 Bill's defeat (224-157); the close vote leading to the 1875 Forsyth Bill's demise — 187-152 on second reading; a majority of 87 against the 1876 Bill (*VM*, 5/76); several Woodall Bills, especially an 1886 one that had a chance of passing, but which Dissolution of Parliament left in limbo; an 1891 Bill that was similarly shelved, and one in 1892 that was defeated 192-175; the two 1889 Bills (during the National Suffrage Society schism) that had no chance of success; and the Registration Bills[24] of 1894 and 1895 that were strongly supported by petitions.[25] Emily also noted some interesting sidelights concerning these Bills. For example, a memorial signed by 18,000 women supporting women's suffrage had been sent to both Benjamin Disraeli and William Ewart Gladstone in 1873. Disraeli replied in the affirmative, that is, very much in favour of granting the vote to qualified women. Gladstone sent no reply; moreover, in 1884 he decided not to include women in the Reform Bill that granted votes to most men in the United Kingdom. Following Disraeli's lead, the National Union of Conservative Associations approved of female suffrage for householders and ratepayers in 1889;[26] on the other hand, the Liberal Party withstood all pleas — even threats — from the Women's Liberal Association[27] concerning votes for women.

Emily's reflections on the House of Commons rump that continued to oppose female suffrage constitute another interesting sidelight. In 1875 she directed these questions (and answers) to that group and anyone who agreed with them:

> "Are women citizens? Yes! when they are asked to pay taxes. No! when they ask to have votes. Does law concern women? Yes, when they are required to obey its commands. No! when they ask to have a voice in electing the legislature. Is direct representation desirable for the interests

of the represented? Yes! if those who wish to be represented are men.
No! if those who wish to be represented are women"

(*W & W*, 7/17/75, 5).

And in 1894 she again addressed them about the growing public
sentiment in favour of women's participation in politics: "We are thus
deemed worthy enough to listen to political speeches, and possibly to
form opinions upon them, though to express these opinions practically at the polling booth is held to be an abominable thing! The
position grows so foolishly inconsistent[28] that it is obviously bound
to end"(*LP*, 2/10/94, 200).

Yet, though convinced that female suffrage at the Parliamentary
level was the prime desideratum, she did not neglect more immediate
successes at municipal and parish levels, in particular the "great
triumph" (*VM*, 7/69, 263) represented by the Municipal Franchise Act
of 1869,[29] the Elementary Education Act of 1870 that enabled
women to vote for and serve as School Board members, and a
comparable Act of 1875 that made it possible for them to be elected
as Guardians of the Poor. She faithfully reported the election of
women to school boards, e.g., Lydia Becker[30] in Manchester and
Emily Davies and Elizabeth Garrett in London in 1870; four London
ladies — Mrs. Westlake, Mrs. Surr, Miss (sic) Fenwick Miller, and
Helen Taylor — in 1876; Mrs. C.P. Scott as successor to Lydia
Becker in 1890; and Mrs. C.P. Scott and Mrs. Jordan in Manchester
in 1894. And, though she herself declined to stand for election to the
London School Board in 1872,[31] she consistently deplored the
reluctance of ladies[32] to accept nomination as school trustees, for
she believed that at least one-third of School Board members should
be women.

She also spoke out strongly about the need for women Guardians.
For example, after Dr. Platt had presented a VDS paper entitled "Our
Poor Law System," Emily asked why he had not laid "greater stress
upon the absence of womanly influence," especially in the "management of workhouses . . . . I venture to say that the exclusion of
women from responsible work in connection with the Poor Law
system has brought about much of the confusion and failure of which
Dr. Platt has complained" (*VM*, 5/74, 46-7). And twenty years later
she elaborated on this need for "educated, tender-hearted women" in
relation to workhouses — as Guardians, managers of poor law
schools, and trained nurses (*LP*, 8/18/94, 221). Indeed, she strongly

encouraged both women[33] and men to stand for election as Guardians, for no work could be more fulfilling: "it is supremely important . . . that the best qualified men and women should be called to the onerous but honourable service of the poor" (*LP*, 10/6/94, 496).

Advocating that women serve on County Councils as well,[34] she recorded her support for the newly organized Society for Promoting the Return of Women as County Councillors in 1888. Then, after "rejoicing" in the election of Lady Sandhurst and Miss Cobden to the London County Council (*LP*, 1/19/89, 86), she registered her annoyance at the Court of Appeals' subsequent ruling that these two women could not "discharge municipal functions" (*LP*, 5/25/89, 726) and therefore could not sit as Councillors.[35]

Emily recognized, of course, that the orbit of female suffrage was still greatly confined, even at the local level. So she felt free to indulge her other political interests. One of these was an independent brand of Conservatism, which ranged from a brief flirtation with Co-operative movements[36] and approval of some parts of the platform of the Independent Labour Party[37] to being "in close touch" with the Conservative government and condemning "Socialists and Revolutionists" and, indeed, anyone who wished "to see the Empire dismembered" (*Women's Penny Paper*, 8/2/90, 481). There is a tinge of Socialism in her 1878 editorial proposing a Metropolitan Board of Works (responsible to Parliament and accountable to the country through Parliament) to supply necessities like pure water, instead of leaving such matters to speculative private enterprise. But by and large she considered Socialism "a great evil"[38] in a world "where the progress from savagery to civilisation is due to individualism" (*LP*, 5/24/90, 775). She also questioned the "wild statements" of Fabian Socialists like Tom Mann, who had denounced Tory landlords, the House of Lords, and Town Councils (*LP*, 3/17/94). However, she was not sure how she should deal with William Morris's prediction that when the Socialists had abolished monopolies and classes conspicuous waste would no longer be a problem; for she herself had lectured on the plague of modern extravagance.[39]

Of one thing Emily was certain, though: the Socialists were wrong when they upheld the principle of "vox populi, vox Dei" — this ultimate form of democratic government was for her "a lie, a hideous blasphemy" (*WLE*, 1/19/78, 27). In fact, she stressed the "peril of placing government in the hands of democracy" (*LE*,

11/16/78, 308), even one like that in America. Though in one way she perceived American democracy as "a gigantic humanitarian scheme" (*VM*, 1/73, 209), in another she saw it as "an utter failure . . . the most corrupt state of politics in the world; the most corrupt jurisprudence; the most corrupt state of religion and morals" (*LE*, 11/16/78, 308). Government, she affirmed, should be resolute and patriarchal, in keeping with the best Conservative traditions. Referring to the Russo-Turkish war, she suggested that "peace is best ensured[40] by [Britain's] being ready for war" (*WLE*, 1/19/78, 31) and she approved of the firm stand of Disraeli's Conservative government that resulted in the dispatch of the British fleet to the Dardanelles. She was so annoyed by the House of Commons's lack of unanimity regarding the war that she recommended the Cabinet, not Parliament as a whole, should conduct future wars. Also, though concerned about the bad features of British rule in India, she approved of the British government's "gagging the native Indian press" to prevent a second Indian mutiny (*WLE*, 3/23/78, 136), thus endorsing decisive action to forestall criticism and potential rebellion.

Her Conservatism took a marked political turn in 1886-7 when the Conservative Party undertook active recruitment of women into its Primrose League.[41] Emily took note that her nephew, Ferdinand Faithfull Begg, had been appointed ruling councillor of the Scott Habitation in Edinburgh. Then she herself joined the newly formed South Manchester Primrose Habitation in May 1887 and was immediately appointed Vice-President. "Miranda," editor of the *Lady's Pictorial* and supporter of the Liberal Party, commented on her inaugural speech as follows: "Miss Emily Faithfull's frank, honest, and outspoken speech . . . will undoubtedly trouble many tender political consciences. Personally . . . I must regret that Miss Faithfull, with her large influence and passionately strong appreciation of all that is best, and wisest, and truest in Liberalism, should find herself compelled — so to speak — to support the Conservative platform. . . . [If] the Primrose League is attracting women like Miss Emily Faithfull to its standard, the politics of England will need greatly to be changed, and I, an unknown unit, may have really to look upon that organisation as a remarkable fact . . . [not as] an ephemeral social eccentricity" (*LP*, 5/28/87, 551). Re-appointed Vice-President of her Habitation in 1888, Emily served as delegate to a huge Primrose League meeting in London; the annual meeting of the Grand Habitation on the second day was, she averred, "a political demonstration . . . [of] the practical support of all the ladies in their (Conservative) fold" (*LP*, 4/28/88, 459).

In 1889 she reported both a Grand Council meeting of Primrose ladies at which Sir William Hardman[42] read the report and a gathering of 14,000 Primrose Leaguers (mostly Dames) to welcome Lady Salisbury and Arthur Balfour. She also undertook a verbal defence of the Primrose Dames, for female Liberal Party supporters were ridiculing them for using badges and official designations (à la Freemasonry), for being adamantly opposed to violent and sudden changes, and for working with the men in the Conservative Party[43] rather than criticizing male prejudices concerning female enfranchisement, etc.[44] A year later she could say of the League that "this magnificent army of volunteer workers has now no less than 900,000 knights, dames, and associates" (*LP*, 4/26/90, 635). So its success was manifest, despite carping criticism of its ceremonies and method of operation. Besides, as she observed in 1894, her Radical (Liberal) friends who made fun of the Primrose League should have recognized that the Women's Liberal Association was involved in the same "amusements" as the Primrose Dames, i.e., trying to get women elected to school boards and boards of guardians, and appointed inspectors of factories (*LP*, 2/10/94, 200).

One question on which Primrose Leaguers, male and female, were unanimous (and Liberals were badly split) was preservation of the Union in the face of Gladstone's Irish Measures Bills of 1886 and 1893. Emily had voiced strong opposition to the concept of Home Rule in 1878, and was glad that all five Tory M.P.'s from the Manchester area had condemned the 1886 Bill. She also had welcomed the Women's Liberal Unionist Association[45] — especially those fine speakers Mrs. Henry Fawcett and Miss Isabella Tod[46] — to unionist ranks. Nevertheless, she resolved to report the activities of the Women's Liberal Association[47] "without the least political personal bias" (*LP*, 9/15/88, 272), despite their support of Gladstone's Bill. In the election years 1885 and 1886 she noted that, though the WLA was not as well organized as the Primrose League, it was commendably active. Three years later she published a brief history of this Association and observed that some of the leading lights of the women's movement — Florence Balgarnie, Eliza Orme, Lady Sandhurst, and Mrs. Jacob Bright — had attended a Conference in Manchester at which Mr. and Mrs. W.E. Gladstone were honoured guests. Also, reporting the 1890 Conference of the WLA, she approved of the topics of discussion: university education of women (especially the lack of degrees at Oxford and Cambridge), combination for trade purposes (formation of the Cigar Makers' Union, etc.) and female enfranchisement. Of their 1891 meeting she was not so complimentary, for Lady Carlisle had ignited a near-rebellion by suggesting that the unnatural silence concerning female suffrage was "out of deference to Mr. Gladstone" (*LP*, 6/6/91, 964 and 10/17/91, 698). When the rebels took up the issue again in 1892, they managed to provoke a "disgraceful scene" which, according to Emily, did great harm to the suffrage cause (*LP*, 5/7/92, 685). The May 1893 meeting re-established a semblance of order, chiefly by keeping to more neutral topics like poverty, and this respect for procedure persisted in a June meeting, though female suffrage was again on the agenda; in fact, the ladies voted for the Parliamentary franchise for all duly qualified women, thus breaking the Gladstone-inspired silence.

Because of this increased political activity of women, Emily had much to say about Parliamentary elections and the part played by women in these elections.[48] In 1885 she concentrated on the electioneering process. Lord Randolph Churchill's political tactics in Woodstock and Birmingham seem to have amused her, particularly his changed views about the franchise for agricultural labourers, and his new-found politeness toward his political rival, the Radical Liberal John Bright, whom only a year before he had called a "plundering cuckoo" (*LP*, 10/31/85, 383). Mr. J.W. Maclure, "the darling of Lancashire Conservatism," also proved newsworthy, if only because he had the backing of Randolph Churchill, "this daring political calumniator" whom Emily found it "impossible to take . . . seriously"[49] (*LP*, 11/14/85, 421). Of greater interest, though, was the part played by women, for example, Lady Randolph Churchill's campaigning on her husband's behalf in Woodstock, where she interviewed the electors and inspired them with more than one "neat little speech" (*LP*, 7/11/85, 25). The Primrose Dames similarly canvassed and addressed the electors. In the early stages of the campaign they even undertook the political education[50] of the newly enfranchised male voters, and in at least one instance — the contest between Jacob Bright and Lord Frederick Hamilton in Manchester — were given credit for the Conservative victory. Girton College graduates also got involved in all phases of the campaign.

Emily observed that political meetings preceding the July 1886 election were either "stormy" or "peaceful," depending on one's political persuasion, for "Mr. Gladstone's Irish Policy . . . engrosses the thoughts by day and the dreams by night of every one who takes an interest in the destiny of the country" (*LP*, 5/8/86, 409). This time Lady Randolph Churchill took up the cudgels against Gladstone's "doomed Bill" in a Primrose League meeting, and Emily demonstrated some preference for the Conservatives by observing that the Liberals were "rent and torn as a party [and] . . . behind-hand in their organisation" (*LP*, 6/19/86, 557). Yet she expressed pleasure that Mr. Peacock, Liberal, had been elected in the Manchester area along with Mr. Maclure, Conservative.

Emily tried to maintain a thinly veiled political neutrality during the next two years. But almost everything she wrote revealed her strengthening Conservative bias, e.g., the clear support of the Primrose ladies for Lord Randolph Churchill in November 1886, her castigation of J.H. Crosfield in 1887 for his "vulgar abuse" of Arthur Balfour (*LP*, 12/3/87, 578), her glowing account of Balfour's Manchester speech in October 1888 — "the toasts were drunk with enthusiasm, and Mr. Balfour's speech cheered to the echo" (*LP*, 10/27/88, 472), and her praise of Lord Salisbury, the Prime Minister, for his "manly, out-spoken recognition of the justice" of women's claim "to female suffrage" (*LP*, 12/15/88, 707). So no one was surprised when she finally threw her political hat into the Conservative ring at a huge Primrose League demonstration in 1889 by publicly declaring her support of Arthur Balfour.[51] She had even altered her perception of Randolph Churchill, now lauding him for "discoursing in the Midlands with all his old fire on the political topics of the hour: the land law, liquor traffic, and unhealthy dwellings" (*LP*, 8/10/89, 205).

Leading up to the 1892 election, she disagreed with Joseph Chamberlain's contention that women should be kept out of the "rough and tumble of political agitation" and re-affirmed her belief that women needed to be even more involved with "all the disagreeable work connected with elections" if they expected to influence legislation on important political matters like the Irish question (*LP*, 1/24/91, 134). She also reported that the Primrose Dames and the Women's Liberal Association were preparing for the "coming struggle," (*LP*, 2/6/92, 216), and she registered the annoyance of Liberal women concerning a proposal by some of Gladstone's followers that lady speakers espousing the Liberal cause be silenced during the campaign.

Another of Emily's political concerns was the rights of married women, as reflected in the laws affecting women, especially the Married Women's Property Acts.[52] She did not take part in the early protests by Barbara Bodichon's group (1854-6) that eventuated in the withdrawal of a Married Women's Property Bill[53] in favour of the Divorce and Matrimonial Causes Act[54] of 1857. But, as she recalled in 1885, she "shared [from 1858 to 1864] in the earliest efforts [by these ladies and by the Social Science Association] to secure for wives the possession of their own property and earnings" (*LP*, 8/22/85, 160).

After her enforced departure from the Langham Place Circle she did not serve on any Married Women's Property committees. Yet she kept her readers informed of the shortcomings of the several Married Women's Property (and related) Acts passed between 1870 and 1892, as well as of the interpretation of those Acts in the law courts, especially in such matters as the protection of a wife's earnings, custody of children, wife beating, the rights of a deserted wife, property rights, and, in general, a wife's unequal treatment under the law. Branding the 1870 Act an "unsatisfactory, stop-gap" Bill which secured only the earnings and property wives acquired after marriage, she observed that it was written by a House of Lords committee after they had "altered" and "mangled" Russell Gurney's Bill "beyond recognition" (*VM*, 12/70, 215). Even after the Act was "repaired" in 1874, magistrates managed to misinterpret it. As Emily pointed out in 1877:

Mr. Barstow, the Clerkenwell magistrate, is not very learned in the law. A woman applied to him for a "protection order" to secure to herself her own earnings, her husband having deserted her. Under the Married Women's Property Act, her earnings are her own in any case. The protection order is waste paper (*WLE*, 12/8/77, 147).

The 1882 Act, which the *Englishwoman's Review* dubbed "the Magna Charta of women" (*ER*, 9/15/82), but which Emily found confusing, likewise did not sufficiently clarify this matter of a working wife's earnings being truly her own, except that it permitted a married woman to deposit money in a Post Office Savings Bank in her name only, and it protected property she possessed at the time of marriage.[55]

As for a mother's having custody of her children, Emily
perceived little change in the law from the Infant Custody Act of
1839 to the reforms of 1886. She found the Custody of Infants Act
of 1873 ineffectual; for, though it extended the term of an "innocent"
mother's care of her children from seven to sixteen years of age, her
husband, as legal guardian of his children, still had to agree to give
her custody of the children. Putting control of the situation in the
husband's hands, Emily contended, meant that a deserted wife often
could not gain custody of a child that her husband meant to harm.
Such was the case in 1875 when a judge gave a father custody of his
three-year-old daughter though he clearly intended to make a
prostitute of her. Emily also pointed out that similar complications
occurred because a father legally controlled his children's education,
whether or not he had granted custody to the mother. Only after
1886, and then only after the death of the father, could the mother
become a joint guardian, along with a guardian of the father's choice.
So the dilemma still existed, even though the welfare of the child was
supposed to be the determining factor.

One consequence of the inferior status of married women was a
rash of brutal wife beating that went for the most part unpunished or
lightly punished. Emily reported a number of these cases: one
husband got only a six-month sentence for disabling his wife for life;
another got three months for repeatedly assaulting his wife; a third
kicked his wife to death and the verdict, surprisingly, was "willful
murder." Referring to this last case, Emily indulged in uncharacteristic irony: "It is not fair, when husbands have got used to regarding
their wives as goods and chattels, to suddenly turn round upon them
and treat them as if the said wives were human beings" (*LE*, 11/9/78,
293). She welcomed a new law[56] allowing the battered wife to
obtain a judicial separation and custody of her children, if the
magistrate so decided.

These various Acts regarding women had allowed another matter
to slip through the cracks, namely, a time limit for desertion. There
was no limit, though most people assumed that seven-years' absence
constituted legal grounds. In 1885, to cite Emily's example, a court
of law committed a "gross injustice" against a deserted wife whose
"brutal lord" had returned after fifteen years to find his wife had
remarried. To a chorus of "permitted laughter," the presiding judge
ruled that her first husband was the "right one" and that she had to

return to him even if he had been away for "fifteen hundred years" (*LP*, 9/26/85, 267).

Emily provided other examples of the unequal treatment of women under laws supposedly designed for their benefit. Divorce laws still favoured men over women: after 1857 a husband could divorce his wife for adultery only, whereas an "innocent" wife had to prove incest, or adultery with desertion, cruelty, or unnatural offences. She could petition for maintenance and property,[57] but both were at her husband's behest. Again, divorces were expensive, so the husband had an economic edge; Emily therefore proposed that the 1882 Act be amended to permit a cheap procedure for suing husbands and obtaining legal custody of children (*LP*, 9/22/88, 305).

Wives were, of course, the lowliest of women under the law. In fact, prior to 1891 when the Clitheroe case, which involved a Mr. Jackson's "forcible detention" of his wife, resulted in women finally being recognized as separate persons, paupers and wives were, as Emily observed in satirical fashion, creatures with no legal rights: the "English Statute Book should be headed by the following legal maxims: — 1. A pauper is a creature who, having no money and no friends, has no rights. It should be designated by the neuter gender. 2. A man may treat his wife as he likes. If he prefers killing her to letting her live, he is only exercising his marital authority" (*LE*, 10/26/78, 261).

As Emily saw it, one means of bringing pressure to bear on legislators concerning women's rights was to participate in and publicize women's congresses. Most groups holding congresses dealt with the demands of women for equality. One of them, however, took a more comprehensive approach. This was the Women's Peace Association founded by Julia Ward Howe in 1872.[58] Emily reported that she and Lydia Becker attended a meeting on July 15, 1872 to hear Mrs. Howe's plans for a Peace Congress in London; they were particularly interested in the speaker's comments about the part women could play in bringing about world peace. Picking up this baton again in 1892, Emily recorded annual meetings of the Manchester Women's Peace Association, voiced her belief that "International arbitration is only a question of time," and concurred with John Ruskin's "bold utterance . . . that at whatever moment women chose they could put an end to war" (*LP*, 10/14/93, 571). She also supported the American Association for the Advancement of Women,[59] which was established in 1873 just after she returned from the U.S.A. Emily wrote a letter to the first Congress of this Association, expressing "the greatest interest" in the Congress and asking the secretary to keep her "duly informed of *all* particulars of your Conference, for the *Victoria.* Your idea is splendid, and practical too."[60]

In the 1870's she got involved with international women's congresses as well. In 1874 she reported on the progress of the International Women's League in Europe, and she agreed to set up the British headquarters of the League at her Industrial and Educational Bureau. Four years later she pronounced the 1878 Women's Congress in Paris "a great success" and listed delegates to the conference from Britain, America, Italy, Switzerland, and the host country France (*VM*, 9/78, 458). She also was pleased to be elected honorary and corresponding member of the Woman's Branch of the World Congress in 1891. And in 1892 she noted somewhat wistfully[61] that delegates were coming from all over the world to the International Congress of Women in Chicago where "every living question related to the education and employment of women may be discussed" (*LP*, 9/24/92, 438).

British women hosted several women's conferences in the 1890's, and Emily reported the ones that took place in the Midlands. She noted that the Birmingham Conference of 1890 featured Francis Power Cobbe's paper, "Women's duties to women," along with discussions of emigration, mothers' unions, the spread of diseases among the poor, free registries, training homes, co-operation of women in charitable efforts, and so on. The next year she reported that the Conference of Liverpool Ladies' Union of Workers Among Women and Girls was attended by "Mrs. Henry Fawcett, Miss Beatrice Potter, Miss Louisa Twining, . . . Mrs. Isabel Cramer-Roberts and her sister Miss Evelyn Faithfull, etc." (*LP*, 11/21/91, 917). Besides dealing with practical topics like girls' clubs and temperance work, this conference took a philosophical approach to such matters as responsibility, duty, love, and sympathy in women's work. Lastly, she observed that a Women's Conference at Leeds in 1893 "ranged from Women's Suffrage to Inebriate Homes," with side glances at Florence Nightingale's letter on "Health Teaching in Villages," housing of the poor, and medical work among Indian women (*LP*, 11/25/93, 819).

Most of Emily's political interests and activities dealt with so far come under the rubric of national politics. But her concerns about health and welfare — sanitation, housing, playgrounds, parks, hygiene, hospitals, physical fitness, mental health, and so on — fit more readily under the heading of municipal politics. Sanitation, of course, subsumes the other topics mentioned, for Victorians defined "sanitary science" as a combination of physiology (the need for pure air and wholesome food) and cleanliness (the need for clean houses, clean drains, and pure water).[62] For the sake of convenience, however, I shall discuss them separately.

It was generally agreed that women could deal with sanitation problems (and hence preventive medicine) better than men could.[63] Therefore, the Ladies' Sanitary Association (LSA) was founded in 1857[64] and the National Health Society (NHS) in 1873.[65] Both were private agencies and both achieved their purposes by providing female lecturers (cultured ladies) to instruct women, especially poor women, in physiology and hygiene or, more simply, the laws of health. Emily apparently got involved with the LSA shortly after she joined the Langham Place Circle, for, as she stated in 1888, she gave the first speech of her life some thirty years ago "on behalf of the Sanitary Association in Aberdeen" (*LP*, 2/18/88). Entitled "Healthy Homes," it dealt with "domestic economy, fresh air, and water" (*LP*, 10/27/88, 472 and *LP*, 8/29/91, 367).

She maintained her affiliation with the LSA (and later with the NHS) in several ways: first, by stressing the importance of health and sanitation to prevent and to combat disease;[66] second, by publicizing the need for Physiology instructors — in 1875 she ran an LSA advertisement encouraging ladies to enroll for a thirteen-lecture course on Physiology applied to health and education; third, by announcing lectures by eminent medical women, e.g., Dr. Frances Hoggan's NHS-sponsored lectures for ladies on the development and physical training of children and her LSA-sponsored health lessons to the poor in the East End of London, and Dr. Longshore Potts's lectures on health; and fourth, by presenting full reports of Hygiene congresses, e.g., one in London in 1891, where Health Councils, hungry school children, polluted water, and diet were discussed, and household coal fires were identified as the chief producers of Manchester's obnoxious fog and smoke.

She also made the public aware of the LSA's and the NHS's continuing need of funds to carry on their good work. For, though the LSA was backed by the Social Science Association until 1885, it was always short of funds, and after 1885 it needed even more financial support as well as additional volunteer workers. So Emily in 1890 was glad to report a successful drawing-room concert in aid of the Ladies' Manchester and Salford Sanitary Association at which the Mayor of Manchester gave a good speech about the advantages of teaching people the value of fresh air, clean homes, and well-cooked food. Of course, one drawing-room concert was not enough to sustain operations; so she had to remind her readers four years later that this Manchester Association (now called the Ladies' Health Society) had not received "the financial support the work merits . . . . To spread among the people . . . a knowledge of the laws of health, to promote cleanliness, temperance and thrift, to obtain a purer atmosphere, to improve the dwellings of the poor and to preserve the lives of their children, are aims which should command a more adequate support from the general public" (*LP*, 2/10/94, 200). In similar fashion she admonished an apparently indifferent public for not giving better support to the National Health Society: "to prevent disease is not only a duty, but a work which even on selfish grounds demands our co-operation. The fever in the city alley brings desolation into the rich man's home" (*LP*, 10/21/93, 604).

The sanitation lectures met with a mixed response at first. Even as late as 1878, Emily stated, the LSA's course of lectures gave "great offence in many quarters," probably because of the lecturers' frank discussion of human physiology; in fact, Baroness Burdett-Coutts resigned from the LSA over this issue (*WLE*, 7/6/78, 5). Yet the Society of Arts Congress on Domestic Economy had recommended school training for girls in Health and Plain Needlework, and Emily gave this Report her blessing. Fortunately, by 1894 the liberals had carried the day and Lady Londonderry could propose without fear of rebuttal that County Councils shoulder the responsibility of providing these lectures on home life and health, for it was vitally important that girls[67] learn "to take care of themselves, what to do with the sick, and the first principles of health" (*LP*, 2/17/94, 230).

Emily took note of every unsanitary situation, and in most cases proposed remedies. She reported in 1891 that male Civil Service clerks were at liberty to leave their offices for lunch or dinner, thus enabling them to fill their lungs with fresh air, whereas their female counterparts had to stay on the job; consequently, the women were on sick leave more often than the men. Perhaps, she continued, the "incivility[68] [from women clerks that] so many people [complained] of" was due to this lack of fresh air (*LP*, 2/28/91, 322). As for the sewage gas that seeped into houses while people were away on vacation, she recommended that "all sinks be well flushed and the house thoroughly ventilated by open windows and doors a few days before coming back, and above all look to the water you drink[69] . . . in these days of cholera scares" (*LP*, 9/26/85, 267). She likewise had much to say about wholesome food and good cooking; she wrote of the need for sanitary regulation to protect the poor from the adulteration of food and from rotten food (*LE*, 9/78), and she recalled the Earl of Shaftesbury's repeated discourses on "the food that is wasted by the poor" because of bad cooking (*LP*, 7/14/88, 36).

Emily also pinpointed industries and locations where disease reared its head. The former included laundries, dairies,[70] and mills; the latter, hospitals,[71] parishes,[72] towns, seaside resorts,[73] barges and boats,[74] and graveyards. She was pleased to report that a limited company, Sanitary and General Laundries, had been authorized to erect "in London and other large towns . . . laundries in which every appliance of modern science will be combined with moderate prices, punctuality, and sanitary arrangements. A separate department for washing linen from infected houses will be built, and every care taken to insure that immunity from infection, which cannot be secured in the crowded dwellings [e.g., suburban cottages] where so much of the washing of English families is carried on" (*VM*, 11/77, 84-5). Conversely, she was unhappy about conditions in the Lancashire mills; so she presented in some detail the Reports of the lady Assistant Labour Commissioners (Eliza Orme, Clara Collet, May Abraham, and M.H. Irwin) that exposed unsanitary conditions, chief of which was the heavy steaming due to bad ventilation (*LP*, 11/18/93, 796).[75]

Manchester was her favourite example of poor sanitation in rapidly expanding urban areas. In 1887 she admitted that she had been taking "complacent and touchy Manchester" to task for its "unloveliness," that is, its unsanitariness (*LP*, 10/15/87, 396). The next year she commented on its smoke and unhealthiness and on the high "death-rate, which is such a disgrace to this city" (*LP*, 12/29/88, 761). Therefore, she urged Manchester citizens to support Lord Derby's appeal concerning the Old Trafford Botanical Gardens, which served as an oasis in "this wilderness of brick and stone, smoke and labour" (*LP*, 11/16/89, 679). And she encouraged Manchester women to take some action to purify their city's "filthy air," as the health of their children was at risk (*LP*, 3/21/91, 436). Still, she did note some improvement in 1894: with the completion of the Thirlmere Water Scheme the city had purer water than before, the installation of electric light to replace gas lamps had reduced (if only marginally) the smoke, and the opening of several parks, recreation grounds and the Manchester Ship Canal had provided much needed open spaces. So she was optimistic that the smoke-abatement discussions held at the International Health Exhibition in Manchester in 1895 would bear fruit, although she concurred with Mrs. Pender, one of the speakers, that "those who lived in the slums and alleys of the towns [like Manchester] were almost entirely deprived of light and air by the dense black smoke, which descended and covered everything like a pall" (*LP*, 5/4/95, 664).

She also believed that Manchester's graveyards constituted a major sanitation problem. Because too many corpses had been interred in the cemeteries, the "leaking" graves[76] were rightly considered a possible source of infectious diseases like cholera, smallpox and diphtheria. In fact, Manchester cemeteries were closed in 1892 because of this danger. Emily and a number of other concerned citizens proposed cremation as a solution to this problem, but most people were opposed to it. Indeed, only two cremations had taken place in Manchester by the end of 1892; Emily's was among the first half dozen performed at the Chorlton-cum-Hardy crematorium she helped to establish. Manchester still deserved the "unloveliness" label she had pinned on it. And so did other large cities in Britain.

Emily also played a small role in providing healthy homes for the London poor. At an 1874 public meeting of the Model Houses Association for the Improvement of the Dwellings of the Industrial Poor she was elected Vice-President. But she gave Octavia Hill full credit for taking the action needed to provide these homes: recommending Hill's paper on woman's work in the homes of the poor; favourably reviewing her *Homes of the London Poor*; agreeing with her that legislation was necessary to force contractors to build better houses for the poor; praising her "rent collector" system whereby volunteer ladies trained by her in property management not only collected rents for houses owned by Hill's Charity Organization Society but also looked after the tenants' moral and physical improvement; and giving her solid backing when she appeared before the Aged Poor Commission — "There is no reformer whose words are more worth listening to than those of Octavia Hill" (*LP*, 4/23/95, 587).

With fresh air and exercise in mind, Emily wrote at length about parks and playgrounds.[77] In 1877 she recommended Octavia Hill's National Health Society lecture on "Open Spaces," especially her proposal that "small open spaces near the homes of the poor should be carefully preserved and made beautiful with plants and flowers. The very old and young cannot go [Hill said,] as far as the parks and the embankments" (*VM*, 6/77, 174). And she later praised Hill and the Kyrle Society[78] she headed for obtaining Vauxhall Park,[79] London, for the people as well as for "planting of trees, . . . laying out gardens of waste patches, . . . promotion of entertainments in the heart of the squalid districts as well as in hospitals and work-houses . . . and prompting the public authorities to follow suit" in a number of English cities (*LP*, 5/12/94, 725). Emily was particularly worried about London parks being built over. There was talk, she said, of erecting buildings in Hyde Park, turning the Mall into a public thoroughfare, and so on. Therefore, citizens had to act to prevent such desecration, for "there is nothing we in London are more concerned to preserve[80] than our unrivalled chain of Parks" (*WLE*, 3/2/78, 101). Parks are "recreation grounds for the whole of the people, and not for one class[81] alone" (*WLE*, 8/10/78, 85).

Parks were only half the answer, however. Playgrounds (play spaces, recreation grounds, recreation rooms, etc.) were equally important. Emily fully agreed with a VDS speaker, Francis Fuller, that people needed to "play rationally and healthfully" (*VM*, 4/71, 527). She admitted that healthful play was not particularly "rational" for young children. They needed playgrounds to run in, instead of darting "in and out between the tramcars and carriages on our public thoroughfares" (*LP*, 9/1/88, 223) or acting like hooligans in Emily's carefully planted garden. For adults and older children, though, all Victorian play appears to have had an intellectual component — from cycling, tennis, and golf for ladies, to "elevating amusements" (*LP*, 5/20/93, 809) for the poor like picture exhibitions, Ladies' Sanitary Association "Park Parties" (*W & W*, 8/22/74), museums and libraries.[82] Sunday Schools and recreative evening classes for the children, "wholesome pleasures" for servants (*LP*, 11/13/86, 444), recreation rooms for shop-girls — all of these, Emily implied, could be justified because they were both rational and healthful.[83]

She had several other environmental concerns. Though she was satisfied with the scheme to pipe water from Thirlmere Lake to Manchester once the project was completed, she appears to have been at one with John Ruskin concerning its effect on the environment: "Poor Mr. Ruskin! The second reading of the Manchester Corporation Water Bill has been agreed to, and the matter involving the Thirlmere Lake scheme referred to a hybrid committee" (*WLE*, 2/16/78, 76). In similar vein she agreed with George Meredith, novelist and poet, that the Ambleside Railway should not be built, and she opposed both the "proposed desecration" of Windermere by a building syndicate (*LP*, 9/28/89, 406) and a plan to spoil Llandudno by an electric railway to the summit of the Great Orme.

Hospitals (especially those for women and children) and homes for the unfortunate were also high on her health-and-welfare agenda. Between 1878 and 1894 she registered a number of strong protests about the inefficient and, at times, neglectful operation of workhouse infirmaries. In June 1878, for example, she took the Boards of Guardians to task for not remedying a bad situation,[84] "for the treatment of the sick in most workhouse infirmaries is a scandal to a Christian country" (*WLE*, 6/29/78, 329). And later that year she angrily denounced specific cases of maltreatment: first, the "gross neglect of duty by a relieving officer" who delayed admitting a dying man into an infirmary (*WLE*, 8/17/78); second, the cruel, inhuman treatment of a sick dock labourer who died the day after he was turned away from the infirmary of the Whitechapel Union and told to go back to work.

She followed Louisa Twining's lead in suggesting improvements to the infirmary system. In 1890 Twining had proposed that untrained pauper nurses be replaced with trained nurses; Emily reported in 1892 and 1894 that Twining's proposal was being put into effect, but many male guardians were opposing it[85] and there was friction among trained nurses, Masters, and Matrons. Again, she and Louisa had tried for years to get more women into workhouse administration, especially as Guardians, but not enough had volunteered. So Emily returned to this theme in the 'nineties, emphasizing that "educated tender-hearted women" were urgently needed (*LP*, 8/18/94, 221) to maintain an acceptable level of improvement[86] to the workhouse system, which "even twenty years ago" had been "hard and tyrannical, with much officialdom and little that was humanising and tender.

It has needed a mother's voice and the element of motherhood" (*LP*, 1/28/93, 122).

Dealing with hospitals for women and children as sanitary measures, Emily focussed on the New Hospital for Women in the early 1870's, for that was the first one administered by women. Under the guidance of Mrs. E.G. Anderson, M.D., it had taken shape in 1872 as a space above the St. Mary's Dispensary in Marylebone. In 1875 it was moved into new premises after a lengthy campaign for public subscriptions. From that point on it met its bills, and its relative prosperity encouraged other London hospitals for women and children to continue their struggle for survival. After her move to Manchester Emily shifted her journalistic support to that city's St. Mary's Hospital for Women and Children. In 1888 she announced that it needed another £10,000 for a new building. Two years later she recognized it as the "most important hospital for women in the North of England" (*LP*, 3/22/90, 417).

She also publicized a number of specialized hospitals and homes and proposed the construction of others. Examples of the former were the Convalescent Home for Infants operated by Caroline Goldsmid, the Chelsea Hospital for women, i.e., gentlewomen of limited means and women of respectability suffering from curable diseases, and a Private Nursing and Convalescent Home for the poorer clergy. The latter category included a Home for Incurables and Infirm Women recommended by both Emily and Louisa Twining, a state-of-the-art hospital where insane people could be treated by well-trained, sympathetic attendants and doctors schooled in the latest methods, and more Female Strangers' Lodging Houses for "fallen" women.[87]

The preventive medicine that Emily believed most effective in keeping women out of hospitals was physical fitness, with an attendant knowledge of Hygiene and Physiology to help gauge one's physical limits.[88] She regarded swimming as the best fitness sport for women; as she stated in 1887, "swimming is the most invigorating sport and it has a moral effect," that is, it induces courage.[89] But, she went on, one must swim regularly — more than once a week — to get the maximum benefit. So she campaigned for public baths for both sexes in every parish[90] and for "gratuitous or cheap instruction" in swimming for the poor (*WLE*, 9/14/78, 169). Of course, she gave other sports their due. In 1882 she remarked on the healthy amusements of American girls — lawn tennis, fencing, and horseback riding — and she expressed concern that the Harvard

Annex girls were getting too little use of the university gymnasium. For she considered gymnastics "a matter of the utmost importance" in the physical training of women (*LP*, 1/20/83, 50). She also noted that British women played tennis in the 1880's, along with golf, badminton and cricket, and she approved of all of these sports because they promoted "physical exercise in a rational manner" (*LP*, 12/10/87, 619). In the following decade she not only stressed the overall importance of physical exercise for women; she favoured a balanced program of swimming, gymnastics, and outdoor recreations as well, especially in higher education. In addition, she recommended dancing and fencing as "innocent recreation" (*LP*, 6/3/93) and good exercise, and she urged all women to take up cycling.

Emily even extended her concern for women's health to include the moral and physical well-being of female prisoners and their children. In 1872 she, Amelia Lewis, and Mary Carpenter spoke up at an International Prison Congress about the need for female administration and guards in women's prisons and the fact that the State was not doing enough to help female prisoners after their discharge. She also reprinted from the *Daily News* a series of articles entitled "Female Prison Life in England" in 1875 and asked her readers for funds to support Princess Mary's Village Homes for the daughters of people serving jail terms. In 1894 she got involved in a flurry of activity: first, supporting the cry of Louisa Twining, Florence Balgarnie and others for matrons[91] at police stations to prevent the "intolerable humiliation" of women in police cells (*LP*, 5/12/94, 712); second, pointing out the need for "lady visitors"[92] in jails housing female prisoners (*LP*, 6/2/94, 830); and third, strongly endorsing the appointment[93] of Eliza Orme to the Departmental Committee of Inquiry into the Administration of Prisons (*LP*, 6/9/94, 897).

*Chapter 9*

# Cultural Reformer: Culture as "great civilizer," the Theatre, Dramatic Reform

Several of Emily's statements indicate her high regard for culture: "Let scientists say what they will, literature and the fine arts[1] ever have been, and ever will be, the great civilisers of the world" (*W & W*, 8/21/75, 5); "general culture . . . makes the good conversationalist" (*LP*, 10/20/94, 551); and "[I delight] in the conversation of intellectual men and women" (*The Women's Penny Paper*, 8/2/90, 481). She believed that women in particular needed an education in culture not only to acquire the cultivated and refined tastes that are the mark of civilized people but also to keep in touch "with all the great movements by which they are surrounded" (*LP*, 5/11/89, 673). Using less exalted phrases like "I am very fond of a good play and delight in music, I am also a great reader . . . " (*The Women's Penny Paper*, op.cit.), she encouraged women to be more enthusiastic about cultural pursuits, for example, by showing their appreciation of a theatrical performance: "A great many ladies seem to me afraid to laugh, and the very idea of applauding would make some of them faint" (*LP*, 11/13/86, 444).

But whether one's approach to culture is down-to-earth or elevated, she contended that everyone should be exposed to these "great civilisers" as often as possible,[2] through direct participation[3] or intellectual discussion,[4] or both. Furthermore, from 1875 on she took every opportunity to inform the public of cultural events. In *Women and Work* she instituted book and magazine reviews and publicized musical and dramatic performances, e.g., a Carl Rosa opera, promenade concerts, "Pops" concerts, drama at the Crystal Palace under Charles Wyndham, a production of *Macbeth*, and one of *Nicholas Nickleby* as a play. Similarly, *West London Express* columns entitled "The Stage" and "Music" informed people about West End shows, concerts, operas, and art exhibitions. The *Victoria Magazine* of the same period dealt with Bach Society and Philharmonic Society concerts, Mlle. Marie Krebs' recital, and a Shakespeare Memorial Benefit, and featured special articles on musicians like Carl Rosa and Mme. Jenny Viard-Louis and actors of the quality of Ella Dietz, Mrs. Madge Kendal, Hermann Vezin, and Kate Pattison. After 1884 Emily maintained this cultural assault with notices and reviews in the *Lady's Pictorial* concerning operas, operettas, plays, music concerts, brass band contests, and art galleries in Manchester, which, though it did not always display "too lively an interest in Italian opera" had "as much true culture . . . as elsewhere" (*LP*, 5/15/86, 453 and 10/30/86, 372).

Most of her operatic items involved Carl Rosa's Company, which was making "laudable efforts to popularise opera" in the mid-1870's. In 1875-6 she observed that this Company had been successful at Birmingham, would open at Drury Lane in London in March 1876 with an English opera, and move to the Lyceum in September 1876. Ten years later she celebrated Rosa's "eminently successful" attempts to entertain Liverpool and Manchester audiences; sold-out houses in the latter city were treated to three operas (*Manon, Faust, Esmeralda*) in one week in September 1885. And "musical Manchester" was equally enthusiastic in March 1886 when Rosa opened with Maillart's *Fadette*. When the maestro died in 1889, Emily mourned her "old friend, Carl Rosa," who, she claimed, had been "another victim to overwork" (*LP*, 5/11/89, 666 and 12/7/89, 816). Still, his company carried on under his name and she noted its repertoire.

She made several other interesting references to opera, for instance, Adelina Patti's accident while performing *Faust* in Paris, from which she apparently recovered quickly; for she had a "great triumph" in St. Petersburg only three months later (*W & W*, 3/6/75). To judge by Emily's frequent mention of Miss Patti, she was her favourite female opera singer, as the following account of Patti's 1882 performance of *La Traviata* in New York demonstrates: "She appeared in her famous role of Violetta, and I never heard her to greater advantage . . . . A more artistic performance of the *Traviata* could not have been given . . . Patti was recalled again and again with every mark of enthusiasm" (*LP*, 12/9/82, 273). Emily also commented on the grand opening of the Metropolitan Opera House on October 22, 1883, just after she arrived in New York from England. Though she did not attend on opening night, she reported that "the sensation of the hour is the opening of Mr. Abbey's new opera house . . ." and continued in her next column, "The Metropolitan Opera House may be open to criticism as to its interior decoration, or rather want of it, but it has achieved a great triumph as far as its performances and audiences are concerned" (*LP*, 11/10/83, 305 and 12/8/83, 366).

Dealing with music other than opera, she displayed an eclectic taste ranging from symphony to "Pops" concerts and Gilbert and Sullivan operettas. One major figure, Charles Hallé, concert pianist and symphony conductor,[5] spanned her London-Manchester musical worlds from 1875 on. Her first reference is to a piano recital at which Hallé played Schumann's *Humoreske*. By 1885 she could report three successful concerts in Manchester, with Hallé now in the role of conductor and master of ceremonies. His November concert, she enthused, was "a grand treat" (*LP*, 11/28/85, 462). But audience support dropped off in the late 1880's; in 1886 Emily referred to a badly attended concert, and in 1888 she pleaded for more public support for this Manchester favourite — after all, this was the thirty-first season of concerts conducted by the newly knighted Sir Charles. Besides carrying on with his concerts in the 1890's — Emily reported Hallé concerts in Manchester in December 1894 and February 1895 — Hallé founded a College of Music in Manchester and Queen Victoria granted it the title "Royal." All in all, he was more responsible than anyone else for establishing a tradition of high-class music in the Midlands (Manchester in particular). As Emily stated in 1892 when comparing the concerts of Charles Hallé with the more popular ones of Mr. de Jong, "What Sir Charles Hallé has done for the classes, Mr. de Jong did for the elevation of the masses" (*LP*, 10/8/92, 486).

She was not being patronising when she made this comparison, for she thoroughly appreciated de Jong's "spirited and successful efforts to give high-class but popular concerts" (*LP*, 3/13/86, 837), and she attended most of them. Here is what she said about de Jong's November 1885 appearance in Manchester's Free Trade Hall: "Miss Sherwin's flute-like voice gave great pleasure . . . and Miss Kate Chaplin's performances on the violin were really admirable. Mr.

Walter Clifford's 'Father O'Flynn' of course evoked the immense applause comic songs are wont to do. Mr. de Jong's flute solo received a loud *encore . . .* " (*LP*, 12/12/85, 501). And, though de Jong was unlucky enough to have Adelina Patti come down with a severe cold in 1886, thus aborting his concert, Emily was glad to report that the long-awaited Patti re-appearance in November 1889 was "wonderful" (*LP*, 11/2/89, 605). She was not at all surprised when de Jong was appointed "commander-in-chief of the musical department" of the forthcoming 1887 Jubilee exhibition in Manchester (*LP*, 10/30/86, 372). Therefore, when de Jong's popularity waned in 1888, she tried to drum up public support for him,[6] for he had contributed a great deal to musical Manchester during the past twenty years.

Harking back to the music scene in London when Emily lived there, we may note her interesting observations on Promenade concerts (called "Proms" even then), on Verdi's *Requiem*, and on a concert-pianist friend of hers. Referring to the 1875 "Proms" she deplored a preponderance of Wagnerian music, particularly "Lohengrin;" on the other hand, she was so pleased with the 1878 "Proms" that she devoted an editorial to them and gave high praise to the "classical nights" when Mr. Arthur Sullivan was conducting (*WLE*, 8/24/78). What impressed her most about Verdi's *Requiem* in 1875 was that the composer himself conducted the work. Regarding her concert-pianist friend, Mme. Jenny Viard-Louis, she took special note of her concerts from 1875 to 1877, for this lady's performance at Emily's first afternoon recital on April 29, 1875 had helped to ensure the success of the series of recitals that preceded Emily's début as actress and manager of a small acting company.

In addition to covering the Hallé and de Jong concerts in Manchester, she reported performances by Arthur Rubinstein (1886) and Paderewski (1892), and presentations of several of Handel's works[7] and the Gilbert and Sullivan operettas. In 1876 she had adopted a "high culture" attitude concerning *Trial by Jury*, the first G & S comic opera, for she apparently assumed it would be just another example of *opéra bouffe*: "Has Mr. Sullivan no capabilities for anything better than this sort of thing? Surely the composer of the 'Light of the World' can write above the Lecocq and Hervé level. He might try at anyrate (sic)" (*W & W*, 2/19/76, 7). But she changed her mind after she saw *The Sorcerer* in London in 1877, partly because of its immense popularity but chiefly, no doubt, because her nephew,

Rutland Barrington, was highly successful in this operetta as actor and singer. Of his acting she reported that he "plays the vicar so well that numbers of clergymen go to see him, and recognize in him, 'a man and a brother'" (*WLE*, 12/15/77, 159). And a particular song he sang so beautifully in *The Sorcerer*, namely, "Time was when love and I were well acquainted," became so popular that sales of the sheet music turned a fine profit for Metzler and Company, Publishers. Emily did not single out Rutland Barrington's G & S performances again, but she retained her high opinion of the operettas after she moved to Manchester. In 1885 she reported "enthusiastic houses" for *Trial by Jury* and *The Sorcerer* (*LP*, 10/31/85, 383); the next year she noted that the *Mikado* was drawing full houses, though attendance at other musical events had fallen off; and in 1888 she commended the *Mikado* and the *Pirates of Penzance* for giving "signal satisfaction . . . during this wet and gloomy season" (*LP*, 8/11/88, 162).

Her knowledge of art appears to have been that of an educated amateur — good enough to criticize selections of art works for academies and to publicize lectures and art exhibitions. No doubt her acquaintance with Anna Jameson and John Ruskin[8] coloured her early perceptions, as did her friendship with Elizabeth Thompson in the 1870's and meeting such people as Harriet Hosmer, American artist, and John Gibson, sculptor, "at one of Lady Cardwell's dinner parties in Liverpool" (*LP*, 2/27/86, 194). With such experts helping to fashion her appreciation of art, she could confidently announce Robert Browning's 1874 lecture on the art treasures of Italy, publish an article entitled "A Saunter Through the Royal Academy" in 1878, and recall the "rare judgement" of Mr. W.A. Turner (*not* the famous artist), at whose house she had many times "listened with infinite pleasure to his keen criticisms on his own art treasures" (*LP*, 6/26/86, 583). She also considered herself competent to criticize the "amateur hangers" of paintings in the Liverpool Autumn Exhibition for their poor selection and haphazard arrangement (*LP*, 9/26/85, 267), to note the artistic qualities of the excellent photographs in Mr. Tabor's "Art Gallery" in San Francisco, and to concur with William Morris and others in the newly formed National Association for the Advancement of Art and its Application to Industry that the Royal Academy was too narrow in its perception of art, especially the relationship of art to one's work (*LP*, 12/15/88, 707).

She also believed she was capable of judging the relative worth of female artists. In 1872 she asserted that women artists in general were not professional[9] for, unlike men, they had "rarely been taught the fine arts as a profession" (*VM*, 7/72, 333); in particular, Mrs. Grundy had prevented their being exposed to a "life school." Still, a few women were proving they could be just as good as the best male artists. Elizabeth Thompson had received John Ruskin's grudging praise in 1875; according to Emily, Ruskin had to admit that Thompson's "Quatre Bras" was a clear exception to his pronouncement that "no woman could paint" (*W & W*, 6/19/75). Emily also reported that Mlle. Dubray had been commissioned to sculpt two statues for a new opera house on the Embankment, that lady artists from Liverpool were well represented at the Royal Academy in 1886 and that two of Charlotte Robinson's artists who had pictures in a Glasgow Exhibition were "on the line" for the Royal Academy (*LP*, 5/12/88, 508).

She publicized art exhibitions as a matter of course, especially those at the Royal Academy and the Manchester Art Gallery. But what really excited her was the new tolerance concerning the opening of art galleries on Sunday[10]. In 1875 she devoted an editorial to the Duke of Westminster's Sunday exhibitions at his Grosvenor Gallery, and three years later she commended him for opening them again at the request of the Sunday Society. In 1886 she accorded similar praise to the Manchester Art Gallery: "The three free Sunday openings proved most acceptable; 30,663 working people, who would never otherwise have visited it, gladly used this generous privilege. . . . We really value pictures in this 'city of sad colours' . . . " (*LP*, 1/16/86, 52).

Emily also valued literature very highly, for it too was a "great civiliser." Like most Victorians she considered the moral effect of literature to be its most important attribute. But her definition of morality was broad in scope. For instance, she regarded Sir Walter Scott's *Rob Roy* as moral, despite its hero being a freebooter. And though she thought that Walt Whitman should have used a pruning-knife before publishing his *Leaves of Grass*, she did not condemn that "eccentric genius" for the sexual references in this work, for she considered him to be "a cultured man" and "a deep thinker" — hence, overall, a decent person who wrote in moral fashion (*LP*, 12/22/83, 391).

On the other hand, she wrote off much Victorian literature as cheap, immoral trash. She even recommended that the Legislature censor the penny and half-penny "awfuls" that led, she believed, to juvenile delinquency. And she pronounced the majority of women's fiction[11] to be "pernicious and deadly," "overly sensational," and mired in "artificial emotion [and] superficial philosophy" (*W & W*, 2/13/75). Pending legislative action, she praised the National Home Reading Union for "advising [its] members to choose the best books" (*LP*, 12/15/94, 924) and for conducting discussion groups, and she asked the Book Clubs, which, she believed, should be "entirely unconnected with a religious or political organisation," to try their best to avoid trash (*LP*, 2/25/93, 280).

Emily likewise was proud of her personal relationship with poets and novelists, e.g., Oliver Wendell Holmes, Joaquin Miller, James Russell Lowell,[12] Walt Whitman, of course, Adelaide Procter, and Frances Power Cobbe.[13] Her close acquaintance with these writers encouraged her to make a few sallies as literary critic. Thus she agreed to judge a story competition for the Ellerslie Union in which she awarded first prize to Edith Cox's "Through Blue Spectacles," a political skit in the form of a love story. And she challenged Coventry Patmore to admit that Alice Meynell's writings had "falsified [his earlier] assertion that no female writer of our time had attained to true distinction" (*LP*, 1/14/93, 48).

But the cultural pursuit with which she felt most at home was the theatre, for she knew many of the actors personally, saw as many plays as she could — at the Lyceum in London she had a private "stage-box" of her own (*W & W*, 3/27/75) — and developed more aplomb as a drama critic than she had as a literary critic. Her references to particular actors and actresses are especially interesting because, though she was casually acquainted with some, she was intimately involved with others. In the first category are Henry Irving, Ellen Terry, Charlotte Cushman, Dion Boucicault,[14] Beerbohm Tree,[15] Hermann Vezin,[16] Laurence Barrett,[17] Wilson Barrett,[18] Sarah Bernhardt,[19] and Lily Langtry.

She stated in 1890 that she had Irving at her house some years earlier to meet a few friends. This gathering probably occurred in 1878 after Irving, Emily and other actors had participated in a Grand Matinée Dramatique. But she had publicized Irving's feats as far back as 1874, when he appeared in *Charles I*, *Eugene Aram*, and *Hamlet*; in 1875, when he triumphed in *Macbeth*; and in 1877 in *The Courier of Lyons*. In late 1883, she reported from America that Irving and Ellen Terry had arrived shortly after she herself had landed, and that he and Matthew Arnold were being lionized. From Manchester she noted in December 1894 that Irving, Ellen Terry and the Lyceum Company as a whole had made the week exciting with *Becket, Nance Oldfield,* and *Lyons Mail,* and that Irving had given a lecture on *Macbeth* at Owen's College. Throughout these citations one senses her respect for Irving as a larger-than-life character.

She first mentioned Ellen Terry in a review of her performance as Clara Douglas in *Money* at London's Prince of Wales Theatre in 1875. In 1877 she again praised her acting in *The Courier of Lyons,* and in 1883 she reported from America that Ellen Terry shoes and caps were all the rage in clothing stores. Almost always, of course, she coupled Terry with Irving.

She also thought highly of Charlotte Cushman's[20] acting ability. In 1873 she attended a dramatic reading by her in Steinway Hall, New York City, and was very impressed. Celebrating Cushman's final performance at Booth's Theatre in 1874, Emily described "her brilliant career [as] an honour to the stage and to womanhood" (*W & W,* 11/14/74, 4). After Cushman died of cancer, she wrote an article praising this "great dramatic artist" (*VM,* 3/79).

One actress about whom she wrote at length was Lily Langtry. In 1882-83 she was critical of the lovely "Jersey Lily," who seemed to her to be relying more on her beauty than on her acting ability to impress audiences. However, she agreed that the American media hyperbole brought on by Mr. Abbey's fanfare welcome of Lily was partly to blame; as a result, the New York theatres were crowded with people who came to see her and not the plays. Then, once they had appreciated her beauty, these New York audiences turned cold, undemonstrative, and hypercritical. They talked to one another during *The Unequal Match,* a "dull, out-of-date, and hackneyed" play; criticized her performance as Rosalind in *As You Like It*; and only came to life during the lively Spanish dance number by Lily and her partner in *The Honeymoon* (*LP,* 12/23/82, 314). Boston crowds proved even less responsive, for they were not as willing as New Yorkers to pay "extra theatrical prices" to see Lily (*LP,* 1/6/83, 7). In Philadelphia her audiences were the "largest . . . ever known," but the media turned against her with "the most cruelly severe newspaper criticisms I ever read on her private character and capabilities, though it must, of course, be acknowledged that she has challenged observation in both directions" (*LP,* 1/27/83, 59). Thus Emily expressed both sympathy for Lily Langtry as a person and doubts about her talent. Two years later, however, she reported that Lily's performance in

*Peril* was "a thoroughly artistic triumph." And she praised her "hard work and devotion to her profession" as thoroughly deserving of "the cordial recognition of all who respect earnest conscientiousness in business or Art" (*LP*, 9/26/85, 267). Langtry's Manchester performances were equally good, she continued: "The performance of *The School for Scandal* was pronounced an unusually fine one; both as Lady Teazle, and Lady Ormonde in *Peril* Mrs. Langtry displayed rare power and finish, and has certainly established herself as a stage favourite in this play-loving, critical city" (*LP*, 10/3/85, 291).

Emily referred even more frequently, of course, to actors she knew well — Genevieve Ward, Mr. and Mrs. Kendal, Kate Pattison, Ella Dietz, and her nephews Rutland Barrington and Walter Bentley. In the summer of 1875, Kate and Ella were part of a small acting company under Emily's direction. Kate proved to be a "natural" actress; therefore, with Emily's encouragement she studied under Hermann Vezin and made her professional début in Manchester in 1877. She was a great success in *The Wandering Heir*, and by October 1878 she had a leading role in the Kendals' production of *Diplomacy*. One might assume that Emily and Kate drifted apart at this point. But they did not; in November 1878 Emily, Kate, and Mr. and Mrs. Kendal took part in a Manchester benefit, in 1880 Emily and Kate lived together in an Edinburgh hotel while Kate was appearing in *Forget-Me-Not* in Glasgow, and in 1882-3 Emily planned her travel itinerary in the U.S.A. to coincide with that of Mr. Abbey's theatrical company, which Kate had recently joined. Ella, a strong supporter of the women's movement, had been successful on the American stage. So her British début in *Money* was, not surprisingly, a triumph, as was her subsequent role as leading lady in *The Hornet*. Her friend Emily recorded these successes; she also gave Ella full credit for *Lessons in Harmony*, the play that Emily's "clever little company" performed in 1875.

Emily established a close relationship with William Hunter Kendal and Madge Kendal (née Robertson) in 1878. Having seen Mrs. Kendal perform at the Gaiety, she published a feature article on her in the August issue of the *Victoria Magazine*. Later that year Emily, the Kendals, and Kate Pattison took part in a dramatic "entertainment" in aid of Dramatic Reform. The following year Mrs. Kendal, Genevieve Ward, and Emily all agreed to serve on the original committee of the Church and Stage Guild founded by Reverend Stewart Headlam,[21] a radical Church of England clergyman who had been a mainstay of the Victoria Discussion Society in the early 1870's. This Guild was closely associated with the Dramatic Reform Association revived by Emily and the Kendals in 1878, for the hallmarks of both groups were respectability and morality. So we may safely assume that because of their mutual interest in these projects, Emily kept in touch with the Kendals, especially Mrs. Kendal.[22]

Emily's close acquaintance with the theatre and her careful reading of Shakespeare's plays — she prided herself on being a student of Shakespeare[23] — emboldened her to become an "occasional" drama critic, especially when Shakespeare plays were at issue. For instance, referring to Henry Irving's role as Macbeth at the Lyceum Theatre in 1875 she stated: "Certainly, Mr. Irving has not, as Macbeth, equalled his Hamlet. Hamlet, indeed, is a character eminently suited to the talents of the artist; the mixture of thoughtfulness, tenderness, and strange humour . . . find entire sympathy in Irving. . . . Yet, if inferior to his impersonation of Hamlet, Irving's Macbeth is still a masterly rendering of a character which, appealing not to our sympathies but to the intellectual side of our nature, makes, so far, greater claims upon the artist, who cannot trust anything to the impulses of his audience . . ." (*W & W*, 12/18/75, 3). In 1878 she again commented on the performance of Shakespeare plays, this time *A Winter's Tale* and *Antony and Cleopatra* at the Drury Lane Theatre, but she avoided further critical sorties into Shakespeare. As for contemporary plays, she eschewed detailed criticism, for she admitted that, though she was usually a "hardened critic," she tended to succumb to touching impersonations of characters like Jo in *Bleak House* and Sydney Grundy in *Deep Waters* (*LP*, 8/29/85, 183 and 9/28/89, 406).

So much for Emily's publicizing of cultural events. Now let us consider her more active contributions to culture as elocutionist, dramatic reader, and actress. As she stated in 1873, her interest in elocution as a prologue to cultural activity was fanned into flame by Frances Anne Kemble's recital of Shakespeare's *Midsummer Night's Dream* in Exeter Hall, circa 1855. Just how she improved on her natural ability to speak well and project her voice remains a mystery. It is sufficient to note that by 1860 she was reading the poetry of Christina Rossetti and other budding female poets at meetings of the Portfolio Club and by 1868 she was lecturing and giving dramatic readings to large crowds. Indeed, her elocutionary skills were universally praised from 1870 on; Alice Le Geyt, for example, regarded her as a model for members of the Victoria Discussion Society to emulate, "for few will deny that she has attained the art of reading and speaking to perfection" (*VM*, 12/71, 155), and others, newspaper reporters included, noted the "power and pathos and the wonderful strength and sweetness of her voice" (*LP*, 6/15/95, 887). In fact, these skills became so widely known that from 1871 to 1878 she was able to augment her earnings by giving elocution lessons to anyone who wished to take them, but particularly to ladies interested in home reading[24] or public speaking.[25]

Emily did not achieve fame as an elocution teacher, but her skills did help her to become a popular lecturer with an international reputation. One reason for this popularity was that dramatic readings usually accompanied her lectures. At the farewell soirée in London preceding her first visit to America, Miss Beedy stated that Emily was already known in the United States "as one of the favourite women speakers" in Britain (*VM*, 10/72, 521). Much of this reputation could be attributed to Alice Le Geyt's "Letter from England" column in *The Woman's Journal*, in which she was adjudged "so eminently qualified to give readings that the lectures will be rare treats to those who are fond of and appreciate good poetry and good elocution" (*The Woman's Journal*, 7/15/71, 219). Nevertheless, American readers of the *Victoria Magazine* — and there were many of them by 1872 — were able to draw the same conclusions as Alice and Miss Beedy. That British audiences were already well aware of her ability is demonstrated by the *York Herald*'s account of two of Emily's lectures during which she read "pathetic pieces" of poetry and gave "with excellent taste and judgment companion passages in poetic prose" from the Old Testament and from Dickens' *Dombey and Son* (*Woman*, 4/20/72, 271).

Usually she combined dramatic readings and lectures,[26] but sometimes she separated them. For instance, in July 1871 she read the "Execution of Montrose" to members of the Victoria Discussion Society; in York in April 1872 she gave a Poetic and Dramatic Reading in the afternoon and a lecture on "Prose Writing Poets" in the evening; at the All Saints' Readings during Easter 1875 she contributed an "extract from *Enoch Arden*" and a "fugitive piece" by Adelaide Procter (*W & W*, 4/10/75, 7); and in 1878 she served as both chairperson and reciter at the St. Mary's Penny Reading.

This separation of dramatic readings from lectures apparently inspired her to include acting in her repertoire. After all, Genevieve Ward, Isabel Bateman, Ella Dietz, Henry Irving, and Ellen Terry had all indulged in these monologues; lecturers and actors trod the same boards. In any event, Emily's readings culminated in dramatic performances in 1875. Early in that year she arranged a series of four music and dramatic recitals[27] at her home. At the first on April 20 she read Alexander Milne's "Jane Conquest" and Elizabeth Barrett Browning's poem "Loved Once," and a quartet of musicians[28] (piano, two violins, cello) played sonatas. For the next recital she intended to read Wordsworth's "Intimations of Immortality" and Procter's "A Comforter," but bronchitis laid her low; so the musicians bore the burden with selections from Mendelssohn, Raffe and Beethoven. Still unable to read well, she recruited Ella Dietz for the third session; she managed to get through "Lady Geraldine's Courtship," Ella read E.B. Browning's "Swan's Nest Among the Reeds," and the musicians did their bit. Completely recovered by June 1, Emily recited James Russell Lowell's "The Vision of Sir Launfal" and Tennyson's "The Lady of Shalott;" and the musicians played works by Raffe, Beethoven and Rubinstein.

These recitals were financial and artistic successes. So Emily decided to mount a Dramatic Performance in aid of her Industrial and Educational Bureau that involved her, Rutland Barrington, Ella Dietz, and Kate Pattison. Her plans for this benefit performance at the Bijou Theatre, St. George's Hall, included a dramatic reading of "Jane Conquest," two short plays — "Not a Bad Judge" and "A Regular Fix" — plus, as was mentioned earlier, a "comedietta adapted from a French play by Miss Ella Dietz" entitled "Lessons in Harmony," and several piano numbers by Amy Stewart. The actual performance substituted Mr. T.F. Dillon's imitations of popular actors for "A Regular Fix," but the rest went according to plan. Ella Dietz's "musical comedietta," with melodies by Ella to words by Swinburne, Tennyson, and Constable, was the hit of the evening (*VM*, 9/75, 946-7).

Emily followed up this triumph with presentations of the same program at the Egyptian Hall, Piccadilly, in July, and a brief provincial tour in August and September. Her "clever little company" put on two shows a day at the Egyptian Hall, and Emily broadened her readings to include American and British poets and prose writers. Otherwise, everything remained the same, except for Grace Greenwood's guest recitation of "Over the Hills to the Poor House" on opening night (*W & W*, 7/10/75, 5). The provincial tour, sans Amy Stewart, took in summer resorts and other towns in the North — Malvern, Matlock Bridge, Southport, Bowness, Ambleside, Ulverstone, Barrow-in-Furness, Fleetwood, Chester, and Derby. Reporting on the opening stages of the tour, *The Era* noted that Emily's reading of Arthur Matthison's "Coffin Ships" was "nightly received with great enthusiasm," that Dietz, Pattison, and Barrington showed "great capacity for acting and singing," and that Barrington's rendition of E.L. Blanchard's clever song "St. George and the Dragon," with which the program concluded, was "deservedly encored" (*The Era*, 8/28/75, rpt. in *W & W*, 9/4/75, 4). The *Derby Advertiser* praised the September 13 performance at the Corn Exchange in Derby, noting that Emily's readings "secured the breathless attention of a large and highly-appreciative audience," and that "admirable acting [in] 'Lessons in Harmony' — interspersed by much excellent singing — provoked uproarious mirth and laughter" (*Derby Advertiser*, rpt. in *W & W*, 9/25/75, 2).

Emily appeared in several other stage performances. Early in 1877 she appeared in an amateur musical and dramatic entertainment at the Gorton home of her friend Richard Peacock; her recitation of "Jane Conquest" "brought tears to the eyes of many in the audience," and her role as Lady Sowerly Creamly in a comic melodrama[29] evoked much laughter (*VM*, 3/77, 451). In November of that same year she took part in a Grand Concert and Evening Assembly to aid the Indian Famine Fund and gave two recitations. And in May 1878 she recited a poem by Miss Evelyn at a Grand Matineé Dramatique in aid of the Vicarage Fund of St. Michael and All Angels; in this instance, Henry Irving and other actors took their turns on stage. So professional actors and managers apparently regarded Emily as both an excellent dramatic reader and a talented amateur actress.

Thespians were also aware of her staunch defence of the theatre as a moral agency and her strong support of "high-class" drama. Even as late as the 1870's the British public considered both theatre and acting to be immoral. So Emily tried to change that attitude, first by observing the close connection between church and stage, and then by attempting to reform the dramatic presentations themselves. Throughout the 1870's and 1880's she cited clerics who regarded the stage as fundamentally moral. For instance, she printed a minister's comments on this issue in 1874, and in the following year she

published two articles, one by Reverend Robert Drummond entitled
"The Theatre, its Bearings on Morals and Religion," the other by
Kate Field on church and theatre. Two years later she quoted the
Chaplain of the Chapel Royal, Savoy, to the effect that "the children
of the [Chapel Royal School] and their parents were directly or
indirectly engaged in the service of the stage" and he "was glad to
report that, contrary to popular and inexperienced prejudice, he had
found the large majority of theatrical *employees* conspicuous for
steadiness, self-respect, and industry. He distinctly denied the
suspicion that all but those who filled the first or second ranks of
dramatic servants were necessarily deteriorated by their professional
occupations. He had found in them, as compared with other classes
of workers, the highest standard of integrity and morality worthy of
all praise and imitation"(*VM*, 8/77, 366). Emily was also pleased that
both Bishops of Manchester believed in the moral possibilities of the
theatre: "Like Bishop Fraser, our new Bishop [Moorhouse] believes
that the theatre may be made an influence for the elevation of the
people as well as a mere source of amusement" (*LP*, 6/19/86, 557).

She herself wrote an article entitled "The Church and the Stage"
in which, after referring to Bishop Fraser's appearance on the stage
of the Manchester Theatre Royal to extol theatre as potentially moral,
she strongly supported his point of view: "We have so often protested
in the pages of the Victoria, against the too common denunciation of
the stage as necessarily exercising a demoralising influence on
society . . . [The profession], though perilous . . . does not exclude
its followers from leading Christian lives" (*VM*, 2/77, 389). This
perception was reinforced by her articles on Mrs. Kendal and Kate
Pattison, both of whom were respectable ladies as well as excellent
actresses, which emphasized the idea that, as *The Era* phrased it, "a
lady of refinement [can combat] the prejudices of society and [win]
an honourable name by honourable means" (*The Era*, 10/13/78, 5).
Emily also observed in December 1883 how church and stage in
America were working together to bring about moderation in the
consumption of alcoholic beverages; thus the bigoted Puritan cry of
"Shut up the theatres, they are hotbeds of vice" was no longer
meaningful; co-operation between Church and Stage was the order of
the day (*LP*, 12/22/83, 391).

Yet the bigots maintained their stand; so Emily continued to
educate them. In answer to an anonymous 1887 pamphlet, "The
Theatre; or the Way to the Pit," she pointed out that "the writer of

this unfortunate pamphlet is evidently absolutely ignorant of the present condition of the stage," particularly of the "earnest Christian lives" led by actresses like Kate Bateman and Genevieve Ward (*LP*, 11/12/87, 499). She likewise deplored the bigotry of Archdeacon Lefroy of Warrington, who had proposed that all entertainments, even those for charitable purposes, be banned. And she strongly disagreed with the House of Commons's decision to ban children from work in the theatre, for she agreed with Mrs. Jeune that the stage training of children was "not injurious or demoralizing" (*LP*, 10/12/89, 489).

In the name of good, uplifting entertainment Emily also espoused a reform movement that would bring about a "literary revival" of the plays of Shakespeare, Ben Jonson, Marlowe, Massinger, Sheridan, Goldsmith, and others of that ilk. That is, she wanted a return to "classic" drama that did not pander to an overweening desire for spectacle or exaggerated acting. From 1874 to 1877 she remained assured that public opinion was in favour of this "legitimate" theatre. So she confined herself, for the most part, to praising theatres that offered this "high-class" entertainment, e.g., the Lyceum[30] for staging *Hamlet* and *Othello*; the Alexandra Palace for its performance of "standard English comedies" like *A School for Scandal, The Rivals, As You Like It,* and *She Stoops to Conquer* (*W & W*, 7/24/75); and the Theatre Royal in Manchester for its careful production of *A School for Scandal*. Yet she could not refrain from attacking the kinds of theatre she disliked, especially *opéra bouffe*[31] and burlesque. She considered *opéra bouffe* to be "burlesque at its worst" (*W & W*, 1/9/75) and queried, "When will public taste learn to condemn it?" (*W & W*, 9/19/74, 5). She also vowed she "would like to see burlesque as obsolete as bull-baiting" (*WLE*, 3/2/78, 101), and confessed that she "never delighted in pantomimes" (*LP*, 11/12/92, 745). As for variety or music hall shows, she recognized the need for "wholesome relaxation," but not at the expense of legitimate drama (*LP*, 2/28/91, 312 and 4/4/91, 530).

By 1878, having become less optimistic about the future of high-class drama,[32] she published an article entitled "Dramatic Reform" in the May issue of the *Victoria Magazine*. In it she revealed all her hopes and fears. Admitting that drama is what society makes it, she asked cultured people to educate public taste so that society would demand "classical plays in the majority." An educated public, she averred, would also want to "raise the standard of acting," "abolish the 'star' system," "utterly banish *opéra bouffe* and burlesque," and "make it worth the while of English authors to write original plays for the stage." High art and high morality go together, she contended, though that morality must not be doctrinaire. But "what we want [to do first]," she asserted, "is to destroy a system that puts a premium on immorality." Because buffo (*opéra bouffe*) and burlesque are "the diseased branches that spoil the tree," they must be chopped off. Legitimate melodrama and honest farce are acceptable, but high-class drama is the chief objective. In summary, she proposed that an Academy of Dramatic Art be established, thus putting "drama on an acknowledged equality with the sister arts of poetry and painting" (*VM*, 5/78, 1-8).

She also got directly involved with the Manchester Dramatic Reform Association in 1878. Early in the year she had merely approved of the appointment of several eminent and useful people — John Ruskin, Bishop Fraser, Hermann Vezin, and Mrs Kendal, in particular — to the executive of this newly founded Association. But by October she herself was organizing a Dramatic Entertainment in aid of the Association. This took place on November 26, 1878: Emily gave the opening address on women's work with special reference to education, Kate Pattison recited, Mr. and Mrs. Kendal presented dramatic readings, and so on. A "large and enthusiastic audience" contributed £70 to £75 (*LE*, 11/2/78 and 11/30/78). Thus Emily moved from concerned observer to active participant[33] within six months, and she apparently maintained her connection with this Association[34] for the rest of her life.

*Chapter 10*

# Writer: Novel and Travel Book

Like most journalists Emily longed to write a novel; like a handful of them she achieved her ambition. In fact, she wrote both a novel and a travel book and thus acquired a reputation, in her day at least, as an author.

The novel was entitled *Change Upon Change: A Love Story* in its 1868 English incarnation and *A Reed Shaken With the Wind* in its 1873 American revival. As the title page indicates, *Change Upon Change* was published by Emily Faithfull, Publisher in Ordinary to Her Majesty, Victoria Press, Princes Street, London; according to the page following, it was printed by her former business partner, W.W. Head, 83A Farringdon Street, E.C. (Office for the employment of women). The American edition, published by Adams, Victor & Co., New York, and "stereotyped at the Women's Printing House" in that city, contains more introductory pages than the British version. First, there is a page dedicating *A Reed Shaken With the Wind* to "my friend, LAURA CURTIS BULLARD, who received me on my first arrival in New York and who, together with her family and many of her noblest countrymen and women, gave me a pleasant experience of *Genuine American Hospitality*, which I shall ever remember with affectionate gratitude." Second, Emily saw fit to include a two-page Preface that spelled out the surface theme (or moral purpose) of the novel[1]:

This story is a simple analysis of one of the most dangerous phases of female character — a phase, alas! but too common in fashionable city life, on both sides of the Atlantic.

I have seen with my own eyes the curious combination of intellectual power and instability of purpose portrayed in Tiny Harewood [the novel's heroine]; I have watched with an aching heart the shifting weakness and faint struggles for redemption described in these pages; I have known women, equally and honestly critical of their own faults, who, while capable of assuming the philosophical and moral tone, occasionally adapted (sic) by my heroine, and displaying a cool acumen and penetration of ethical questions, like her, persistently 'the wrong pursued.' Gifted with physical and mental attractions, although conscious of higher and nobler aspirations, some appeared unable to resist the temptation of exercising their perilous love of power, and accordingly drifted hopelessly away into the shallows and quicksands of life, extinguishing God's light in the soul by the myriad *conventional* crimes which are under the shelter of social, but not within the pale of moral, laws.

If the delineation of the chameleon nature of my English heroine, and the gradual crucifixion of the higher purpose beneath the destroying influence of a frivolous butterfly existence, enables one American reader to detect in time

> "That little rift within the lute
> Which by and by will make the music mute,
> And gently spreading, slowly silence all — "

the publication of this tale will not be in vain.[2]

After the introductory pages — and allowing for a differing number of pages (411 in the English version and 286 in the American) — the text of *A Reed Shaken With the Wind* is identical with that of *Change Upon Change*. Both consist of thirty-five short chapters — some only three pages long — and each chapter is preceded by an apt quotation, following a pattern established in the introductory pages. For example, on the title page of *Change Upon Change* Emily quotes Owen Meredith: "Women have so many natures:/I think she loved me well with one," and, on that of *A Reed Shaken With the Wind*, these lines from Sir Walter Scott's *Marmion*: "The variable as the shade,/By the light quivering aspen made." In the opening pages of both versions she uses Henry Alford's verse,

> Whirling away
> Like leafs (sic) in the wind,
> Points of attachment,
> Left daily behind,
> Fixed to no principle,
> Fast to no friend,
> Such our fidelity,
> Where is the end?

Chapter 1, which deals with the separation of the lovers Wilfred and Tiny, is introduced by quotations from Swinburne and Browning, the latter from "Two in the Campagna" stressing "Infinite passion, and the pain/Of finite hearts that yearn." And Chapter 2 is similarly captioned by a line from Byron that accords well with Wilfred's attempt to find an intellectual basis for his strong emotions: "Is human love the growth of human will?" Thus the quotations[3] march in step with the developing plot.

Here is a brief summary of that plot. Wilfred Lane watches a steamer leave for France with his sweetheart, her mother, and two sisters aboard. In flashback we learn that at Lady Harewood's instigation and with Wilfred's compliance they are heading for Rome, ostensibly to test Tiny's and Wilfred's love but actually, in Lady Harewood's eyes at least, to prevent Tiny's marrying Wilfred, her cousin, because he is poor and therefore unsuitable. Tiny, an incorrigible flirt, has not confessed to Wilfred that she had previously fallen in love with a Captain Foy and was heartbroken when he got engaged to another woman. She recovered from her heartbreak when Wilfred got her interested in intellectual and artistic pursuits; subsequently they fell passionately in love. But Lady Harewood would not permit them to marry until their love had been tested by absence.

Wilfred is unhappy about letting Tiny take the trip to Rome, for he has misgivings about her incomplete development. But Tiny writes letters to him in which she insists that his love for her will bring her best self to the fore and put an end to her fickleness. Besides, she is learning so much about great art in Rome with the help of Ruskin's books on art and Robert Browning's poetry that she feels sure she is developing just the way Wilfred wants her to. At this point Wilfred is convinced that her love for him is not just physical but also spiritual and intellectual.[4] In the meantime, Tiny gets bored, somewhat depressed, and in need of change. So she persuades her mother to return home early; she hopes that Wilfred's physical presence and her marriage to him will keep her safe from undesirable flightiness.

The lovers' reunion is passionate, but they have to accede to Lady Harewood's wish for another year's grace before they marry, even though Wilfred has received a promotion and a higher salary. Wilfred admits to Tiny that he had a brief love affair when he was young, but she tells him nothing about Captain Foy. However, when they go on a cruise with Sir Anthony Claypole, a family friend, and

Foy appears, she confesses to Wilfred that she loves both him and Foy. Wilfred, unable to accept this "bigamous" situation, wants his ring back, but when Tiny assures him by letter from a friend's home that her life is bound up with his, he forgives her and sets out to join her. Meanwhile, Tiny flirts with Reginald Macnaghten, another guest at her friend's place. When Wilfred arrives, Reginald is jealous and rude. So Wilfred reproves Tiny for coquetry and, when he catches her flirting with Reginald again, leaves for London in disgust. Tiny is astonished at this "desertion" but Wilfred insists on her using her free will to resist temptation. She writes him that she is ashamed and he, still infatuated, thinks he perhaps was too hasty. But Tiny, restless and changeable again, has teased Reginald into proposing to her, given him a passionate kiss, and then rebuffed him.

When Wilfred arrives once more on the scene, she confesses that she craved excitement, but pledges her love to him. On the strength of that statement, Wilfred returns to London, buys a cottage and writes Tiny that he wants them to get married right away. Tiny is wild with joy, but shortly after, writing from Scotland where she is now visiting Lord Lothian and his family, she admits she has developed strong feelings for her host. Wilfred, heartbroken, finally realizes that Tiny is too unstable for him, and he breaks off their relationship.

There is little character development in the novel. Wilfred is too noble, too good. And he is too optimistic that his "ardent impulse for seeking the truth" (183-4) will inspire Tiny to do likewise. He knows that Tiny's "nature capable of change upon change" (70) could change for the worse as well as for the better, but right to the very end he assumes that the consummation he desires will occur. In other words, though he prides himself on his intellect, he acts according to his feelings. Tiny Harewood is flighty throughout. Her one virtue is that she recognizes this flightiness and sometimes fights against it. With Wilfred we approve of her attempts to bring out her best self — intellectually, artistically, spiritually. But we disapprove — and Victorian readers would disapprove even more than we — of the way she succumbs to errant emotions and of her irresponsible assumption that her lovers should accept her feckless flirting as part of her charming self. Above all, she does not develop as a character. The other characters — Lady Harewood, Tiny's two sisters, Sir Anthony Claypole, Captain Foy, the Wroughtons, and Reginald Macnaghten — are so undeveloped that they serve merely as foils to the two main characters. A bad-tempered mother, snobbish sisters, rude lovers — these are fairy-tale figures, not characters in a realistic novel.

Descriptions of the English setting are much too brief. But those of the Italian scene, particularly Rome as witnessed by Tiny Harewood, are unexpectedly complete and convincing. And the epistolary style of these passages makes Tiny (and, by reflection, Wilfred) seem much more alive than do the face-to-face encounters of the two lovers.

The language of the novel is generally acceptable, e.g., apt references to the "warm, subtle, and half-perverse nature of Tiny Harewood" (13) and to Lady Harewood who, "with all her apparent refinement . . . could sometimes say and do very rude things — so can everyone whose school of manners has not been an honest and true heart, but a smooth false world" (25). Sometimes Emily lapses into cliché and pathetic fallacy — "a fair young face," "a slight figure of a girl," the "cruel rapidity" of the departing ship, Wilfred's "generous unselfish character" and "high tone of mind." But overall she refrains from the exaggerated language common to second-rate Victorian novels.

The novel's surface theme so clearly stated in Emily's Preface to *A Reed Shaken With the Wind* appears to be a condemnation of Tiny Harewood's "frivolous butterfly existence" that gradually destroys her "higher purpose." But I detect a hidden moral in the evident sympathy (or pity) that the author sometimes extends to her heroine.[5] I believe her real purpose in writing this book was to air a major concern of hers, namely, the plight of unfortunate middle- and upper-class female "butterflies" of the Victorian period: women who were too poorly educated (morally and intellectually) to deal with the real world; idle, often pampered to the point of feeling useless; and able to exercise sexual, but not legal or political power. Given these deplorable conditions the obligation of holding fast to a "higher purpose" was bound to prove too difficult for many Victorian women. How urgent it was, therefore, that they should have access to meaningful education, training, and work — this is the underlying message of *Change Upon Change*, which was written less than four years after Emily disentangled herself from Mrs. Codrington, a living example of the wayward Victorian butterfly.

Even though *Change Upon Change* proved immediately popular — the second edition came out within a month of the first — reviewers noted more weaknesses than strengths in the novel. "A love story with a vengeance," said *The Queen's* reviewer — that is, "too much of the love, and not enough of the story" — and concluded that "love stories are not [Emily Faithfull's] forte." This reviewer also complained that "the young lady's [Tiny Harewood's] letters are full of accounts of scenery and towns, but we don't want them in a novel" (*The Queen*, 6/13/68, 473). Most modern readers would, I believe, agree with me that these accounts of Italian scenery, towns, and art works liven up what is otherwise a rather dull novel. But the dearth of story and character development are weaknesses every reader would note. Also, though some Victorians very likely approved of the obvious theme or moral purpose — the whole of chapter twenty-nine, for example, is a sermon on the power of ruling oneself, of soul controlling flesh — this preachiness is a clear weakness for today's readers. It no doubt deterred many Victorian readers as well, for unsold copies of the second edition were still on Victoria Press shelves in 1877 despite Emily's reprinting favourable reviews[6] in *Women and Work* and the *West London Express*.

Other journals referred to *Change Upon Change* in the 1880's and 1890's. An interviewer from *The World* stated that "many of her friends regret that the authoress of *Change Upon Change* could never be tempted to try another novel" (*The World*, 10/31/88, 6). And, citing Emily's "considerable literary talent," the writer of her obituary in *Woman* made specific reference to it: "I suppose few people know her novel, *Change Upon Change* . . . but it is a book full of originality and readableness" (*Woman*, 6/12/95, 5).

Emily herself had little to say to interviewers except that this novel was "my first and only effort in this direction" (*Women's Penny Paper*, 8/2/90, 481). She showed one reporter favourable notices of her travel book, but none of *Change Upon Change*. So by 1890 she seems to have accepted the fact that her novel, though it had some good points, was by and large a failed effort. Even the testimonial accompanying the Civil List [Literary] Pension she received in 1889 for "distinguished services as a writer and a worker on behalf of the education and employment of women" made no mention of *Change Upon Change*. Yet Queen Victoria and everyone else associated with that pension regarded *Three Visits to America* as both a valuable record of women's work in Britain and America and a stimulus to women's education and employment in both countries.

*Three Visits to America* was published by David Douglas of Edinburgh in October 1884 and was printed by four different printers in Edinburgh, London, Cambridge, and Glasgow. In addition, as a letter to Mr. Baynham and an item in *The Queen* indicate,[7] Emily had arranged for simultaneous publication in America.

Though, as she admitted in her Preface, this travel book was chiefly a compilation of the articles she had already submitted to the *Victoria Magazine, Lady's Pictorial, Pall Mall Gazette* and other English and American publications, she did add some "fresh records." More importantly, she refashioned these articles into a "bright, chatty, and amusing"[8] account of her impressions of Americans in major American cities, some of which she returned to seven or eight times over the period 1872 to 1884. She also deserves credit for piecing the book together in less than four months (May-August 1884). Working, as she says in *Three Visits*, "in the noise and smoke of London,"[9] she produced a smooth, unrepetitive record of her travels that apparently pleased everyone, even her critical self.

Most of the details about Emily's travels and her investigation of the "changed position of women" in America have already been presented. However, one group of Americans — the Mormons — requires further treatment. For Emily devoted a whole chapter[10] of *Three Visits* to these people, whom she visited in Salt Lake City in 1884 at the suggestion of several American newspapers, e.g., the *Chicago Inter-Ocean*, who thought she should explore the "inwardness" of this new religion because so many of its "victims" came from Britain.

During the first days of her stay in Utah Emily was treated with kindness and consideration, but she was keenly aware that the Mormon leaders (President John Taylor, in particular) and some of the women (e.g., Sister Eliza Snow) were trying to convert her to Mormonism. She even got calls from wives praising polygamy. On the other hand, a number of women offered "secret[11] testimony" of the "forced consent" that allowed their husbands to take extra wives. In this initial phase of her investigations Emily also noted that Mormons were generally thrifty and industrious, but most families were poor.

She soon realized that the "essential characteristic doctrine" of the Mormon religion was "that revelation is perpetual" (*Three Visits*, 185). From Joseph Smith, whose "convenient revelations" were set down in the *Book of Mormon*, through Brigham Young, who used his revelations to justify polygamy and "blood atonement" (*LP*, 9/6/84, 214), to the milder but still dogmatic John Taylor, these special instructions from God formed the basis of Mormon male tyranny. Girls in this society were brainwashed into believing that they had only two choices — "sin or polygamy" — and that "without a husband no woman can enter the kingdom of heaven" (*LP*, 8/30/84, 182). Thus husbands were empowered both to teach their wives "the law and will of God" and to serve as their only guarantee of eternal life (*Three Visits*, 157). To assist the cause of polygamy, courtships were made easy through entertainments designed to bring married men[12] and single girls together, e.g., dances, literary and choral unions, glee clubs, musical parties, and theatres (*LP*, 9/13/84, 230).

Emily's conclusion was that this iniquitous system of polygamy had resulted in the "hopeless degradation of Mormon women" (*Three Visits*, 152), for it reduced woman to an "inferior creature."[13] So, even though she hated "the employment of force and law against mistaken beliefs in religion and politics," she called on "those who have the interests of women at heart never [to] rest satisfied until they are freed from the worst sort of slavery the heart of man ever yet invented, and justified on biblical and religious grounds" (*Three Visits*, 197). In practice this meant lobbying the Congress of the United States to pass laws outlawing polygamy[14] (*Three Visits*, 199), for it was "full of danger to the well-being of the entire [American] Republic" (*Three Visits*, 190).

Reviews of *Three Visits* were uniformly laudatory. As *Manchester Faces and Places* noted in 1892 (p. 134), "a leading New York newspaper" said of the book that Emily Faithfull had "looked at us with a highly cultivated mind, and a shrewd but kindly nature . . . . [She is] an earnest, intelligent, and enthusiastic summariser of her impressions, recollections, and convictions." A Boston reviewer, similarly praising the writer more than the book, asserted, "No living woman has a warmer place in the affections of the American people" (rpt. in *The Women's Penny Paper*, 8/2/90, 481). The *Lady's Pictorial* called Emily "a large-minded woman" and favourably compared her impressions of America with those of Harriet Martineau and Mrs. Trollope (*LP*, 11/22/84, 478). And *The Queen* reporter, after recommending the parts of *Three Visits* that dealt with the opening up of jobs and higher education to American women, concluded by noting "many other points of similar interest in the book . . . much interesting information on the social status of American women at the present moment" (*The Queen*, 11/15/84, 530-31).

*Chapter 11*

# Conclusion

Although there is little information about Emily Faithfull as a private person, it is possible to assess her life's contribution in terms of the ideas, commitments, and experiences underlying her public achievements. For instance, three characteristics emerge from a consideration of her upbringing: first, a strong sense of responsibility for people less privileged than she; second, an urge to rebel against male figures of authority; and third, abundant energy with which to pursue her objectives. No wonder Bessie Parkes was impressed with but wary of this keen young recruit for the *English Woman's Journal*, carpet bag in hand and bursting with resolve to aid the cause of women.

Emily certainly worked hard for the *Journal*, SPEW, and the SSA during her first year and a half with the Langham Place ladies. But when she founded the Victoria Press in 1860 she undertook the greatest single task of her life. Within a few months this achievement established her reputation for providing jobs for women and proved that women were capable of managing business enterprises. Even the *Saturday Review*, usually critical of women working, applauded her initiative. And, in spite of financial difficulties and the vehement, at times vicious, opposition of the male printers' union, this publishing endeavour lasted twenty-one years — a monument to Emily's determination.

Her foray into journalism by launching the *Victoria Magazine* in 1863 was both a tribute to her ability to get financial backing[1] and further evidence of her confidence in undertaking new pursuits. That the *Victoria* was recognized in the late 1860's as internationally important to women attests to her success as its conductor. It also served as harbinger to Emily's other journalistic triumphs: *Women and Work, West London Express,* two columns in the *Lady's Pictorial,* and her travel book *Three Visits to America.*

Given her steady succession of victories from 1858 to 1864, Emily must initially have been devastated by the consequences of the Codrington divorce trial. Yet, traumatic as it was, this court case proved to be the most important event in her life. One can imagine her mixed emotions during and after the trial: angry with male authorities and burning to get even; guilty about the harm she had done to the women's movement[2] and wanting to make amends; utterly lacking in confidence but determined to regain it. Fortunately, this mixture turned out to be more positive than negative; tempered with commonsense and newly acquired prudence, it sustained her during a doldrums period and formed the basis for a fresh start.

She maintained a low profile from early 1865 to mid-1868, when she published her novel, *Change Upon Change,* in which one can discern an undertone of rebellion beneath surface adherence to conventional morality. This was the first evidence of her recovery. During the next four years new activities helped to exorcise Emily's bad memories of the Codrington fiasco. Most significant were her lectures on the condition of women. Her decision to serve as the first regular lecturer on women's rights in Britain was bold, for even in the 1860's women were ridiculed for daring to speak in public. Yet it was not a rash move; Emily was justifiably proud of her elocution-ary skills honed in the Portfolio Club and SSA Congresses.

To make sure everything went well at her first official public lecture in December 1868, she took personal charge of all arrange-ments. Venue: Hanover Square Rooms; no sponsors; no pre-arranged chairman — just Emily herself on stage. The lecture dealt with women's education and employment, but also with the female franchise, with Emily carefully introducing this last topic as general redress sought by her sex for evils to which they were subject. That is, she avoided the "strong-minded," agitated tone of most advocates of female suffrage; instead, she assumed an intelligent audience and got a thoughtful response. And she maintained this calm approach in subsequent lectures, with similar results. Thus she could congratulate herself concerning the impact of her lectures, even when the subjects dealt with were literature, the economy, Queen Victoria, the Mormons, and so on. Most importantly at this juncture, her self-confidence got a mighty boost from this activity, chiefly because of favourable — and immediate — feedback from the Press and her live audiences.

Another confidence-building enterprise was the Victoria Discussion Society. After a year's experience as lecturer, Emily concluded that women needed training if they were to speak knowledgeably in public. So she provided a friendly forum where they could air their ideas and convictions without fear of male derision. Indeed, Emily took full advantage of this situation herself: most of her outbursts concerning female suffrage occurred in the relative privacy of VDS meetings.

To exact a kind of revenge on male authorities for publicly debasing her in the Codrington divorce trial, she also exercised her renascent courage in selective attacks on men. Her strong criticism of William Wilfred Head, her partner in the Victoria Press for three years (1864-67) and purchaser of part of the company from her in 1867, is a case in point. In 1869 Head published a pamphlet containing inaccuracies about the origins of the Press. When Emily pointed out these mistakes in the correspondence section of the *Victoria Magazine*, Head made a tactical error: he wrote a letter to the editor of the *Victoria* (Emily) and demanded she print it. She complied, thus recording Head's complaints that Emily had taken too much credit for inaugurating the Press and making it a success, was idle much of the time (and thus left the hard work for him), and had wrongly claimed she sold the Press to him cheaply, whereas his purchase price was more than generous. She then proceeded to demolish his arguments in concise footnotes. Head emerged from this contretemps a victim where he had believed himself to be prosecutor.

Emily also publicized her litigious victories. In 1869 Reverend James Grant wrote a book entitled *The Religious Tendencies of the Times* in which he accused her of preaching atheism in Sunday Schools as a member of the Ladies' Secular Society. Emily, who affirmed her horror of atheism and denied any connection with the Ladies' Secular Society, brought a libel action against Grant "for the vindication of her character." She demanded that Grant publish a retraction "as widely as the libel itself had been published," and she agreed to drop the suit only after he promised not only to expunge the objectionable paragraph from every unsold copy of his book but also to retract it in journals that would reach those who had already read the libel (*Times*, 8/9/69, 11). Truly a *femme formidable*.

In 1874, James Coleman, a compositor who said Emily owed him two weeks' wages in lieu of notice, sued her for £3 12s. She conducted her own case and won it with the defence that Coleman was a "grass hand," not a regular employee, and had not done any work since being hired. The male business manager of the Victoria Press and two female compositors bore out the truth of her statements. And all proceedings were duly published in Emily Faithfull's *Women and Work* (*W & W*, 9/19/74, 5). She also sued Bernard Heldmann for not paying a printing bill in the amount of £7 8s. Heldmann, who had been ordered by the court in September 1877 to pay instalments of £1 per month, had failed to do so, and pleaded "infancy" (to an outburst of laughter concerning this "large infant"). The judge severely rebuked Heldmann and ordered him to pay the full sum. This time Emily published the item in her *West London Express* (*WLE*, 12/8/77, 149).

These carefully planned litigious sorties[3] call into question Arthur Munby's[4] assertion, after visiting the Victoria Press offices in 1871, that she was "irrepressible and inconsistent."[5] Most observers admired her practical, commonsensical, orderly approach to business. So Munby's comment may be largely discounted, though one should not rule out Emily's strong emotional reactions on occasion — Westwater rightly notes "something untameable" in her nature. After all, she was venting her anger when she sued these men. And, though she risked harsh criticism for daring to compete with male lawyers in a *public* court of law, she no doubt relished these feminine triumphs.

By early 1872 Emily's self-reliance appears to have been largely restored by these small revenges, her new activities, and increasing public recognition of her achievements. For in January of that year she had the audacity to ask Barbara Bodichon, who had been in Algeria during the Codrington divorce trial, for a letter of reference to Laura Curtis Bullard, a potential sponsor of Emily's upcoming visit to America. Barbara wrote Emily Davies about this request, and she answered as follows: "It *is* very vexing about E.F. but I don't see what we can do. You might explain to Mrs. Bullard that she is not a friend of yours. I should not like [to] make such an adroit manager of people our active enemy."[6] Emily Davies was clearly convinced that Emily Faithfull, "adroit manager of people," had recovered her earlier formidability. Duly warned, Barbara doubtless couched her letter of reference in terms generally favourable to Emily's objective.

Her three visits to America constitute the second most important influence of her life. In fact, these trips produced more obvious changes in Emily's personality than the Codrington divorce trial had done. For they enlarged both her outlook and her character, whereas, though the Codrington trial had severely tested her character, it had had little effect on her parochial view of the world. Admittedly, these American experiences were not all sweetness and light; painful bouts with asthma constantly demanded stoic endurance. But even these life-threatening attacks helped develop Emily's understanding of the needs of others, especially women and children. Her intimate friendships with Kate Pattison and Charlotte Robinson, both of whom accompanied her to America, exemplify this increased sensitivity. Emily's earlier relationships with women had lasted less than six years (allowing for the five years the Codringtons were stationed in Malta); the one with Kate lasted from 1869 to 1883, that with Charlotte from 1883 to 1895. Moreover, these latter friendships were much deeper than the earlier ones. During her 1882-3 visit to America, when Emily had no official companion, she arranged her itinerary to suit that of the theatrical company with which Kate was travelling. And Emily and Charlotte were apparently inseparable from their first encounter.

Emily's sisterly feelings for particular American women likewise illustrate this broadened perception of female friendship. Their generosity, hospitality, and frank appreciation of her talents struck a responsive chord in her. Also, her realization that American women in general suffered the same inequalities as British women made Emily more concerned than previously about the millions of badly treated women in both countries. Even her outspoken criticism of Americans and their political system is evidence of her empathy with women on both sides of the Atlantic.

After every visit to America, especially the first one, Emily's solicitude about suffering womankind manifested itself in heightened activity. For instance, her 1873 founding of the Industrial and Educational Bureau for Women was an important first step in changing public attitudes about the employment of women. That same year she worked with Emma Paterson in an attempt to get apathetic women to combine meaningfully in women's trade unions, co-operatives, and clubs. Two years later she got directly involved in creating jobs for women by persuading the Postmaster General to hire them in the General Post Office, and in 1889 she witnessed the fruits of her fifteen-year campaign to get a watchmaking factory — similar to the one in America that hired women — established in England. Influenced in part by American women's clubs, she also promoted jobs for women in artistic endeavours and tried to convince the British public that women needed culture as individuals and as rightful repositories of the nation's culture. She was especially interested in making the theatre a place where respectable lady actresses could work without stigma.

Emily's 1870's agitation for better housing for the poor and better sanitation in their dwellings is further evidence of her newfound concern for *all* struggling and distressed creatures, not just women. In the 1880's she directed this compassion toward animals and children, the most helpless members of our "civilized" society. Indeed, she became a strong proponent of three inter-related groups: the Society for the Prevention of Cruelty to Children, the Society for the Prevention of Cruelty to Animals, and the Church of England Waifs' and Strays' Society. At the time this last institution came into being she had this to say: the "Cry of 'Save the Children' must surely touch every womanly heart. It is terrible to think that there are thousands of helpless little ones in our large cities wandering almost uncared for, exposed to the inhuman brutality of those who surround them, and trained to vice as soon as they can speak" (*LP*, 5/26/88, 587). Homes, hospitals, boarding-out arrangements, emigration — all these options and more,[7] said Emily, had to be explored, for "as long as our children are practically uncared for, our gaols, reformatories, and workhouses will never lack inmates" (*LP*, 1/12/95, 64). In upholding these remedial measures she condemned such practices as baby farming, which was supposed to ensure that wet nurses — for payment — provided milk and tender loving care to babies whose mothers could not do so, but which often resulted in these infants being locked in cupboards or tied to bedposts; the flogging of non-paying children at board schools; the "horrifying and disgusting" perversion of flogging girls for a price (*LP*, 12/7/89, 825); the suffocation of infants by drunken mothers; and the murders committed by parents to collect child life insurance — not to mention the continued employment of six to eight-year olds (in rural areas, at least) as chimney sweeps and (throughout the country) as hawkers of every ware imaginable. The statistics concerning abused children, e.g., 1,026 cases affecting 2,895 children in the year 1894 in the Manchester district alone, provided ample warrant, Emily asserted, for widening the mandate of "the noblest [society] of them all, the Society for the Prevention of Cruelty to Children" (*LP*, 6/30/94, 1006). Furthermore, for Emily SPCC activity was clearly woman's work: "Surely never was there a work in which beyond all cavil women may find ample and unquestioned scope" (*LP*, 2/10/94, 200).

Looking back in 1893 on the improvement in children's welfare in Britain, Emily selected these matters for commendation: increased number of crèches; emigration to Canada, thanks to the efforts of Misses MacPherson and Rye; homes for crippled children; boarding-out of workhouse children; Princess Mary village homes; the Orphans' Association; the SPCC; and the County Holiday Fund. All the same, she continued to plead for womanly help in the never-ending struggle to protect helpless children.[8]

Emily's concern for animals was just as strong as that for children. After being attacked in 1894 for her criticism of hypocritical churchgoers who were more involved with profit and loss than with the welfare of children and animals, she defended her stand by quoting Ruskin to the effect that "the one Divine work is to do justice" to God's creatures (*LP*, 9/15/94, 436). She also cited the sermons of the Bishops of Manchester and other church worthies to support this point of view. More specifically, she targeted groups of people who consciously or inadvertently were cruel to animals. For instance, she backed the construction of drinking troughs for thirsty cattle being driven to market and strongly approved of the establishment of a Cattle Trough Association to ensure that brutal or thoughtless keepers allowed their cattle to drink at these watering holes. She also deplored the unthinking cruelty of boy drovers of sheep and cows and asserted that lessons in kindness to animals "would be far more practical and salutary [for these boys and for other children][9] than lessons respecting original sin and eternal punishment" (*LP*, 9/9/93, 365). As for cart horses,[10] she condemned the cruel "two-cart system" — which subjected a single horse to a double burden — that was still permitted in the outskirts of London and queried, "Why is not more humanity taught in our Board and Sunday Schools?" (*LP*, 6/9/94, 898). In similar vein she worried about the cruel treatment of riding horses, especially the "pernicious cruelty" (*W & W*, 4/3/75) of bearing reins tied nose to tail on fashionable ladies' horses, presumably for safety's sake (the safety of the lady, not the horse). In 1887, when this cruel custom had finally been outlawed, Emily observed that "It was my good fortune years ago to know Mr. [Edward Fordham] Flower, and to join in his crusade against sharp bits, bearing reins, and blinkers" (*LP*, 4/23/87, 425).

Because she had two dogs of her own, Emily also spoke out against mandatory muzzling of dogs, which she believed would be unnecessary if children were taught to be kinder to animals. And she deplored the dog poisonings apparently perpetrated by victims of the hydrophobia scare who had initiated the muzzling order. Yet she was not a doctrinaire animal lover; she did not oppose fox hunts[11] or the hunting of grouse and snipe. For her these sports did not involve the inhumane, wanton killing that the Society for the Protection of Birds rightly lamented when they condemned both the skinning alive of humming-birds to fashion aigrettes for ladies and the killing of birds for their plumage alone.

She had strong views about vivisection. In the mid-1870's she appears to have favoured controlled vivisection, though even then she proposed severe restrictions on scientists to prevent unnecessary suffering of animals, and she worried about the "pernicious moral effects" on the vivisectors: "Well may the supporters of the [Anti-Vivisection] society ask whether it is possible for men to practise such awful cruelties upon dumb brutes and yet remain sensitive to the sufferings of human beings" (*W & W*, 6/26/75, 5). From the late 'seventies, however, Emily was adamantly opposed to vivisection, as well as to casual treatment of pets[12] and blood sports using animals. Therefore, she frequently publicized the activities of the Anti-Vivisectionist Society, with special reference to Frances Power Cobbe, leader of the movement. And she praised the research of Drs. George and Frances Hoggan[13] on human muscles, for it had been conducted "without the infliction of the smallest pain even on the meanest of God's sensitive creatures" (*VM*, 3/77, 457).

The breadth of outlook due in large part to her American experiences mellowed many of Emily's other ideas and opinions as well. An interviewer's observation in 1878 that she was "free seemingly from the cramped prison of sectaries, political or theological"[14] is borne out by her balanced views about crime and punishment, temperance and teetotalism, marriage and divorce, equality of the sexes and the spiritual nature of women. With respect to violent crimes, she consistently favoured harsh punishment, opposing light sentences and even advocating flogging for women. She likewise dismissed the granting of mercy to youthful murderers as "weak sentimentalism" (*W & W*, 7/31/75, 5). Yet, she later stated, "nothing will ever reconcile me to capital punishment" (*LP*, 8/17/89, 239). For her a criminal had to be made a *living* example of the cause-and-effect relationship between crime and punishment.

After 1875 she also deplored the "intemperate zeal" of women's temperance crusaders in Britain and the United States and denounced teetotalism as "a moral mistake. It goes upon the principle not of temperate use, but of entire abstinence, and the same principle would abolish many things besides alcohol, because many things — good in themselves — are abused by certain numbers of people. We are second to none in our horror of drunkenness . . . but the assumption that the glass of wine, or the glass of beer at dinner, must inevitably end in the most odious of vices, is not only monstrous in itself, but is disputed by actual fact" (*W & W*, 6/19/75, 4). Emily admired the "faith and determination" of Lady Henry Somerset, head of the British Women's Temperance Association, especially in 1893 when she and Frances Willard, president of the Women's Christian Temperance Union in the U.S.A., undertook a world tour to collect signatures to a temperance petition, but she could not agree with their idea that drunkenness could be prevented through prohibitive law[15] rather than persuasive reason. She appreciated receiving a letter from Frances Willard pointing out that the temperance movement was but one branch of the women's work she was involved in, and she enjoyed being interviewed by Miss Willard in 1894 for the *Woman's Signal*, a paper edited by Lady Somerset. Still, she could not entertain the "monstrous" teetotalism of the WCTU.

Nevertheless, as she was very concerned about drunkenness, she set forth her remedies for this disease at every opportunity. Most were preventive measures, though she did support Lady Somerset's 1894 proposal that habitual drunkards be cared for in institutions. Emily particularly liked the idea of an industrial farm for inebriate women where the patients could undertake "outdoor activities" such as "fruit growing, poultry farming, gardening, bee keeping and butter making — as well as cookery, dressmaking, embroidery, and lace-making" (*LP*, 5/26/94, 712).

She believed the best means of preventing drunkenness were occupational and recreational therapy. Provide more sources of public amusement, she suggested — on Sundays as well as weekdays. Open up "well-organized and cheerful coffee houses" to rival the "gin palaces;" after all, "the reformer's true wisdom lies in offering something which shall compete in the open market with such seductive pleasures . . . [as] drinking, gambling, debasing spectacles, and cruel sports" (*Three Visits*, 95). Encourage dancing in Girls' Clubs, for dancing is "innocent recreation," not the "promiscuous" activity that the Temperance Union and the "Scotch (sic) Free Kirk" have labelled it. Cultivate a greater taste for music, pictures, and books among the working-class, for literature and the fine arts are "the great civilisers of the world" (*W & W*, 8/21/75, 5). On Sunday, in addition to the churches, public houses, and coffee houses, open up the art galleries, museums, libraries, and public parks; arrange for Sunday concerts in the Parks, encourage cycling and outdoor games, and provide toys for children and newspapers for adults.

Next, reduce the number of public houses, but do not abolish them or close them on Sundays, for that would amount to having one law for the rich, who have easy access to alcohol, and another law for the deprived poor. In the interests of educating the children, she continued, do not show drunkenness on the stage as something comical. And, if there must be temperance "missions," make them educational and persuasive, not condemnatory, and send them out to enlighten *all* classes of society, for drunkenness is no respecter of caste. Finally, encourage women to be better cooks: "those interested in the temperance cause should never forget that a good nourishing diet keeps many a man from dyspepsia and the undue use of stimulants" (*LP*, 9/10/92, 358).

Emily considered marriage to be both woman's finest destiny and society's strongest pillar. She was not in favour of any legislation that tended to loosen the tie of wedlock; citing the "loose" laws of the U.S.A. that permitted easy divorce, she "hoped that what saps at the very foundation of home life will not spread in our own country, but the laws should certainly be made equal for both men and women" (*LP*, 1/27/94, 108). If a marriage had to be dissolved, she believed legal separation was "the only remedy for the wrongs husbands and wives may suffer at each others' (sic) hands" (*LE*, 12/7/78, 364). She also suggested, though not too seriously, that adulterers be imprisoned. Prevention would, of course, be preferable to such a harsh "cure," Emily opined. Society should provide new opportunities for Victorian men and women to get to know one another before marriage. And, though a woman should not sacrifice "heart to money-bags," she should not enter into a strictly romantic marriage[16] that had a good chance of foundering "on the shoals of poverty" (*LP*, 7/23/92, 117).

During the 1870's Emily also managed to accommodate two apparently incompatible beliefs: equality of the sexes and the Victorian idea that woman is by nature spiritual, religious, and domestic. With reference to the latter, she insisted that women retain these qualities no matter what rôles they might play outside the home. She contended too that women should make themselves inconspicuous in public unless the course they pursued was clearly devoid of scandal or ridicule.[17] Thus she deplored the actions of a Mrs. Pearce, who sued a skin specialist for extortion and in so doing placed "herself in the pillory" (*WLE*, 2/23/78, 91) of public opinion for being so weak and credulous as to trust the man. For the same reason she disapproved of "Miss [Sophia] Jex-Blake, who became so notorious during her career as a medical student at Edinburgh" (*WLE*, 3/9/78, 113) and of a "Lady Champion Walker" who walked 1500 miles in 1000 hours, a feat which Emily found "repulsive. . . . [It] shocks all one's ideas of the refinement which should belong to the female sex" (*WLE*, 5/25/78, 245). Likewise, though she admired the "courage" of female mountain climbers and their "desire to explore regions monopolized by men," she criticized a team of women who climbed the Matterhorn in poor weather for undertaking "hazardous and useless exploits" (*LP*, 7/30/92, 169) that brought them (and women in general) into disrepute. Emily also believed women should play only those musical instruments "calculated to display [their lips] to advantage" (*LP*, 6/20/85, 588) and should not make themselves conspicuous by using cosmetics. Apropos of this last point, she noted that women in the "fast society" of 1883 Philadelphia left themselves open to criticism by wearing heavy makeup and brightly coloured dresses suited to negroes but not "true-born" Americans (*LP*, 12/29/83, 407).

Emily's acceptance of these Victorian conventions was, however, offset by her insistence on the equality of men and women[18] and the need for women to attain, assert, and exercise their independence. Her argument that men and women were equal was based on her interpretations of the Bible and John Ruskin's essays, particularly *Of Queen's Gardens*. In the *Victoria Magazine* she averred that the Bible "teaches us that the promises to the two sexes of the life that now is and that which is to come are equal, their hopes identical, that each has to play its own part in the advancement of the truth which is so vital to both, each to be a helpmeet for the other, that 'neither is the man without the woman, nor the woman without the man'" and therefore there should be "honest cooperation of both in all that pertains to the highest interests of humanity" (*VM*, 2/72, 398). She credited Ruskin with noting the characteristic differences of men and women (wherein neither sex was superior) and she called for "absolute freedom of action"[19] for both sexes in pursuing the interests of humanity (*LP*, 4/2/92, 505). Anticipating a rejoinder that Ruskin attributed heart and emotions to women and head and intelligence to men, Emily added a proviso that it is dangerous to draw arbitrary lines of distinction between masculine and feminine characteristics. She concluded from this that men and women should work side by side as equal partners and was delighted when the Church of England put her theory into practice by having the men and women deliberate together at their Church Congress in Manchester in August, 1888: "As a rule I do not care for separate meetings; much more good is done when men and women think and act together" (*LP*, 9/1/88, 223). Again, as a strong advocate of mixed clubs for men and women, she observed that the evident success of the Manchester Social Club by 1893 had fully justified the brave act of opening it to both sexes two years earlier. Above all, she celebrated the fact that the "wisest and best men" welcomed the advance of women (*LP*, 1/5/89, 14).

Emily included matters other than mixed meetings, training and employment under the heading "independence for women." First, she felt that girls should be encouraged to be tom-boys. For the sake of their health (mental and physical) they should be permitted at girls' schools to play cricket, go boating, play football (with some modifications to the game played by boys), and take part in all games requiring "running, jumping, and free exercise of the limbs" (*W & W*, 2/19/76, 4). They should not be confined, as they usually were, to such "ladylike" games as croquet and *la grace*. Second, women should begin thinking for themselves and doing things that up to now they had expected men to do for them. In 1875 Emily was pleased that Mlle. Tietjens, a famous opera singer, had laid the first brick of a new opera house, but she regretted that she got a man to respond to the toast to her health instead of undertaking that task herself.

She also proposed that women read newspapers, take part in discussion of public matters, and get involved in public affairs — all highly unconventional ideas. But she was even more radical in suggesting that they rebel against the dictates of fashion. As one might expect, she was denounced for making the following commonsense observations concerning women's dress: a crinoline "cage" could prove embarrassing in a high wind or when sitting down; high-heeled boots are "frightful engines of deformity" (*WLE*, 3/16/78, 104); décolleté dresses are unsuitable in cold drawing rooms and draughty opera houses; "tight-lacing is a flagrant abuse" of a woman's body (*LP*, 9/28/89, 394), and stays should be abolished; and a walking skirt should be several inches off the ground, not dragging in the mud. Furthermore, though she insisted she was not a dress reformer, Emily consistently opposed the fashion-mongers themselves, with such statements as "woman is the slave of a crushing, grinding, paralysing, morally annihilating despotism" (*WLE*, 9/28/78, 201) and "[she is] sacrificed to the Moloch of personal adornment, doomed to long tresses and long trains, and compelled to give up all comfort and individuality in order to avoid that deadly sin of not being in the fashion" (*LP*, 1/7/88, 18).

In 1878 she made the extremely radical suggestion that young, unmarried girls not be chaperoned; but after visiting America in the 1880's and observing the behaviour of unchaperoned American girls, she modified her initial stance by recommending a "happy medium course" between the "prudish barriers" in Britain (i.e., close chaperoning) and the "freedom which can easily be distorted into licence" in the U.S.A. (*Three Visits*, 321). Still, as if to say, "I would like to be unconventional more often concerning the position of women," Emily occasionally applauded sheer rebellion, though she took care to keep her own actions within bounds — after the Codrington divorce case, at least. For example, she expressed her admiration of Dr. Mary E. Walker of Washington, D.C., who insisted on wearing male attire and claiming a salary for doing nothing for two years, in accord with her male boss's decision to give her nothing to do after he was forced to hire her: "Well done, Dr. Mary E! There is something truly sublime in such impudence" (*WLE*, 1/5/78, 4).

Though greatly influenced by her visits to America, Emily did not accept the American version of democracy. Her political convictions did shift from small "l" liberal to small "c" conservative, and ultimately to large "C" Conservative because of her strong Unionist views. Yet she preferred to identify with Queen Victoria's dual role as sovereign and mother in her search for a political model[20] for herself and women in general. With the Queen[21] in mind, she expressed her conviction that "the purification of society must be wrought out by individual example and individual efforts to maintain the highest ideal." Therefore, Emily did not approve of "vehement denunciations" (*LP*, 8/20/92, 260) of society,[22] and she was not generally in favour of political agitation. To illustrate how the latter could result in undesirable animosity, she cited Mrs. Emmeline Pankhurst's outspoken condemnation of the Boards of Guardians for serving the ratepayers instead of the poor. The resulting uproar defeated (or at least nullified) Mrs. Pankhurst's purpose, Emily contended, for "the rancour excited was keen and perhaps it would have been best avoided" (*LP*, 3/16/95, 372). Emily believed in dealing with important issues and she was willing to work hard to bring about reform, but she preferred to set an example rather than demand immediate remedy. As she stated in the same context as her comment on Mrs. Pankhurst, "it is always the women who are at work [in the cause of women] who are so different from the women who simply agitate" (*LP*, 3/9/95, 322).

In 1891 Emily Faithfull said she was satisfied with the part she had played in changing public attitudes concerning women's place in the scheme of things. She could also take pride in being personally responsible for a number of significant achievements, especially the Victoria Press, her many journalistic endeavours, her public lectures, the Victoria Discussion Society, the Industrial and Educational Bureau for Women, and her leading role in getting women admitted to universities. Having undertaken most of these tasks in response to the challenges of the Codrington divorce trial and her American experiences, she had proved herself "most noble"[23] with or without the "unforeseen grace of God" that Bessie Parkes had worried about in 1862. Indeed, the "particular screw loose"[24] that Bessie detected in Emily had been well and truly tightened.

# NOTES

## Chapter One

1. Deborah Gorham, *The Victorian Girl and the Feminine Ideal,* London: Croom Helm, c1982, p. 5.
2. *Ibid.*
3. Constance L. Maynard, "From Early Victorian Schoolroom to University: Some Personal Experiences," *The Nineteenth Century and After,* November 1914, p.1068 — Even in 1914 Maynard, though a Girton College graduate and a women's rights' advocate, agreed with John Ruskin concerning the noble, pure ideal of woman and the educator's responsibility to keep "the treasure unblemished."
4. John Ruskin, "Of Queen's Gardens," in *Sesame and Lilies,* London: George Allen, 1890 — Ruskin opined that the knowledge women received should be related to feeling and judging (i.e., be moral, not intellectual).
5. Sir William Blackstone's comments concerning women (in his *Commentaries on the English Law*) still applied in the 1850's, i.e.,wives were classed with minors and idiots and "Property, liberty, earnings, even a wife's conscience, all belonged to her husband, as did the children she might bear." (Duncan Crow, *The Victorian Woman,* London: George Allen & Unwin Ltd., 1971, p.147.)
6. *Eliza Cook's Journal,* 9/25/52, 337.
7. M. Jeanne Peterson, "No Angels in the House: Victorian Myth and Paget Women," *American Historical Review* 89: June 1984, p.708.
8. Even in the 1850's women were "brought up to believe men were superior to them mentally, physically, and morally. Education, therefore, would be wasted on them, responsibility would overwhelm them, and work would make them ill"(Ray Strachey, *"The Cause": a Short History of the Women's Movement in Great Britain,* London: G. Bell & Sons, 1928, p.16.)
9. In the eighteenth century girls were taught cooking and housekeeping, but girls of the early Victorian period were sadly deficient in these domestic arts. Mistresses-to-be were not even schooled in the management of servants.

10. *English Journal of Education*, 8/1/59, 255-256.
11. *Saturday Review*, VI, 1858, 128-29.
12. There were over 500,000 more women than men, according to the 1851 census, over 800,000 more in 1861, and over 1,000,000 more in 1871.
13. Crow, p.63.
14. Dinah Craik, *A Woman's Thoughts About Women*, London: Hurst and Blackett, 1858, p.61.
15. *English Journal of Education*, 7/1/62, 238.
16. Most nineteenth- and twentieth-century women continued to pay more than lip service to this myth. Indeed, from 1870 to 1925 American and British women avoided blue collar jobs because they thought they were not strong enough, mentally and physically, to undertake them (Dorothy C. Wertz, "Social Science Attitudes Toward Women Workers 1870-1970," *International Journal of Women's Studies* 5:161-171, March-April 1982). And even in the 1970's female students were merely trickling into university engineering courses.
17. For more than half of her reign Queen Victoria also objected to the entry of women into medicine and other male preserves.
18. Novelist and playwright Aphra Behn (1640-1680); Mary Astell (1668-1731), who stressed education as a solution; the intellectual Bluestockings of the late eighteenth century, especially Lady Mary Wortley Montagu (1689-1762), a political journalist who preached woman's superiority over man; and Catherine Macaulay (1731-1791), author of *Letters on Education* and *A History of England* — all of these women (and others) constituted an early continuum of protest concerning women's rights. But most of them were effectively discredited by men. So their protests were either "disappeared" or rendered insignificant. In any case, they had little influence on those working for women's emancipation in Britain in the 1850's.
19. Crow, p.144.
20. But George Eliot, who cheered the "pioneers" from the sidelines, wrote an essay in 1855 entitled "Margaret Fuller and Mary Wollstone- craft," in which she noted the mutual concern of these two women with the "intellectual existence of women." In this essay Eliot took care to retain her own "reliability and respectability," but she also was determined to preserve the ideas of these unorthodox women concern- ing "the feminist tradition as it has existed in a male-dominated society." (Dale Spender, *Women of Ideas and What Men Have Done to Them*, London: Routledge and Kegan Paul, 1982, pp.173-176).
21. I have selected only a few of the precursors of the nineteenth-century British women's movement. For other important women (British and American) consult Dale Spender, *Women of Ideas*.

22. Spender, p.154.
23. The term "feminism," meaning "advocacy of the claims and rights of women," was not used until 1895 (*Shorter Oxford English Dictionary*, Third Edition, p.688).
24. *Eliza Cook's Journal*, 6/22/50, 115.
25. Ibid., 2/21/52, 271.
26. Ibid., 9/25/52, 338.
27. Ibid., 1/5/50, 145.
28. Ibid., 1/5/50, 147.
29. When Eliza Cook died in 1889, Emily Faithfull credited her with giving "impetus to the educational interests of her sex" through the publication of her journal (*LP*, 10/5/89, 43).
30. In America Elizabeth Cady Stanton and Lucretia Mott organized the Seneca Falls Convention of July 1848 to discuss social, civil, and religious rights of women; and in 1850 Lucy Stone presided over the first of twelve annual Women's Rights' Conventions. These conventions no doubt influenced the women's rights' advocates in Britain, but it is hard to measure that influence until the 1860's and 1870's.
31. In her article entitled "Women's Work, Official and Unofficial," *The National Review*, July 1887, Louisa Twining credits Florence Nightingale and Anna Jameson with getting the British women's movement started.
32. Clara Thomas, *Love and Work Enough: The Life of Anna Jameson*, London: Macdonald, 1967, p. 209.
33. Bessie Rayner (Parkes) Belloc, *In a Walled Garden*, London: Ward and Downey Ltd., 1895, p.67.
34. Thomas, p.157.
35. Anna Jameson, *Sisters of Charity and the Communion of Labour*, London: Longmans, Brown, Green, Longmans, and Roberts, 1859, pp. xxx-lii.
36. The Married Women's Property Committee included Elizabeth Barrett Browning, Harriet Martineau, Anna Jameson, Charlotte Cushman (an actress of note), Amelia Edwards (writer and, later, Egyptian archeologist), and Mary Howitt (friend of Anna Jameson and strong supporter of women's rights). So the appeal of the committee to intellectual and artistic women was compelling.
37. Sheila R. Herstein, *A Mid-Victorian Feminist, Barbara Leigh Smith Bodichon*, New Haven: Yale University Press, 1985, p.18.
38. Barbara Leigh Smith Bodichon, *Women and Work*, London: Bosworth and Harrison, 1857, pp.16-17. This pamphlet was first published in the February 7, 1857 issue of the *Waverley Journal* edited by Bessie Parkes.
39. Ibid., p.18.

40. Kathleen E. McCrone, "The NAPSS and the Advancement of Victorian Women," *Atlantis*, Fall 1982, p. 52. Quoted from *Transactions* of NAPSS, *EWJ*, viii, 59.
41. The later work of the Langham Place ladies will be dealt with in the chapters that pertain to them (e.g., emigration, employment, education, etc.). This introduction confines itself to the exploits of the group prior to Emily Faithfull's arrival in 1858.
42. Margaret Maison, "Insignificant Objects of Desire," *The Listener*, July 22, 1971, p.105.
43. George Eliot, *Letters*, Gordon S. Haight, ed., New Haven: Yale University Press, 1955, VII, 15.
44. Herstein, p.129. According to Gorham, pp. 103-4, "strong-minded" meant "overly learned" and hence "dogmatic, presumptuous, self-willed and arrogant, eccentric in dress and disagreeable in manner."
45. *Saturday Review*, 10/7/65, 459-60.
46. Martha Westwater, *The Wilson Sisters: A biographical study of upper middle-class Victorian life*, Athens,Ohio: Ohio University Press, 1984, p.1.
47. *Spectator*, 5/3/62, 490.
48. *The Alexandra Magazine and English Woman's Journal*, June 1864.
49. Ibid.


Chapter Two

1. Entitled *The Descendants of William Faithfull for Seven Generations* and privately printed for Reverend R.C. Faithfull in 1906 by C. Edwards, Printer, Peterborough, England. In 1983 Brian Faithfull of Lara, Victoria, Australia, updated this family tree to embrace ten generations.
2. A cleric was of good social standing in the eighteenth and nineteenth centuries—not at all the way it is now. In fact, it was generally understood that only gentlemen could undertake clerical studies.
3. Even the women maintained this dual interest in church and education. George's daughter Isabel married Bishop Francis Cramer Roberts, and another daughter, Evelyn, married Reverend Canon Cooper. Emily's sister, Maria, married the Rt. Rev. James Begg; another sister married a vicar; a cousin married Sir Monier Monier Williams, professor of Sanskrit at Oxford; and another of Emily Faithfull's sisters, Elizabeth, became a Sanskrit scholar.

4. Three Faithfull women—Eveline R. Faithfull, Una Maude Faithfull, and Lilian Mary Faithfull—graduated from Somerville College, Oxford in the 1880's and 1890's. The first received a certificate and the second a diploma, which was all Oxford would permit until 1920. Lilian, who also received a certificate, obtained a degree from Trinity College, Dublin, in 1889.

5. A number of biographical sources give sketchy and, in some cases, inaccurate information about Emily Faithfull, e.g., (1) Frances Hays, *Women of the Day*, Philadelphia: Lippincott, 1885. (2) G. Washington Moon, *Men and Women of the Time: A Dictionary of Contemporaries*, 13th Edition, London: George Rutledge and Sons Ltd., 1891. (3) John Foster Kirk, *A Supplement to Allibone's Critical Dictionary of English Literature and British and American Authors*, London: J.B. Lippincott Co., 1891. (4) *Manchester Faces and Places*, 1892. (5) *Chambers's Biographical Dictionary*, London, 1951 [1897]. (6) Joseph Adelman, *Famous Women*, New York: The Outlook Company, 1928. (7) *Encyclopedia Americana* (1937 Edition). (8) Frederic Boase, *Modern English Biography* (Supplement to Vol. II) London: Frank Cass & Co. Ltd., 1965. (9) Olive Banks, *The Biographical Dictionary of British Feminists, Vol. 1, 1800-1930*, New York: NYU Press, 1985.

6. Emily's favourite "permissible" author was Grace Aguilar, whose "wholesome" tales were "the most exciting" of her youth (*LP*, 11/3/88, 503).

7. Lady Morgan had written *Woman and Her Master* in 1840.

8. At the Codrington divorce trial, Emily said she had met Mrs. Codrington in 1854 while she (Emily) was staying with her married sister, Esther Faithfull Fleet, at Walmer, Kent.

9. "An Interview [with] Emily Faithfull," *Women's Penny Paper*, 8/2/90, 481.

10. *Parkes Papers at Girton College*, BRP V 86 and 87, Letters to BB 5 Jan and 30 Jan 59.

11. *Times*(?) 10/1/60—from Bessie Parkes's newspaper clippings at Girton College.

12. In her August 21 (1859 or 1860, but probably 1859) letter to Barbara Bodichon, Bessie refers to her "visiting Mr. Faithfull's at Headley" (*Parkes Papers*, BRP V, 158).

13. "BRP to BB, 8 Dec 61," *Parkes Papers*, BRP V 108/2.

14. "BRP to BB, Sept/62," *Parkes Papers*, BRP V 115/1.

15. The Portfolio Club, an all-female association, was founded in 1854. As Emily stated in 1895, she was made a member "at Miss Adelaide Proctor's (sic) suggestion as the reader of the poems sent by friends not present or who were too shy to read their own productions . . . For

the latter reason I had entrusted to me the one written by Christina Rossetti" (*LP*, 1/12/95, 64).

16. Robert Browning's letter to Isabella Blagden in January 1865 referring to the Codrington divorce case suggests this interpretation: "Mrs. Procter [Adelaide's mother] . . . told me of a lie she [Emily] had invented to interest Adelaide, about as pretty a specimen as I ever heard, though familiar with such sportings of the fancy." (Edward C. McAleer, ed., *Dearest Isa: Robert Browning's Letters to Isabella Blagden*, Austin: University of Texas, 1951, p. 204).

17. A month earlier Adelaide Procter had objected strongly to the suggestion that Bessie Parkes hand over the editorship of the *English Woman's Journal* to Emily Faithfull or someone close to her: "anything which throws the *E.W.J.* into E. Faithfull's power, which giving it to Isa Craig does, is a positively wrong & wicked thing" (*Parkes Papers*, BRP VIII 24, July 4 [1862]).

18. *Parkes Papers*, BRP VIII 26, Aug 7 [1862].

19. *Women and Education 1849-1921: The Papers of Emily Davies and Barbara Bodichon from Girton College, Cambridge*, Brighton, Sussex: Harvester Press Microform Publications Ltd., 1985, Reel 14, letter dated January 3, 1863.

20. Bessie Parkes admitted that as a Unitarian she could not "deal very well" with Church of England people like Emily Davies, Jane Crowe, Isa Craig, and Emily Faithfull. According to her, they had "no floors to their interior domains," that is, their systems of ethics were too weak to sustain their religious faith (*Parkes Papers*, BRP V, 121/2, letter to Barbara Bodichon, 1863). So Emily Faithfull was only one of Bessie's "bêtes noires," though she was the most notable in 1863.

21. Emily apparently held no grudge against Bessie for deserting her so quickly. She often referred to her as "one of the earliest and wisest workers" in the cause of women (*LP*, 10/11/90, 626), the one who more than any other "bore the heat and the burden" of those opposed to women working (*VM*, 7/74, 192). She also lauded Bessie as a pioneer in sanitary reform and praised both the content and style of her *Essays on Women's Work* (1865) and *Vignettes* (1866) (*VM* 6/65, 173 and 7/66, 374).

22. *Papers of Emily Davies and Barbara Bodichon*, pp. 337-8.

23. Isa Craig Knox's poem, "These Three" in a collection of poetry entitled *English Lyrics* that was reviewed in *VM*, 11/70, commemorated B.R. Parkes as "Love" or "Charity," A.A. Procter as "Faith," and Emily Faithfull as "Hope." Here is the stanza dealing with EF:

> My Hope is ruddy with the flush
> Though day had darken'd and the rush
> Of morning joy, that keeps its place

Of rain is on her face.
Her clear eyes look far, as bent
On shining futures gathering in;
Nought seems too high for her intent,
Too hard for her to win.

Apparently Isa wanted to publish something that did justice to Emily,
if only in verse. The other members of the Langham Place Circle held
their tongues.

24. Bessie Parkes stated in 1861 that Matilda Hays was also "morally
    unsettled" (*Parkes Papers*, BRP V, 108/2) and that Emily Faithfull
    was "not half so mad or tiresome" as Matilda (*Parkes Papers*, BRP V,
    115/1). But Robert Browning was much harsher concerning Matilda.
    In 1852 he described her relationship with Charlotte Cushman as that
    of two women making "vows of celibacy and of eternal attachment to
    each other—they live together, dress alike . . . it is a female marriage."
    (Edward C. McAleer, ed., *Dearest Isa: Robert Browning's Letters to
    Isabella Blagden*, Austin: University of Texas Press, 1951, p. 27, fn.
    12). So Matilda's reputation had apparently been "teetering on the
    edge of respectability" for at least twelve years prior to the Codrington
    divorce trial.

25. For details concerning this "intense friendship" see Westwater, *The
    Wilson Sisters*.

26. Their friendship cooled in 1868 when Emilie married Russell Barring-
    ton, but they remained on good terms. In 1893 Emily recommended
    Emilie's novel, *Lena's Picture*, as "a story of simple, unpretentious
    goodness and uncompromising sense of duty" (*LP*, 1/21/93, 103).

27. Sir William Hardman, *A Mid-Victorian Pepys: Letters and Memoirs
    of Sir William Hardman*, S.M. Ellis, ed., London: C. Palmer, c. 1923,
    p. 230.

28. The press referred to the sleeping arrangements as "curious," no doubt
    also implying a lesbian relationship. But I believe there was nothing
    more than a strong feeling of sisterliness between the two women.

29. On November 1, 1863 Admiral Codrington had his cabman tail his
    wife to Emily's home and afterwards to the residence of Colonel
    Anderson.

30. Martha Westwater sees Emily Faithfull's vacillation as mirroring "the
    aching confusion of a whole generation of Victorian women who had
    to face up to the changing demands being made on their sex. . . .
    [Emily] saw herself, on the one hand, as the young nineteen-year-old
    girl duped by a powerful female friend; and, on the other hand, as the
    twenty-nine-year-old spinster, staunch defender of the sanctity of the
    home" (Westwater, *The Wilson Sisters*, p. 120).

31. Mr. Few, Mrs. Codrington's lawyer, swore in court that on November 3 or 4, 1863 Emily Faithfull had called on him in his office, that he had "asked her in express terms whether the Admiral had had connexion with her, and her answer was in the affirmative" (*Times*, 11/21/64, 11). So Few's contention that Admiral Codrington had succeeded in committing rape went beyond Mrs. Codrington's story of attempted rape. Mr. Few was clearly pulling out all the stops!

32. The final judgment for costs occurred on June 30, 1866. So the divorce proceedings were in the news for almost three years.

33. Hardman, p. 227.

34. Hardman, p. 229.

35. McAleer, p. 204.

36. Hardman, p. 231. Lionel Robinson, a close friend of Hardman's, disagreed with him. He told him he had met Emily Faithfull "before now" and "was rather pleased than otherwise" (Ibid.).

37. Twentieth-century feminists must understand that when I use the word "ladies" in preference to "women" I am noting a distinction which Emily and her colleagues, even her American friends, were careful to observe. For they approved of a caste system wherein upper-middle class and upper class women were regarded as "untitled gentle-women"—hence "ladies." Emily likewise used the term "girls" not only to indicate nonage but also to make it clear that these budding women were not and would not become "ladies" unless birth entitled them to that condition.

38. The SSA apparently did not invite EF to any of their annual conferences from 1864 to 1868; nor did they ask her to present a paper during that period. However, she attended the 1869 conference; and she presented two papers at the 1870 conference—probably at her instigation, though her success with the Victoria Discussion Society (VDS) no doubt convinced the SSA Executive that she was once more a power to be reckoned with (*VM*, 11/70).

39. Jessie Boucherett also identified EF as the "private hands" that established the Victoria Press, but she depreciated EF's accomplishment by stating (not entirely accurately) that the women compositors at the VP merely set type, whereas those at the Women's Printing Society set type, composed, corrected in galley, proofread, and even did some of the heavy work. (Jessie Boucherett, "The Industrial Movement," in Theodore Stanton, ed., *The Woman Question in Europe*, London: G. Putnam's Sons, 1884, p.98).

40. When the Victoria Press began printing a few tracts in March 1860, Bessie Parkes wrote enthusiastically to Mme. Bodichon, " . . . so here are women in the trade at last! One dream of my life!" (*Parkes Papers*, BRP V 96/2).

41. Emily bequeathed these pictures of her mother, grandfather and grandmother, along with portraits of Queen Victoria and the Queen of Romania, to Charlotte Robinson. Again there is no mention of her father (*Last Will and Testament of Emily Faithfull*, Somerset House, London).
42. A year after their father died Emily and her sister Esther collaborated in publishing *38 Texts*. Designed and illuminated by Esther, this book celebrated "texts" most favoured by their father in his preaching. So Emily apparently continued to respect her father, whatever his attitude toward her had been.
43. In her *Lady's Pictorial* columns of 1887 and 1888, Emily said that she had in her library "several books of newspaper cuttings from the year 1858 and onwards" (*LP*, 11/12/87, 499) and "cherished volumes of autograph letters . . . from the men and women of 'light and leading' of this generation" (*LP*, 10/20/88, 438).
44. According to references in her journalistic columns and comments by Emily Davies and Bessie Parkes, Emily Faithfull lived in Taviton Street in Gordon Square from 1862 to 1864, and moved to lodgings in Belgravia (near Buckingham Palace) from mid-1864 to sometime in 1865 (i.e., during the Codrington divorce trial). Her address was 50 Norfolk Square, Hyde Park, from 1871 to 1880 (and perhaps from 1865 to 1871 as well). Then she bought a "bijou house" (*LP*, 8/15/85, 144) at 50 Bryanston Street, Hyde Park, in 1880 and lived there until her departure for America in 1882.
45. Bessie Parkes Belloc, *A Passing World*, London: Ward and Downey Ltd., 1897, pp.32-33.
46. Bessie Parkes had also avoided any clear reference to EF in her *Essays on Women's Work*, London: A. Strahan, 1865.
47. *A Handbook for Women Engaged in Social and Political Work*, Helen Blackburn, ed., Bristol: J.W. Arrowsmith, 1895 (Second Edition) listed EF in an obituary of women who had been leaders and pioneers during the reign of Queen Victoria, but it provided no details.
48. The *Englishwoman's Review* mentioned a few of EF's accomplishments, but more often than not this journal omitted her name when commenting on projects Emily was closely associated with, e.g., her Industrial and Educational Bureau for Women, the part she played in the Social Science Association, and her contributions to the *English Woman's Journal*.
49. Veva Karsland also managed to avoid any reference to EF in her book *Women and Their Work*, London: Sampson Low, 1891, though headings such as "Compositor," "Lecturer," and "Journalist" cried out for EF's name.
50. *National Review*, 7/97, 659-667.

51. London, 1912. Mrs. Fawcett also said nothing about EF in her reminiscences entitled *What I Remember*, London: Fisher Unwin, 1924 and her book entitled *Some Eminent Women of Our Time*, London: Macmillan, 1889.

52. Christopher Kent, "Image and Reality," in Martha Vicinus, ed., *A Widening Sphere: Changing Roles of Victorian Women*, Bloomington: Indiana University Press, c. 1977, p.106.

53. Despite Bessie Parkes's and Jessie Boucherett's assurances that EF established the Press as a private venture, the rumour that SPEW had founded and financed it took hold. Even Louisa Hubbard, editor of the annual *Englishwoman's Year Book and Directory*, was fooled. In her 1888 edition of this directory she gave SPEW the nod and stated that EF was merely the manager. As a result Edwin A. Pratt, *Pioneer Women in Victoria's Reign*, London: G. Newnes, 1897, perpetuated this false rumour, as did several twentieth-century writers (see endnote #61).

54. Lee Holcombe, *Victorian Ladies at Work (1850-1914)*, Hamden, CT: Archon Books, 1973.

55. Crow dismisses the Victoria Press, EF's greatest accomplishment, as but "another small development in the field of [women's] employment" (Crow, p.160).

56. Ibid.

57. William E. Fredeman, "Emily Faithfull and the Victoria Press: an experiment in sociological bibliography," *The Library*, XXIX (June 1974), 139-64.

58. James S. Stone, "More Light on Emily Faithfull and the Victoria Press," *The Library*, XXXIII (March 1978), 63-67 and James S. Stone, "Emily Faithfull" in *The Biographical Dictionary of Modern British Radicals*, Vol. 2, eds. N.J. Gossman and J.O Baylen, New York: Harvester Press, 1984.

59. Pauline Nestor, "A New Departure in Women's Publishing: *The English Woman's Journal* and the *Victoria Magazine*," *Victorian Periodicals Review*, XV (1982), 93-106.

60. Martha Westwater, *The Wilson Sisters: A Biographical Study of Upper Middle-Class Victorian Life*, Athens, Ohio: Ohio University Press, 1984 and Martha Westwater, "Victoria Magazine" in *British Literary Magazines 1837-1913*, Alvin Sullivan, ed., Westport, CT: Greenwood Press, 1984, pp.443-445.

61. Most twentieth-century writers have adopted the pattern set in EF's time. Some have ignored her achievements, e.g., Martha Vicinus, *Independent Women: Work and Community for Single Women 1850-1920*, Chicago: University of Chicago Press, 1985; Patricia Hollis, *Women in Public 1850-1900: Documents of the Victorian Women's*

*Movement*, London: George Allen and Unwin Ltd., 1979; Cynthia White, *Women's Magazines 1693-1928*, London: Michael Joseph, c. 1970; and Nancy Fix Anderson, *Women Against Women in Victorian England*, Bloomington: Indiana University Press, 1987.

Others have mentioned EF but have compounded the errors or omissions originally designed to disparage her contributions, e.g., the mistaken idea that EF did not establish and/or conduct the Victoria Press. Like Lee Holcombe, Josephine Kamm in her two books, *Hope Deferred: Girls' Education in English History*, London: Methuen & Co. Ltd., 1965 and *Rapiers and Battle Axes: The Women's Movement and its Aftermath*, London: George Allen & Unwin Ltd., 1966, credits SPEW with starting VP, though she notes that it was under the direction of Emily Faithfull, "a most capable enthusiast" (*Rapiers*, p.96). Harold Goldman, in his *Emma Paterson: She Led Woman into a Man's World*, London: Lawrence & Wishart, 1974, wrongly states that W.W. Head started and ran VP, with Emily acting only as "Proprietor." Dale Spender, in her *Women of Ideas and What Men Have Done to Them*, London: Routledge & Kegan Paul, 1982, gives Emily credit for starting VP but mistakenly asserts that Emma Paterson was involved in the planning stages of the Press. And Sir James Hammerton, *Emigrant Gentlewomen*, London: Croom Helm, c. 1979, contends Jessie Boucherett ran VP, with Emily merely helping her. Incidentally, Jessie Boucherett's deprecatory statement that Emma Paterson's women compositors in the Women's Printing Society carried out all the printing tasks whereas Emily Faithfull's women merely set type is reborn in Angela V. John, ed., *Unequal Opportunities: Women's Employment in England 1800-1918*, Oxford: Basil Blackwell, 1986.

Several writers give EF too much credit and thus err in another direction. Barbara Drake, *Women in Trade Unions*, London: George Allen & Unwin, c. 1920, is one of these. She wrongly claims that EF established printing societies in both Edinburgh and London and trained women compositors in both towns. And she errs again in crediting EF with hiring only women to staff her Press. The following writers follow Drake's lead in some or all details: Dame Anne Godwin, "Early Years in the Trade Unions," in Lucy Middleton, ed., *Women in the Labour Movement: The British Experience*, London: Croom Helm, 1977; Sheila Lewenhak, *Women and Trade Unions*, London: Ernest Benn Ltd., c. 1977; Susan Raven and Alison Weir, *Women in History*, London: Wiedenfeld & Nicolson, 1981; and Philippa Levine, *Feminist Lives in Victorian England*, Oxford: Basil Blackwell, 1990.

E.H. Behnken is another writer who seems to have bent over backwards to give EF her due. Not only does (s)he correctly identify her as founder and manager of VP and editor of the *Victoria Magazine*. She also mistakenly asserts that she was the editor of the *English Woman's Journal* (E.M. Behnken, "The Feminine Image in the *English Woman's Journal*," *Ball State University Forum*, 19: 71-75, Winter 1978). And Philippa Levine similarly errs in saying that EF was editor of the *Alexandra Magazine* (Philippa Levine, *Victorian Feminism 1850-1900*, Tallahassee: Florida State University Press, 1987, p. 89), as does Candida Lacey in crediting her with two novels instead of one (Candida Ann Lacey, *Barbara Leigh Smith Bodichon and the Langham Place Group*, New York: Routledge and Kegan Paul, 1987, p. 279).

Finally, a number of twentieth-century writers (in addition to biographical sources listed earlier) have very briefly but accurately noted some of EF's accomplishments. These are:

(1) Ray Strachey, *"The Cause": A Short History of the Women's Movement in Great Britain*, London: G. Bell & Sons, 1928.

(2) Janet Courtney, *The Women of My Time*, London: Lovat Dickson, 1934.

(3) Mary Agnes Hamilton, *Women at Work*, London: The Labour Book Service, 1941.

(4) Hester Burton, *Barbara Bodichon (1827-1891)*, London: John Murray, 1949.

(5) Clara Thomas, *Love and Work Enough: The Life of Anna Jameson*, London: Macdonald, 1967.

(6) Kathryn Taylor, *Generations of Denial*, New York: Times Change Press, c. 1971.

(7) E.M. Palmegiano, *Women and British Periodicals 1832-1867: A Bibliography*, New York: Garland Publishing, 1976.

(8) Patricia Branca, *Women in Europe Since 1750*, London: Croom Helm, 1978.

(9) Carol Bauer and Lawrence Ritt, *Free and Ennobled: Source Readings in the Development of Victorian Feminism*, New York: Pergamon Press, c. 1979.

(10) Edward Ellsworth, *Liberators of the Female Mind: The Shirreff Sisters*, London: Greenwood Press, c. 1979.

(11) Andrew Rosen, "Emily Davies and the Women's Movement 1862-67," *Journal of British Studies* 19:101-121, Fall 1979.

(12) Kathleen E. McCrone, "The National Association for the Promotion of Social Science and the Advancement of Victorian Women," *Atlantis* 8:1, 44-66, Fall 1982.

(13) Sheila Herstein, *A Mid-Victorian Feminist, Barbara Leigh Smith Bodichon*, New Haven: Yale University Press, 1985.

(14) Jane Rendall, *The Origins of Modern Feminism 1780-1860*, London, Macmillan, 1985.

(15) Barbara Kanner, *Women in English Social History 1800-1914* (a guide to research in three volumes), Vol. 2, New York: Garland Press, 1987.

(16) Jane Rendall, ed., *Equal or Different: Women's Politics 1800-1914*, Oxford: Basil Blackwell, 1987.

(17) Daphne Bennett, *Emily Davies and the Liberation of Women (1830-1921)*, London: A. Deutsch, 1990.

(18) Barbara Caine, *Victorian Feminists*, Oxford; Toronto: Oxford University Press, 1992.

(19) Mary Lyndon Shanley, *Feminism, Marriage and the Law in Victorian England, 1850-1895*, Princeton, N.J.: Princeton University Press, c1989.

(20) Eric Ratcliffe, *The Caxton of Her Age: The Career and Family Background of Emily Faithfull 1835-95*, Upton-Upon Severn, U.K.: Images Publishing (Malvern) Ltd., 1993.

62.  Kate Pattison was secretary of the Victoria Discussion Society throughout its existence. She also worked on the *Victoria Magazine* and she accompanied EF to America as her secretary in 1872-3. Kate made her professional début as an actress in 1877.

63.  Kate Hillard, whom Emily later described as "one of my oldest and most valued friends" (*Three Visits*, 21), gave the Sorosis women's club a glowing report of Miss Faithfull's character and abilities (*VM*, 1/73, 268) that apparently removed any lingering doubts Sorosis might have had about inviting her to America in 1872.

64.  Amelia Lewis was a teacher, public lecturer, novelist, and editor and conductor of *Woman*. Emily and she shared several activities in 1872: the Victoria Discussion Society, a Prison Congress, Amelia's public lecture on the art of teaching that Emily chaired (*VM*, 5/72), and a meeting of "the first trades union of women" (*Woman*, 5/18/72, 331). Amelia was much impressed by Emily's energy and capabilities, but their friendship does not appear to have outlived Emily's first visit to America.

65.  Emily Faithfull, "American Industries in Their Relation to Women," *VM*, 9/73 and 11/73, 417-32.

66.  She visited both Harvard and the University of Michigan during this first visit to America.

67.  More encouraging for Emily was her meeting with "General Lee, late Governor of Wyoming, under whose leadership woman's suffrage became a law in that State" (*VM*, 4/73, 542).

68.  "Half-an-hour with Miss Emily Faithfull," *North British Daily Mail*, 9/16/78, 4.

69. Emily did appreciate the Pullman cars, and on occasion she engaged a "small stateroom" for herself and Kate Pattison. But this luxury accommodation was expensive, and she still had to undergo the "misery of travelling at night," when the "dust of the beds [was] provocative of asthma." So they travelled by day as much as possible (*VM*, 3/73, 451-2).

70. Emily apparently became a favorite of the Moultons during this visit, for Francis Moulton, Louise's husband, led the praise of their English visitor at a farewell banquet aboard the *Oceanic* on May 9, 1873. Mrs. Moulton visited Emily in England in 1888.

71. Letter of presentation read by Mr. W.F. Wilder, dated May 5th, 1873 (*VM*, 7/73, 264).

72. In 1869 Jennie June Croly was president of the Sorosis Club, one of the first women's clubs in America. She no doubt had much to do with EF's being made an honorary vice-president of Sorosis in 1869. Mrs. Croly also contributed a column entitled "American Notes" to EF's journal *Women and Work* (*W & W*, 7/18/74, and ff.).

73. Grace Greenwood made EF's 1873 visit to Washington enjoyable. Grace was Sara Jane Clarke, author, in the early 1850's, became an editor after marrying the publisher L. Lippincott in 1853, and was later a journalist and actress. Like Emily, she suffered from asthma; therefore, she recommended that she take the Colorado "cure" that improved her health greatly, if only for a while. Emily thought Grace was the "wittiest woman in America" (*VM*, 6/73, 162).

74. Kate Field was a foreign correspondent for American papers in the late 1850's and she covered the Spanish Revolution of 1873. By the late 1860's she had become a public lecturer and one of the founders of Sorosis. In 1874 she tried acting, and in 1882 she founded the Co-operative Dress Association, but it failed despite her and EF's high hopes for it. Emily's visit to Salt Lake City in 1884 was inspired by Kate's earlier lecture tour among the Mormons.

75. Mrs. Stanton took EF to the home of the late Hon. Gerrit Smith for Christmas 1872. They met again in London just after Emily returned from America. Stanton and Anthony were considered so radical in England in 1883 that "even the officers of the suffrage societies did not dare sign the invitation" inviting people to a testimonial dinner in their honour. Yet EF and Grace Greenwood had no qualms about dining with them at Mrs. Mellon's London home (Stanton, Elizabeth Cady, Susan Brownell Anthony, Matilda Jocelyn Gage, and Ida Usted Harper, eds., *The History of Woman Suffrage*, Rochester, N.Y., 1881-1902, iii, 942 and iv, 353).

76. After meeting Dr. Sarah Hackett Stevenson, "one of the most agreeable women I know on either side of the Atlantic" (*LP*, 8/28/86,

167), in Chicago in 1872, Emily persuaded her to visit London and present a paper entitled "Physical Science as the True Key in Social Science" to the Victoria Discussion Society. She was able to repay Stevenson's Chicago hospitality in 1890 when the doctor visited Manchester hospitals while on her way to a medical congress in Berlin (*LP*, 8/2/90, 212). Sarah Stevenson was not only an eminent medical doctor; she also served as president of the Chicago Women's Club and she wrote an acclaimed medical book, *Boys and Girls in Biology*.

77.  In Boston a men's literary group, the Papyrus Club, also welcomed Emily at a festive dinner on their first "ladies' night" of the season (*LP*, 1/13/83, 26-7).

78.  In her article "A Clerical View of Woman's Sphere" (*VM*, 8/71, 355-58) Emily had strongly criticized clerics who asserted that sexual equality was counter to the word of God.

79.  The many references to "we" and "our" in Emily's "Across the Atlantic" columns of 1882-3 indicate that, whenever possible, Emily and Kate Pattison travelled together and stayed in the same hotels. But Kate appears to have been very busy with her theatrical activities; so most of the time Emily was on her own.

80.  Charlotte Robinson was the daughter of a well-known and well-to-do Yorkshire solicitor. She was educated at Queen's College and for a while resorted to the pleasures of society and a few unfocused philanthropic exercises (*Manchester Faces and Places*, 1892, 119-120). Emily does not tell us when she met Charlotte, but their friendship, the strongest and most enduring of Emily's life, apparently blossomed during the summer of 1883.

81.  Emily paid particular attention to an "ardent" follower of Whitman's who was "one of the most brilliant contributors" to the discussion, namely, Dr. Buck, head of the Canadian State Insane Asylum for Women (*LP*, 12/22/83, 391).

82.  Emily was impressed that "in seventeen years of most radical co-education not a whisper of scandal has disturbed the social life of the [Kansas State] university" (*LP*, 4/19/84, 367).

83.  "Life Among the Mormons" appeared weekly in the *Lady's Pictorial* from August 6 to September 20, 1884.

84.  Emily Faithfull was present in 1885 when a delegation asked Peacock to stand as Liberal candidate for Gorton, Openshaw, and Denton. He was admired by many Conservative supporters because he had established "gigantic [industrial] works" in the Gorton district, fought to get ladies employed in the machine drawing department of one of those huge foundries, and aided every movement concerned with the "educational interests and social progress" of people in the Manchester area (*LP*, 6/20/85, 588).

85. Emily and Charlotte Robinson probably shared an apartment in London from June to December 1884. For after their return from America and prior to their move to Manchester, Charlotte studied decorative art in London.

86. It appears that the Lord Chamberlain sent the letter of appointment to Emily, no doubt because Queen Victoria was aware of the part she had played as Charlotte's sponsor (*Fawcett Library Collection*, Vol. XVIII, December 14, 1887).

87. Shortly after I decided to write about Emily Faithfull, I asked her great-niece, Dorothy Faithfull, who was ten years old when Emily died, what she could remember about her grandmother's sister. "She loved smoking cigars and catching streetcars on the run," was her reply.

88. Emily Faithfull had known Lady Strangford (née Emily Beaufort) before her marriage. In fact, she recalled that Lord Strangford had proposed to Miss Beaufort over "her book of favourite characters, in which they were inscribing their preferences at my request" (*LP*, 4/2/87, 341). Lady Strangford later made her mark as an independent woman when she established hospitals and staffed them with English nurses to treat sick and wounded Bulgarians and Turks in their 1877 war and more sick and wounded soldiers in Egypt during the war between British soldiers and those of Arabi Pasha in 1882. For this latter mission of mercy Queen Victoria personally invested her with a Red Cross decoration.

89. The "dog" lounge was for Koko (fox terrier) and Gradel, "a much cherished dachshund" (*The World*, 10/31/88, 6).

90. That she suffered greatly from asthma-related illnesses in the winter of 1894-95 is evident from the more-than-occasional absence of one or both of her *Lady's Pictorial* columns during the three months preceding her death. Neither "Woman" nor "Northern Gossip" appeared on February 23 and May 25. And only the latter made its appearance in the issues of April 6, April 20, May 11, and—rather eerily—June 1, the day after Emily died.

91. One can only guess why her brother George (d. 1900) and sister Esther (d. 1902) were not at Emily's funeral. Her other sisters had died earlier: Mary in 1880, Elizabeth in 1891, and Maria in 1892; her other living brother, Henry, was in Australia.

Chapter Three

1.  On the twentieth anniversary of SPEW, Jessie Boucherett recalled
    Harriet Martineau's article entitled "Female Industry" in the *Edinburgh
    Review* (April 1859) that gave her the idea for a Society for Promoting
    the Employment of Women. Jessie said the first meeting of SPEW
    took place on June 19, 1859 and the Society was fully organized by
    November 1859 (*Englishwoman's Review*, 6/79, 289-297). A Society
    for the Employment of Women had been suggested in the *North
    British Review* of February 1857, and Eliza Cook had mooted the idea
    as far back as 1850. But Boucherett and the ladies of Langham Place
    gave substance to the proposal.

2.  An account of this meeting and subsequent developments appeared in
    the *English Woman's Journal*, 9/59, 54-60.

3.  Mrs. Jameson had advocated voluntary, mostly unpaid, jobs for women
    in hospitals, prisons, workhouses, and reformatories. But the chief
    concern of the SPEW committee was the promotion of remunerative
    employment for the increasing number of destitute or near-destitute
    middle-class women.

4.  Jessie Boucherett personally financed this Commercial School for Girls
    (SPEW) from 1860 to 1876 (*ER*, 5/15/76).

5.  Maria S. Rye, *Emigration of Educated Women*, London: Emily
    Faithfull and Co., Victoria Press, 1861, p. 3 (rpt. from *English
    Woman's Journal*).

6.  Emily Faithfull, Preface to *The Victoria Regia*, ed. Adelaide A.
    Procter, London: Printed and published by Emily Faithfull and Co.,
    Victoria Press, 1861, p.v.

7.  Bessie Parkes's 1859 SSA Conference paper, "The Market for
    Educated Female Labour" and Jessie Boucherett's "Industrial Employ-
    ment of Women" undoubtedly helped to convince male SSA members
    of the necessity for extending the field of women's employment in
    Britain. For both papers stressed the urgent need for action in a
    situation where there were fifty applicants for every governess position
    and where "three-fourths of the unmarried, two-thirds of the widowed,
    and one-seventh of the married women, were maintaining themselves
    by their labours, exclusive of those who, as wives, daughters, or
    sisters, were sharing in the industry of their relatives, attending to the
    counter, plying the needle or the pen" (Emily Faithfull, "On Some of
    the Drawbacks Connected with the Present Employment of Women,"
    London: Emily Faithfull and Co., Victoria Press, 1862, p.2 (rpt. of
    1862 SSA paper).

8.   According to EF, Anthony Ashley Cooper (1792-1885), Seventh Earl of Shaftesbury, exercised "a broad and comprehensive sympathy with every form of suffering" and therefore exerted himself mightily "in aid of some of the most progressive movements of the day." In supporting the women's movement he espoused higher education and advocated "fresh channels for the remunerative employment of women" (*LP*, 10/17/85, 336). He worked closely with or encouraged EF in almost every undertaking, e.g., SPEW, SSA, the Victoria Press (which he publicly praised in 1862), VDS, her deputation to the Home Secretary on behalf of Milliners and Dressmakers, and her "Modern Extravagance" lecture.

9.   *Manchester Faces and Places*, 133.

10.  Boucherett recalled a much larger committee of twenty-two. No doubt the committee of twelve was the working group, and the others — including such eminent people as the Bishops of London and Oxford, William Ewart Gladstone, and Sir Page Wood — were non-working members (*ER*, 6/79, 289-97).

11.  In an account of EF's Victoria Press the *Illustrated London News* credited EF with identifying the November 1859 committee as Lord Shaftesbury, Hon. A. Kinnaird, M.P., Mr. E. Ackroyd, Mr. Hastings, Mr. Horace Malin, Mr. W.S. Cookson, Mrs. Jameson, Miss Parkes, Miss A. Procter, Miss Boucherett, Miss Craig, and Miss Emily Faithfull (*ILN*, 11/30/61, 538).

12.  A contemporary report of the June 29, 1860 meeting of SPEW indicated that after G.W. Hastings read EF's paper on the Victoria Press to an invited audience of influential people, some of whom, it was hoped, would become customers of the Press, the whole assemblage was taken to a lower room where EF exhibited specimens of printing by her female compositors (*Friend of the People*, 7/7/60, 378).

13.  Hester Burton, *Barbara Bodichon*, London: John Murray, 1949, p. 113.

14.  Rev. Dr. James Begg, married to Emily Faithfull's sister Maria, was a charter member of the Edinburgh SPEW and served on its executive in 1862 (*EWJ*, 2/62). He also presented several papers at SSA Conferences in Edinburgh (1863) and Glasgow (1874). No doubt Emily got him interested in SPEW's objectives, and she may even have persuaded him to get involved in its activities.

15.  The Queen's Institute of Dublin (for the industrial training of women), a counterpart of Boucherett's training school, was established in 1863 to help the Dublin SPEW achieve its objectives. This Institute was in turn replaced in 1884 by the Irish Association for Promoting the Training and Employment of Women.

16.  Emily Faithfull and Bessie Parkes had already written letters to the *Times* in 1859 and 1860 to explain SPEW's objectives and invite any

interested women to call at the office of the *English Woman's Journal* for more information. (For EF's letters see *Times*, 11/12/59, 7 and 7/23/60, 9.)

17. In 1885 the women of Britain raised money for the construction of a drinking fountain in Embankment Park, London, in memory of Henry Fawcett, M.P., who had done so much for their cause. It still (1992) stands and is in good condition.

18. In 1878 Queen Victoria sent £50 "in answer to the late appeal for funds from the Society for the Employment of Women" (*W & W*, 2/78, 361).

19. The *EWJ* of July 1863 reported a meeting of SPEW in which Lord Shaftesbury lauded "Miss Faithfull's printing press" as an inspiration to the thousands of British women needing employment (*EWJ*, 7/63, 422). But *EWJ*'s successor took pains in November 1864 to divorce SPEW from Emily Faithfull and her Victoria Press (*Alexandra Magazine and the English Woman's Journal*, 11/64, 445-46). Sic transit gloria!

20. Jessie Boucherett, "Local Societies for Promoting Employment of Women," A Paper presented at the 1861 SSA Conference, *EWJ*, 12/61, 217.

21. SPEW opened type-writing offices in London in 1884 (*ER*, 10/15/84) and in Liverpool and Oxford in 1886 (*ER*, 5/15/86 and 11/15/86).

22. The best accounts of the Social Science Association (a.k.a. The National Association for the Promotion of Social Science) that I have found are the following:
    Kathleen E. McCrone, "The National Association for the Promotion of Social Science and the Advancement of Victorian Women," *Atlantis*, Vol. 8, No. 1, Fall 1982, pp. 44-66;
    and
    Frances Power Cobbe, "Social Science Congresses and Women's Part in Them," *Essays on the Pursuits of Women*, London: Emily Faithfull, 1863 (rpt. from *Macmillan's Magazine*, Vol. V, 12/61, 81-94).

23. Cobbe, "Social Science Congresses . . .," p. 2.

24. John Stuart Mill, a member of the General Committee of the SSA, took part in some discussions at SSA headquarters in 1864 (*Papers of Emily Davies and Barbara Bodichon*, Letter from Emily Davies to Barbara Bodichon 4/14/64), but he had declined office as President of the Social Economy Department of SSA in 1860, and he declined the chairmanship of the Ladies' Sanitary Association, a subsidiary of the SSA, in 1871. Evidently the SSA was too conservative for Mill's liking. In particular, the Association disapproved of female suffrage, whereas Mill was one of its chief advocates.

25. *Times* report on Emily Faithfull's paper "The Unfit Employments in which Women are now Engaged," SSA Congress October 1863, wherein the reporter observed that Emily Faithfull received loud applause for stating that women "did not want a social revolution, but a readjustment of social machinery" (*Times*, 10/15/63, 5).

26. The *Times* reporter also was not paying enough attention, for he incorrectly recorded the title of Emily Faithfull's paper as "The Useful Employments in which Women are now Engaged" (*Times*, 10/15/63, 5).

27. Isa Craig's appointment as Assistant Secretary of the SSA in 1857 was regarded by the women members as "the first major step toward women's participation in public policy" (Herstein, pp. 132-33).

28. As Bessie Parkes Belloc recalled in assessing the SSA, "for the first time in English history, a full opportunity was given to women to state their thoughts and contribute the results of their experience on subjects of social importance" (Belloc, *A Passing World*, pp. 17-18).

29. The SSA and the Society for Promoting the Amendment of the Law merged under the SSA banner in 1863 (*VM*, 12/63).

30. SSA's annual Congresses were attended by 1,500 to 2,000 people.

31. The last SSA Congress took place in 1884. But the Association was not officially disbanded until a motion to dissolve was passed at a special meeting in April 1886 (*The Queen*, 4/24/86, 455).

32. According to the records of the SSA Congresses provided in *Transactions*, the *English Woman's Journal*, and the *Victoria Magazine*, Emily Faithfull attended SSA congresses in spurts: all annual congresses from 1859 to 1863, three from 1869 to 1871, and one in 1875. The hiatuses from 1863 to 1869 and 1873 to 1875 can no doubt be accounted for by the snubbing she received during and after the Codrington divorce case. After 1875 she avoided the SSA congresses because she had decided they were no longer interesting.

33. Despite her apparent silence during the 1859 Congress sessions EF must have made the gentlemen of the SSA aware of her feelings about the need to train women for vocations other than teaching, for right after the congress they appointed her secretary of the SSA committee on the employment of women.

34. In her *Victoria Magazine* Emily speaks of the "scanty and depressed audiences" at this dull SSA congress at Brighton in 1875, and she recalls the early congresses replete with "clever and earnest lady speakers . . . . The association then coveted the presence of persons who are now directly snubbed, made to fear that they are not valued or required"(*VM*, 11/75, 92).

35. Emily Faithfull also read Jessie Boucherett's paper, "Local Societies for Promoting the Employment of Women" at the 1861 SSA Congress (*EWJ*, 9/61).

36. Five of Emily Faithfull's six SSA papers were published in the SSA's *Transactions of the National Association for the Promotion of Social Science*:
    (1)  "The Victoria Press" (*Transactions*, 1861)
    (2)  "Women Compositors" (*Transactions*, 1862)
    (3)  "On Some of the Drawbacks Connected with the Present Employment of Women" (*Transactions*, 1863)
    (4)  "Unfit Employments in Which Women are Now Engaged" (*Transactions*, (1864)
    (5)  "The Influence of Working Men's Clubs on Their Homes" (*Transactions*, 1871).

    Though a sixth paper, "Special Training of Women and the Consequences of the Want of It," was presented at the same Congress as the one on working men's clubs, it was not published in the *Transactions* or anywhere else.

    The first two papers listed above were also published in the *English Woman's Journal*; the third was published by the Victoria Press as a separate item; the fourth and fifth were published in the *Victoria Magazine*; and the sixth was cited in the *Victoria Magazine* (*VM*, 11/70).

37. These two papers are dealt with in detail in Chapter 4.
38. Emily Faithfull, "Drawbacks . . . ," p. 3.
39. Ibid., pp. 7-8.
40. Later (1886) she admitted that she had been wrong to exclude women totally from such objectionable work. For she noted that these pit-brow women were healthy and fit.
41. *Transactions*, p. 523.

Chapter Four

1. The letter reads:
    "Dear Miss Bethell
    I have been asked by a Mr. Aird who for some years has done much to aid me in introducing women into the printing business to bring the enclosed petition before Lord Westbury, and I venture to hope you will not think me very troublesome for doing so.

The petition tells its own tale . . .

> Ystruly
> Emily Faithfull"

The Fawcett librarian has appended this note to the letter:

> "Miss Bethell was a relation of Richard Bethell, 1st Lord Westbury, appointed Lord Chancellor in 1861"

(Fawcett Library, Vol. IIA, c.1862).

2. Anthony Trollope, *North America*, ed. Donald Smalley and Bradford A. Booth, 1958, p. 258, as quoted in Fredeman, op. cit., p. 139.

3. Derek Hudson, *Munby, Man of Two Worlds: the Life and Diaries of Arthur J. Munby 1828-1910*, London: J. Murray, 1972, p. 162.

4. In commenting on one printer's statement that intelligent workmen and printers did not disapprove of the introduction of women into the printing trade, Miss Thackeray stated, "I feel bound to add that I have seen exactly a contrary statement in another little pamphlet written by another member of the [printers'] society" (Miss Thackeray, *Toilers and Spinsters*, London: Smith and Elder, 1874, pp. 18-19).

5. Emily Faithfull's reference to George W. Hastings (1825-1917) in 1893 may well serve as a starting point for a footnote on him: "Mr. G.W. Hastings, the late M.P. for Worcester [1880-1892], and the mainspring in days gone by of the Social Science Association, [is] now unhappily undergoing the penalty of his misappropriation of trust-money [£20,000 to £30,000]. It seems difficult to believe that a man in his position could have been guilty of the breach of faith of which he was convicted, and equally extraordinary that after his successful escape he should have run the fatal risk of returning to England" (*LP*, 9/9/93, 360.)

Hastings served first as Secretary to the SSA (1857-68), then as President (1868-83). He was particularly helpful to the cause of women: hiring Isa Craig as Assistant Secretary of SSA in 1857, providing financial backing for the Victoria Press, serving as a member of the SSA Committee that affiliated with SPEW, and supporting (both in and out of Parliament) the long struggle to improve the education and the legal status of women. When Hastings was convicted of embezzlement in 1893, he was immediately expelled from the House of Commons. He lived out his last years in complete disgrace.

6. Queen Victoria waited until September 1860 to officially approve of the employment of women in printing and of the use of her name in the title of the Victoria Press. Here is a paragraph from the *Times*, as reprinted in the *English Woman's Journal*: "The Queen has graciously signified to Miss Emily Faithfull her approval of the establishment of the Victoria Press, at 9, Great Coram Street, for the employment of

7.       female compositors, adding, that all such useful and practical steps for the opening of new branches of industry to educated women must meet with Her Majesty's entire approbation" (*EWJ*, 9/60, 72).

7.       SPEW, by this time under the control of the SSA Committee for the Employment of Women, gave the Victoria Press its blessing, though it decided not to finance it beyond the premiums paid for its apprentices.

8.       In a letter to the editor of *EWJ*, H.W. Porter, a printer, advised EF to deal with the heated-type problem by having her compositors frequently cool their hands and arms in cold water. But he could offer no remedy for dust in their eyes (*EWJ*, 9/60, 69).

9.       That is, apprentices were "paid on an hourly basis according to productivity and the stage of their training" (Fredeman, p. 149). Presumably they got the same pay as the men when they reached the men's levels of skill.

10.     Matilda M. Hays' partnership was apparently of short duration, for it was never mentioned again. Nor did Matilda invest in the Press. Emily had to struggle on with limited finances until William Wilfred Head became a paying partner in 1864.

11.     No doubt his Radical beliefs prompted Austin Holyoake to accept this job; most printers would have shied away from it because their union strongly disapproved of women compositors. In 1868 Austin Holyoake carried this radicalism further by founding the Women's Printing Office "as a means of finding employment for educated ladies," thus rivalling Emily Faithfull's Victoria Press (Fredeman, p. 160).

12.     Emily said that she personally spent several weeks of "assiduous labour" to prove that the printing trade was suitable for women (Preface to *The Victoria Regia*, p. vii).

13.     Six months to a year appears to have been the length of the apprenticeship that EF favoured, a much shorter period than the seven-year apprenticeship required by the printers' union.

14.     W. Wilfred Head, *The Victoria Press: Its History and Vindication, with an account of the movement for the employment of females in printing*, London: Victoria Press, 1869. As I did not locate this pamphlet, I have relied on Fredeman, op.cit., for references to it.

15.     W.W. Head, Ibid., p. 10.

16.     These wages were good in comparison with those paid women in some jobs; e.g., governesses in 1874 got £20 (or less) per annum; sackmakers in 1875 received 2s a day for 15 hours work; and East-end London wages in 1889 for artificial flower makers, bookbinders, box makers, collar and cap makers, etc. averaged about 12s a week, with match-girls getting less than 7s a week (*LP*, 10/26/89, 566). And even in 1888 the average wage for unskilled women was 10s a week (*ER*,

4/15/88). Moreover, none of these women was fortunate enough to work only an eight-hour day for five days a week; ten hours a day for a six-day week appears to have been the norm.

17. Miss Thackeray, *Toilers and Spinsters*, op.cit., p. 17.

18. *ILN*, 6/15/61, 555 and 11/30/61, 538; *Queen*, 12/7/61, 261.

19. In the *ILN* print "twenty-two girls and two men are shown working together at various tasks, the compositors at three double tiers of cases jutting into the room from the window wall" (Fredeman, p. 150). The *Queen* sketch shows two men working with fifteen girls, but it also includes an authority-figure (probably Emily Faithfull) and, behind her, a woman visitor still clad in her outdoor garments.

20. During the first nine months of the Press's operation, contract printing was the order of the day — *Transactions* for the SSA (from the October 1860 Glasgow Conference), the *English Woman's Journal* (from the September 1860 issue on), and job printing for individuals and organizations (of which no record remains, except for two works for the SSA on jurisprudence and on trade societies).

21. M.M.H., in an *English Woman's Journal* article entitled "A ramble with Mrs. Grundy: A Visit to the Victoria Press," June 1860, p. 271, attributed this statement to Emily Faithfull.

22. Quoted in Emily Faithfull, *Three Visits*, 26 and in "Women Compositors," *W & W*, 10/10/74, 5.

23. Fredeman, p. 151. I have drawn freely from Fredeman's account of the printers' attacks on the Victoria Press, especially for matters relating to the Publishers' Circulars of 1 Sept 69 and 16 Aug 69 and to W.W. Head's pamphlet, *The Victoria Press: Its History and Vindication*.

24. Ibid.

25. Ibid., p. 152. This favourable conclusion about the employment of female compositors is in accord with that of the American and French (Parisian at least) societies of compositors. In America, the Women's Typographical Union was established in 1869, and women were fully accepted as compositors by 1873, as EF noted somewhat enviously when she visited Harper's Works and the Riverside Press. In 1874 Paris printers voted in favour of employing women as compositors (*VM*, 6/74). Yet British printers continued to regard their employment as "an experiment" (*VM*, 8/73, 381).

26. Article in the *Printer's Register*, reproduced in Chapter II of Head's pamphlet, *The Victoria Press: Its History and Vindication*. This passage is from Head, p. 26, as quoted in Fredeman, p. 152.

27. This was not an advertisement for a woman compositor to work at the Victoria Press. When Emily Faithfull wanted a female apprentice, she advertised openly for her.

28. Even in 1894 the Secretary of the Society of Compositors contended that women compositors did inferior work (*LP*, 9/22/94, 384).
29. *Women in the Printing Trades*, 1904, p. 28, as cited in Fredeman, pp. 152-53.
30. As Fredeman says of the recalcitrant printers' union, "If the only test of the ultimate success of Emily Faithfull's experiment with the employment of women in printing were to be that of an ever-burgeoning membership of ladies in the London Society of Compositors, then the Victoria Press would have to be rated a resounding failure. Fortunately, there are other criteria . . . " (Fredeman, p. 153).
31. Mary Agnes Hamilton, *Women at Work*, London: The Labour Book Service, 1941, p. 51.
32. *Women's Penny Paper*, 8/2/90, 481.
33. The SSA declined to provide financial support for the Victoria Press, though individual members of the Association were no doubt among the "rich and generous friends" who helped EF weather this storm.
34. After she received this royal appointment, EF fashioned a coat of arms for the Press in which "Victoria Press By Appointment" encircled the Royal coat of arms (Fawcett Library, Vol. II A, Letterhead in April 21, 1871 letter).
35. In a letter to "Dua" dated January 27, 1864, Emily Davies informed her friend that the Press needed not only an infusion of money but also "a responsible manager who knows the business," for all the men and women printers "seem to have been cheating tremendously." She added that "Fido [Emily Faithfull]" was "in good spirits, poor thing, having closed with Mr. Head & pretty nearly accomplished the sale of Farringdon St" (*Papers of Emily Davies and Barbara Bodichon*, Reel 1, p. 337 F(2).).
36. In a letter to the *Times* in October 1867, EF stated that the reason for the dissolution of their partnership was Head's "sole addition" to the publications of the Press of a weekly newspaper consisting of extracts from the "public papers" (*Times*, 10/15/67, 7). Evidently she thought that such a second-hand publication was of little worth. Nevertheless, it appears that financial problems were the underlying cause of her sale of part of the Press to Head.
37. Head also printed the April 1868 issue of the *Englishwoman's Review*. So, with only two short published works and sixteen printed items in a four-year period, he must have had much unrecorded job printing to keep the Press busy.
38. The addresses of the Victoria Press over the span of its lifetime tell their own story of the changes that occurred from 1860 to 1881:
    (1)    Emily Faithfull & Co. for the Employment of Women, 9 Great Coram St. 1860-62.

(2)     Emily Faithfull, Printer and Publisher In Ordinary to Her Majesty, 9 Great Coram St., 1862; 83a Farringdon St. 1862-64; 14 Princes St. Hanover Square 1863-64.

(3)     Emily Faithfull & Co. [EF & Head], 14 Princes St., 83a Farringdon St., 1a Princes Mews Westminster (1864-67).

(4)     Emily Faithfull, Printer & Publisher, etc., 14 Princes St. 1867-73, 85 Praed St. Paddington 1874-77, 117 Praed St. 1878-79.

(5)     Emily Faithfull & Co., etc. 117 Praed St. 1880-81.

(6)     Head [William Wilfred], successor in part to Emily Faithfull & Co. 1a Princes Mews 1868, 83a Farringdon St. 1868-69, 11, 12 & 13 Harp Alley 1870-71.

(Philip A.H. Brown, *London Publishers and Printers c1800-1870*, London: British Library, 1982, pp. 65-66).

39.   One must, of course, allow for the relative inactivity of the Press during EF's nine-months' tour of the U.S.A. in 1872-73.

40.   Emily had high hopes that this new Steam Press would attract job printing business, as these 1874 advertisements in *Women and Work* indicated:

(1)     "Reports, Trade Circulars & Cards, Memorandums, Bill Heads, and all kinds of Colour and General Printing at the Victoria Press, 85, Praed St. W." (*W & W*, 10/3/74, 8).

(2)     "Printing of every description executed with neatness and despatch at the Office of 'Women and Work,' Victoria Press, 85, Praed St., Paddington W." (*W & W*, 10/3/74, 18).

41.   Here is a half-page advertisement in the *West London Express* in December 1877: "Owing to the large increase of business, the entire front part of 117 Praed Street will, in future, form part of the Printing Office" (*WLE*, 12/8/77).

42.   There are only ten located titles for these final eight years of the Victoria Press's existence.

43.   Fredeman, p. 153. Fredeman provides full bibliographical descriptions of *The Victoria Regia* and two other prestige publications of the Victoria Press, namely, *A Welcome: Original Contributions in Poetry and Prose* and *Poems: An Offering to Lancashire*. See Fredeman, p. 153, Plate II, and pp. 155-57 for these descriptions.

44.   For example, Alfred Tennyson, W.M. Thackeray, Anthony Trollope, Owen Meredith, Harriet Martineau, Coventry Patmore, Matthew Arnold, Leigh Hunt, F.D. Maurice, Caroline Norton, Adelaide Procter, Edwin Arnold, George Macdonald, and Isa Craig. Incidentally, Anthony Trollope's contributions to *Victoria Regia* ("The Journey to Panama") and to *A Welcome* ("Miss Ophelia Gledd") resulted in his inviting "that female Caxton of the Age Emily Faithfull" to his home

on June 14, 1863. (Anthony Trollope, *The Letters of Anthony Trollope*, N. John Hall, ed., Stanford: Stanford University Press, 1983, p. 220).

45.  Adelaide Procter's mother, who was "brought into company with Lamb and Coleridge, Keats and Leigh Hunt and who became a close friend of Thackeray and Dickens, Tennyson and Browning" (*ER*, 3/15/88, 105), no doubt helped Adelaide solicit contributions to *The Victoria Regia*.

46.  Brother and mother of Anthony Trollope, both of whom were novelists.

47.  Emily Faithfull's praise of Queen Victoria and of Royalty in general was not always restrained.

48.  Here are a few lines from Parkes's dedication poem:
     "Victoria Regia! — Never happier name
     A Flower, a woman, or a Queen could claim

                    . . .

     Victoria Regia! May our blossom hold
     In pure white leaves a heart of gold."
                              (Dedication page, *The Victoria Regia*)

49.  Preface to *Poems: An Offering to Lancashire*, as cited in Fredeman, p. 156.

50.  The contributions to these three anthologies consisted, for the most part, of previously unpublished poetry or prose, most of which was second-rate.

51.  *Te Deum Laudamus* was also chromolithographed by M. & N. Hanhart.

52.  This Appendix provides a list of Victoria Press publications.

53.  Bessie Parkes was especially pleased that the Victoria Press was "superintended by a woman . . . our moral sympathy is chiefly due to the Press on the score of Miss Faithfull's superintendence" (*EWJ*, 7/62, 343). And even the *Saturday Review*, which was usually very critical of women's rights' advocates, recognized the importance of a woman's undertaking such a project: "Miss Faithfull . . . has shown so much promptitude of resource, so much spirit and ingenuity, and so true a benevolence in her management of the Victoria Printing Press that, if she is spoken of at all, she deserves to be spoken of with great respect" (*Saturday Review*, Jan-June 1864, Vol. XVII, p. 524).

54.  As early as 1861, *The Queen* commended EF for opening printing to women, and giving "those women, whose education and ability qualify them to undertake skilled labour, the opportunity of freeing themselves from the slopseller's sordid tyranny and the dull drudgery of the mill" (*The Queen*, 12/7/61, 261).

Chapter Five

1. The term "correspondent" applies to EF's contributions as foreign correspondent while visiting America in 1872-3, 1882-3, and 1883-4. Her "Letters from America" were published in the *Victoria Magazine* in 1872-3; during the other two visits the feature appeared in the *Lady's Pictorial*, the first column being entitled "America Revisited by a Lady," the subsequent columns, "Across the Atlantic."

2. Emily Faithfull's searching but polite interview of "Carmen Sylva," a.k.a. Queen Elizabeth of Rumania, in September 1890, contrasted sharply with rude interviews of EF by male American reporters, who not only "invariably published the remark [she was] drawn into at some unguarded moment" (*LP*, 9/4/86, 197), but also had no regard for her mental or physical condition. She recalled a Chicago interviewer who woke her late at night and printed an imaginary interview when she refused to see him. Another opened her bedroom door when she was in bed with neuralgia and put questions to her. A third said he would invent an opinion for her when she refused to give one; when she "indignantly replied that she should contradict it if he did . . . he rejoined smilingly, 'Ah, but that will not matter — my statement will be a day ahead of your denial'" (Fanny L. Green, "Journalism," in *Ladies at Work*, London: A.D. Innes & Co., 1893).

3. "The Lady Journalist," *Women's Penny Paper*, 6/1/89, 4.

4. Fanny L. Green, op.cit., pp. 31-2.

5. In reporting that EF was resident in Manchester in 1886, *The Queen* noted that "the social doings of that city as well as of Liverpool and other centres around Cottonopolis find sprightly record through her pen [in the *Lady's Pictorial*]" (*The Queen*, 10/16/86, 436).

6. Other good examples of her style are her description of the Cincinnati flood of 1883, a disaster at the Clifton Colliery in 1885, the celebrations attendant on the passing of the Manchester Ship Canal Bill in 1885, a terrible storm in Scotland in 1886, and the effective way in which the Manchester police quelled a riot in 1886. More mundane, but still effective, examples are items concerning a ladies' tennis tournament, attempted smuggling through American Customs, and the deaths of F.D. Maurice and Mary Carpenter, notable workers in the cause of women.

7. She delighted in pointing out what she called grammatical errors in such phrases as "luxuriant (for "luxurious") hotel," (*WLE*, 9/28/78, 201) and she apologized to her readers for using neologisms like "danceable waltz" (*LP*, 1/12/89, 56).

8. Martha Westwater, "Emily Faithfull: Folly Reconsidered," unpublished paper presented before the Pacific Coast Studies in British Literature at the University of California (Santa Barbara), 1981, p. 10.

9. Martha Westwater, "*Victoria Magazine*," op.cit., p. 444.

10. Martha Westwater calls this self-praise "indelicate self-aggrandizement," though earlier in her paper she puts the matter more positively: "Deliberately, as if to debunk the women's subservience and humility myth, Emily Faithfull advertised all her achievements" ("EF: Folly Reconsidered," pp. 15 and 6).

11. Some of the more enthusiastic members of the Victoria Discussion Society went overboard concerning EF's attributes and achievements and every word was recorded in *VM*. For example, Alice B. Le Geyt called her a "pillar" and a "great magnate" (*VM*, 1/70, 312). But most of the praise for her work with the Society was well deserved. And, after all, readers of the *Victoria Magazine* expected full reports — praise and all — of the proceedings of the VDS.

12. As Pauline Nestor says, "Emily Faithfull herself was the centre of much of the [*Victoria*] *Magazine*'s mythologizing" (Pauline Nestor, "A New Departure in Women's Publishing: The *EWJ* and the *VM*," *Victorian Periodicals Review*, XV (1982), p. 102).

13. Volume XXI of the *Victoria Magazine* also reported every nuance of EF's tour of America with more "Letters from America," articles entitled "The Farewell Banquet to Miss Faithfull," "American Journalism" (by EF), "American Industries in their Relation to Women" (by EF), "An Afternoon in a Lunatic Asylum" (by EF), and more reprints entitled "Miss Faithfull in America." And the praise was almost as over-generous as that in Volume XX. For example, successive speakers at EF's farewell lecture at Steinway Hall, New York City, on April 3, 1873 referred to the "gracious and womanly manner" of this "sweet-voiced and high-minded . . . true hearted, gifted, cultivated woman" who possessed so much "intellectual and moral force." Also, at the farewell banquet for Emily on May 9, 1873 Francis Moulton lauded her as "the most effective of all workers in behalf of working women" (*VM*, 5/73, 117-128 and 7/73, 259).

14. Westwater, "Emily Faithfull: Folly Reconsidered," p. 4.

15. Emily Faithfull's words, as reported in Frances E. Willard's interview of Emily Faithfull, *The Woman's Signal*, 3/1/94, 138.

16. The Empress Frederick of Germany was Queen Victoria's oldest daughter.

17. Probably Evelyn, who was still unmarried in 1891 when she attended a conference in Liverpool with her sister Isabel.

18. She also reported visits by the Duke of Connaught and the Duke and Duchess of York, as well as a planned visit by the Duke and Duchess of Westminster.

19. Frances Willard's description of Emily Faithfull, *The Woman's Signal*, 3/1/94, 138.

20. Emily always referred to Walter Bentley by his stage name. His family name was Walter William Begg.

21. I have already mentioned Dr. James Begg as a participant in SSA Conferences.

22. Dr. Begg visited New Zealand in 1874 and was impressed with the independent bearing of New Zealanders (*VM*, 1/75, 204).

23. Ferdinand Faithfull Begg (1847-1926) emigrated to New Zealand in 1863, returned to Edinburgh in 1872, and married a New Zealand woman in 1873. He became an M.P. in 1895. In 1897 he moved the second reading of a Women's Franchise Bill that passed with a majority of 71 but was talked out and eventually shuffled into committee (*Dictionary of National Biography* and *Lady's Pictorial* columns by Emily Faithfull).

24. In 1886 Emily proudly recorded that her nephew F.F. Begg had been invited by the British Columbia government to inspect land opened up for immigrants by the Canadian Pacific Railway (*LP*, 7/24/86, 49).

25. Walter Bentley was very successful as actor and manager in New York from 1883-5. He had a starring role in *The Silver King* from August 1883 to May 1884. As actor-manager he also presented *Love or Money*, a play adapted from Charles Reade's *A Perilous Secret*, from March to May 1885 (George C.D. Odell, *Annals of the New York Stage*, Vol. 12, New York: Columbia University Press, 1940).

26. "Marcus Ward has published a pretty little volume *Roses with and without Thorns*, by Mrs. Esther Faithfull Fleet, very tastefully and effectively illustrated . . . charming coloured pictures . . . letter press really delightful. . . . Altogether the book is as pretty a Christmas gift as auntie or grandmama could give to the little ones" (*W & W*, 12/19/74, 3-5).

27. In 1893 Emily reported that Rutland Barrington had just returned from a holiday with Sir Arthur Sullivan (*LP*, 1/28/93, 145).

28. The *DNB* states that two unsuccessful plays bankrupted Rutland Barrington's operation at St. James's Theatre.

29. Sometimes the young men at the Reverend George Faithfull's "crammer" in Storrington got involved in pranks that caused public mischief.

30. Emily especially noted Monier Williams's *Indian Wisdom* (*W & W*, 4/13/75), "Facts of Indian Progress" (*VM*, 5/78, 73), "The Progress of Indian Religious Thought" (*VM*, 10/78, 545), and "Afghanistan and the Punjab" (*LE*, 12/7/78, 364).

31. Emily pursued this "family" connection even further with congratulations to Mrs. Stanley Monier Williams for a successful exhibition of her sketches of children in 1893 (*LP*, 4/1/93, 472).

32. Emily admitted that Mrs. F.G. Faithfull's story was "slight in construction;" yet she pronounced it "singularly attractive" (*W & W*, 7/31/75, 6).

33. Published monthly for seventeen years and two months, a total of 206 numbers in 35 volumes, the last one containing only two numbers.

34. Emily Davies, who had edited the *English Woman's Journal* from September 1862 to February 1863, agreed to be editor of the *Victoria Magazine* on March 15, 1863 at a salary of £100 a year plus 5 shillings a page for an article contributed by the editor, and a contract signed by both Emily Davies and EF was drawn up to that effect. However, Davies said she got only one quarter's salary and nothing for anything she wrote (*ED Papers*, 3 and 4/63, 288-289).

35. Emily Davies noted that Mr. Gunning was a partner with EF in the early days of the *Victoria Magazine* (*ED Papers*, 289). But this partnership could not have lasted very long, for Gunning is not mentioned after Emily Davies resigned as editor.

36. Westwater, "EF: Folly Reconsidered," p. 15.

37. One of these generous friends was Mr. Nassau Senior (*LP*, 2/11/93, 206).

38. Nowadays, advertising is an important source of revenue for any publication. In the nineteenth century it was not so vital. Moreover — and this is still true today — advertisers refused to pay well until a journal had achieved a good circulation. Therefore, the *VM* could not rely on advertising to fund even the smallest part of its operation.

39. Emily Davies's resignation as editor was partly due to the impending Codrington divorce case, but chiefly to the reorganization of the *Victoria Magazine* that would not permit her to pay for good articles and stories. As she put the matter in a letter to Anna Richardson on March 15, 1864, "I could not edit a light magazine, nor can I edit one at all, unless I may go to the best writers, and pay them properly" (*ED Papers*, 349).

40. Before commencing publication of the *VM*, EF and Emily Davies agreed that the magazine should employ "chiefly men [as writers] at first, and not . . . press our special subject [the cause of women] till we have got a character" (*ED Papers*, Letter to BB, 3/12/63).

41. The Social Science section lasted only until volume VI, that is, to April 1866. "Miscellanea" appears to have replaced it.

42. The worst poem was the anonymous "opener" to Vol. I, No. I entitled "Victoria Regina." Besides being extremely jingoistic, it achieves a

dreadful monotony with the repetition of "Victoria!" at the end of every verse.

43. Other well-known writers who were almost certainly paid for their contributions to the *VM* were Richard Holt Hutton ("The Unspiritual World of Spirits"), Frances Power Cobbe ("The Humour of Various Nations"), Mrs. Oliphant ("The Story of a Voice"), Thomas Hughes ("An Afternoon in Whitechapel"), Moncure Conway ("Robert Browning") and Matthew Arnold ("Marcus Aurelius"). Christina Rossetti contributed another poem entitled "L.E.L.," as did Hood ("A Reason for Beauty").

44. *ED Papers*, 290-291.

45. Nestor, though she notes the political sophistication of the *Victoria Magazine*, contends that the firm "establishment ties" of the journal and constant "deference to the sovereign" resulted in a kind of "restrictive moralism" that the *English Woman's Journal* did not manifest (Nestor, op.cit., p. 102).

46. *The Revolution*, 12/30/69, 414 and 1/13/70, 23, as cited in Westwater, "EF: Folly Reconsidered," p. 18.

47. Praise of the *Victoria Magazine* in British newspapers was more restrained than Mrs. Wilbour's: "Takes high rank among its contemporaries" (*Daily Telegraph*); "discusses the special questions that affect the status of women with a knowledge and ability altogether its own" (*Spectator*); "not an article too dry for a lady's reading or too frivolous for a man" (*Examiner*) — all of which were reprinted in *WLE*, 9/22/77. *The Queen* had recognized the merits of *VM* much earlier: "The *Victoria Magazine* always has some claims upon our respect. . . . [It] is always sober, if not serious, but intellectual readers will enjoy it . . . always abounds in that which is instructive and solid . . . always brings wise and sober utterances, and at the same time offers us specimens of a lighter style" (*The Queen*, 1/13/66, 25; 4/7/66, 262, 5/12/66, 363; and 8/11/66, 95).

48. "Miss Faithfull the Guest of Sorosis," report from American newspaper as rpt. in *VM*, 1/73, 265.

49. In this same context Westwater notes that the *VM* was "surprisingly modern in advocating the integration of the sexes in education and the importance of physical education for girls" (Westwater, "*Victoria Magazine*," p. 445).

50. Pauline Nestor says the *English Woman's Journal* and the *Victoria Magazine* provided "a galvanizing focus for the disparate forces of the women's movement" (Nestor, op.cit., p. 103).

51. The original name of the society was the Victoria Debating Society. No doubt "debating" connoted argument and the ladies tended to shy away from that hitherto forbidden ground; thus "discussion" seemed

preferable in 1870. By 1876, however, after the Victoria Discussion Society had whetted their appetite for controversy, many of them joined the Ladies' Debating Club (*W & W*, 1/22/76).

52.  In 1884 EF defined this two-fold object of VDS more briefly: "to afford a neutral meeting-point for all interested in women's work and to give ladies an increased opportunity of oral utterance" (*Three Visits*, 100).

53.  The *VM*'s detailed accounts of VDS meetings provide no evidence of "gaffes" by the ladies present. So I assume EF edited them out.

54.  Women occasionally chaired meetings, usually when the appointed man was unable to preside. Emily Faithfull, as one might expect, chaired several meetings. Julia Ward Howe of Boston, Mass., chaired one session, as did Mrs. Cora Tappan (another American) and Alice B. Le Geyt.

55.  Emily usually assigned chairmen to topics dealing with their particular political or social concerns; for example, Lord Shaftesbury presided over a paper and discussion on "Women and Work;" Sir Erskine Perry, "Married Women's Property Bill 1870;" Lord Houghton, "Medicine as a Profession for Women;" Sir Charles Trevelyan, "The Poor Law System;" and Sir George Grey and Sir Charles Clifford, separate sessions on emigration.

56.  Of the forty-three papers over the five-year span of the VDS, at least nineteen were by women.

57.  Emily seems to have filled *all* the offices of the VDS — founder, director, president, chairperson on occasion, presenter of papers, participant in discussions, dramatic reader, and, above all, mother hen. With reference to this last office, when Elizabeth Cady Stanton and Mrs. P.W. Davis invited EF to the 20th Anniversary celebration of the Woman Suffrage Movement in the U.S.A. in October 1870, she declined the invitation with this observation: "the discussion society [VDS] I have started up in London is still too young to run alone, and yet promises such good things for the future that I feel it ought to be carefully tended" (*The History of Woman Suffrage*, op.cit., Vol. II, p. 440).

58.  Mrs. Horace St. John, "The Position of Women," *VM*, 1/70, 193-99.

59.  J. McGrigor Allan, "A Protest Against Woman's Demand for the Privileges of Both Sexes," *VM*, 8/70.

60.  Mr. Hoskins, "Women's Franchise," *VM*, 7/70.

61.  Emily had several names for this bureau. One was "Victoria Educational and Industrial Bureau" (*VM*, 11/73, 30); another was "Educational, Industrial, and Domestic Bureau" (*W & W*, 10/10/74, 6); a third was "Industrial Bureau for Women" (*Times*, 9/2/73, 9). But the

name she appears to have settled on or, at least, to have used most often, was "Industrial and Educational Bureau."

62. The "American Notes" column in an April 1875 issue of *Women and Work* consisted of the first annual report of the New York Women's Educational and Industrial Society that EF had helped bring into being during her first visit to America. Proudly announcing that the Society had sent 6,000 women into employment in the past two years, Mrs. C.L. Hodges, author of the column, asked Miss Faithfull for "any new plans or revelations which might be a stimulant to this end that your noble industry has devised" (*W & W*, 4/3/75, 2). So the "New York model" to which Emily referred was apparently inspired by her.

63. Dr. Frances Hoggan gave these lectures in human physiology (*W & W*, 6/6/74, 4).

64. *Papers and Letters Presented at the First Women's Congress of the Association for the Advancement of Women, October 1873*, New York: Mrs. William Bullard, 1874, p. 186.

65. Mr. Rundell started instructing women at the Industrial and Educational Bureau in May 1874, and his classes were still going strong in 1876 when Emily handed over the operation of the Bureau to other members of her family. He used a system quite different from Pitman's; according to *The Queen*, Pitman's system was speedier, but Rundell's was more accurate (*The Queen*, 11/21/74, 349).

66. In her article "American Industries" EF announced that lessons in the use of this American sewing machine would be given at the Bureau (*VM*, 11/73, 30).

67. In August 1874 EF became Managing Director of the Victoria Dressmaking Company, located at the offices of the *Victoria Magazine*, *Women and Work*, and the Industrial and Educational Bureau, under the management of Madame Burston, court dressmaker (*W & W*, 8/29/74). No doubt Mme. Burston gave some instruction to women wishing to become professional dressmakers.

68. In the first issue of *Women and Work* EF noted the deplorable lack of training for women. The remedy, as she saw it, was a concerted demand for job training by concerned parents and an educated public (*W & W*, 6/6/74, 4).

69. In May 1874 the *Standard* observed that no one was more fit than EF to conduct the Industrial and Educational Bureau for Women (*VM*, 5/74, 69, rpt. from the *Standard*). And in July Queen Victoria wished Miss Faithfull "every success in the laudable undertaking by which new branches of industry are opened to the female portion of her subjects" (*W & W*, 7/25/74, 6, rpt. from the *Times*).

70. In fact, EF claimed this success even earlier in a letter to *The Queen*: "Thanks to the numerous offers of various employments from public

bodies and private persons, a wonderful success has been achieved; organised with our leading cities and colonies, generous gifts have not been wanting from those who appreciate and understand the difficulties surrounding such a movement, and a staff of unpaid as well as salaried workers is connected with an office which desires to be practical rather than merely charitable" (*The Queen*, 4/11/74).

71. To give unemployed women a break, EF set the fee for non-subscribers at five shillings a month.

72. *Women and Work* ceased publication on February 26, 1876. Its function was assumed in April 1876 by the "Women and Work" column in the *Victoria Magazine*, and later by the "Work for Women" column in the *West London Express*.

73. In its 1878-79 listings the *Newspaper Press Directory* offered this comment on the *West London Express*: "The *Express*, though a local organ for West London, can hardly be classed with the usual order of papers for suburban districts, for while giving in an attractive form all the news, it contains many novel features interesting to all" (*Newspaper Press Directory*, 1878, p. 34).

74. This "Work for Women" column, begun in August 1878, included short notes in reply to correspondents who had asked EF for advice on qualifications for particular jobs, home employments, literary work, secretarial work, nursing, etc.

75. Advertisements about the Victoria Steam Press, Kate Pattison, EF's lectures and elocution lessons, the contents of *VM*, the publications of the Victoria Press, the International Women's Congress in Paris, openings for more apprentices in VP — all of these were almost certainly printed free.

76. After EF had recommended the coupon system of the General Expenditure Assurance Company in her "Modern Extravagance" lecture that she gave to large audiences throughout the United Kingdom, that firm took out three-page advertisements in twelve successive issues of *WLE* (8/31/78 to 11/16/78). So these "ads" must have paid well.

77. Her first "Northern Gossip" submission appeared in the June 13, 1885 issue of the *Lady's Pictorial*. The last one made a rather eerie appearance on June 1, 1895, the day after Emily died.

78. The final "Woman" column appeared in the May 18, 1895 issue of the *Lady's Pictorial*, thirteen days before Emily's death. Apparently the "Northern Gossip" column was easier to prepare during her final illness than "Woman."

79. Emily Faithfull insisted that as a journalist she could not deal with "the important communications and proofs which leave London on

Saturday and must be dealt with by return of post" unless Sunday delivery of the post was maintained (*LP*, 11/20/86, 455).

80. In 1889 EF expressed her pleasure at having electric light on the trains, "a great advantage to busy people who, like me, are accompanied by a bag full of letters and papers, which can be arranged and answered during the four hours' journey" (*LP*, 6/8/89, 834).

81. Male journalists in Manchester had little to say about EF or any other female journalist. As Margaret Beetham writes, "In terms of gender the press in Manchester remained largely a male preserve. This was despite the activity of Lydia Becker and the Women's Suffrage Movement, whose Journal she edited, and despite the city's association with Emily Faithful (sic), founder of the first women's press, known locally as The Lancashire Witch" (Margaret Beetham, "Healthy Reading: The Periodical Press in Late Victorian Manchester," in Alan J. Kidd and K.W. Roberts, *City, Class and Culture: Studies of Social Policy and Cultural Production in Victorian Manchester*, Manchester: Manchester University Press, 1985, p. 175).

82. Other articles by EF may have been published in these journals. As she herself said in an 1890 interview, "I also contribute articles to a Paris-American Syndicate and to various other papers and magazines" (*Women's Penny Paper*, 8/2/90, 481). I have been able to locate only the two I have commented on. Incidentally, *The Queen* noted in 1873 that EF had been "appointed correspondent of the *New York World* and *Harper's Bazar* (sic)" (*The Queen*, 6/28/73, 534).

83. *The Hull and Eastern Counties Herald* reported that in presenting this lecture in Hull in April 1870 EF not only advocated jobs, better education, and legal protection for women. She also asserted women's claim for "some share of political power" (rpt. in *VM*, 4/70, 567).

84. This February 1871 lecture in aid of French Female Refugees made special reference to women serving on School Boards and to women's share in the great educational movements of the day (*VM*, 3/71, 453-4).

85. In this paper read before the Society of Arts on March 29, 1871, EF called for a national effort to provide training and jobs for the millions of surplus women needing employment to stave off starvation (rpt. from the *Arts Journal* in *VM*, 7/71, 308-22).

86. Reporting on EF's March 13, 1872 lecture in Gloucester, Amelia Lewis noted that EF had again referred to the "hardships consequent upon woman's exclusion from the suffrage" (*Woman*, 3/23/72, 195).

87. According to Amelia Lewis, theatre seats for EF's lectures in 1872 sold for prices ranging from five shillings for "Stalls," to 2s 6d for "Balcony," to one shilling for "Unreserved" (*Woman*, 7/13/72, 435). The speaker's fee is not mentioned.

88. This was an impromptu lecture, given at the special request of Julia Ward Howe (*VM*, "Letters from America," 5/73, 39). Emily also gave an impromptu lecture to female medical students at the University of Michigan on "the movement in England in favour of female education and women doctors" (*VM*, 2/73, 350).

89. She presented this lecture to a working women's audience on February 1, 1873, the ninth anniversary of the American Working Women's Protective Union. It drew a full house to New York's Association Hall; indeed, hundreds were turned away (*VM*, "Miss Faithfull in America," 4/73, 564-5).

90. Writing his *Annals of the New York Stage* in the 1930's, George Odell quipped, "Emily Faithfull, on April 3rd [1873] spoke at Steinway Hall *Last Words on the Woman Question*; many then and years later might have wished they could have been the last" (George C.D. Odell, *Annals of the New York Stage*, Volume 9, New York: Columbia University Press, 1937, p. 337).

91. In November and December 1873 she delivered these lectures (plus others on American orators and poets) five nights a week (*VM*, 1/74).

92. As late as 1877 she was giving the odd lecture on America, e.g., "Nine Months in America" (*WLE*, 11/3/77), and in November 1878 she gave a short opening address to a dramatic entertainment in which she spoke of woman's work with special reference to education (*LE*, 11/2/78). Moreover, her popular lecture short-titled "Modern Extravagance" filled most of her lecture slots in 1878. But, with these exceptions, most of her lectures from 1875 to 1882 dealt with American and British literature.

93. Odell, *Annals*, Vol. 12, p. 144.

94. *Three Visits*, 139.

95. When EF stayed at the Antlers Hotel in Colorado Springs in late 1883, Miss Warren, manager of the hotel, told her that a lecture she (EF) had given in Cincinnati on woman's work had inspired her to accept the job at the Antlers (*Three Visits*, 140).

96. Emily noted in 1884 that travelling theatrical companies were taking over from lecturers; however, she still drew good crowds in 1882-3 (*Three Visits*, 80).

97. Letter from EF to "Hen. Watson," n.d. but probably 1885, Manchester Central Library.

98. A lecture entitled "General Literature," first mentioned in 1872, appears to have dealt with the same material as "The Best Society: Your Bookshelf," for during this lecture EF "denounced the novel reading tendency of the present day" and regretted that so many women were "both . . . consumers and . . . producers of pernicious books" (*VM*, 2/72, 375).

99. In the summer of 1888 EF informed her readers that her lecture on "The Best Society: Your Bookshelf" would be one of Mr. Charles Rowley's course of lectures being presented in the Public Hall in Ancoats during the winter of 1888-89. Emily was in good company, as William Morris, Mrs. Henry Fawcett, and Walter Crane had also agreed to take part in this lecture series (*LP*, 8/11/88, 162).

100. She gave this lecture to a variety of audiences — students at the City of London College, working men and women in Working Men's Clubs, parishioners of the Lower Clapton Congregational Church, and students in Mr. Lewis's Chapel Schools — not to mention Mr. Charles Rowley's "students" in Ancoats (see previous note).

101. In her "Letter from England" to *The Woman's Journal* (Boston) Alice Le Geyt wrote, 'during this month and the next she [EF] is to give three lectures at the Salle de Lecture . . . London, on "Our English Poets," "The American Poets," and "Our Prose-Writing Poets"' (*The Woman's Journal*, 7/15/71, 219).

102. The other lectures in this course were given by men; they were entitled "The Wives of Great Men," "Astronomy," "The Life of John Howard," and "Selections From Shakespeare" (*WLE*, 11/24/77).

103. Emily reported that she had lost a "valuable travelling bag" when she left Chicago in December 1872. It contained the lecture "English Orators," "a beautiful portrait of Queen Victoria set in gold . . . and some valuable notes of her visits to the schools and University of Michigan" (*VM*, 2/73, 369, rpt. from *The Queen*).

104. *The Queen* reported in 1880 that "Miss Emily Faithfull has accepted an invitation to lecture in America during the autumn season on 'Modern Extravagance, its Cause and Cure'" (*The Queen*, 4/17/80, 356). But EF obviously had to decline this invitation during the summer; she did not visit America until 1882.

105. *The Queen* reported that the National Thrift Society met soon after EF's lecture and decided that "in consequence of the success attending Miss Emily Faithfull's lecture on 'Modern Extravagance' at the Kensington Town Hall on the 18th ult. [i.e., March 18], [they would] deliver a series of such lectures in London and the suburbs" (*The Queen*, 4/16/81, 389).

106. George Odell noted that "Emily Faithfull, on November 9, [1883] treated [a New York] audience to a lecture on Modern Shams, a topic pertinent to life in 1940" (Odell, op. cit., Vol. 12, 1940).

107. Emily apparently expanded this lecture to include her travels through Colorado and California that preceded and followed her stay in Utah among the Mormons (*LP*, 10/6/94, 497).

108. Emily prepared this address at the request of the Mayor of Manchester. It was printed along with the addresses of the Bishops of Manchester

and Salford, and EF had the honour of presenting the slim volume to the Princess of Wales "at a reception in the Town Hall on the day of the opening of the Jubilee Exhibition" in 1887 (*Manchester Faces and Places*, 1892, 133). Copies were also sent to Queen Victoria and Princess Beatrice in 1887, and to the Duchess of York in 1893 (*The Queen*, 5/21/87, 629 and *LP* 7/15/93, 102).

Chapter Six

1.  The University of Scotland Bill, which would have authorized Scottish universities to grant degrees to women, was defeated in 1875 by a vote of 194 to 151. Scottish women had to await degree-granting privileges until the House reversed this decision in 1888.
2.  Emily viewed American education more positively than Mrs. Stanton did. In a letter to the *Times* from America in 1872 she had this to say: "While we in England are only beginning to think seriously about female education, American educators have long since repudiated our miserable process of dipping girls in a thin solution of accomplishments which will not bear the test of time, and both sexes have shared alike in the splendid opportunities afforded by the Free School system, which has forced even the private schools here to maintain a far higher standard than that achieved by ladies' schools in England" (*Times*, 12/31/72, 9).
3.  Queen's College professors came from King's College, those at Bedford from University College.
4.  Adelaide Procter, Dorothea Beale, and Frances Mary Buss attended lectures at Queen's College in 1848. Julia Smith and Barbara Leigh Smith attended lectures at Bedford College in 1849 (Herstein, p. 19), and George Eliot was there in 1851 (*George Eliot Letters*, op.cit., Vol. I, p. 343).
5.  "The Helen Blackburn Pamphlet Collection from Girton College, Cambridge," *Voices of the Women's Mov't*, Brighton, Sussex: Harvester Press Microform Pubs. Ltd., 1987, Reel 2.
6.  Emily gives Barbara Leigh Smith (Bodichon) credit, "as one of the pioneers in education reform," for her work with Portman Hall School and Girton College (*LP*, 1/19/95, 98).
7.  Portman Hall School lasted from 1854 to 1864.
8.  Emily Faithfull's editorial about the success of the "mixed" (co-educational) system at the Working Women's College lauded mixed education as a beneficial extension of "the principles of family life"

(*W & W*, 10/17/74, 4). She also approved of two colleges established as co-educational institutions, namely, Josiah Mason College, Birmingham, and University College, Bristol. Conversely, she labelled the City of London College an "anachronism" in 1879 because it refused to admit women (*VM*, 1/79, 308).

9. For instance, EF praised Miss Adela Brooke for putting her reading-room and library in Combe House, Woodstock, at the disposal of working-class readers (*LP*, 8/24/89, 250).

10. During its inquiries the Commission became aware of the ironic fact that working-class girls attending government-endowed schools for both sexes received a much better education than middle-class girls attending private schools at their parents' expense. For the former, taught by certificated teachers, were subjected to a relatively rigorous co-educational curriculum, whereas the latter were taught "accomplishments" designed to make them shine in society (and thus to attract husbands) by non-certificated teachers or governesses (Hollis, op.cit., p. 133). Incidentally, the certificated teachers were not allowed to teach at schools other than the government's elementary schools, so Miss Buss and Miss Beale had to hire non-certificated teachers until 1878 at least (Hollis, p. 140).

11. This investigation took place from 1864 to 1867. At first it was confined to boys' education, but Frances Buss, Dorothea Beale, and Emily Davies gave early evidence before the Commission that convinced the male members (of whom Matthew Arnold was one) that girls should be included in its scope. Indeed, the Commission eventually realized that girls' education was much in need of reform. Josephine Kamm did not exaggerate when she stated, "The work of the Schools Inquiry Commission was the turning-point in girls' education" (Josephine Kamm, *How Different From Us: Miss Buss and Miss Beale*, London: The Bodley Head, 1958, p. 92).

12. By 1890 the Girls' Public Day School Trust had established almost forty schools with a total enrolment of 7,000 girls (Hollis, p. 134).

13. Before 1868 girls' schools received no endowments, though boys' schools, for the middle and upper classes at least, were well endowed. By 1875 the situation had changed very little.

14. In 1878 the National Union established Maria Grey College, the first training college in Britain for non-elementary school teachers (Hollis, p. 134).

15. Maria Grey and Emily Shirreff founded the English branch of the Froebel Society in 1874. Maria then got much involved with the Girls' Day Schools Co. Ltd. But Emily Shirreff made kindergartens her main interest and activity. There were no kindergartens in the government-controlled public school system until the 1890's.

16.  Friedrich Froebel's system of kindergarten education differed markedly
     from the traditional methods of education in elementary and secondary
     schools. These excerpts from EF's précis of Emily Shirreff's Froebel
     Society paper, "The Kindergarten in relation to the School," provide
     some idea of that system:
     > In the schools children were taught that they were recipients of
     > knowledge; in Fröbel's system they were beings with faculties of
     > many kinds that must develop freely according to their nature, that
     > must not be urged in this direction or cramped in another, but be
     > placed in the most favourable circumstances to attain their full
     > growth. . . . Fröbel rejected all kinds of instruction for little
     > children that [were] directed to the memory alone; he presented
     > objects to them — form, colour, tangible and visible properties, not
     > words and symbols. He asked them to learn nothing that they could
     > not understand, and he did not seek to make them understand
     > anything but what they could observe and compare for them-
     > selves. . . . Besides the faculties of observation, discrimination,
     > reasoning, and imagination, a most important quality was trained,
     > without which the rest lost their highest value — the quality of
     > accuracy. . . . Experience shows that the Kindergarten is not merely
     > play — that it is a part of education (*VM*, 1/78, 268).
17.  Emily stated that she had met Miss Peabody in Boston during her
     previous trip to America in 1872-3. So she knew of Froebel's system
     at least a year before Mrs. Grey and Miss Shirreff founded the British
     branch of the Froebel Society.
18.  In 1884 EF donated the proceeds of two of her lectures in Chicago and
     San Francisco to the Kindergarten Associations in those cities. Her
     generosity led to a San Francisco kindergarten being named the Emily
     Faithfull Kindergarten (*Three Visits*, 222).
19.  Before the San Francisco kindergartens were incorporated into the
     public school system, the Golden Gate Kindergarten Association could
     boast of forty-four free kindergartens, of which the Emily Faithfull
     Kindergarten was one (Agnes Snyder, *Dauntless Women in Childhood
     Education 1856-1931*, Washington: Ass'n for Childhood Education
     International, 1972).
20.  "Boarding-out" involved living in foster homes and attending Board
     Schools.
21.  In December 1878 EF announced that Lord Shaftesbury was making
     another appeal for funds for the Ragged Schools, whose urchins were
     apparently not genteel enough to be registered in Board Schools (*LE*,
     12/21/78). Mary Carpenter, a fellow supporter of Ragged Schools for
     neglected children for many years, had died in 1877; so Shaftesbury
     was conducting the appeal on his own.

22. Emily favoured compulsory education of children in principle, but she noted some problems, e.g., an eleven-year old girl being forced to attend school , thus depriving her working mother of a baby-sitter and her job (*W & W*, 5/8/75). So she suggested that authorities "Exercise the law [concerning compulsory education] firmly where you must; but make some allowance for actual necessities" (*W & W*, 15/22/75, 2). Nevertheless, she would compel factory owners to educate children in their factories (*W & W*, 5/11/75), and she praised Henry Fawcett for introducing a motion in Parliament favouring compulsory education of children of agricultural labourers (*W & W*, 3/6/75, 4).

23. Writing from America in 1882, Emily commented on the bad effects of cramming on female scholars in women's colleges (*LP*, 12/2/82, 244).

24. Emily approved of Elizabeth Cady Stanton's insistence on a liberal education to help women recover their self-respect: "What is the secret of this want of self-respect among women? Man's want of respect for them. They have been educated in superstition and subjection" (E.C. Stanton, "American Notes," *W & W*, 2/20/75, 2).

25. Emily, for example, contended that a student should get an historical training in the classical manner *before* dealing with "present day history and politics" (*LP*, 6/28/90, 1048).

26. She was referring to Victoria University here (*LP*, 7/11/85, 25).

27. Emily reported that a Miss Leach had proposed that elocution be a school subject (*LP*, 4/15/93, 526), and she was pleased that King's College had appointed a lady professor of elocution (*LP*, 7/15/93, 104).

28. Referring to Dr. Alfred Russel Wallace's opinion that "reformed humanity" would result from "rapid development and higher education of women," EF stated that the "goal in view is to give woman such a training that she will be rendered economically independent" and therefore not be compelled to make an "uncongenial marriage" (*LP*, 1/20/94, 80). Here, of course, she was expressing in positive terms the argument she had presented negatively in her 1862 SSA paper "On Some of the Drawbacks Connected with the Present Employment of Women," when she asserted that the "chief drawback" was "defective education."

29. In 1874 she quoted a Dr. Wilks on this subject: "My own experience is that the strong, active, right-minded girls are those who have been well educated at school or colleges, and who are constantly engaged in work for themselves and others, who are employed at drawing, sculpture, languages, or even science" (*W & W*, 8/1/74, 2). To these "employments" Emily added physical exercise as a reason for their being healthy. And in 1892 she cited Dr. Elizabeth Garrett Anderson as another authority who had observed that freer lives and better

education had resulted in taller, stronger, better-looking and happier girls (*LP*, 7/9/92, 55).

30. In 1872 and 1883 EF visited Vassar, the most famous of women's colleges in America. Though she was impressed by the wonderful facilities there, she asserted that American college girls were not as healthy as British girls, chiefly because they did not get enough exercise, especially in winter (*VM*, 4/73, 541).

31. Emily cited the examples of single women like Emily Davies, Anne Clough, and Miss Gladstone to show that higher education did not "unfeminise" girls (*LP*, 1/12/89, 54).

32. Elizabeth Garrett and Emily Davies applied for admission in April 1862 because a new charter for the University of London was being drafted and they hoped that this charter could be amended to extend the privileges of the university (admission, granting of degrees, etc.) to women. (E. Moberly Bell, *Storming the Citadel: The Rise of the Woman Doctor*, London: Constable & Co. Ltd., 1953, p. 57).

33. Jessie Meriton White was the first woman who tried (unsuccessfully) to gain admission to a British university, the University of London (1856).

34. Emily Faithfull listed these people as participants in the 1862 breakfast discussions at her home on Taviton Street, London: the Earl of Shaftesbury, Lords Lyttleton and Houghton, Reverend F.D. Maurice, Mr. Nassau Senior, Emily Davies, and "distinguished educationists" (*LP*, 6/29/89, 938). To this list Emily Davies added Harry Chester, Russell Gurney, R.H. Hutton, G.W. Hastings, Mr. Shaen (of University of London), Barbara Bodichon, Isa Craig, and Bessie Parkes (*ED Papers*, 262).

35. Emily Davies gave tangible support to EF's claim that she was an ex-officio member of the expanded committee when she informed a correspondent that copies of this pamphlet could be obtained at "Princes St. (Miss Faithfull's shop and the office of the *Victoria Magazine*)" (*ED Papers*, 304).

36. Frances Power Cobbe's 1862 SSA paper, "The Education of Women and How it Would be Affected by University Examinations," which was published by the Victoria Press in 1863, and Emily Davies's 1863 article entitled "The Influence of University Degrees on the Education of Women" (*VM*, 10/63) provided further grist for the Oxford and Cambridge mills in which the "Proposed Admission of Girls to Local University Examinations" petition was being ground so fine.

37. The SSA got involved in 1864; it was their memorial to Cambridge that led to the three-year arrangement concerning local examinations for girls.

38. The University of Edinburgh admitted girls to the local examinations in 1864, Oxford did so in 1870, and by 1873 Durham, Ireland (Dublin) and Queen's (Belfast) had jumped on the bandwagon. Other universities and colleges soon followed these leaders.

39. Emily applied the term "girls" to the earlier examinees; by 1869 she referred to them as "ladies" and "women," thus implying a dignified maturity.

40. Another women's college comparable with Girton and Newnham was Holloway College, built at Egham, a good distance out of London, according to the grandiose plans for a ladies' university of an American millionaire, Thomas Holloway, who no doubt had Tennyson's "The Princess" in mind when he designed his palace. The 1874 plans called for a huge building to house and provide classroom and laboratory space for 400 women students, with twenty or more female professors to teach them (*W & W*, 3/6/75). Honnor Morten described Holloway College as "somewhat lonesome and detached," with "an empty and cheerless air" (Morten, op.cit., p. 39). But EF apparently believed it had potential, particularly in the sciences; in 1888 she noted that, though it had only a population of forty-six students, Holloway had an "excellent laboratory . . . working room for twenty-two students in chemistry, and two smaller rooms for biology and physics" (*LP*, 10/27/88, 472). She also published the names of Holloway College's scholarship winners in 1893 (*LP*, 7/29/88, 169) and listed the 1894 graduates — all four of them! (*LP*, 7/14/94, 48). Of course, her second cousin Lilian Faithfull was a lecturer at Holloway from 1889-1894, so EF probably felt she had to speak well of the institution.

41. Hollis, op.cit., p. 135.

42. Letter from Emily Davies to Mr. H. Sidgwick, 31 December 1870, in Hollis, p. 153.

43. In 1875 EF reprinted a *Fraser's Magazine* article entitled "Girton College" that gave full credit to Emily Davies and Barbara Bodichon for their part in ensuring the success of Girton College (*VM*, 5/75).

44. After Emily Davies had refused to locate her women's college in the heart of Cambridge, Henry Sidgwick, with the aid of Mr. and Mrs. Henry Fawcett, founded Newnham Hall (later Newnham College) and appointed Anne Clough, who had been the organizing secretary of the North of England Council for women's education, as principal. The philosophy of education at Newnham was based on the idea that "women should obtain a higher education that suited their needs and resources, whether they stayed a term or a year" (Hollis, p. 135).

45. Hollis, p. 154, quoted from B.A. Clough, *Memoir of Anne Jemima Clough*, 1897, pp. 175-7.

46.  An 1888 petition for admission of women to Cambridge degrees was signed by these influential women (among others): Lady Goldsmid, the Dowager Lady Stanley of Alderley, Miss Buss, Miss Beale, Barbara Bodichon, Mrs. Henry Fawcett, Mrs. Elizabeth Garrett Anderson, M.D., Amelia B. Edwards, Florence Nightingale, Emily Shirreff, Mrs. Humphrey Ward, Lydia Becker, Elizabeth Blackwell, M.D., Arabella Shore, and Louisa Hubbard. And these eminent men also signed: R.H. Hutton, Professor Thomas Huxley, John Bright, Wilfrid S. Blunt, Robert Browning, Richard Haldane, Thomas Hughes, J. Cotter Morison, and James Sully. But it was all to no avail.

Women university students and ex-students also submitted petitions. When the university council finally voted on April 22, 1897, the tally was 1707 to 661 against granting degrees to women — hardly encouraging (*ED Papers*, Reel 8).

47.  Emily Davies, in her article "Women in Universities," published in *Tracts on Female Suffrage*, said that Cambridge admitted women to degrees in music in 1882. But that appears to have been the only degree Cambridge granted to women until after World War II.

48.  At the instigation of the London Ladies' Educational Association, University College professors lectured to ladies at the College in a broad spectrum of subjects from 1869 to 1877 (*VM*, 11/77, 78-80). King's College professors gave lectures in Science and Art at the South Kensington Museum; EF mentions Professors Huxley, Guthrie and Oliver in particular (*VM*, 11/69 and 11/70).

49.  Emily was aware that American lawyers were also strongly opposed to women entering their profession. As late as 1893 the University of New York agreed to provide law courses to women students, but only if they were not pursuing a law degree (*LP*, 1/7/93). However, some American women had received degrees from other American universities and were practising law before 1879, the year that Mrs. Bella Lockwood, who had graduated in law in 1873, became the first woman attorney in the U.S.A. Certainly Mrs. Lockwood, who practised law in the District of Columbia, still had to deal with the strong prejudice against female lawyers; for example, in 1878 a Maryland judge refused her admission to the Circuit Court of Prince George's County, Maryland (*VM*, 4/79, 596). Nevertheless, American women had access to law degrees and law practice much sooner than their British counterparts did.

50.  Westfield College, Hampstead, built in 1882, was the first permanent residence for women registered at the University of London. So University of London degrees for women were not legally valid until 1882.

51. There were two false alarms, the first in 1874 and the second when the University of London Senate had voted in 1877 to admit women to medical degrees (*VM*, 4/77), only to have their vote temporarily rescinded by the House of Commons (*VM*, 6/77), which was in the throes of passing the Medical Act Amendment Bill that enabled women to enter the medical profession.

52. A permanent hall of residence was built at the University of Wales in 1891; so its degrees for women were legally valid in that year. This university was co-educational from its inception.

53. Edinburgh, Glasgow, Aberdeen, and St. Andrew's were the universities of Scotland. The Scottish Universities' Bill authorizing these institutions to admit women to degrees was passed in 1888, though St. Andrew's had admitted women to its LLA degree since 1877. Thus Queen Margaret College, Glasgow, a women's college, comparable with Girton, Newnham and Royal Holloway, was eligible to affiliate with Glasgow University, and it did so. As EF observed, women students of this college were given special correspondence classes to prepare them for university and other examinations (*LP*, 11/24/88, 596).

54. The *Englishwoman's Review* stated that women were admitted to Durham University and to the first degree in Arts in 1881 (*ER*, 6/15/81). The 1895 date refers to the year Durham opened all its degrees to women.

55. Emily reported that Australian universities received women for degrees from 1876 to 1882. Women were also eligible to become professors and lecturers at these universities but they were excluded from membership in Senate. So even Australian universities did not grant the full rights and privileges that University of London did (*LP*, 7/27/89, 120). Canada was far behind Britain. In 1891 only McGill University was considering a women's college (*LP*, 1/20/91, 1097).

56. The Royal Academy of Music admitted women to its ranks and a new school of Music was established in South Kensington in 1875 (*W & W*, 6/26/75). Emily Faithfull also noted that Sir Charles Hallé's College of Music had opened in 1893, with seventy-four students (men and women) from all over the country (*LP*, 10/7/93, 534). The universities, however, do not appear to have regarded music as a serious academic discipline. Nor did they welcome Schools of Art. Therefore, separate Schools of Art were established for women.

57. This building, built in 1883, housed the Women's Department of Owen's College.

58. Victoria University consisted of three colleges: Owen's College, Manchester; University College, Liverpool; and Yorkshire College, Leeds.

59. Emily gave credit to Sir Henry Roscoe, head of the School of Chemistry, and to Dr. Greenwood for being concerned about equal education facilities for women at Owen's College and Victoria University (*LP*, 12/26/85, 557 and 10/6/94, 497).

60. In 1872 ladies registered at the Birkbeck Institute (later a college of the University of London) were also given the title of Associate if they gave proof that they possessed a good sound English education. So "Associate" appears to have been an honorary title of little use in the marketplace (*VM*, 2/72, 375).

61. In her SSA paper, "Middle Class Schools for Girls."

62. Emily did not hold governesses entirely responsible for the low standard of their teaching. She also blamed the parents, "who are not at all particular how their children are taught . . . the root of the whole evil lies in the disregard for education which is a disgrace to the English people" (*W & W*, 1/15/76, 4).

63. Emily Faithfull, "Woman's Work; with special reference to industrial employment," London: Victoria Press, 1871 (read before the Society of Arts, March 29, 1871).

64. In 1875 EF listed pharmacy as an employment for women in her "Guide to Employments for Women" column and indicated that the five-month course cost £4.14s 6d (*W & W*, 4/17/75, 7).

65. In 1858 the *Lancet* praised women for founding the Ladies' Sanitary Association, "which concerns itself with all things womanly in the homes and habits of the poor . . . healthy homes, the feeding of infants, how to manage when pregnant, etc.," for none of these activities encroached on the medical doctor's domain (*Lancet*, 11/13/58, 507).

66. Midwives attained some measure of independence by undertaking courses and examinations at the Female Medical College established by the Female Medical Society.

67. Emily attended the seventh annual meeting of the Female Medical Society in 1871 and, at the Earl of Shaftesbury's urging, moved the adoption of a report concerning women who had passed the Female Medical College's examinations in midwifery. She "saw no reason why this movement should not be supported because it did not aim at securing for women the position to which Mrs. [Elizabeth Garrett] Anderson with larger means and power could attain" (*VM*, 7/71, 282). The Female Medical Society, incidentally, was established "to promote the employment of educated women in the practice of midwifery and the treatment of the diseases of women and children" (*VM*, 5/67, 28).

Despite these attempts of midwives to be independent, the Medical Council decided in 1875 to take steps to ensure more efficient education and examination of midwives (*W & W*, 9/25/75, 5). Women midwives who passed these examinations and gained a Diploma were entitled to a place in the Medical Register and could get jobs in obstetric departments of medicine and surgery (*W & W*, 1/27/76).

68. In 1849 Elizabeth Blackwell, a graduate of Geneva College, was the only woman with a medical degree in America.

69. By 1894 this total of British women doctors — at least those who were members of the British Medical Association — had increased only slightly to twenty-one (*LP*, 1/13/94, 47).

70. The only universities in Europe where a woman could get a medical degree up to 1878 were Zurich and Paris.

71. The plight of the University of Edinburgh women students from 1871 on and the pressing need for women doctors in India were also contributing factors. However, the long struggle of Elizabeth Garrett Anderson engaged the public imagination more than anything else did.

72. The best known of these women were Sophia Jex-Blake and Edith Pechey.

73. After granting Elizabeth Garrett its diploma, the London Society of Apothecaries would not accept any more women for diplomas. So EF wrote an editorial in 1874 in which she proposed a separate medical school for women (*W & W*, 10/10/74).

74. The impasse at the University of Edinburgh was not resolved satisfactorily before 1895. Instead, an Edinburgh School of Medicine was established and in 1891 its female students were admitted for hospital instruction to the Edinburgh Royal Infirmary (with separate ward visits and clinical lectures). Scottish medical degrees were granted through the Scottish Association for Medical Education, and through St. Andrew's University (*LP*, 10/10/94, 551).

75. Because of religious restrictions, especially among cloistered ladies of the Zenana, male doctors were not allowed to treat Indian women. As a Dr. Cornish had explained it to EF, "no one but a woman doctor could have a chance of dealing with the native patients, who were not allowed to see the masculine doctor, and at most could only put their hand out through a screen to have the state of their pulse ascertained [by him]" (*LP*, 7/26/90, 148).

76. The King's and Queen's College of Physicians and Surgeons in Dublin jumped the gun by granting medical degrees to women in 1877. Two of their degrees went to Sophia Jex-Blake and Edith Pechey (*VM*, 6/77, 173).

77. Emily noted in her *West London Express* that "one of the best, if not the best, speeches on the opening of the Medical Schools [at the University of London in October 1878] was made by Miss Pechy (sic), M.D., of the Medical School for Women" (*WLE*, 10/5/78, 213).

78. In 1894 EF felt constrained to condemn the callousness and utter indifference of many fathers to "the claims of their girls . . . I have never wished to incite any girl to leave the shelter of a home, but no man has a right to keep his daughters there without making a provision for their future" (*LP*, 11/10/94, 680). And she went on to castigate fathers who assumed "ownership" of daughters "where only guardianship was intended" (*LP*, 12/1/94, 801).

79. The *Times* of February 21, 1878 had published an article blaming women for contributing to "too much of the bad work which is done in the world." Emily Faithfull answered in a letter to the *Times'* editor that this bad work was due to "want of definite training. Take the very case you instance, and I reply it is only within the last year or two that women have had a fair chance of being even trained as cooks. They have had to scramble into all occupations as best they could. . . . Those who do "bad work" are for the most part driven for dear life into pursuits for which they have neither taste nor inclination" (*Times*, 2/22/78, rpt. in *VM*, 3/78, 449-50).

80. In "Our Daughters" EF gave Bessie Parkes credit for originating this idea that every girl should be trained for some trade. Incidentally, as EF was happy to report in a subsequent column, this article resulted in both the Shorthand Association and the Massage Therapists offering to train girls in their trades (*LP*, 5/5/88, 478).

81. Emily insisted on workers being thoroughly trained. She was quite upset when she learned that women compositors in Glasgow might not be required to undergo full apprenticeship (*W & W*, 8/28/75, 2).

82. Emily attended the first meeting of the Quebec Institute in November 1874 and seconded the vote of thanks to Mr. John Walter, M.P., who had presented a paper on the advantages of a course in the masterpieces of English Literature (*W & W*, 11/28/74, 2).

83. When the New Society for Employment of Women opened in Manchester in 1891, EF reminded the founders that technical training should be the first objective of the Society, for it "alone can raise a woman's work above the level of mere charity" (*LP*, 3/21/91, 436).

84. In 1874 EF published an article on the Queen's Institute, Dublin, which conducted "technical" training in all of these art-related jobs, as well as in scrivenery and telegraphy (*W & W*, 10/24/74).

85. Emily Faithfull's *W & W* column entitled "Guide to Employments for Women" contained brief references to training for certain employments, e.g., "respectable and honest tuition" for women wishing to become actresses, (*W & W*, 12/4/75, 7); courses from the Female School of Art, the South Kensington School of Art, and the School of Art Needlework; and on-the-job training for printer's readers, law copiers, dispensers, and hairdressers (*W & W*, 4/17/75, 7).

86. Emily reported in 1894 that the Certificated Society of Sanitary Inspectors, some of whom were women, had suggested at its annual meeting that a training programme be organized for its members, and that they gain more knowledge of their job through reading books on the subject (*LP*, 4/7/94).
87. In 1894 EF noted a need for technical schools connected with the manufacture of silk (*LP*, 6/9/94, 898).
88. Emily contended that ladies needed training before undertaking political work: "I am often astounded to see how difficult it is to discover any one really fit to undertake such work" (*LP*, 6/17/93, 950).
89. Emily believed that a training in domestic economy was more essential for women than higher education: "No one has taken keener interest than I have in higher education of woman, yet I have always felt that education in home life and duties must be the groundwork on which all other branches of education are built" ( *LP*, 9/8/94, 338).
90. Emily noted that Miss Cock's school, St. Martha's School of Domestic Economy at Walthamstow, also included a St. John's Ambulance course in first aid in its curriculum (*LP*, 1/14/93, 48).
91. Middle-class and upper-class girls in 1850 and even later got no training in domestic economy. As Josephine Kamm says, "The eighteenth-century woman might be ignorant of geography and history, but she was learned in domestic lore; while in the prosperous nineteenth century the idea had developed that she should not be expected to cook, keep house, or even wait on herself" (Josephine Kamm, *How Different From Us: Miss Buss and Miss Beale*, London: The Bodley Head, 1958, p. 9).
92. In her "Letter from England" Alice B. Le Geyt reported that EF was busy "organizing a training school for cookery and housekeeping" (*The Woman's Journal*, 7/1/71, 203).
93. Prior to this meeting EF wrote a letter to the Duke of Argyll that referred to an "undertaking of great significance to middle-class English homes" and said that she was empowered by the "committee of the proposed Training Institute" to ask him to be a Vice-President "as signifying his Grace's interest" in this project (Fawcett Library, Vol. IIA, letter dated 7/29/71).
94. Emily was closely associated with this campaign. Not only did she solicit funds; she also wrote to the Duke of Westminster to request that he open the new premises of Miss Romley Wright's School of Domestic Economy and informed her readers that the Duke had regretfully declined her invitation (*LP*, 4/26/90, 632). She also reported that money for the School was coming in slowly, thus implying that Manchester people should contribute more to this worthwhile project (*LP*, 5/31/90, 831).

95.   In 1875 EF reported that the London School Board had arranged for
      three hundred girls to be taught cookery at the National Training
      School of Cookery at Marylebone and Greenwich (*W & W*, 10/2/75,
      3). Students in this programme were trained to "instruct in Training
      Schools, Board Schools, &c. Also to become lecturers and public
      instructors in the provinces" (*W & W*, 4/17/75, 7).
96.   In 1877 EF pointed out that some schools of cookery needed help
      from the Department of Education (*VM*, 9/77, 457).
97.   Honnor Morten disagreed with EF about the importance of domestic
      economy for Board School girls; she contended that these girls should
      take such courses at evening schools and polytechnics, and that Board
      Schools should concentrate on teaching the three R's (Morten, op.cit.).
98.   Emily recommended Mrs. Marshall's lectures in high-class cookery in
      1887 and 1892 (*LP*, 8/20/87, 184 and 10/1/92, 468).
99.   Emily recommended an apprenticeship in cookery for teachers of
      cookery, not just courses in Schools of Domestic Economy (*LP*,
      3/19/92, 428).
100.  Emily believed that if more women were elected to School Boards,
      Schools of Domestic Economy under the wings of these Boards would
      be better supported. But not enough women stood for election to
      School Boards; so men controlled the Boards and hence the fate of
      courses in Domestic Economy.
101.  Lydia Becker was the first woman to serve on the Manchester School
      Board. She was elected in 1870 and served for seven consecutive
      terms.
102.  The *OED* defines "sloyd" as "a system of manual instruction in
      elementary woodwork, etc., originally developed and taught in
      Sweden" (*Shorter Oxford English Dictionary*, Oxford: Clarendon
      Press, 1959, p. 1920).
103.  Fawcett, intro. to Honnor Morten, *Questions for Women (and Men)*,
      London: Adam & Charles Black, 1899, pp. 4-5.

Chapter Seven

1.    In her paper "Women and Work" presented to the Victoria Discussion
      Society in June 1874 EF stressed the "physical necessity" for women
      to work; i.e., they had to work or starve. She noted that other VDS
      participants had dealt with the abstract moral right of women to work,
      but she suggested that her *practical* approach would have to apply for
      years to come (*VM*, 7/74, 191-202 and 8/74, 308-311).

2.   Emily noted that Parliament, no doubt acting on the belief that women were mentally and physically inferior to men, had imposed several restrictions on women, e.g., a limitation on the number of hours they could work in factories and workshops, and an attempt to remove pit-brow women from their "too strenuous" jobs (*LP*, 4/10/86, 315). And she recorded Mrs. Fawcett's observation that Parliament had further restricted women's employment by not permitting them to be members or professors of universities and by opening only one branch of the Civil Service — the Post Office — to them (*LP*, 7/22/93, 118).

3.   In 1875 EF commented on the plight of resident governesses when they were compelled to take unpaid holidays because their employers were out of town. EF suggested that these families should take their governesses with them (*W & W*, 8/7/75, 5). And she noted in a letter to the *Times* from Montreal in 1883 that governesses who had emigrated to Canada had become charity cases because they could not adapt to new habits and new jobs when they realized that the field for governesses and teachers was as overstocked in Canada as it was in Britain (*Times*, 4/23/83, 11). Even as late as 1893 EF observed that governesses, if they were lucky enough to be employed, received poor salaries and suffered indignities (*LP*, 3/18/93, 378).

4.   Teaching was the only profession fully open to educated women in 1895, but women teachers in Britain received only forty percent of the salary paid to comparable male teachers. Conditions were somewhat better in America, but even there women had difficulty getting jobs for which they were qualified. And with very few exceptions they received poor wages for the work they did. (*VM*, 11/73, 79-80).

5.   The same situation prevailed in America. Very few of the women working in government offices in Washington in March 1873 were promoted to higher ranks. Indeed, having only recently been introduced into government employ during the Civil War, they were there "on sufferance," Grace Greenwood told EF (*VM*, 5/73, 31-2 and 11/73, 79-80).

6.   Honnor Morten, op.cit., p. 7.

7.   To mark the end of the first year's successful publication of *Women and Work*, EF asked for three things:
     (1)   Women be allowed to do work for which they were specially fitted.
     (2)   Women be allowed to compete on equal terms with men in work done by either sex.
     (3)   A "fair field and no favour."
                    (*W & W*, 6/5/75, 4).

8.   Changes in the economy that forced employers to hire women in proliferating white-collar jobs seem to have been more responsible for

      this change in attitude than the demands of reformers or the economic circumstances of individuals.

9.   Emily noted this change in 1892, though she was not assured that all women recognized it: "I have survived the prejudices of my youth, when I thought that gentlemen were alone to be found in the army, navy, and the church. I have lived to see the day when they can enter upon any professional or commercial work without loss of social position; perhaps before I die I may find that idleness will be looked upon as discreditable in a woman" (*LP*, 4/2/92, 508).

10.   Emily objected even more strongly to selling these home-made items at bazaars, for she agreed with Louisa Twining that bazaars constituted "an immoral method of raising money for charity purposes" (*LP*, 1/19/89, 85).

11.   Emily Faithfull, "The Progress of Woman in Industrial Employment," *The Universal Review*, December 1888, pp. 642-3.

12.   Emily set up a Christmas "Fund for Destitute Ladies" in the 1860's and she continued to solicit money for that fund until the 1890's. But she frankly admitted that it did little to alleviate the distress of these gentlewomen.

13.   Emily Faithfull's Letter-to-the-Editor, *Times*, 7/12/69, 610.

14.   After announcing the formation of the Ladies' Work Society in May/69, EF received confidential letters from hundreds of women, along with examples of their work. Even she was "unprepared for the mass of misery" revealed in these letters (*VM*, 7/69, 195).

15.   No member's name was made public and numbers were assigned to the ladies so that their work could be identified when the finished product was sold (*VM*, 7/69, 194).

16.   The sale took place daily from 10 a.m. to 5 p.m. at the offices of the Victoria Press. In December 1869 the Princess of Wales, patron of EF's Ladies' Work Society, purchased some of the items to encourage other ladies to do likewise (*VM*, 12/69).

17.   A.C. Twynam, Lady Superintendent, set up day classes in choral conducting, photograph colouring, wood engraving, carving, modelling, gutta percha work, reading, illumination, shorthand writing, mapping for surveys, and French and Italian conversation. She also arranged for evening lectures on such popular subjects as Physiology, Domestic Economy, Astronomy, Practical Chemistry, Music, Education, Art, Eminent Women, Botany, Tapestry, Watch Making, Practical Medicine and Nursing, Female Costumes, Flemish Wood Carving, and Etching. Classrooms were also open on Sunday for rest and quiet reading between church services (*VM*, 11/69, 80-81).

18.   In 1885 EF reported that the annual return to the 200 ladies in the Manchester Ladies' Work Society averaged only £3. "Not a very

substantial maintenance surely!" was EF's British understatement to describe this pittance (*LP*, 12/12/85, 501).

19. Ladies' settlements were established in the poor areas of the big cities, and the ladies lived and worked there. They performed functions similar to those of the College of Women Workers (the "Grey Ladies"), e.g., visits to the poor; superintendence of Bible classes, needle societies, parochial clubs, mothers' meetings, Sunday schools; dressmaking, drawing, and singing classes; sanitation lectures, and so on. EF praised these settlements in 1895: "It is pleasant to know, in spite of the talk of the New Woman, that so many ladies are ready to devote their energies to the ministrations needed by the sick and suffering. Every ridiculous step [of the New Woman ] is recorded throughout the newspapers in the kingdom, but how slowly is modest, good, womanly work recognized" (*LP*, 2/2/95, 150).

20. In 1890 EF mentioned a House of Help in Bristol for ladies willing to help the sick and distressed and pay £40 a year for board and lodging (*LP*, 2/1/90, 166).

21. In 1892 EF referred to a party in Whitechapel for crippled children at which female philanthropists presented mechanical dolls, clothing, and "buns galore" to the children. Four thousand people attended (*LP*, 6/18/92, 984).

22. EF had met Amelia Edwards "at the earliest attempts at a club for ladies in Langham Place in 1859" (*LP*, 4/30/92, 677). By 1886 Edwards had become famous as an Egyptologist. She received honorary degrees from Smith College and the College of Sisters of Bethany. She also gave a keynote address at an Oriental Congress in Vienna (*The Queen*, 7/24, 8/7, and 8/14/86).

23. In 1894 EF noted that Miss Smith occupied a professorial chair in the Ladies' Department of King's College but that no women had yet been appointed to professorships at King's College (*LP*, 8/4/94, 166). Lilian Faithfull, recently elected by King's College "to fill the important post of Vice-Principal of the Ladies' Department," was in the same situation as Miss Smith.

24. Though Emily confessed that "reared in all the prejudices of English Episcopalianism few things seemed to me more strange in America than the claim of lady preachers to the title of Reverend" (*LP*, 2/23/89, 252), she nonetheless supported the right of women in other denominations to become "clergywomen."

25. With uncharacteristic modesty EF neglected to point out that by 1878 she herself had published and edited the *Victoria Magazine, Women and Work*, and the *West London Express*.

26. Emily noted this need in 1872 (*VM*, 7/72), stressed its urgency in 1877 (*VM*, 3/77, 458) and 1890 (*LP*, 7/26/90, 148), and gave credit in 1894

to Lady Dufferin and Lady Lansdowne for enabling medical women to assume responsible positions in India.

27.  In 1874 EF quoted Florence Nightingale as saying that nursing the sick poor in their homes was the "most important aspect of nursing" (*W & W*, 9/12/74, 6). And in 1891 she congratulated the nurses who had received Queen's badges for taking charge of the sick poor in their homes (*LP*, 3/7/91, 338).

28.  Emily also gave credit to Louisa Twining for establishing the Workhouse Infirmary Nursing Association for trained female nurses (*LP*, 5/24/90, 775).

29.  In 1883 EF was impressed with the work at the School of Young Lady Potters in Philadelphia where "the students are taught the chemistry of colours and anatomy, and find not only a delightful occupation, but a very remunerative one" (*LP*, "Across the Atlantic," 1/27/83, 59).

30.  In 1874 EF reprinted an article from *Pictorial World* entitled "Artistic Employment for Women" that described two alternatives to wood engraving. The first involved drawing on waxed plates with an etching needle; the second entailed photographic reproduction of pen-and-ink sketches. Both procedures were more suitable than wood engraving with letter press (*W & W*, 7/4/74, 1).

31.  In her travel book EF commented on the many jobs opened up by ingenious American women after they had received a thorough art education. These included glass-painting, illuminating, crayon photography, specimen-mounting, etching, designing, china-painting, and wood-carving (*Three Visits*, 286).

32.  Decorative art, as practised by Charlotte Robinson, EF's good friend, and others, comprehended a number of artistic talents including interior and exterior decorating (of house or town hall or what have you), painting knick-knacks, designing wallpaper and furniture, ribbon and velvet embroideries, even dress designing (*W & W*, 10/3/74, 2).

33.  In 1878 EF reprinted an item from the *Englishwoman's Review* announcing the opening of "an artistic table-glass depot" by two enterprising ladies and suggesting that women with "sufficient *esprit de corps*" should make their Christmas purchases there (*VM*, 1/78, 269).

34.  In her "Guide to Employments for Women" column EF inserted this item: "China painters at Minton's (pottery work) South Kensington earn from £80 to £170 per annum" (*W & W*, 12/4/75, 7).

35.  Emily highly recommended Miss Downing's photographic studio (the North London Photographic Fine Arts Repository Company), where Ella Dietz, Kate Pattison, Rutland Barrington and EF herself had had their photos taken: "We can say, without hesitation, that more beautiful

specimens of photographic art it would not be easy to find" (*W & W,* 8/21/75, 2).

36. Isa Craig had worked with some of these women at the Telegraph Station in 1861, and she had encouraged the privately-owned postal telegraph companies to hire more women (*EWJ,* 11/61).

37. Janet Courtney remembered her parson father telling her "as a little girl, that a Miss Faithfull had got women into the General Post Office," i.e., that she had persuaded "the Postmaster-General of the period to introduce women as postal sorters . . . " (Janet E. Courtney, *The Women of My Time,* London: Lovat Dickson Ltd., 1934). According to EF, Lord John Manners, Duke of Rutland, opened jobs for women in telegraph offices, and Henry Fawcett did likewise in post offices (*LP,* 4/27/89, 575). But Emily also noted that both Manners and Fawcett were involved in the 1875 hiring of women to work in the Post Office Savings Banks (*W & W,* 4/10/75, 4/24/75 and 8/28/75).

38. At a meeting of the Victoria Discussion Society in April 1875, EF quoted from a letter she had just received to the effect that female clerks would be hired to do Savings Bank work. So it is clear that she was one of the first to be informed of this important change in hiring policy (*VM,* 5/75, 599-600).

39. Emily reported in 1883 that, though many women were employed in the American Civil Service, their pay was generally lower than that of women in the British Civil Service. For example, the women working in the U.S. Mint received only $1.50 a day (*LP,* "Across the Atlantic," 1/27/83, 59).

40. Referring to these civil service jobs in Britain, EF stated, "I am glad to say that while girls entering as second-class clerks receive £65, rising by £3 a year to £80, there are promotions by merit to clerkships rising to £110 a year and a few to £170. Three lady superintendents receive £400, and four assistant superintendents £200. The work is not difficult and the hours seven a day, and an annual holiday of a month is given" (*LP,* 4/11/91, 566).

41. In 1874 the British Civil Service employed 3000 women (*W & W,* 10/10/74, 6); in 1881 the census figure had risen only to 4,353 for Post Office and Telegraph workers.

42. In 1875 female book-keepers were hired to make abstracts from invoices for the goods traffic carried by the London and Northwestern Rlwy. Co., and when it was found that these women were neater and more accurate than male clerks, more women were hired (*VM,* 2/78, 357). Incidentally, in an attempt to convince ladies that book-keeping done at home was less remunerative than that done in a supervised office setting, EF published these comparative salaries: "Indoors, £15

to £30 per annum. Out of house 10s to 30s per week [i.e. £26 to £78 per annum]" (*VM*, 12/76, 183).

43. In Oct/76 a Miss Crosby opened a Ladies' Tracing Office in London. And several firms in Scotland had already hired women to trace engineers' plans (*VM*, 12/76, 178-9).

44. Emily Faithfull, "The Progress of Woman in Industrial Employment," op.cit., p. 640.

45. William Robson, a London tea-merchant, offered "genteel and easy employment" for ladies as "corresponding agents" (selling tea by mail, presumably)(*W & W*, 9/18/75, 4).

46. British publishers apparently did not hire gentlewomen as sales agents, though working-class women were employed as "Bible-women" to sell the good book to their own class (*VM*, 12/76, 182). In America, however, many ladies were hired as newspaper canvassers and as encyclopedia saleswomen (*Three Visits*, 299).

47. Of course, EF approved of ladies undertaking management of "a house of business," for that was just what she had done when she established the Victoria Press in 1860.

48. In 1875 EF announced, "Numerical printing is a trade now open to women . . . . Mr. White of Shoe-lane offers permanent employment and training" (*W & W*, 8/21/75, 5).

49. In 1875 EF reported that 13,000 women were employed in watchmaking in Switzerland (*W & W*, 12/18/75, 5). No doubt she hoped that an equal or greater number would be employed in British watch factories in years to come.

50. The 1875 figure is drawn from *Women and Work*, in which EF stated that there were 12,000 operatives, mostly women, in 156 silk factories in the U.S.A. (*W & W*, 8/21/75), the 1884 one from *Three Visits to America*, wherein the total was 50,000 (again mostly women) employed in 400 silk factories (*Three Visits*, 224). Incidentally, in this chapter of *Three Visits* EF provides full details of the cultivation of silk (planting and growing of mulberry trees, hatching and feeding of the silkworms, spinning of the cocoon, reeling of silk from the cocoon, etc.).

51. In 1889 EF reported a scheme for an "English colony" of men and women willing to invest and work in vineyards in Fresno, California (*LP*, 6/29/89, 938).

52. Emily was concerned that most dairy products were imported into Britain from the European continent. "Home" dairying was needed; so here was another opportunity for gentlewomen (*LP*, 2/7/91, 216).

53. In 1875 EF announced that fifty-seven women were editing journals in America (*W & W*, 5/19/75). She did not give the figure for Britain.

54. Emily claimed that in Canada and America, where there were few jobs for governesses and teachers but great need of good dressmakers, ladies could become dressmakers without stigma (*W & W*, 8/22/74).

55. London needlewomen were starving in 1874. However, EF noted, there was a "need for a thoroughly plain good needlewoman at Hayward's Heath, Sussex" (*W & W*, 9/19/74, 5) and no doubt in other small towns outside London.

56. *The Englishwoman's Review* listed some jobs for women that EF did not mention, e.g. brickmaker, glass grinder, brushmaker, coachbuilder, fur sewer (*ER*, 9/15/76); boot and shoe maker, mantle japanner, corset maker; maker of leather bags and millinery; and winder of silk and cotton (*ER*, 4/15/88); also umbrella manufacturer and handloom weaver (*ER*, 2/15/77 and 8/15/77) and woman overseer (*ER*, 5/15/85).

57. In the early 1890's EF strongly urged the Board of Guardians to fund Lady Frederick Cavendish's scheme to set up a laundry to provide jobs for "feeble-minded" or "morally deficient" women (*LP*, 4/5/90, 506). She was able to report in 1893 that the laundry had been established and that the occupation had "brightened" these women considerably (*LP*, 6/24/93, 1017).

58. In 1884 she reported that there were still about 30,000 women "driving and steering canal boats" along the English canal system (*Three Visits*, 299).

59. Emily Faithfull's *Women and Work* also announced that there were many jobs for good household servants in America (*W & W*, 6/6/74).

60. Home work, i.e., doing piece work at home, was still much in evidence in 1894, when EF averred that "it was the home work [in relative isolation] which prevented these girls [who were making trousers, ties, and umbrellas] from combining to get a better price for their work" (*LP*, 3/17/94, 377). Therefore, EF concluded, home work "is one of the greatest hindrances to the success of unionism, and a fruitful source of 'sweating'" (*LP*, 10/31/91, 798).

61. Even in 1866 EF was in favour of the early closing movement for shop assistants (*VM*, 8/66, 467). In 1890 she approved of agitation as a means of shortening their hours of work (*LP*, 7/12/90, 66).

62. In 1875 EF proposed these women be granted "recesses" to occasionally sit down (*W & W*, 10/30/75, 3); and in 1894 and 1895 she noted that two women (Miss Margaret Irwin and Lady Jeune) were conducting "inquiries" into working conditions for shop assistants (*LP*, 8/25/94 and 1/26/95, 134).

63. In 1892 EF observed that 65.5% of the teaching body in America were women, that an American Commissioner of Education had commended these women teachers for achieving better results than the men, but that their salaries were 60% lower than the men's (*LP*, 1/23/92, 126).

The exception was California, where equal pay for male and female teachers had been in effect since 1875 (*W & W*, 7/17/75, 5).

64. From 1871 to 1894 EF demanded again and again that the government appoint women factory inspectors to check on sanitary conditions, illegal prolonging of hours of work, and safety standards in factories and workshops employing women. In 1872-3 she noted the urgent need for women factory inspectors in both Britain and America. In 1875 she agreed with a Miss Simcox that factory inspection by men was a sham (*W & W*, 10/23/75, 2). She also applauded the TUC's approval of female factory inspectors in 1889, and wrote a letter to the *Times* in 1891 asking the editor to call attention to the fact that women factory inspectors were "essential" (*Times*, 2/19/91, 14). And in 1893 she reported a deputation to the Home Secretary similar to the one she herself had headed in 1871; this later deputation concentrated on the need for female inspectors, requesting that "working women, not ladies, be appointed . . . Asquith [the Home Secretary] pledged himself to two 'peripatetic' women inspectors based in London and Glasgow" (*LP*, 2/4/93, 177). In the event Asquith appointed only one woman factory inspector, Clementina Black, and she was a lady. So paternalistic legislation triumphed once again.

Incidentally, in 1894 Mr. Asquith received another deputation of women from the Women's Industrial Defence League (representing bookbinders, shirt and collar makers, tailoresses, laundresses, box makers, etc.) concerning legislation interfering with adult labour and treating women as children. EF commented in this instance on Mr. Asquith's "courtesy and consideration" (*LP*, 7/7/94, 6). But as usual nothing came of it.

65. In 1878 EF disapproved of male trade unions, "which ought to be good and useful combinations, [but which] are practically vast engines, not for protecting, but for crippling trade" (*LE*, 11/16/78, 312), and went on to blame the working classes for the current recession: "There can be no doubt that the bulk of the present distress is owing, directly or indirectly, to the reckless misconduct of the working classes, to strikes, short hours, and improvidence" (*LE*, 12/28/78, 403).

66. Before the TUC came into being, women who tried to join male unions were often rebuffed, e.g., the unsuccessful bid to get women admitted to the National Agricultural Labourers' Union in 1874 (*W & W*, 6/20/74). After the TUC was formed and representatives of women's unions were invited to attend their annual congresses, such refusals were less common. Incidentally, EF was pleased when many of the men on the London Trades Council were in favour of the formation of "Trades Societies" among women (*W & W*, 9/12/74).

67. Amelia Lewis, who attended several meetings of this society, contended that it was not just an ad hoc embryo union; she described it instead as "the first trades union of women" (*Woman*, 5/18/72, 331). EF, however, made no such claim for it. She credited Mrs. Emma Paterson with establishing the first women's trade union (the Book-binders) under the aegis of the Women's Protective and Provident League in 1874 (*W & W*, 9/19/74, 3).

68. Observe the innocuous wording. Even male unions were barely legal in 1872; so euphemisms were constantly employed to avoid the offending term "trade(s) unions," e.g., "Friendly Societies," "Associations," "Protective and Provident Societies," "Benefit and Protection Societies," etc.

69. Anne Godwin, "Early Years in the Trade Unions" in Lucy Middleton, op.cit.

70. Goldman, op.cit., p. 78.

71. The *Englishwoman's Review* (July 15, 1876) stated that the Women's Printing Society was a co-operative venture in that workers could acquire shares.

72. Emily noted that John Ruskin approved of the Women's Protective and Provident League (*VM*, 5/76).

73. Sickness and unemployment insurance for women was urgently needed. In 1892 Clementina Black reported that half the women "unengaged" (i.e., unemployed) over the age of sixty died as paupers (*LP*, 10/15/92, 556).

74. The *Englishwoman's Review* described the WPPL as a self-help group with a library, halfpenny bank, swimming club, employment register, etc. (*ER*, 11/15/79).

75. In 1891 EF referred to a United Sisters' Friendly Society. This was apparently a kind of trade union, for it provided funds during sickness, funeral expenses, and pensions for superannuation (*LP*, 11/7/91, 824).

76. Emily and the other women producing the *English Woman's Journal* in 1860 proposed the formation of industrial associations among workwomen, e.g., an association of needleworkers who would be both capitalists and labourers à la the Rochdale Co-operative Movement founded in 1844. So EF apparently approved of Co-operation when it was not yet respectable.

77. Margaret Llewelyn Davies had this to say about the Guild: "The members who form the Guild are almost entirely married women belonging to the artisan class. . . . The Guild stands for the organized purchasing or consuming power of the working-class community of the country" (M.L. Davies, *Women's Co-operative Guild 1883-1904*, 1904, p. 57 as quoted in Patricia Hollis, op.cit., p. 275).

78. Emily observed that conditions in this Confectionary Co-operative, where the girls worked in "airy workrooms" and enjoyed "satisfactory hours" of work, contrasted sharply with those in the jam and sweet-making industry in the East End of London, where nearly 3,000 women worked long hours in unsanitary conditions for poor wages and were subjected to numerous fines by overseers (*LP*, 7/16/92, 104).

79. Emily visited a number of women's clubs in America, she was an honorary member of Sorosis, the New York club, from 1869 on, and she kept in touch with the executive of that club (Jane Croly, Ella Dietz Clymer, and so on) over the years. So she knew whereof she spoke when she commented on the "clubbable" American women, their highly successful clubs and the aims of the most important of those clubs. Her first observation was that these American women's clubs, unlike their British counterparts, were not primarily designed for social enjoyment (*LP*, 8/27/92, 304). American clubwomen were chiefly interested in women's work and welfare, and to that end they joined forces in a General Federation of Women's Clubs in 1889. Individual women's clubs opted for other activities as well. As EF reported in 1884, the New Century Club in Philadelphia concerned itself with music, literature and cookery (*Three Visits*, 83), and the Ebell Society in Oakland concentrated on art, science, and literature (*Three Visits*, 235). The New England Club in Boston, "the acknowledged centre of intellectual culture and literary work" was a headquarters for various reform movements (*Three Visits*, 97-99). And EF's Sorosis Club, according to Jane Croly, had Standing Committees in Literature, Science, Education, Art, Philanthropy, House and Home, Drama, and Current Events (Jane C. Croly, *The History of the Woman's Club Movement in America*, New York: Henry G. Allen & Co., 1898).

80. The Royal Geographical Society decided not to admit any more women in 1893, though they agreed that the "twenty-two ladies already elected must be borne with" (*LP*, 7/15/93, 104).

81. Emily reported in 1893 that Queen Victoria was a patroness of one of the new female branches of the Ancient Order of Foresters (*LP*, 7/15/93, 104).

82. Making a plea for funds to get this self-supporting business under way, EF stated, "We hope the Princess House may prove to be only the nucleus from which many like institutions will spring throughout, but especially in the West End of, London" (*WLE*, 11/10/77, 100).

83. Emily was in favour of these girls' clubs inculcating "self-reliance and repugnance to licence of all kinds." However, she did not believe in prohibition and protection, and she insisted that the "good, wholesome

recreation" provided be not too dull or too narrow (*LP*, 5/10/90, 700 and 8/9/90, 236).

84. Emily believed there was an urgent need for more clubs like this one: "As it is estimated that 30,000 women are employed in factories and workshops in the metropolis, and many are without regular homes, this is an undertaking worthy of support" (*WLE*, 3/2/78, 100).

85. Emily was particularly impressed by the facilities of the YWCA in New York: circulating library, employment bureau, social parlour, classrooms, art rooms, gymnasium, relief committee for the sick and needy, Bible class, etc. (*LP*, 6/22/89, 904). This YWCA operated on a grander scale than its counterpart in Britain that EF had praised in 1878 for befriending young girls.

86. William R. Greg, "Why are Women Redundant?" *National Review*, 4/62, 434-460.

87. Emily termed W.R. Greg's harsh proposal "enforced transportation in a benevolent disguise" (*VM*, 6/71, 321).

88. The three acknowledged British pioneers in nineteenth-century female emigration were Mrs. Caroline Chisholm, Maria S. Rye, and Mrs. Caroline Howard (later Mrs. E.L. Blanchard). Referring to the last two EF stated: "Emigration is a desirable outlet for our surplus population, but it has to be conducted with great care and knowledge. Fortunately, there have been several ladies whose devotion to the work has only been equalled by their judgement, notably, Mrs. E.L. Blanchard and Miss Rye, who were the earliest in the field, and have both gone round the world in the interests of women and children they are anxious to aid" (*LP*, 6/23/94, 950).

89. The *English Woman's Journal* reported in October 1862 that the 39 women sent to British Columbia and the 20 sent to New Zealand were chiefly mill hands, but most of them had experience in domestic work as well. And the December 1862 issue of that journal, which featured Bessie Parkes' article, "The Departure of Miss Rye for the Colonies," noted that, of the 100 women Maria Rye had escorted to New Zealand, eight were governesses, 30 were factory girls, and the rest were domestic servants. So Rye had revised her emigration policy by the Fall of 1862.

90. Jane Lewin admitted in 1874 that she had not been able to help very many ladies to emigrate — only 158 in fourteen years. (*ER*, 4/74).

91. In March 1862 *EWJ* printed a letter addressed to EF suggesting that she personally arrange to send out the Hartley widows and their children to the colonies, following the colliery disaster at Hartley. So her letters to the *Times* and her fame as the woman who had established the Victoria Press had apparently persuaded some people that she was an emigration specialist.

92. The *Englishwoman's Review* provided additional details about the kinds and numbers of women Rye sent to Australia in 1866. In October it announced that she was sending out single domestic servants and young married couples. And it reported that 93 single women and ten families had sailed for Melbourne in December, that another 100 singles and ten couples were due to go early in the New Year, and that two other shiploads had left before December (*ER*, 12/66 and 1/67).

93. This information on "Carina" may be found in a column EF devoted to this extraordinary woman (*LP*, 8/3/89, 165).

94. Emily got some information about New Zealand from relatives. Her favourite nephew Ferdinand Faithfull Begg's nine years of N.Z. experience, though not concentrated on emigration matters like Mrs. Caroline Howard's, would have been of some use to EF. And the Right Reverend James Begg's impressions would have augmented Mrs. Howard's.

95. Emily described Carina as a lady "who works in connection with our office in giving aid and advice to intending emigrants" (*W & W*, 8/28/75, 2). But an advertisement in the same issue referred to "passages arranged for by [her]." Carina apparently took care of most of the emigration business for EF, though the latter no doubt had to handle public relations and some of the paper work.

96. This was also the address of EF's Victoria Press, *Victoria Magazine*, *Women and Work*, and her Industrial and Educational Bureau.

97. Carina also identified the Captain, Surgeon Superintendent, and Matron of the *Western Monarch* and stressed their experience and concern for the emigrants. And she reported that the ship had two hospitals: one for general use and one for contagious diseases (*W & W*, 12/25/75, 5).

98. Emily said she established the Manchester branch of the Colonial Emigration Society at the "urgent request" of Lady Strangford. But Lady Strangford was off to Egypt shortly after; therefore, EF formed a working partnership with Mrs. Blanchard (*LP*, 6/18/87, 652-3), secretary and workhorse of the Society. When Lady Strangford died suddenly in 1887, Mrs. Blanchard assumed full operation of the London headquarters of the Society.

99. Mrs. Blanchard and Lady Strangford established the Women's Emigration Society in 1880. Most of the emigrants sent out by that Society went to Queensland because it was the best place for educated women. The Colonial Emigration Society appears to have been better funded than the Women's Emigration Society; moreover, it had a broader scope (emigration to both Queensland and Canada). So it enfolded the Women's Emigration Society in 1881.

100. At a Bristol Women's Conference in November 1892 EF noted that of 12,000 women Mrs. Blanchard had sent to the colonies only 5% had "come to grief" (*LP*, 11/26/92, 827). And none of the 10,000 women she had sent out by 1887 had been lost at sea (*LP*, 2/12/87, 174).
101. Emily noted that she found 60 to 70 unemployed at the CES Emigration Office, Manchester, in May 1886 (*LP*, 5/22/86, 478).
102. Lord Ripon replied that he could not attend the meeting on May 30 because he would be fully occupied during his stay in Manchester (Fawcett Library, Vol IIB, 18/4/86).
103. Lady Egerton's reply stated that Lord Egerton was away from home and she did not know what his engagements were (Fawcett Library, Vol. IIB, Feb. 6 [1887?]).
104. Lord Carmarthen sent his regrets. He believed it would represent a conflict of interest if he, as secretary to Sir Henry Holland, the Colonial Secretary, agreed to be a patron (Fawcett Library, Vol. VIII B, 28/9/[87]).

      Because he received so many applications similar to EF's, Lord Rosebery also declined the invitation to be a patron. However, he said he would "endeavour to introduce such an allusion as [you desire] if it falls within the scope of the few remarks which [I have] to make this evening" (Fawcett Library, Vol. VII B, 28/9/87). No doubt the "allusion" was to the importance of women's emigration and the need for funds to support that cause.
105. In an 1888 interview EF commented on the "much correspondence" that being President of the Northern and Midland Branch of the Colonial Emigration Society demanded of her (*The World*, 10/31/88, 6).
106. In May 1886 EF received a letter from Edward Stanley, the 15th Earl of Derby, saying he would send £100 "in aid of her plans" (Fawcett Library, Vol. II, 5/5/86).
107. Emily also reported F.F. Begg's 1891 "lecture at Prince's Hall, over which the Prince of Wales presided," in which Begg dealt with "Lord Carrington's criticisms [of the League?]" (*LP*, 2/28/91, 312). So the heir to the throne appears to have been strongly supportive of the League, and EF's nephew was moving in noble company.
108. Emily was pleased that "this movement [the Imperial Federation League] is happily not a party one, Conservatives and Liberals on both sides of the ocean are working hand in hand to secure what they believe will be of benefit to the whole English (sic) Empire, and they 'won't be happy till they get it'" (Ibid.).
109. The *Women's Herald* reported in March 1891 that the "Imperial Federation League has taken a new departure by forming a women's branch. Amongst its members are Lady Aberdeen, Lady Brooke, Miss

Clough, Miss (sic) Arthur Walter, and Miss Emily Faithfull" (3/21/91, 340). Emily of course had been a member of the League since its inception; in 1891 she became a spokeswoman for the Britannia Roll as well.

Chapter Eight

1.  Martha Westwater mistakenly labels EF "antisuffrage," chiefly because she was against married women getting the vote (Westwater, *The Wilson Sisters*, p. 118).
2.  Olive Banks appears to have been the only one to go to the other extreme. There is no evidence to support Banks's assumption (in the *Biographical Dictionary of British Feminists, Volume 1, 1880-1830*, New York: New York University Press, 1985, p. 74) that EF was involved in the Langham Place ladies' attempts to establish a women's suffrage society in the 1860's.
3.  Here the *Manchester Evening News* was repeating EF's very words in an interview granted to *The Women's Penny Paper* in 1890. During that interview she added the proviso that female suffrage was not "the end and aim of all things. Women as ratepayers should certainly vote, and doubtless will before long" (*The Women's Penny Paper*, 8/2/90, 481).
4.  Shortly after Mill's election to Parliament the Langham Place ladies and others, e.g., Helen Taylor, formed the Kensington Ladies' Discussion Society that later evolved into the London National Society for Women's Suffrage. The Kensington Society prepared the petition that Mill presented to Parliament in June 1866; that is, Helen Taylor wrote a draft of the petition and a committee consisting of Emily Davies, Bessie Parkes, Barbara Bodichon, Jessie Boucherett, Elizabeth Garrett, and Isa Craig revised it (Herstein, op.cit., p. 153).
5.  In August 1866 EF wrote, "*We* do not ourselves at present feel very troubled about political rights for women, believing that other questions (as, for instance, that of education) have necessarily a prior claim" (*VM*, 8/66, 289).
6.  Emily was fully cognizant of the activities of the supporters of women's suffrage in 1867 and 1868 after Mill's 1867 Parliamentary motion had been defeated. Chief among these was the formation of a National Society for Women's Suffrage in London. Barbara Bodichon and Emily Davies were charter members of this Society, but they resigned from it within a few months of its formation, leaving Mrs.

P.A. Taylor, Frances Power Cobbe, and Millicent Garrett Fawcett on its Executive, with John Stuart Mill and Helen Taylor as Grey Eminences. A Manchester branch of the Society was formed in 1868, with Jacob Bright and Lydia Becker as its leaders; the latter also undertook editorship of the *Women's Suffrage Journal.*

7. Eliza Lynn Linton (*Saturday Review*, 3/30/67, 385-6) had claimed that women were "non-political creatures" and not "independent." She believed the development of a higher sense of honour among men would protect women from male brutality better than electoral reform. Other *Saturday Review* writers were much harsher than Linton concerning votes for women; for the most part, they based their strong objections to women's suffrage on the eminent medical journal *Lancet*'s "scientific proof" that women were not physically or mentally fitted for the franchise (*Lancet*, 3/30/67, 401). Emily Faithfull gave them all a dose of commonsense.

8. According to Emily, Mrs. Fawcett and Lady Amberley began speaking in public about women's rights early in 1869, but only after she (Emily) had tested the waters in 1868 ((*VM*, 5/72, 119-120).

9. In 1892 Emily gave this reason for restricting female suffrage to taxpaying single women and widows: "to a certain extent the married women have made their choice, but the single are forced by circumstances, over which they have no control, to accept the duties of citizenship, although at present denied its privileges" (*LP*, 4/2/92, 505).

10. This September 1869 issue of *VM* also contained a copy of Mill's speech given at the July meeting of the National Society and a review of his book *The Subjection of Women.*

11. In 1884 EF commented on American women who could not understand "the intimate connection between political representation and the higher education and industrial employments of women, and therefore they fail to see that it is a matter of urgent necessity, rather than abstract justice" (*Three Visits*, 327).

12. Probably because of her involvement in the Codrington divorce case, EF was almost never asked to sign petitions supporting female suffrage or any other cause. However, in 1877 the National Society for Female Suffrage did ask her, as a woman qualified for the Parliamentary vote, to sign a "standing protest against the deprivations of the Parliamentary franchise attached to the household or property qualification" she possessed (*VM*, 9/77, 458). Though EF apparently approved of this declaration and listed the names of eminent people who had already signed it, she did not confess to having added her name to the list. So she seems once again to have exercised public caution.

13. Like Emily Davies, EF feared a backlash concerning women's employment and education if women's rights' supporters took too strong a stand on female suffrage.

14. A.P. Martin, author of "Female Suffrage in Victoria" had no doubts about EF's strong support of female suffrage: "In the whole field of politics, there is no other question on which so many noble-minded men and women are unanimous. In what other cause do we find such "agitators," as the late John Stuart Mill and his wife, Professor Fawcett and Mrs. Fawcett, Mr. and Mrs. Peter Taylor, Florence Nightingale, Viscount and Lady Amberly, Mr. Jacob Bright, Sir Chas. Dilke, Miss Emily Faithfull; Harriet Martineau, Miss Cobbe, and Lady Anna Gore Langton, etc." (*VM*, 10/73, 558-559).

15. Thanks to Laura Curtis Bullard, EF was also able to talk to Horace Greeley about female suffrage and other matters just before his election defeat by Ulysses S. Grant for the office of President of the United States of America: "I told him that Englishwomen traced to their exclusion from the suffrage three of the principal hardships of which they complained, namely, the injustice of the laws relating to the property of married women; the misappropriation to boys of educational endowments intended for the benefit of both sexes; and last, but not least, the unwillingness of landlords to receive or even to retain women as tenants. Landlords wish to find in tenants possible voters; and therefore they want men instead of women" (*VM*, 5/73, 124).

16. Amelia Lewis, editor of *Woman*, reported that at a VDS meeting in 1872 concerning women's suffrage EF had said much the same thing: "Miss Emily Faithfull, who re-opened the debate, said that the argument which was now moving Mr. Gladstone's mind was precisely that which first induced her to advocate female franchise — viz., the fact that from year to year more and more women were becoming self-dependent members of the community. The census had compelled the Premier to acknowledge that self-dependent women had become an important section of the community, and she believed it would soon be impossible to deny to women what we were now granting to every class, the right to be consulted in the choice of a representative." (*Woman*, 2/10/72, 53).

17. EF also informed her British readers whenever other countries granted the franchise to women: Victoria (Australia) in 1873, the Isle of Man in 1881, six American States by 1890, New Zealand in 1891, and South Australia in 1894.

18. Stanton, E.C., Anthony, Susan Brownell, and Matilda Joslyn Gage, eds., *The History of Woman Suffrage* [microform], Rochester, N.Y.: S.B. Anthony, [1881]-1922, Volume II, p. 440.

19. EF's article attacking Captain Maxse's position elicited congratulations from Helen Blackburn, Secretary of the National Suffrage Society (*W & W*, 11/28/74).

20. Emily's friend, Emilie Barrington (née Wilson), and her five sisters all signed this anti-suffrage Appeal, thus maintaining their support of a political system that denied parliamentary votes to women.

21. A year earlier EF had stated categorically that "it is generally allowed by all but thoughtless fanatics that the exclusion of women from public affairs has been a mistake" (*LP*, 9/15/88, 272). And only two months before publication of the "Appeal Against Female Suffrage" she had asserted that "[few] now attempt to dispute the powerful influences women have, even without votes, on the political tendencies of the day" (*LP*, 4/20/89, 532). So no wonder she called the "Appeal" arguments outdated.

22. Some of these reports are interesting: e.g., John Stuart Mill, Henry Fawcett, and John Morley attended an 1870 meeting (*VM*, May-Oct/70); in an 1874 meeting Frances Power Cobbe and others attacked Goldwin Smith, "Knight of the Rueful Countenance" and the meeting dragged on for 3½ hours in a "crowded, badly ventilated hall." (*W & W*, 7/11/74, 4).

23. In January 1872 EF made further comment on this schism: If it has "put an end to cliqueism . . . we independent advocates . . . of women's suffrage will not view the event with unmixed feelings" (*VM*, 1/72, 282). Incidentally, according to the *Later Letters* of John Stuart Mill, the split occurred because the Manchester group (chiefly Jacob Bright, Lydia Becker, and Caroline Biggs) wanted to link women's suffrage with repeal of the Contagious Diseases Acts and John Stuart Mill and Helen Taylor were dead against such linkage. (J.S. Mill, *Later Letters* in *Collected Works, Vols. 14-17*, ed. Mineka and Lindley, University of Toronto Press: Toronto, 1972, p. 1818 n2).

24. In January 1895 EF stated that the time had come "when registration reform should effect the abolition of all disqualification and the creation of one register for parochial, municipal, parliamentary, and all other elections, to include all present registered electors, both men and women" (*LP*, 1/26/95, 134).

25. Emily reported in July 1894 that 248,674 people had signed these petitions (*LP*, 7/28/94, 136).

26. In 1892 EF praised Lord Salisbury, Conservative leader, for openly proclaiming "his sympathy with 'relaxing the restraints imposed upon women' in relation to representation" (*LP*, 3/12/92, 392).

27. Gladstone refused to receive a deputation from the Women's Emancipation Union in 1893 (*LP*, 7/22/93, 118). And Lord Rosebery, who became Prime Minister after Gladstone resigned, refused to accede to

the threats of the Women's Liberal Association. As EF phrased it, "Mrs. Charles McLaren held out the threat that if Lord Rosebery did not fall in with the advance line in politics, the strength of the [Women's] movement might yet sweep him away" (*LP*, 5/12/94, 712).

28. Emily also pointed out how illogical and inconsistent it was for women to be willing to work for their husbands, brothers, and friends on the hustings but to remain doubtful of the wisdom of granting the vote to women householders (*LP*, 7/11/85, 25). And, EF contended, it was equally illogical and inconsistent for Parliament to grant the vote to the "male masses" in 1884. It would have been more sensible to enfranchise women ratepayers, most of whom were educated, than these men, whose ignorance was so manifest in the 1886 election (*LP*, 7/17/86, 30).

29. Emily assumed, as did many other women, that Parliament's granting suffrage to women at the municipal level presaged early passage of a national franchise Bill: "The admission of women to the Parliamentary franchise is now only a question of time." She added her usual proviso, however: "Our advocacy is strictly limited to the enfranchisement of single women who are householders" (*VM*, 7/69, 263).

30. Emily also noted successive re-elections of Lydia Becker to the Manchester School Board from 1871 to 1889, the year before Becker died.

31. A deputation of Marylebone voters asked EF to stand for election to the London School Board in 1872 after Thomas Henry Huxley had resigned, but she "reluctantly declined on account of other pressing engagements" (*Daily News*, rpt. in *VM*, 3/72, 444) such as lecture tours, VDS meetings, the *Victoria Magazine*, and preparations for her first visit to America.

32. In 1891, for example, she expressed her disappointment that there was only one lady candidate for the Manchester School Board and one for Liverpool (*LP*, 11/21/91, 917).

33. Emily expressed "anxiety" about getting women elected as Guardians in 1893 (*LP*, 4/8/93, 498), and she observed that male guardians did not always welcome women to their ranks (*LP*, 5/12/92, 388). However, in 1895 she was able to note with satisfaction that 875 women now served on Boards of Guardians (*LP*, 3/30/95, 434).

34. Even before County Councils came into being, EF and other Manchester ladies, among whom was Mrs. Gaskell, took the bold and unusual step of proposing and seconding male candidates for Manchester City Council (*LP*, 11/5/87, 472).

35. The Court of Appeals compounded this bad decision in 1890 by ruling once again that women could not sit on County Councils (*LP*, 12/6/90, 932). Indeed, subsequent efforts to give women this right proved

fruitless until 1907. So EF had to remain dissatisfied in this matter. Incidentally, to EF's surprise, Gladstone, who was so opposed to female suffrage, approved of women serving on County Councils (*LP*, 4/4/91, 518).

36.  Emily compared Miss Beatrice Potter's "Fabian Socialism" and George Jacob Holyoake's "Co-operation" in an 1891 column, and appeared to favour Holyoake's idea of Co-operatives making profits, though she probably did not entirely agree with Holyoake's view that the workers, not the capitalists, should share those profits (*LP*, 9/19/91, 494). Moreover, EF, following John Stuart Mill's lead, approved of women's co-operatives of various kinds, for they had proved effective in combatting male-dominated capitalism.

37.  Reporting on an 1894 conference of the International Labour Party (founded 1893), EF approved of their resolutions that women's guilds be promoted and that there be an increased number of women factory inspectors. She also made favourable note of ILP's disapproval of the use of physical force to resolve social questions (*LP*, 2/17/94, 231).

38.  Emily applied this phrase to German Socialism in particular (*WLE*, 6/8/78). However, she condemned the German government's arrest and exile of German Socialists in 1878, for she contended that "Socialism is a power in Germany, not a mere hobby." Besides, she did not want these "banished firebrands" in England (*LE*, 12/7/78, 358).

39.  Emily contended that individual initiative was more effective than collective action in dealing with poverty and unemployment. She disagreed with "the Socialists' cry — the bread and shoes all round policy is not a practicable one; but we are our 'brother's keeper' and in times like these self-sacrifices are imperatively required of us . . . [The] poor and unemployed [constitute a] national question; before it can be solved it must be treated as an individual one" (*LP*, 12/11/86, 533).

40.  In 1875 EF agreed with Cardinal Manning that the "best way for nations to preserve peace [is] to be powerfully armed. What do the Peace Society say to this man of peace? Yet his Eminence is right" (*W & W*, 12/11/75, 7).

41.  The Primrose League encouraged Primrose Dames to get involved in political campaigns, particularly after Gladstone introduced his Irish Home Rule Bill in 1886.

42.  This is the same William Hardman who at the time of the Codrington divorce case in 1864 had described EF, "the Lady Manager of the Victoria Press, [as] simply a fool" (Hardman, p. 231). It is ironic that both Hardman and EF were closely involved with the Primrose League in 1890.

43. Primrose Dames worked behind the scenes to convince Conservative men that the enfranchisement of women was a reasonable demand. Emily, for example, apparently persuaded her nephew, Ferdinand Faithfull Begg, to announce his advocacy of female suffrage at a gathering of Primrose Leaguers at his London residence three days after Mrs. Faithfull Begg and EF had entertained a "very large number of literary, political, and social celebrities" at that residence. (*Woman's Herald*, 7/26/90, 478). And F.F. Begg remained faithful to that cause, particularly during his years as a Conservative M.P. when, as one of the Parliamentary advisers to the National Union of Women's Suffrage Societies in 1897, he moved the second reading of a Women's Disabilities Removal Bill in his maiden speech.

44. "Miss Faithfull and the Primrose League," *Woman's Herald*, 5/18/89, rpt. from *Primrose League Gazette*.

45. Emily Faithfull's strong Unionist bias is evident in her recognition of the Women's Liberal Unionist Association as a group with which she was willing to ally herself because they were "trying to preserve the unity of the empire and maintain the proud position this country has always held in the eyes of the whole civilized world" (*LP*, 11/21/91, 926).

46. In 1891 EF praised Miss Tod as both a Unionist and a women's worker: "Her life has been entirely devoted to the political, educational, and industrial interests of women, and she is now, without doubt, one of the best and pleasantest platform speakers" (*LP*, 6/13/91, 1021). And later that year she referred to Mrs. Fawcett's "trenchant address" to Unionist ladies in Birmingham (*LP*, 12/5/91, 1022).

47. The Women's Liberal Association was established in 1885, partly because the Liberal Party needed it to counter the success of the Primrose Dames, but also because women of Liberal persuasion wanted to influence Liberal policies for the benefit of women. The Women's Liberal Association saw eye to eye with the Women's Liberal Unionist Association except in the matter of Irish Home Rule.

48. Prior to the 1885 election, EF confined herself to comments on political personalities. For example, in 1878 she made these observations:

Lord Beaconsfield
(Conservative) -      "the first statesman in Europe" because of the part he played in the peace talks among Russia, Bulgaria and Turkey that resulted in the Berlin Treaty (*WLE*, 7/20/78, 36).

W.E. Gladstone
(Liberal) -             lacked boldness in dealing with the Ameer of Afghanistan (*LE*, 11/2/78 and 11/16/78).

Joseph Chamberlain
(Radical Liberal)- "showy, reckless, and shallow," makes an "incessant appeal to feeling and prejudice rather than reason" (*LE*, 11/2/78, 280-81).

49. In 1885 EF was not yet committed to Conservatism. Therefore, she had some fun at the expense of Randolph Churchill and J.W. Maclure. Her favorite in this campaign seems to have been Sir Charles Dilke, Radical Liberal, who eventually did not contest the election; for he had wrecked his political life by getting involved in what was possibly the most sensational divorce action of the nineteenth century. Emily, mindful no doubt of the scandal of the Codrington divorce case, hoped in vain that Dilke would "emerge unscathed from the cloud which overshadows him" (*LP*, 10/17/85, 336).

50. Emily, noting that ladies (both Liberal and Conservative) "induced waverers" to vote for their party, wondered if this action contravened the Corrupt Practices Act (*LP*, 11/28/85, 462).

51. Emily meted out further praise to Arthur Balfour in 1891 and 1892. In October 1891 she declared that "a kinder-hearted or more genial man than the young statesman — misrepresented by the Radical press as a cynic — does not exist" (*LP*, 10/31/91, 795). In November she voiced her pride that he was "Leader of the House of Commons who has done such splendid work in Ireland [as Irish Secretary]" (*LP*, 11/21/91, 926). And in April 1892 she expressed her pleasure that Balfour had again visited Manchester to drum up support for the upcoming election (*LP*, 4/9/92, 546).

52. Married Women's Property Acts were passed in 1870, 1874, 1882, and 1893, but eighteen Bills concerning married women's rights were introduced in Parliament between 1857 and 1882.

53. The object of this 1857 Bill presented by Lord Brougham and Sir Erskine Perry was to ensure that all married women would have control over their property and earnings. The Marriage and Divorce Act which replaced this Bill did not protect property or earnings except where a woman was deserted, and even then it protected only the property and earnings acquired after the divorce.

54. As William Fredeman rightly observes, this unsatisfactory Act "forestalled for nearly a quarter of a century a proper and acceptable Married Women's Property Bill" (Fredeman, p. 140).

55. In 1879 EF, reporting a meeting of the committee devoted to obtaining the reform of the laws regulating women's property, quoted Mrs. Arthur Arnold concerning the confiscation of a woman's property by her marriage: "A married woman had in fact no existence of her own in this country. Her position was founded on the barbarous laws of the

heathen two thousand years ago" (*VM*, 4/79, 592). So the 1882 Act provided some relief.

56. Despite this Matrimonial Causes Amendment Act, the battering continued. In 1888 EF noted a "rising flood of brutality" toward women, particularly through "despotism in family life" (*LP*, 10/13/88, 403).

57. Only after 1883 could a "guilty" wife petition for maintenance.

58. In 1893 EF gave Julia Ward Howe credit for setting peace societies in motion in England (*LP*, 10/14/93, 571).

59. The AAW was created by Sorosis (chiefly by Jennie June Croly) on October 15, 1873. It "became a proving ground that strong-minded suffragism and Domestic Feminism were not mutually exclusive." After 1881 the AAW was dominated by Julia Ward Howe of the Boston-based moderate American Woman Suffrage Association, to the disgruntlement of Mrs. Croly. The AAW was succeeded by the General Federation of Women's Clubs (Karen J. Blair, *The Clubwoman as Feminist*, London: Holmes and Meier, 1980, p. 45 and ff.).

60. Letter from EF to the Congress, op.cit., p. 186.

61. Emily regretted that she was too ill to answer the letter announcing her election to the Women's Branch of the World Congress at the time she received it (*LP*, 8/15/91, 316) and that she was unable to attend the International Congress of Women in Chicago in 1892.

62. At the Liverpool Sanitation Institute meeting in 1894 sanitary science was viewed in terms of the need to train girls (rich and poor alike) concerning sanitary laws and the knowledge of hygiene and sanitation (drainage, ventilation, lighting, purity of water, milk and meat, etc., proper preparation and cooking of food, care of children and nursing of the sick, management of infectious diseases, etc.) (*LP*, 10/6/94, 496).

63. At the very first VDS meeting in 1869 EF expressed this idea as follows: "We cannot doubt for one instant that there is much disease which is preventible, and that it is woman who must chiefly take the initiative in measures directed toward an end so desirable. Men may suggest, but it will be after all for mothers and sisters in the homes to carry out such suggestions" (*VM*, 12/69, 137).

64. The Social Science Association took the Ladies' Sanitary Association under its wing shortly after the latter came into existence in October 1857.

65. Dr. Elizabeth Blackwell was the founder of the National Health Society.

66. For example, in 1889 EF referred to "one of Mr. Ruskin's brilliant lectures" concerning knowledge of the health and sanitation of our

bodies and minds and how to take care of them. Then she recommended *The Family Physician* to women who wished to learn the elements of physiology (*LP*, 3/16/89, 361). Similarly in 1885 she stressed the importance of sanitation in dealing with Manchester's persistent cholera epidemic (*LP*, 8/29/85, 183).

67. Some lecturers believed that both men and women should be taught Hygiene. Emily noted in 1895 that "Miss Dorothy Butler . . . another fresh worker in the field of reform . . . has been lecturing on Health and Nursing to both sexes" (*LP*, 3/30/95).

68. Emily also contended that brutality among the working classes was due in large part to their living in "dens of filth and foul air" (*W & W*, 10/10/74, 3).

69. Emily did not trust Manchester water; so she drank soda water (*LP*, 8/27/87, 210).

70. In 1877 EF praised the Aylesbury Dairy for instituting sanitary methods to ensure the purity of its products (*WLE*, 11/3/77).

71. In 1889 EF appealed to rich women to support the removal of St. Mary's Hospital in Manchester from its present unsanitary location. That is, a new hospital had to be built (*LP*, 3/30/89, 433).

72. Emily took British parishes to task in an 1877 editorial entitled "Strongholds of Pestilence" in which she referred to the "miserably defective sanitary organisation of our parishes" (*WLE*, 11/3/77).

73. In 1890 EF expressed her concern about the lack of sanitation at seaside resorts (*LP*, 7/12/90, 66).

74. Emily wrote an editorial in 1874 about the lack of sanitation on barges and boats. She also stressed the need to send barge children to school to learn hygiene, among other subjects (*W & W*, 10/3/74, 4).

75. Emily strongly supported the idea of female sanitary inspectors in factories and workshops. Therefore, she took special note of the 1893 appointment of two ladies by Kensington vestry, both of whom had been trained by the National Health Society. "They will inspect all workshops where women are employed, and report respecting defective ventilation and drainage." Emily hoped this action might be "followed . . . with advantage throughout the country" (*LP*, 10/28/93, 642).

76. In 1890 Sir Spencer Wells criticized the unsanitary condition of Manchester cemeteries; in particular, he noted that the graves were leaking because there were far too many corpses buried in the space allotted (*LP*, 10/11/90, 616).

77. Emily also recommended fresh air holidays for the poor. In 1892, for instance, she praised the Openshaw Club for setting up "encampments for city lads" (*LP*, 6/18/92, 984) and pronounced the Factory Girls' Country Holiday an "excellent scheme" (*LP*, 7/9/92, 55) comparable

with Brooklyn, New York's "Fresh Air Fund" for taking poor children to the seaside and elsewhere (*W & W*, 9/4/75, 5).

78. The Kyrle Society, founded in 1876, initially was scorned for beautifying parks, constantly pestering public authorities about preserving open spaces, and entertaining the poor.

79. Octavia Hill also worked with Henry Fawcett and the Commons Preservation Society to protect Wimbledon, Epping Forest, and Hampstead Heath.

80. In this same issue of *WLE*, EF wrote an editorial entitled "The People and the Parks" which deplored the recent destruction of flower beds in Hyde Park. In a second editorial she referred to trees as the "noblest of all growing things," and she scolded the citizens for their "careless indifference to the trees of London" (*WLE*, 5/25/78, 249). And in a later editorial she suggested that trees be planted along London's streets, thus transforming them into boulevards (*WLE*, 6/8/78).

81. When there was evident need of an additional park in a slum area, EF advocated affirmative action, e.g., she proposed a new park in Paddington especially for the poor, though open to other classes (*WLE*, 9/28/78).

82. Many Free Libraries contained much more than books. Emily Faithfull mentioned one that had baths, billiards room, smoking room, and refreshment room, i.e., a coffee tavern (*LP*, 7/21/94, 90).

83. Emily, referring to a Church Conference in Exeter in 1894, had this to say about mental health as a sanitary measure: "It is well for ladies engrossed in sanitary work among the poor, to hear of efforts connected with clubs for girls, the reforms needed in the management of our workhouses, the establishment of village libraries, &c; health in mind and many useful hints are insured by such conferences when rightly managed" (*LP*, 8/18/94, 221).

84. A letter-to-the-editor of *WLE* agreed with EF about the bad treatment of the sick in workhouses and suggested that the authorities be exposed. This letter was signed "One who visited for three years the sick and dying in a Metropolitan Workhouse Infirmary" (*WLE*, 7/13/78, 23).

85. In 1892 lady Guardians were taking action to substitute trained nurses for pauper nurses, but male Guardians were dragging their feet (*LP*, 2/13/92, 245).

86. In 1893 EF admitted that the workhouse system had improved: "[It is] a far cry from Miss Louisa Twining's first attack on that citadel of ignorant prejudice to Lady Meath's successful scheme for providing suitable occupation for workhouse men and women" (*LP*, 9/2/93, 318).

87. Emily noted in 1894 that there were two of these lodging houses in Piccadilly and Manchester. They operated as open night shelters (to

facilitate rescue work) and were designed to give these unfortunate women a new start. Emily praised this institution as "valuable and benevolent" and stated that these houses needed both volunteer help and money to continue their rescue work (*LP*, 5/26/94, 804).

88. In 1891 EF attended a demonstration at the Hampstead Physical Training College for Girls that Mrs. Grundy would not have approved of, for the girls took energetic part in gymnastic feats, fencing, and swimming. They also demonstrated their grasp of "anatomical, physiological, and hygienic subjects." In the same context EF imagined how aghast Mrs. Grundy would have been if she could have witnessed ladies' cricket matches and ladies' rifle shooting at Bisley, both of which were now common occurrences (*LP*, 7/25/91, 176).

89. In 1889 EF wanted swimming made compulsory for boys and girls because it not only improved one's physical health and cleanliness; it also was a means of saving lives (*LP*, 10/5/89, 431).

90. She was annoyed to discover in 1878 that only five public baths in London were open to women (*WLE*, 7/6/78, 5).

91. In August 1894 EF reported that Mr. Asquith, Home Secretary, had promised to appoint police matrons sometime in the future. But, EF insisted, that answer was not good enough, for police matrons were needed right now (*LP*, 8/11/94, 207).

92. Emily stated that these "visitors" should be ladies of "infinite tact and experience and judgment and sympathy" (*LP*, 6/2/94, 830).

93. Emily described Miss Orme's appointment as "another recognition of the value of women's co-operation and advice in matters which concern their sex" (*LP*, 6/9/94, 897).

Chapter Nine

1. For EF the fine arts embraced theatre (opera and drama) in addition to music, painting, sculpture, and architecture.

2. In 1894 EF approved of musical entertainments "for charity and the improvement of the people" (*LP*, 4/28/94, 631). And she did not rule out technological improvements as contributors to culture, either as labour-saving devices (e.g., sewing machines, potato peelers and mashers, extension-grate stoves, travelling wardrobes, painting machines) or as useful adjuncts (e.g., the telephone, electric light, phonographs). Of this latter group EF noted that she took part in experiments with telephones in 1878 and phonographs in 1887 and 1893, and she lauded the telephone as "this marvellous adjunct to

nineteenth-century civilisation" (*LP*, 10/12/89, 488). She also noted that at the Shakespeare Memorial Benefit at the Gaiety Theatre in London in 1878 she was privileged to hear "sounds from Stratford" over the telephone (*VM*, May-Oct/78).

3.      Emily opposed a "Music at Home" proposal whereby musicians would be hired to perform in one's home. This would be all right for cripples who could not attend concerts, EF asserted, but not for healthy, active people . . . "the average girl would be totally discouraged in her efforts to play or sing well enough to give pleasure to the home circle and . . . the money could be better spent elsewhere. Fancy what can be had in the way of the best music for a shilling at the Saturday and Monday Popular Concerts!" (*LP*, 1/5/89, 14).

4.      Emily was pleased that she was able in 1873 to engage in "animated conversation" with Arthur Rubinstein about "the relative merits [of] poetry, painting, and music," during which "the great Russian pianist" used his "splendid playing" to enforce "his arguments in favour [of music]"(*LP*, 6/5/86, 510 and 12/8/94, 868).

5.      George Eliot reported that she and George Henry Lewes had gone to hear Hallé perform on piano at a St. James's Hall Monday concert in 1860 and at the Grosvenor Gallery in 1878. Mrs. Hallé (Mme. Wilma Maria Norman-Neruda) had also played for GE and GHL — at the Priory in May/77 (George Eliot, *Letters*, op.cit., Vol. VII, pp. 20-21). And EF noted in 1893 that it was forty-five years since Hallé had first performed in Manchester (*LP*, 4/22/93, 589). So he was well known as a concert pianist long before EF first heard him. Incidentally, Hallé concerts are still being presented in Britain at the time of writing, almost a century and a half after Sir Charles's first performance.

6.      In 1891 EF also asked the public to save the Gentlemen's Concerts from oblivion. She observed that this concert group was one of the oldest in England (established 1774) and that it had provided Manchester with some memorable musical experiences. So she suggested that Manchester ladies could support it with afternoon recitals and the public in general could purchase subscriptions (*LP*, 1/28/88, 82 and 10/31/91, 795).

7.      Emily noted that Handel's *Messiah* had been very popular in Manchester in December 1888: "there were no less than six performances within ten days in the Manchester Free Trade Hall. On Saturday (22nd) I found the hall so crowded it was difficult to get to our seats . . ." (*LP*, 1/5/89, 14).

8.      Announcing the opening of the Manchester Art Museum in Ancoats (Manchester area) in October 1886, EF noted a strong interest by Ruskin, as evidenced in his notes to the Turner paintings on exhibition there (*LP*, 10/16/86, 318).

9. Establishment of the Female Artists' Society in 1856 strengthened the claim of the Female School of Art that women artists should be recognized by the Royal Academy and that the Academy should accept female students. The Academy did enrol women in 1860, but it withheld admission of women artists to its life school, thus relegating them to a subordinate position.

10. In 1894 Emily mounted an even stronger attack on Sunday naysayers than she had on teetotallers, for she held the former in contempt for their hypocrisy: "[those] crooked Sabbatarians . . . enjoying ill-gotten gains, and heaping up riches even at the expense of the widow and orphan, and yet [parading] as 'churchgoers' on Sunday, present a spectacle no one who respects religion can regard without pain" (*LP*, 9/29/94, 436). She noted that bigots, some of whom served on City Councils and Lord's Day Observance Societies, were responsible for cancelling Sunday concerts in the parks — even those consisting only of sacred music — and for vandalizing libraries and art galleries opened to the public on Sundays. So she took pleasure in recording the Sabbatarians' "groans" when Sunday afternoon recitals were presented at St. George's Hall, Manchester, in 1886 and when the Manchester Art Gallery was opened on Sundays in 1887. And she was happy that her views were in accord with the Bishop of Manchester's sweeping condemnation of the puritanical attitude lying behind Sabbatarianism that ruled out all amusement — innocent or otherwise — associated with dancing, cards, theatre, and art (poetry, painting, music and fiction).

11. Among the very few contemporary women novelists EF praised was George Eliot (*W & W*, 2/13/75).

12. In late 1883 EF expressed pleasure that J.R. Lowell had been elected Rector of St. Andrew's University. She had met him on an earlier visit to America (*LP*, "Across the Atlantic," 12/15/83, 378).

13. Emily, who had known Frances Power Cobbe since the early 1860's, recommended her novel, *Peg Woffington*, in 1878 (*VM*, 10/78).

14. Of Dion Boucicault, actor, playwright, director, and producer, EF wrote often. For example, she praised his acting in *The Shaughraun* in 1875 (*W & W*, 10/23/75) and the quality of his melodrama *After Dark* in 1877 (*VM*, 10/77).

15. In 1891 EF, writing about Manchester theatre, stated, "The dramatic event of the week was Mr. Tree's appearance as Hamlet" (*LP*, 9/19/91, 493).

16. Emily devoted a *VM* article to Hermann Vezin in 1878. She was particularly grateful to him for teaching her friend Kate Pattison the fundamentals of acting.

17. Emily saw two of Laurence Barrett's performances in America (in Boston and New Orleans) in 1882 and 1883. Of his leading roles in *Yorrick's Love* and *Francesca da Rimini* she stated, "I have never been more moved by Salvini or Bernhardt . . . . These are the performances which restore one's faith in the modern drama . . . Mr. Laurence Barrett is certainly America's greatest tragedian . . ." (*LP*, "Across the Atlantic," 2/24/83, 136).

18. In 1886 EF commented favourably on Wilson Barrett's Manchester performances in *Clito* and *Hamlet* (*LP*, 9/11/86, 218).

19. Emily reported in 1887 that she had seen Sarah Bernhardt perform in Manchester and had been "carried away" by her (*LP*, 7/23/87, 84).

20. Charlotte Cushman (1816-1876) was American, but she often acted in Britain. Emily described her as having a "tall, commanding, and even masculine appearance" (*W & W*, 2/26/76, 3).

21. According to Christopher Kent, the "original committee included Emily Faithfull as well as Genevieve Ward and Mrs. Kendal, two of the most respectable of their profession" (Christopher Kent, "Image and Reality," in Vicinus, *A Widening Sphere* . . ., op.cit., p. 108).

22. In 1893 EF noted that Mrs. Kendal was playing roles of wicked women (*LP*, 9/23/93, 428). Even Mrs. Grundy was apparently accepting the fact that a respectable actress could undertake the role of a bad woman as long as virtue was rewarded and vice punished.

23. In 1889 EF criticized a paper on *Hamlet* in her *Lady's Pictorial* column (*LP*, 1/26/89, 119).

24. In November 1871 the *Victoria Magazine* reprinted this item from the *Daily News* — "*Reading aloud* — We hear that Miss Faithfull has organised under high auspices a series of lectures to ladies on elocution. They will shortly commence at her new residence 50 Norfolk Square, Hyde Park, and will doubtless induce those who value home pleasures to take an interest in this rare accomplishment" (*VM*, 11/71, 90). *The Queen* said the object of these lectures was to popularize "the art of reading as a drawing-room amusement" and recommended that ladies sign up for it because of EF's "good taste, feeling, and excellent elocution" (*The Queen*, rpt. in *VM*, 6/72, 267).

25. Emily also advertised her lessons in elocution from 1873 to 1878; advertisements in *W & W* and *WLE* informed the public that she was continuing these private lessons and classes in home reading, public speaking, pronunciation, English composition, etc., and that "resident pupils would be received for a period of six to eight weeks" (*W & W*, 10/17/74, 6).

26. This was particularly true of her lectures on literature. For example, her lecture entitled "American Poets" consisted in large part of

recitations from Bryant, Longfellow, Lowell, O.W. Holmes, Bret Harte, Colonel John Hay, and others (*W & W*, 3/13/75).

27. Emily charged for these recitals — two guineas for a course of four sessions and 10s 6d for single sessions (*W & W*, 4/17/75, 7).

28. These "artistes" were Madame Jenny Viard-Louis, M. Sainton, Herr Ries, M. Zerbini, and M. Lasserre (*The Era*, 4/25/75, 11).

29. Appearing with EF in this melodrama were Kate Pattison, Rutland Barrington, and Mrs. Morgan (*VM*, 3/77, 451).

30. She also approved of the offerings of the St. James's Theatre in 1876 (*W & W*, 2/26/76).

31. In 1871 the *New York Herald* expressed its distaste for *opéra bouffe* as follows: this "lower school of music" is "only a passing exhileration (sic). Like champagne too, in large doses, it has proved nauseating . . . The purer taste is returning, and Offenbach, Hervé and the lesser lights are being thrown aside for the great lyric masters of the high school [of opera]" (*New York Herald*, 9/12/71, cited in Odell, *Annals of the New York Stage*, p. 7). The *Herald* also noted that *opéra bouffe* was more "indecent" in English than in French.

32. In 1885 EF hoped that Manchester audiences would take to "classic" plays. But when attendance at these plays dropped off in 1888 because most people preferred pantomime, she decided her adopted home town was "utterly incapable of supporting legitimate drama" (*LP*, 12/22/88, 739).

33. Mrs. Kendal credited EF with most of the "behind the scenes" organization of this Entertainment (*LE*, 11/30/78, 348).

34. Frances Hays claimed that EF founded the International Musical, Dramatic and Literary Association in 1881 to protect the copyright of composers, playwrights, and authors (Frances Hays, op.cit., p. 67). But EF never mentioned this Association; nor did anyone else except biographers following Hays's lead. I think Hays confused the Dramatic Reform Association with the International Musical, Dramatic, and Literary Association.

Chapter Ten

1. A page at the end of *A Reed Shaken With the Wind* advertising *The Abominations of Modern Society* by De Witt Talmage and *Get Thee Behind Me, Satan* by Olive Logan also stresses this moral purpose. The first is described as "A truly noble book! and especially suggestive to young men and young women" concerning the vices and follies

of the big city. The second is credited with informing women about all
stages of their lives, especially the dangerous ones.

2.  This Preface is signed EMILY FAITHFULL and dated Brooklyn,
    N.Y., May 1, 1873, just nine days before her departure from America.

3.  Besides the poets already mentioned, EF quotes from Landon, Shelley,
    Shakespeare, Tennyson, Mrs. Jameson, Goethe, Elizabeth Barrett
    Browning, Frances A. Kemble, Adelaide Procter, George Eliot, George
    Macdonald, Ruskin, George Herbert, and the Marquis of Montrose.

4.  Wilfred recognizes that Tiny, though intelligent, is at the mercy of her
    mercurial emotions. As Ray Strachey observed, Florence Nightingale
    in her novel *Cassandra* also deplored this incomplete development in
    miseducated Victorian women: "Woman has nothing but her affec-
    tions — and this makes her at once more loving and less loved"
    (Strachey, *The Cause* . . . , p. 411). But Wilfred mistakenly believes
    he can "train Tiny's feeling" (*Change Upon Change*, p. 71).

5.  In 1893 EF stated that Mrs. Gaskell's *Ruth* was her favourite novel
    because it awakened the world's compassion for the "unfortunate
    woman" who too often was hunted down "without remorse, however
    much her error has been repented of and her character purified by the
    pain and sorrow she has passed through" (*LP*, 2/11/93, 206). Thus EF
    was suggesting that society was perhaps as much to blame as the
    "fallen woman."

6.  The *Contemporary Review* praised EF for "her reading, her vivacity,
    and the freedom of hand with which she sketches what she sees;" the
    *Civil Service Gazette* compared her with W.M. Thackeray: "Social life
    of the higher class is hit off without exaggeration in a manner forcibly
    reminding us of some of Thackeray's shrewd and exquisitely perfect
    sketches;" and *John Bull* stated, "The moral is excellent, the plot
    natural, well-conceived, and ably worked out" (rpts in *WLE*, 9/22/77).

7.  Emily's letter to Mr. Baynham dated August 31, 1884 informed him
    that she had just finished writing *Three Visits to America*, "which shall
    shortly appear both there [America] and here [Britain]!" (Fawcett
    Library, Vol. IIB, 31/8/84, p.1). The news item in *The Queen* told
    readers that before she left America in April 1884 she had arranged for
    simultaneous English and American publication of her travel book
    (*The Queen*, 9/20/84, 303).

8.  According to the *Women's Penny Paper*, 8/2/90, 481, American
    newspapers had described *Three Visits* in these flattering terms.

9.  Emily said she wrote the book in London, probably in the temporary
    lodgings where she and Charlotte Robinson lived prior to their move
    to Manchester in December 1884. The Preface, dated October 1, 1884,
    gives Ferdinand Faithfull Begg's Edinburgh home as her address, so
    she was apparently staying there in September and early October to

take care of last minute proofreading for David Douglas, the publisher. After her return from America in May she had spent "many weeks" at the home of Richard Peacock near Manchester, and while there she very likely worked on *Three Visits*. In return for his hospitality EF "affectionately inscribed" the book to him "in remembrance of the unvarying kindness received from him and his family" (*Three Visits to America*, inscription page).

10. Chapter 12 of *Three Visits* is a shortened version of the series of weekly articles entitled "Life Among the Mormons" that EF wrote for the *Lady's Pictorial* from August 16 to September 20, 1884.

11. If these discontented wives complained publicly they faced bitter punishments, e.g., having their children pronounced illegitimate and being themselves damned through all eternity (*LP*, "Life Among the Mormons," 8/30/84, 182).

12. Divorce also was made easy for husbands, but wives were denied this privilege (*LP*, "Life Among the Mormons," 9/13/84, 230).

13. Elizabeth Cady Stanton did not consider the position of Mormon women to be as "inferior" as EF did. Referring to the visit she and Susan B. Anthony made to Salt Lake City in 1871, she recalled a "thoroughly democratic gathering [of Mormon women] in the Tabernacle" who could vote but not hold office (E.C. Stanton, *Eighty Years and More (1815-1897)*, New York: European Publishing Co., 1898, p. 285). And the writers of a 1984 article concurred with Mrs. Stanton that women in plural marriages got greater autonomy than other women (Mary Ryan et al, *Feminist Studies* 10: 504-36, Fall 1984). Emily Faithfull was certainly aware that Mormon women had the franchise, but she thought it was of little use to them, for they still had to surrender their dowers to their husbands. Moreover, a husband could take his wife's goods at any time (*Three Visits*, 187). So for EF this kind of autonomy was meaningless.

14. When pressure from Congress caused the Mormon leaders in 1890 to abandon the practice of polygamy, EF heaved a sigh of "intense relief" (*LP*, 10/18/90, 661), for after her return from America in 1884 she had kept a tally of misguided British "victims." In September 1885, for example, she regretfully reported that "329 men, women, and children left in charge of fourteen elders for Salt Lake City — the fourth party of Mormons in the present year, making up a total of 1331 persons" (*LP*, 9/5/85, 215).

Chapter Eleven

1.  Referring to the possibility of Emily Faithfull's starting up a women's journal, Emily Davies assured Barbara Bodichon that "people are very ready to lend her money" (*ED Papers*, Reel 14, letter to Barbara Bodichon, January 3, 1863).

2.  Emily must have realized that she had damaged the cause of women and that she somehow had to make matters right. For after 1864 she demanded increasing devotion to that cause from all women, especially leaders of the movement: "Every woman who fails to do her duty in the work she has taken up does an injury to the whole sex, and every false move on the part of so-called leaders of the progressive movement inflicts an injury on the cause" (*LP*, 4/30/92, 677).

3.  Emily appears to have lost only one legal battle, and that was not of her choosing. In 1864 Captain Mayne Reid sued the Earl of Essex and Emily Faithfull for printing and publishing a set of rules for croquet which he claimed were plagiarized from his book. The judge decided in favour of the Captain: the publication of Essex's *Cashiobary Croquet* had to be discontinued and all unsold copies given to Reid, along with £250 and costs "for the damage done by the piracy" (*The Queen*, 9/3/64, 140).

4.  Munby disapproved of women being in charge of anything other than domestic matters, and preferred humble working-class women to educated middle-class women. So he was doubly prejudiced against EF before he visited her Press.

5.  Michael Hiley, *Victorian Working Women*, London: Gordon Fraser, 1979, p. 43.

6.  *ED Papers*, January 1872 letter, Reel 13, no page number.

7.  Emily also advocated such positive measures as
    (1) Kindergartens to "help in the rescue of little waifs from three to six years old," as per the example of Mrs. Cooper in San Francisco (*LP*, 4/14/94, 520)
    (2) More Home and Day Care nurseries for the children of widows, and crèches for new mothers
    (3) Dinners for destitute children, as proposed by "Lord Shaftesbury and other benevolent gentlemen" (*LE*, 11/30/78, 348).

8.  Here is one of her many cries for help in rehabilitating abused children: "I trust that more friends will rally around these efforts to aid the helpless little ones to whom the word home conveys no sense but misery. Surely the sympathy of every true woman will be roused by the cry of the ill-used children" (*LP*, 7/14/94, 65).

9.  Only a month before she died EF reported that an S.P.C.A. meeting had dealt with two important matters: providing right harnesses for horses and educating children to be kind to animals (*LP*, 4/20/95).

10. In 1874 EF recommended Baroness Burdett-Coutts's horse and donkey show designed to "promote humanity among carters, waggoners, cabmen, and donkey drivers" (*W & W*, 10/3/74, 4).

11. Emily recalled early days when she "enjoyed many a run after Reynard," and risked her neck over fences. She approved of fox-hunting because it trained men and women to be "prompt and self-reliant" (*LP*, 1/26/89, 119).

12. Emily was appalled at the cruel treatment of stray dogs. So she appealed for funds to support the Manchester Home for Lost Dogs, whose policy was to keep the dogs for six days, then either sell or painlessly destroy them, but not to sell any animal "for the purpose of physiological or other experiments" (*LP*, 3/3/94, 300).

13. Dr. Frances Elizabeth Hoggan was a friend of Emily's from 1874. She got her degree in medicine at the University of Zurich in the early 1870's and subsequently practised in London, but the British Medical Association did not recognize her until she passed Dublin examinations in 1877. Emily informs us that Frances lectured for the National Health Society on the development and physical training of children (*W & W*, 10/31/74), served as visiting physician at the New Hospital for Women and Children (*W & W*, 1/16/75), offered gratuitous instruction in specimen mounting to destitute ladies so they could get paying jobs that were going a'begging (*W & W*, 4/10/75, 4/17/75, and 6/26/75), and lectured on sanitation to poor women in London's East End (*VM*, 1/77, 264).

14. "Half-an-hour with Miss Emily Faithfull," *North British Daily Mail*, Glasgow, 9/16/78, 4.

15. Emily publicly disapproved of Sir Wilfrid Lawson's Permissive Bill that allowed people in a given area to decide in favour of prohibition if two-thirds of their number voted for it. She in turn was attacked by a member of the Women's Temperance Association in a letter to the editor of *Women and Work* (*W & W*, 7/10/75).

16. Yet, though EF asserted that French marriage contracts had much to recommend them, she also believed that the growing incidence of divorce was to be traced in the main to the "increasing tendency in every class of society to marry for worldly motives (money and position) rather than pure affection" (*LP*, 1/4/90, 26).

17. In 1876 EF stated unequivocally that she did not support "in any cause, religious, political or social, anything that tends to excite ridicule and obloquy" (*W & W*, 1/29/76, 5).

18. Like most human beings, Emily could not maintain mental equilibrium in all matters. For instance, though she opposed slavery and condemned the lynching of American blacks, she accepted the "scientific" theory that negroes were mentally inferior. Agreeing with the *Brisbane Telegraph* that blacks were "an anthropological difficulty," she added, "no one but the bigots who uphold Sambo as the equal of the white men would be inclined to deny the aptness of the definition" (*W & W*, 12/25/75, 5). Such a statement would be termed "racist" and "highly prejudiced" today; in 1875, however, it was regarded as relatively liberal, as was her objection to a black man's marrying a white woman: "one would imagine that the most enthusiastic of abolitionists — surely even Mrs. Beecher Stowe herself — would hardly 'look and watch along the deep' for Pompey or Sambo" (*W & W*, 9/11/75, 2). For Emily, as for most middle- and upper-class English people, it was only just that blacks should be free, but, like the English working class, they could not be considered equal in intelligence to civilized white people.

19. Emily's many references to Professor Frederick D. Maurice and John Ruskin, whom she also called "Professor," suggest that she attended some of their lectures. She greatly admired Ruskin as "the chief of art critics" (*LE*, 11/30/78, 342) and a "perfect master of prose" (*LP*, 5/13/93, 733); she recalled afternoons spent with him at Denmark Hill "enthusing over coins," (*LP*, 9/25/86, 256) and was very concerned about him when he was ill in 1878. In this context she went well beyond Ruskin's argument in *Of Queen's Gardens* when she suggested that a woman should have "absolute freedom of action." Ruskin preferred to think of women as cloistered, domestic, and limited in their actions, even though, as Emily noted in 1894, "the great master" wanted women to be educated so that they could "understand and even . . . aid the work of man" (*LP*, 12/1/94, 802). Incidentally, a *Victoria Magazine* review of Ruskin's *Sesame and Lilies* (probably by Emily Faithfull) took issue with his contention that girls should be educated only for the sake of their husbands' talents (*VM*, 11/65 and 12/65).

20. As EF's 1887 letter to the *Times* indicated, she took pride in playing "an active part in the movement for enabling the women of England to express their respectful affection for the Queen, both as woman and Sovereign" (*Times*, 5/3/87, 10). This activity included collecting money for Manchester's Jubilee project and a public lecture praising Queen Victoria.

21. Profound respect for the Queen and unswerving faith in a hierarchical government were probably responsible for EF's inventing a family motto and crest that she displayed on her watch and in personal letters

from 1884 on. The motto "Fidelis et firmus" was set in an oval around a unicorn (statant). Neither the motto nor the crest is mentioned in *Fairbairn's Crests of Families of Great Britain and Ireland* (1968). Fairbairn lists two Faithfull family crests: the first, "a key, in pale, wards upward, surmounted by a crosier and a sword, in saltier" (Fairbairn, Plate 4, Crest 8), obviously did not inspire Emily; the other, "a talbot (statant)" (Plate 120, Crest 8), could have been the source of the unicorn (statant). Quite probably Emily became tired of being referred to as "faithful Fido"; so she transformed dog to unicorn, thus superimposing "virtue of mind and strength of body" on mere fidelity.

22. In line with her church's stand, she withheld her approval of the Salvation Army and any evangelical preaching that bordered on the sensational. She was unimpressed by American preachers, "formerly great sinners" (*LE*, 12/14/78, 374), who crossed the Atlantic in search of souls. As for General Booth, founder of the Salvation Army, she questioned his extravagant "claim to an exclusive interest in the submerged masses" (*LP*, 4/11/91, 566), for the Church of England had been involved in rescue work, prison-gate missions, etc. long before General Booth appeared on the scene. Such claims as Booth's smacked of "self-glorification," said Emily, and she wanted to see how he would use the money he had collected "in the interests of humanity" (*LP*, 3/5/92, 344).

23. Robin de Beaumont, noted British antiquarian, recently unearthed what he calls "an extraordinary entry [about Emily Faithfull] in an Album I found" (Letter to James Stone, 7 November 1991). It appears in a quiz about one's likes and dislikes, hopes and fears that is dated October 27, 1878 and signed "Elizabeth Rhodes." Here are a few of the questions, with Elizabeth's revealing answers in parenthesis:

Your favorite occupation. (Reading)
Your chief characteristic. (Anxiety)
Your idea of happiness. (Plenty of Money and Nothing to do)
Your idea of misery. (Not able to pay your debts)
Your favorite poets. (Mrs. Hemans & Longfellow)
Your favorite heroes in real life. (My four sons)
Your favorite heroines in real life. (Emily Faithful [sic] & Miss Nightingale)

A heroine no less, and on the same level as the lady with the lamp! Elizabeth Rhodes, representative middle-class Victorian woman, proves to be a more evenhanded witness to Emily's nobility than any of Emily's fellow pioneers in the cause of women.

24. *Parkes Papers*, BRP V 115/1.

*Appendix*

# A Tentative Short-Title Listing of Victoria Press Publications

In accord with the pattern in William Fredeman's *Library* article, "Emily Faithfull and the Victoria Press," titles are arranged within six chronological groups, followed by a section on proceedings, periodicals, and miscellaneous publications. Works printed at the Victoria Press but not published by Emily Faithfull are so indicated, as are special features of works. Items marked with a single asterisk were submitted by Victor Berch, librarian at Brandeis University, Waltham, Massachusetts; those with a double asterisk were located by James Stone; and those without asterisks were listed by Fredeman in the above-noted article.

## 1860

**1. *Trade societies and strikes: Report of the NAPSS committee.*

*2. Sir James Moncrieff. *An address on jurisprudence and the amendment of the law.* (Rpt. from *Transactions of NAPSS 1860.*)

## 1861

*3. Edwin Lankester. *Notes on recent sanitary legislation in the metropolis.* (Rpt. from *Transactions of NAPSS.*)

*4. Sir Edwin Chadwick. *Address as vice president of the Public Health Section to the general meeting of the National Association for the Promotion of Social Science.*

5. Ellen Barlee. *Individual exertion: A Christmas call to action.* (Issued in blue wrappers with decorative printed border.)

6. Frances Power Cobbe. *The workhouse as an hospital.*

7. _____. *Friendless girls and how to help them: Being an account of the Preventive Mission at Bristol.*

8. Adelaide A. Procter, ed. *The Victoria Regia: A volume of original contributions in poetry and prose.* (2nd edition, 1863.)

9. Maria S. Rye. *Emigration of educated women.* (Rpt. from *EWJ.*)

10. Frank Ives Scudamore. *Post Office Savings' Banks: A few plain words concerning them.*

11. _____. *Life insurance by small payments: A few plain words concerning it.*

### 1862

*12. Florence Nightingale. *Hospital statistics and hospital plans.* (Rpt. from *Transactions of NAPSS 1861.*)

13. [E.H. Maling]. *Birds and flowers; or, The children's guide to gardening and bird-keeping.* (With a coloured lithographed frontispiece.)

14. Frances Power Cobbe. *Female education and how it would be affected by university examinations.*

15. C. Coker. *The Round Robin.* (Nursery poems on the fruits and vegetables.)

16. Walter Crofton. *A brief description of the Irish convict system.*

17. Manockjee Cursetjee. *Female education in India.*

18. T. Pelliam Dale, ed. *Deaconess' institutions.* (Speeches by several authors.)

19. Emily Davies. *Medicine as a profession for women.*

\*\*20. \_\_\_\_\_. *Thoughts on some questions relating to women.* (Rpt. from a Northern daily paper.)

21. Amelia B. Edwards. *Sights and stories: Being some account of a holiday tour through the north of Belgium.* (With nine illustrations by the author.)

22. Sarah Stickney Ellis. *Janet: One of many. A story in verse.* Uniform with 'The votive offering.'

23. Emily Faithfull. *On some of the drawbacks connected with the present employment of women.*

24. *Flowers for window gardens, in town and country. What to grow and how.*

25. *Gourds for the many: How to grow and cook them.* (For the 1862 International Exhibition.)

26. R. J. Hoyne. *Preventive helps before penitential remedies.*

27. Richard Holt Hutton. *The relative value of studies and accomplishments in the education of women. A lecture.*

28. Anne Jellicoe. *Woman's supervision of women's industry.*

29. Frances Smith Marriott. *The votive offering.* (With a lithographic frontispiece of Ulcombe Church and Rectory in Kent, and six other lithographs.)

30. *Memories of Madame Luce of Algiers.* (Rpt. from *EWJ.*)

31. Mary Merryweather. *Experience of factory life: Being a record of fourteen years' work at Mr. Courtauld's silk mill at Halstead in Essex.* (3rd edition contains a preface by Bessie Parkes.)

32. Y.S.N. *The sparrow and the primrose.* (Sold for the benefit of the Hospital for Sick Children.)

33. S. Hadden Parkes. *Flower shows of window plants for the working classes of London.* (Items 17, 19, 28, 32, and 33 appear in advertisements in *EWJ*, March 1863; dating is therefore uncertain.)

34. *Principia pauperismatis: Considerations regarding paupers.*

35. *Report on the Commission Appointed by the Imperial and Royal Academy of the Fine Arts of Venice to examine the Salviati Mosaic Establishment at Venice.* Translated from the original in the *Transactions* of the Imperial and Royal Institute of Venice, Vol. vi, series iii, no. x.

36. Frederica Rowan, trans. *Meditations on death and eternity.* (By J.H.D. Zschokke; printed by EF, for private circulation.)

37. Frank Ives Scudamore. *Orthography: A few plain words concerning it.*

38. Louisa Twining. *Our poor laws and our workhouses.*

39. _____. *A few words on social science to working people.*

40. *What to cook and how to cook it.* (From advertisement in No. 37 above.)

41. James Wild. *An essay on co-operation, showing the necessity of attaining self-knowledge, self-reliance, and self-respect.*

42. *Endowed schools: their uses and shortcomings.* With a table showing the number of endowed schools and their scholars in every county.

43. *How to learn cookery.*

44. *A letter to young Christians.*

45. *Six weeks in Ireland* by a Templar. (1862 dating confirmed in *The Queen*, 6/3/65, 361.)

*46. Baron George John Shaw-Lefevre Eversley. *The discipline of the bar.*

## 1863

*47. Society for Promoting the Amendment of the Law. *Report of the Special Committee on the marriage laws of the United Kingdom.*

*48. Frances Power Cobbe. *Rejoinder to Mrs. Stowe's reply to the address of the women of England.*

*49. George W. Hastings. *The history and objects of the National Association for the Promotion of Social Science.*

*50. J.R. Fowler and Martin Ware, eds. *The transportation of criminals, being a report of a discussion at a special meeting of the [National Association for the Promotion of Social Science] held at Burlington House, on the 17th February 1863.*

51. Ellen Barlee. *Friendless and helpless.*

52. _____. *Helen Lindsay; or, The trial of faith.*

53. Jessie Boucherett. *How shall I educate my daughter?* (Tracts for Parents and Daughters, No. 1.)

54. _____. *Shall my daughter learn a business?* (TPD, No. 2.)

55. J.E. Cairnes. *Who are the Canters?* (Tract No. 3, published for the Ladies' London Emancipation Society.)

56. Frances Power Cobbe. *The red flag in John Bull's eyes.* (Tract No. 1, published for LLES.)

57. _____. *Essays on the pursuits of women.* (Six essays rpt. from *Macmillan's magazine* and *Fraser's* plus a paper on female education.)

58. Isa Craig. *The essence of slavery.* Extracted from 'A journal of a residence on a Georgian plantation,' by Francis Ann Kemble (Tract no. 2, published for LLES.)

59. ___, ed. *A welcome: Original contributions in verse and prose.* (2nd edition, 1865).

60. ___, ed. *Poems: An Offering to Lancashire.* 'Printed and Published for the Art Exhibition for the Relief of Distress in the Cotton Districts'.

61. Edward Dicey. [Tract No. 4, published for LLES, announced as forthcoming in No. 55 above.]

62. [J.G. Faithfull]. *Wayside thoughts, by a Christian pilgrim; The recreation of weary days. The solace of suffering nights, 1860-62.* (Printed by EF.)

63. M. Goldschmidt. *The solace of virtue at Rome.*

64. Henry Grant. *Mariquita.* (Long narrative poem; a subscription volume with a photographic frontispiece.)

65. *Prayers, texts, and hymns for those in service.* (By the author of 'Count up your mercies,' and 'Tracts for railway men,' and others. A third edition is advertised in No. 117, below.)

66. *A letter of remembrance.* By an old curate.

67. *Plain words about cookery.* By the author of 'Birds and flowers'. (Items 66 and 67 appear in advertisements in No. 65 above.)

## 1864

*68. William Robert Bertolacci. *Christian spiritualism; wherein is shown the extension of the human faculties, by the application of modern spiritual phenomena, according to the doctrine of Christ.*

*69. Sir Edwin Chadwick. *The comparative results of the chief principles of the poor-law administration in England and Ireland, as compared with that of Scotland.*

*70. William Dougal Christie. *Suggestions for an organisation for restraint of corruption and expenditure at election.* (2nd edition, with additions. NAPSS paper.)

*71. Sir Walter Crofton. *The present aspect of the convict question.*

*72. John Henry Freese, ed. *The philosophy of the immortality of the soul and the resurrection of the human body.*

*73. Thomas Hare. *The facilities which the law may give for small investments in real property, and the means they would afford of improving the dwellings of the people and the condition of the working classes.* (NAPSS paper.)

*74. George Woodyatt Hastings. *On a proposed new court of ecclesiastical jurisdiction.*

*75. *Annual report of the Ladies' London Emancipation Society.*

*76. Edwin Lankester. *First annual report of the Coroner for the central district of Middlesex from August 1st, 1862 to July 31st, 1863.*

*77. Frederick Denison Maurice. *Corruption at elections with speeches by John Stuart Mill and Edwin Chadwick, and report of standing committee of jurisprudence and amendment of the law.*

*78. *Report of a [NAPSS] discussion on the proposed admission of girls to the university local examinations.*

*79. Florence Nightingale. *How people may live and not die in India.* (Longman, Green, Longman, Roberts, and Green are listed as publishers of record, but on verso of title page Emily Faithfull is also listed as printer and publisher.)

*80. G. Harry Palmer. *Suggestions for the amendment of the law of appeal in criminal cases. Read at a meeting of the Department of Jurisprudence and Amendment of the Law, February 6, 1864.* (NAPSS paper.)

*81. Neptune, pseud. *Oyster tattle and truthful digest of the Herne Bay, Hampton & Reculver oyster fishery, read a third time and passed in the House of Lords, with a few words upon existing oyster companies, and their vexatious opposition.*

82. Jessie Boucherett. *Choice of a business for girls: Artistic and intellectual employments.* (*TPD*, No. 3, Pt. I.)

83. _____. *Choice of a business for girls: Dressmaking, sick nursing, domestic service, and some other employments and handicrafts.* (*TPD*, No. 3, Pt. II.)

84. Helen Dagley. *Told at last: A novel.* 2 vols.

85. W.B. Hodgson. *Lecture on the education of girls.*

86. J. Smith. *The excellency and nobleness of true religion*, by John Smith, Fellow of Queens' College, Cambridge, from 1640-1652, Being a Reprint from that Date. (From an advertisement in Publishers' circular, 1864.)

## 1865-80

*87. Emily Davies. *The application of funds to the education of girls.* 1865. (NAPSS paper, with publishers of record being Longman, Green, et al, but with Emily Faithfull listed as printer and publisher on verso of title page.)

88. [Mary Louisa Boyle]. *The court and camp of Queen Marian*. By a contemporaneous historian. [1865]. ('Printed only by EF,' no VP imprint; dated 1890 in British Museum catalogue.)

**89. *The bath-tatting book*. (VP imprint only; mentioned in *Alexandra Magazine and EWJ*, 5/65, 316.)

90. *Words for meditation during the season of Lent*. [1865]. (Dated 1867 in BM catalogue.)

*91. Sir Walter Crofton. *A speech on the treatment of life-sentenced convicts*. 1866. (NAPSS paper, VP imprint only.)

*92. John Frederic La Trobe Bateman. *On a constant water supply for London*. 1867. (Faithfull and Head.)

**93. Emily Davies. *Report of an examination of girls*. 1868. (VP imprint; W.W. Head, printer.)

94. *Te Deum Laudamus*. Illuminations by Esther Faithfull-Fleet, chromolithographed by M. & N. Hanhart. (Two eds. in 1868, the first undated.)

95. Emily Faithfull. *Change upon change: A love story*. 1868. (Published by EF at VP, printed by W.W. Head.)

*96. *Report of the [NAPSS] council to the annual business meeting of members July 16, 1868*. 1868. (W.W. Head.)

*97. *Constitution and laws [of NAPSS]; with list of officers and members*. 1868. (W.W. Head.)

*98. William Ballantyne Hodgson. *Exaggerated estimates of reading and writing, as means of education. A paper read at the Belfast meeting of the Social Science Association, 24th September, 1867*. 1868. (W.W. Head.)

*99. Sir Walter Crofton. *The criminal classes and their control. Prison treatment and its principles. Addresses.* 1868. (W.W. Head.)

100. *Crinoline.* Rpt. from *The illustrated news of the world.* [1868?]

101. W. Wilfred Head. *The Victoria Press: Its history and vindication, with an account of the movement for the employment of females in printing.* 1869. (Printed at VP, 11, 12, 13 Harp Alley.)

102. Motley's *Dutch Republic.* 1869. (Printed at VP according to Head's pamphlet, but unlocated.)

*103. Thomas Beggs. *International arbitration and reduction of armaments.* 1870. (W.W. Head, printer.)

*104. William Ballantyne Hodgson. *Competition. A lecture delivered by W.B. Hodgson . . . on . . . March 15, 1870.* 1870. (W.W. Head.)

105. Mary Taylor. *The first duty of women.* 1870.

106. Emily Faithfull. *Woman's work; with special reference to industrial employment: A paper read before the Society of Arts, March 29th, 1871.* 1871. (Rpt. from *VM*, 6/71, 308-322.)

107. *38 texts.* Designed and illuminated by Esther Faithfull-Fleet. 1872.

108. J.G. Fitch. *Working women's college: An address.* 1872.

**109. Emily Faithfull, ed. *Women's work and wages.* [1874.] (Advertised in *W & W*, 10/3/74.)

110. Mary Louisa Boyle. *Biographical notices of the portraits at Hinchingbrook.* 1876. (Printed only at VP.)

**111. *Tales from the German.* [1877?] (Advertised in *WLE*, 2/2/78.)

112. William Thomas Blair. *Female Suffrage*. An article rpt. from *VM* of 1874, with some remarks on the late debate in the House of Commons. 1876.

113. _____. *A letter to Lord Ebury, on liturgical revision*. 1876.

**114. *Village lanes and country life*. [1878.] (Advertised in *WLE*, 6/29/78.)

115. R.J. Gilman. *Guzman the Good: A tragedy. The secretary: A play, and miscellaneous poems*. 1878.

**116. W. T. Blair. *Emigration of pauper and other destitute children to Canada*. 1878.

117. Gina Rose. *Modesta*. 1880.

118. *Allegorical sketches. For the mothers, wives, and daughters of Great Britain.*

119. H.G.B. *Women compositors: A guide to the composing room. Also giving particulars of the time required to learn the business, scale of remuneration, &c, &c.* (Items 118 and 119 appear in advertisements in No. 117; dating is therefore uncertain.)

Proceedings, Periodicals, and Miscellaneous Publications

120. *Transactions of the National Association for the Promotion of Social Science 1860-61.* (Printed by EF at VP.)

121. _____. 1862. (Five parts, four of them printed and published by EF, one printed only.)

**122. _____. 1863-4. (Longman, Green, et al listed as publishers of record, but EF also listed as "printer and publisher.")

**123. _____. 1865. (Printed by VP, with Longman, Green, et al listed as publishers.)

**124. _____. 1866. (Printed by Faithfull and Head at VP.)

\*\*125. ____. 1867-69. (Printed by W.W. Head at VP.)

126. *The law magazine.* (Some issues printed by VP; see *Transactions of NAPSS 1862*, p. 685.)

127. *The Victoria magazine.* 1863-80. (Edited by EF, this journal was printed at VP and most volumes were published by her.)

128. *The English woman's journal.* 1858-64. (Printed at VP from September 1860 to January 1864.)

\*\*129. *The Englishwoman's review.* January 1868. (Printed by W.W. Head at VP.)

130. *The Victoria Press almanack.* 1868. (Broadside published by W.W. Head at VP.)

\*\*131. *Women and work.* 1874-6. Edited by EF.

132. *The reformatory and refuge journal.* 1861-72? (EF published numbers 5-12.)

133. *The West London express.* 1877-8. Edited by EF.

\*\*134. *All Saints' Parish magazine* (Paddington). 1877-8. (Advertised in *WLE*, 9/22/77.)

### Last-minute additions

135.  John Shirley. *The Golden Gleanings: being Sketches of Female Character from Bible History.* 1863. (From Robin de Beaumont's *Catalogue Thirteen 1990.*)

136.  Henry Toby Prinsep. *Specimens of Ballad Poetry, Applied to the Tales and Traditions of the East.* 1862. (Acquired by William E. Fredeman several years after publication of his article, "Emily Faithfull and the Victorian Press.")

137.  Adelaide A. Procter. *Legends and Lyrics*. 5th Edition. Printed at Victoria Press. 1861.

138.  [G.A. Paley]. *Saul of Tarsus, A Dramatic Sketch*. (Revision of a Rivington 1855 edition.) 1862.

139.  Alexander P. Stewart and Edward Jenkins. *The Medical and Legal Aspects of Sanitary Reform*. Robert Hardwick. Printed at Faithfull and Head. 1867.

N.B.  Items 137-9 were submitted by Robin de Beaumont, as were corrections to other items.

# Selected Bibliography

*The Alexandra Magazine and English Woman's Journal* (1864-5).

Bauer, Carol and Lawrence Ritt. *Free and Ennobled: Source Readings in the Development of Victorian Feminism.* New York: Pergamon Press, c 1979.

Bell, E. Moberly. *Storming the Citadel: The Rise of the Woman Doctor.* London: Constable & Co., 1953.

Bennett, Daphne. *Emily Davies and the Liberation of Women (1830-1921).* London: A. Deutsch, 1990.

"The Helen Blackburn Pamphlet Collection from Girton College, Cambridge." *Voices of the Women's Movement.* Brighton, Sussex: Harvester Press Microform Publications, 1987.

Blair, Karen J. *The Clubwoman as Feminist.* London: Holmes and Meier, 1980.

Boase, Frederic. *Modern English Biography* (Supplement to Vol II). London: Frank Cass & Co. Ltd., 1965.

Bodichon, Barbara Leigh Smith. *Women and Work.* London: Bosworth and Harrison, 1857.

Branca, Patricia. *Women in Europe Since 1750.* London: Croom Helm, 1978.

Brown, Philip A.H. *London Publishers and Printers c 1800-1870.* London: British Library, 1982.

Burton, Hester. *Barbara Bodichon (1827-1891)*. London: John Murray, 1949.

Caine, Barbara. *Victorian Feminists*. Oxford; Toronto: Oxford University Press, 1992.

Cobbe, Frances Power. *Essays on the Pursuits of Women*. London: Emily Faithfull, 1863.

Courtney, Janet E. *The Women of My Time*. London: Lovat Dickson Ltd., 1934.

Croly, Jane C. *The History of the Woman's Club Movement in America*. New York: Henry G. Allen & Co., 1898.

Crow, Duncan. *The Victorian Woman*. London: George Allen and Unwin Ltd., 1971.

Davies, Emily. *Thoughts on Some Questions Relating to Women 1860-1908*. Cambridge: Bowes and Bowes, 1910.

Eliot, George. *Letters*. ed. Gordon S. Haight. New Haven: Yale University Press, 1955.

*Eliza Cook's Journal* (1849-1856).

Ellsworth, Edward. *Liberators of the Female Mind: The Shirreff Sisters*. London: Greenwood Press, c 1979.

"Emily Faithfull," *Women Manchester Remembers*: the Margaret Ashton Memorial Lecture delivered by Alderman Mary L. Kingsmill Jones, C.B.E., M.A., J.P., Tuesday 26 June 1951.

*English Woman's Journal* (1858-1864).

*The Englishwoman's Review* (1866-1895).

Faithfull, Lilian M. *In the House of My Pilgrimage*. London: Chatto and Windus, 1924.

*Fawcett Library Collection of Material on Women's Work.*

Fredeman, William E. "Emily Faithfull and the Victoria Press: an experiment in sociological bibliography." *The Library*, XXIX (June 1974), 139-64.

*The Friend of the People: A Journal of Social Science and of Charitable Institutions* (1860).

Godwin, Anne. "Early Years in the Trade Unions," in Middleton, Lucy, ed., *Women in the Labour Mov't: The British Experience.* London: Croom Helm, 1977.

Greg, William R. "Why are Women Redundant?" *National Review*, April, 1862, 434-60.

Gorham, Deborah. *The Victorian Girl and the Feminine Ideal.* London: Croom Helm, c 1982.

Goldman, Harold. *Emma Paterson: She Led Woman into a Man's World.* London: Lawrence and Wishart, 1974.

Hays, Frances. *Women of the Day.* Philadelphia: Lippincott, 1885.

Herstein, Sheila R. *A Mid-Victorian Feminist, Barbara Leigh Smith Bodichon.* New Haven: Yale University Press, 1985.

Holcombe, Lee. *Victorian Ladies at Work 1850-1914.* Hamden, Connecticut: Archon Books, 1973.

Hollis, Patricia. *Women in Public 1850-1900: Documents of the Victorian Women's Movement.* London: George Allen & Unwin, 1979.

Jameson, Anna. *Sisters of Charity and the Communion of Labour.* London: Longmans et al, 1859.

Kamm, Josephine. *How Different from Us: Miss Buss and Miss Beale.* London: The Bodley Head, 1958.

_____. *Rapiers and Battleaxes: The Women's Movement and its Aftermath.* London: George Allen & Unwin, 1966.

Kanner, Barbara. *Women in English Social History 1800-1914* (a guide to research in three volumes). New York: Garland Press, 1987.

Christopher Kent. "Image and Reality," in Martha Vicinus, ed. *A Widening Sphere: Changing Roles of Victorian Women.* Bloomington: Indiana University Press, c 1977.

Lacey, Candida Ann. *Barbara Leigh Smith Bodichon and the Langham Place Group.* New York: Routledge and Kegan Paul, 1987.

*Lady's Pictorial* (1882-1895).

Levine, Philippa. *Victorian Feminism 1850-1900.* Tallahassee: Florida State University Press, 1987.

McCrone, Kathleen E. "The National Association for the Promotion of Social Science and the Advancement of Victorian Women." *Atlantis*, 8:1, 44-66, Fall 1982.

Maison, Margaret. "Insignificant Objects of Desire." *The Listener*, 22 July 1971, 105-107.

Maynard, Constance L. "From Early Victorian Schoolroom to University: Some Personal Experiences." *The Nineteenth Century and After.* November 1914, pp. 1060-73.

Mill, John Stuart. *Later Letters,* in *Collected Works*, Vols. 14-17. ed. Mineka and Lindley. Toronto: University of Toronto Press, 1972.

Moon, G. Washington. *Men and Women of the Time: A Dictionary of Contemporaries* (13th Edition). London: George Rutledge & Sons Ltd., 1891.

Morten, Honnor. *Questions for Women (and Men)*. London: Adam and Charles Black, 1899.

Nestor, Pauline. "A New Departure in Women's Publishing: The *English Woman's Journal* and the *Victoria Magazine*." *Victorian Periodicals Review*, XV (1982), 93-106.

_____. *Female Friendships and Communities*. Oxford: Clarendon Press, 1985.

Odell, George C. *Annals of the New York Stage*, Vols. 9 and 12. New York: Columbia University Press, 1937 and 1940.

Palmegiano, E.M. *Women and British Periodicals 1832-1867: A Bibliography*. New York: Garland Publishing, 1976.

*Parkes Papers at Girton College* (unpublished papers).

Pratt, Edwin A. *Pioneer Women in Victoria's Reign*. London: G. Newnes, 1897.

*The Queen* (1861-1895).

Ratcliffe, Eric. *The Caxton of Her Age: The Career and Family Background of Emily Faithfull 1835-95*, Upton-Upon-Severn, U.K.: Images Publishing (Malvern) Ltd., 1993.

Rendall, Jane. *The Origins of Modern Feminism 1780-1860*. London: Macmillan, 1985.

Rover, Constance. *The Punch Book of Women's Rights*. London: Hutchinson, 1967.

*Saturday Review of Politics, Literature, Science and Art* (1858-1895).

Shanley, Mary Lyndon. *Feminism, Marriage and the Law in Victorian England, 1850-1895*. Princeton, N.J.: Princeton University Press, c1989.

Spender, Dale. *Women of Ideas and What Men Have Done to Them.* London: Routledge and Kegan Paul, 1982.

Stanton, Elizabeth Cady. *Eighty Years and More (1815-1897).* New York: European Publishing Co., 1898.

_____, Susan Brownell Anthony, Matilda Jocelyn Gage, and Isa Usted Harper, eds. *The History of Woman Suffrage.* [microform]. Rochester, New York: S.B. Anthony, [1881]-1922.

Stanton, Theodore, ed. *The Woman Question in Europe.* London: G.P. Putnam's Sons, 1884.

Stone, James S. "Emily Faithfull," in *The Biographical Dictionary of Modern British Radicals,* Vol. 2. eds., N.J. Gossman and J.O. Baylen. New York: Harvester Press, 1984.

_____. "More Light on Emily Faithfull and the Victoria Press." *The Library,* XXXIII (March 1978), 63-67.

Strachey, Ray. *"The Cause": a Short History of the Women's Movement in Great Britain.* London: G. Bell and Sons, 1928.

Thackeray, Miss. *Toilers and Spinsters.* London: Smith and Elder, 1874.

Thomas, Clara. *Love and Work Enough: The Life of Anna Jameson.* London: Macdonald & Co., 1967.

*Times* (1858-1895).

*Transactions of the National Association for the Promotion of Social Science* (1857-1884).

Vicinus, Martha. *Independent Women: Work and Community for Single Women 1850-1920.* Chicago: University of Chicago Press, 1985.

*Victoria Magazine* (1863-1880). ed. Emily Faithfull.

*(West) London Express* (1877-78). ed. Emily Faithfull.

Westwater, Martha. "Emily Faithfull: Folly Reconsidered." Unpublished paper presented before the Pacific Coast Studies in British Literature at the University of California (Santa Barbara), 1981.

_____. *The Wilson Sisters: A biographical study of upper middle-class Victorian life.* Athens, Ohio: Ohio University Press, 1984.

_____. "Victoria Magazine," in *British Literary Magazines 1837-1913.* ed. Alvin Sullivan. Westport, CT: Greenwood Press, 1984, pp. 443-5.

*Women and Education 1849-1921: The Papers of Emily Davies and Barbara Bodichon from Girton College, Cambridge.* Brighton, Sussex: Harvester Press Microform Publications Ltd., 1985.

*Women and Work* (1874-76). ed. Emily Faithfull.

# Index